History, Education, and Public Policy

THE NATIONAL SOCIETY
FOR THE STUDY OF EDUCATION

Series on Contemporary Educational Issues
Kenneth J. Rehage, Series Editor

The 1978 Titles

History, Education, and Public Policy: Recovering the American Educational Past, Donald R. Warren, Editor
Aspects of Reading Education, Susanna Pflaum-Connor, Editor
From Youth to Constructive Adult Life: The Role of the Public School, Ralph W. Tyler, Editor

The National Society for the Study of Education also publishes Yearbooks which are distributed by the University of Chicago Press. Inquiries regarding all publications of the Society, as well as inquiries about membership in the Society, may be addressed to the Secretary-Treasurer, 5835 Kimbark Avenue, Chicago, IL 60637. Membership in the Society is open to any who are interested in promoting the investigation and discussion of educational questions.

History, Education, and Public Policy

EDITED BY

Donald R. Warren

University of Illinois at Chicago Circle

McCutchan Publishing Corporation
2526 Grove Street
Berkeley, California 94704

ISBN 0-8211-2258-4
Library of Congress Catalog Card Number 77-95251

Cover design and illustration by Terry Down, Griffin Graphics

Series Foreword

In choosing the selections to be included in this volume, Professor Donald Warren has taken great care to have represented the most significant thrusts emerging from the recent work of those engaged in the study of American educational history. The selections will enable the reader to see the nature of current disagreements among educational historians, particularly those between the "revisionists" and their critics. More than that, however, the chapters in this book will provide the reader with a basis for seeing more clearly how the study of history can contribute to the broader study of American education and of public policy. Thus, the concern of this book fits very neatly into the overall plan for the series of which it is a part—the NSSE Series on Contemporary Educational Issues.

The National Society for the Study of Education appreciates the efforts of Professor Warren, who has applied his scholarly talents and devoted a considerable portion of his time over the past three years to the design of this volume. The Committee responsible for planning this series shares his hope that the book will serve a very useful purpose both for the general reader and for the serious student of American educational history.

Kenneth J. Rehage

for the Committee on an Expanded
Publication Program of the
National Society for the Study
of Education

Preface

Although its title may suggest otherwise, this volume is not addressed directly to historians of American education. As befits a publication of the National Society for the Study of Education, it is intended for a larger audience of scholars and lay people who share an interest in educational history. The chapters offer a selective survey of recent developments in the history and historiography of American education. Consisting in the main of material originally published elsewhere, the volume highlights disagreements among practitioners of the art, significant research, book reviews, and contributions of history to the broader study of American education and to public policy. Historians will immediately notice the lack of comprehensiveness and systematic critique. Space limitations prohibited the former, and readers will find references to recent attempts at the latter in notes following each chapter. The numerous critiques reflect the volume of research activity and the sometimes heated discussions that have come to characterize American educational history and those who work that field. To continue the metaphor, there is a frequent need to examine the quality of the crop. In attempting to serve a larger audience, this collection pursues a more general objective. Historians may view it as more of a recollection, but students of the history of American education should find it useful as an introduction to the area of study. An essential point bears emphasis. In the pages that follow readers will encounter some, although obviously not all, of the highly gifted scholars who are responsible for the current vitality in the history of American education.

In addition to those whose work is included in this collection, several colleagues have provided advice and encouragement. Geraldine Clifford, whose impressive bibliographic essay, "Education: Its History and Historiography," could not be reprinted because of copyright restrictions, was generous with both. Paul Mattingly, editor of the *History of Education Quarterly,* offered both detailed recommendations and a comprehensive plan for the book. He surely is not responsible for either its content or organization, but he directly influenced both. Maurice J. Eash, dean of education at the University of Illinois at Chicago Circle, provided valuable comment from the perspective of an informed and interested "nonhistorian." Herbert J. Walberg, another colleague from outside the history field, has been particularly supportive. Charles A. Tesconi, Jr., a social philosophy colleague who occasionally ventures into historical inquiry, delivered typically wise and cogent advice. Ms. Allene Robinson, secretary of the department of policy studies, typed various sections of the manuscript. Finally, I am especially grateful to the Committee on an Expanded Publication Program of the National Society for the Study of Education for seeing the need and providing the vehicle for publishing a volume such as this.

As is always the case, there are intellectual sources that cannot be cited through the usual mechanisms of notes and bibliography. For me, these include Clarence Ayres, Paul Tillich, Joseph W. Mathews, and William R. Cozart, as diverse a crew of idea peddlers as one could imagine. The book is dedicated to Robert L. McCaul in partial acknowledgment of an enormous debt.

Donald R. Warren
University of Illinois at
Chicago Circle

Contributors

R. Freeman Butts, William F. Russell Professor in the Foundations of Education, Emeritus, Teachers College, Columbia University; Visiting Distinguished Professor of Education, San Jose State University

Sol Cohen, Professor, Graduate School of Education, University of California, Los Angeles

Jill K. Conway, Professor of History, and President, Smith College

Lawrence A. Cremin, Frederick A. P. Barnard Professor of Education, and President, Teachers College, Columbia University

Barbara Finkelstein, Associate Professor of Social Foundations of Education, University of Maryland, College Park

Maxine Greene, William F. Russell Professor in the Foundations of Education, Teachers College, Columbia University

Neil Harris, Professor, Department of History, University of Chicago

Carl F. Kaestle, Professor of Educational Policy Studies and History, University of Wisconsin, Madison

Michael B. Katz, Professor of History, York University

Marvin Lazerson, Professor of Education, University of British Columbia

Robert L. McCaul, Associate Professor, Department of Education, University of Chicago

Michael R. Olneck, Assistant Professor in Educational Policy Studies and the Institute for Research on Poverty, University of Wisconsin, Madison

Diane Ravitch, Assistant Professor of History and Education, Teachers College, Columbia University

Maxine S. Seller, Associate Professor of Social Foundations of Education, State University of New York at Buffalo

David B. Tyack, Professor of Education and History, Stanford University

Donald R. Warren, Associate Professor and Head, Department of Policy Studies, University of Illinois at Chicago Circle

Contents

FIVE

Strangers at Home: Schooling, Exclusion, and Acculturation   149

SIX

The Control Problem   225

SEVEN

A Past for the Future: Historiographical Perspectives   271

ONE

A Past for the Present

Donald R. Warren

In few periods prior to the past two decades have historians of American education enjoyed their quarrels more or, conversely, taken them more seriously. Nor have their research productivity and its relevance to public policy been higher. Of recent developments in the field, revisionism easily ranks among the most widely and hotly debated, and not merely among educational historians. In the process, the traditional story of American education and the historians who wrote it have been challenged fundamentally. The familiar accounts depicted unqualified success: the construction, despite strenuous opposition, of a well-intentioned public school system to which American children of whatever race, sex, or social class eventually gained access. Revisionists tend to view the educational past differently. First, they see it as encompassing more than schools. Second, when they focus on schools, they provide more critical accounts of institutional openness and the school's record in promoting educational opportunity. They present evidence suggesting that schools have exhibited a greater concern with moral training than education and that the goals of those who have controlled schools have been ambivalent at best relative to the education of minorities and working-class people. Equally pointed criticisms have been leveled against earlier generations of educational historians. Viewed as a Whiggish cadre given to the retelling of distorted tales, they are charged with sharing unfounded assumptions about the value of schools, erring collectively in equating education

1

and schooling, and producing pietistic histories of formal education.[1]

Intrinsically valuable in most instances, debate over these criticisms has also drawn attention to recent significant gains in American educational history and historiography. A closer kinship with general history is being established. Comparative and interdisciplinary approaches provide concepts and resources for assessing educational development in the United States. There is also a discernible trend away from survey history in favor of basic research and case study. A wealth of new literature has appeared that utilizes new sources and techniques, employs fresh critical perspectives, and, in turn, generates new research questions. That conflicting interpretations of the American educational past have surfaced is on the whole a healthy sign. More significant, however, are advances in the sophistication and subtlety by which complex educational phenomena are analyzed and explained.

The infusion of vitality and self-esteem may be the most striking development of all. Over the past two decades, the *History of Education Quarterly* has grown in stature as a quality research journal. The worth and volume of historical research in education have earned increasing recognition among academic scholars generally and other historians in particular. As annual meetings of the History of Education Society make clear, no new consensus history has yet emerged; nor does there appear to be much urgency to force one. Instead, one finds conflict, controversy, and general confidence that significant findings are being unearthed and important issues confronted.

HISTORY AND EDUCATION

Common to the field of history generally are problems of method, source, and perspective. These problems reflect triangular approaches to interpreting historical developments and ideas. Recovering the past is literally impossible. The sources, being partial records in more than one meaning of the term, do not permit it. Documents that survive do not, by that fact alone, shed clear, unassailable light on the past. They were, after all, written by someone with a particular perspective. Empirical data contain limits and possible flaws of their own. They lend themselves to sophisticated statistical analyses, but require context and corroboration before they become intelligible. And they are incapable of penetrating all aspects of the past. Valuable and tough-minded, quantitative history risks being unreadable and enigmatic.

The weaknesses of documentary history run in the opposite direction toward subjectivity and imprecision. Each can produce similar results: accounts cleansed of human content.

Even if all the puzzle pieces come to light, the "oceans of facts," to use Alfred North Whitehead's phrase, there remain the difficulties of identifying, analyzing, and articulating their interactions and relations, including the complex, usually unrecorded feelings, hopes, and desperations of another age. As time-bound people, historians open windows onto a past which, in the final analysis, remains elusive because it, too, is finite. They use perspective to illuminate a past, and, in the end, what they produce is perspective. That limitation, however, is not a license. Historical interpretation is a bounded field. There is evidence to be obtained and context to be protected. Reflecting its reliance on both the humanities and the social sciences, history is a science of perspective.

As a general guideline, that observation has limited utility. In the history of education as in other branches of the parent discipline, disagreements inevitably arise over which poles of the interpretive task deserve the greatest emphasis: data gleaned from the sources, analytic techniques intended to transform data into evidence, or the historian's developed intuition. Alone, each poses difficulties. History as mere technique relinquishes descriptive power. Attempts to write histories that permit the educational past to speak for itself from within its own setting stumble finally over the limitations of the sources and of historians themselves. On the other hand, reconstructing the past as a reflection of the present or, more restrictive still, forcing it to serve political ideologies, produces superficial history and, ultimately, fantasy or propaganda. Writing what Carl Kaestle might term "elegant" history is not simply a matter of balancing the poles of the interpretive task.[2] It follows, rather, from the historian's discipline: knowing that sufficient reliable sources have been consulted, that the context is clearly retained, that the mode of analysis can explain the data, and that the historian's perspective has not imposed alien forms on the past. No historian avoids tangling with this dilemma. Nor are there formulas at hand to ease its resolution. With that in mind, Arthur Schlesinger, Jr., cautioned an audience of his peers against misplaced arrogance. "All any of us can do," he advised, "is descry a figure in the carpet—realizing as we do that contemporary preoccupations define our own definitions."[3] "That is all right," he added, "so long as we recognize what we are doing." M.I. Finley has put the matter more bluntly: "The study and writing of history, in short, is a form of ideology."[4] He is not sanctioning "crude, politically motivated distortions, falsifications, and suppressions" in history, but, rather, he employs the term in its more neutral sense, as defined in the *Shorter Oxford English Dictionary*: "a system of ideas concerning phenomena, esp. those of social life; the manner of thinking characteristic of a class or an individual." History, therefore, has a temporal quality. Heartfelt denials notwithstanding, all history, even or perhaps most especially the dry, textbook variety, is interpretation.

The interpretive task may be completed with authority and grace, but portions of it are bound to be repeated. Out-of-print books are not readily available. New sources come to light. Other historians arrange the parts to form a different whole. A new story will be told. The history of education, like history generally, is a labor of Sisyphus.

It does not follow that all history contains revisionist elements or that historical revision is akin to a natural process. At a crude level, historical revision occurs, as M. I. Finley observes, because historians are inevitably ignorant of the future.[5] Revision itself, however, is not so much inevitable as problematic. Such is the case particularly when it challenges fundamental assumptions in accepted accounts. Like uninspected memories, the latter tend to acquire lives of their own and devoted defenders. Quarrels among historians over revisionist interpretations thus can assume political proportions, with vested interests forming on all sides. The heat of battle, and the argument can reach that level of intensity, is sometimes necessary to ascertain soundness of interpretation, that is, adequacy relative to sources, technique, and perspective. But it is equally important not to suppress or lose sight of fresh questions and perspectives, however inadequately pursued, which carry the potential for significant additions to the body of historical knowledge.

Revision in the history of the American Reconstruction period, which has been gathering momentum since the early 1960s, illustrates the range and dimension of conflicts that can arise among historians representing traditional and antitraditional perspectives.[6] The American Reconstruction represents an authentic episode in social problem solving. There has been general agreement as to what the problems were. At issue were national purpose, constitutional questions, economic recovery, political stability, the role and status of black Americans, and, in general, the easing of regional hostilities. Other questions have proved far more provocative in historical reanalysis. What solutions were attempted? With what results? Were the problems susceptible to the ministries of special programs, such as those of the Freedmen's Bureau, or to the long-range amelioration promised through public schools? Could they be eased and finally resolved through rational debate and negotiation? Or were they systemic and national, thus requiring, in addition to moderate strategies, a redistribution of political and economic power and an extension of the franchise to black people nation-wide? Not surprisingly, historians' answers have proved to be almost as controversial as the original issues. The debate has forced reconsideration of ground once thought settled: Who did or attempted to do what to whom? When and for how long? Why? To what effect? Documentary and quantitative sources and techniques have been employed, with stunning achievements and pratfalls scored on all sides. Final results are not in, but a richer understanding of a complex and pivotal period of the American past is evident.

Substantial revision in the history of American education has occurred during the same period. Educational revisionists, like their counterparts among Reconstruction historians, represent a diverse group. Beyond the necessity of expanding the scope of their field, they recognize the importance of social and cultural factors in examining educational phenomena. Beneath this general consensus, there are differences over assumptions, techniques, and sources. It is not a simple matter to identify the revisionists or to date precisely the beginning of their efforts. Not all historians grouped as revisionists accept the label, and, indeed, some are not even historians.[7] Nor is there convincing evidence that revisionists are more susceptible to unfounded assertion than their peers, as some critics have charged. One difficulty is that, since the late 1950s, there have been two distinct, if nonetheless related, revisionist trends in educational history.[8] The earlier one, represented most strongly in the work of Lawrence Cremin, expanded the field by adopting a broad definition of education, sought new and more rigorous research methodologies and drew educational history closer to general history, particularly intellectual and political history. So much controversy has centered around a more recent and more radical revisionist trend, however, that the term is frequently applied solely to those historians designated in some quarters and occasionally by themselves as "radical."

Historical revision seldom constitutes an unprecedented, complete break with past interpretations. That is at least true in educational history. The work of Michael B. Katz, who has been instrumental in initiating radical revisionism, includes a thorough critique of the origins of American public schools.[9] He views them as detrimental to the working class, racist, and sexist. They were intended to suppress and pacify marginal groups—goals shared with such other nineteenth-century educational agencies as reformatories. He judges them successful, not as vehicles for educational opportunity but as barriers to hope and liberation. Freeman Butts, the dean of American educational historians, accepts none of these conclusions. For him, the American public school represents a "great idea."[10] It is not a romantic notion. His research over the past forty years touches on persistent themes: patterns of educational exclusion, church-state conflicts, violations of civil rights, and struggles to advance educational opportunity for minorities.

Public schools have not always succeeded in matching their promise, Butts finds, and they have been guilty of exclusion and unequal treatment of particular groups. But, on balance and in the long run, they have provided learning opportunities for Americans. Fundamentally, it is the continuation of the idea of public education within the American "experiment" that Butts explores and seeks to defend.

In large measure, these two positions are irreconcilable; their assumptions and perspectives are worlds apart. There are also threads of continuity and differences in emphasis and opinion. Both, for example, tend to focus the history of education on schools and related issues. Merle Curti's critiques of American school reformers even more strikingly illustrate the connections between past and current research in the field.[11] The point is that there are antecedents to the radical critique. Themes evident in earlier works are developed with a vengeance in the more recent revisionist ones.

But substantive and methodological departures have also occurred, and these constitute major contributions to the history of education. The later revisionists trend to treat the goals, policies, organization, and outcomes of schooling more as issues to be examined than as portions of a chronology. Their research emphasizes developments in selected periods or cities, the rise of school bureaucracy, and the impact of organizational forms of education on learning. Of special interest have been differences in educational opportunity and achievement for females, racial minorities, immigrants, and working-class people generally. The methodologies of the later revisionists encourage case study and the use of new sources, quantitative data, interdisciplinary approaches, and explicitly stated perspectives in examining educational outcomes from the client's point of view.

It is not yet clear where, for example, social-class analyses of American educational history will lead. That there have been social-class differences in the delivery and outcomes of American public schooling can hardly be debated. Far more telling is research that seeks to establish when, where, and under what circumstances the differences occurred. And, of course, there must be some reason why the public schools attracted working-class children, which they increasingly did throughout the nineteenth century. In pursuing such questions, Marxism and anarchism have proved to have little more utility than liberalism, if only because such metatheories tend to encourage historians of limited ability and insight to precategorize and simplify educational and social-class phenomena. Quantification offers limited assistance. It represents one among several possible approaches to rigorous historical analysis of social-class variables.[12] Qualitative data from documentary sources or literature also may be needed to account for apparent connections between cultural and social-class characteristics of educational outcomes. There remains the often repeated, but not necessarily lame, conclusion familiar among scholars: more research is needed. What is essential, however, is the realization that social-class analyses are undoubtedly legitimate in the attempt to understand educational development in a nation where equal opportunity enjoys a rich oral and written tradition, if not a very strong history.

EDUCATION AND PUBLIC POLICY

Historians of education cannot proceed very far without an understanding of how and through what kinds of agencies and experiences people learn. They cannot proceed at all without marking the boundaries of their specialization. What is education? In his multivolume history, *American Education,* Lawrence Cremin views it "as the deliberate, systematic, and sustained effort to transmit or evoke knowledge, attitudes, values, skills, and sensibilities, a process that is more limited than what the anthropologist would term enculturation or the sociologist socialization, though obviously inclusive of some of the same elements."[13] That definition, or some version of it, now dominates the history of American education. As employed by Cremin, it enables investigation of the formal and informal agencies that "have shaped American thought, character, and sensibility over the years and . . . the relationships between these agencies and the society that has sustained them."[14] Hypothetically, the range of variables is limitless. Nor should one be put off by such qualifiers as "deliberate, systematic, and sustained." As Cremin sees them, such educational agencies as families and television follow curricula and assess their results.[15]

When education is defined as both institution and process, its history becomes more encompassing and complex. Intellectual, political, and cultural factors emerge as necessary resources for full-bodied chronicles. Indeed, during the years since the late 1950s, historians of education have produced a richly varied research literature utilizing perspectives and analytic tools borrowed from literature and the arts, social change theory, theology, church history, demography, economics, and psychoanalytic theory.[16] Although some have been used with greater frequency and confidence than others, the list of potential sources is far from complete. Maxine Greene has argued persuasively that poetry, drama, film, and novels remain largely untapped as sources in the history of education.[17] On the other hand, among historians in various specialties, including education, there is enormous interest in cultural phenomena and ethnicity within the American context.[18]

Expanding the concept of education, however, has not solved one basic dilemma of historians. It has, on the contrary, become more acute. Learning theories abound, and, while the state of knowledge is not so fluid that one can be selected by tossing a coin, historians of education have inevitably assumed positions on the nature and value of education. With equal necessity, they have adopted criteria for locating and assessing its outcomes. Openly, covertly, or indirectly, their work displays attitudes and philosophical assumptions of education. If learning is perceived as essentially cognitive development, its history differs from chronicles that start by assuming that education involves feelings and behavior to significant degrees. The surest course touches all bases: cognition, affect, skill, and morality — in short, the phenomena necessary for creating flesh-and-blood histories. That, of course, only restates the problem. Balanced, presumably neutral, approaches risk offering little more than dull comfort. Identifying and sifting the sources remain the historian's essential labors. But while these tasks can possibly be begun, they cannot be completed without the aid of a point of view. Granted, examples of incompetent, witless history can still be found.

It is more accurate to admit that the educational point of view colors and shapes historical research on education from the outset. If the latter has integrity, the former is altered and honed in the process. Without that dialectic, some fairly dreadful history appears in print. Consider two examples. What constitutes the history of American Indian education? Without at least crude knowledge of the characteristics distinguishing the various tribes and nations of Native Americans, historians blunder at the outset. A general history is possible, although none has yet been published, but only if built on analyses of relatively discrete elements of culture and tradition.[19] Such precision remains necessary even if historians limit their focus to the forms of education imposed on Indians by white people. Educational policies, programs, and practices intended for Indians, whether devised at federal or state levels, varied over time and often by locality. There were, in short, several histories in the making — a point that raises a more profound question for historians of education. Is the history of Native American education solely or even primarily the story of white attempts to school, train, or acculturate Indian peoples? Here is a legitimate area of research. When done well, important contributions to knowledge follow. But they constitute a partial account, resting possibly on the assumption that education only occurs in forms and processes familiar within Western European traditions. Vast segments of the story are omitted: the forms, processes, and traditions of learning indigenous to the various tribes and nations. Admittedly, a history from that perspective is a difficult achievement, written primary sources being almost nonexistent, but the effort brings us closer to telling the whole story. Furthermore, it may shed light on American Indians' astonishing capacity for cultural survival.[20]

The history of Native American education helps to illustrate other general problems in educational historiography. Analyzing the points of cultural conflict and imposition encourages one to move beyond mere description to weigh the gains and losses. Simplistic notions of

progress or failure become difficult to defend. Without the aid of narrow provincialisms, one cannot conclude that white people civilized
Indians, or failed to do so. Even assuming that the effort issued from
humane and pious intentions, and quite often it did not, the ultimate
result was altered civilization. Native Americans had civilizations of
their own well before the white invasion. And in those instances of
relative assimilation or even acculturation, the effective forces may
not have been white education or the attraction of European culture
but technological progress and insurmountable economic and military
power. That hypothesis points to the history of American Indian
education as a possible testing ground for assumptions about education as a principal agent of social development and reform. Although
much research remains to be done, what appears to be emerging as
the history of Native American education is a tale rife with ambiguity
and anguish, few heroes, and an ending not yet in sight—in other
words, history on a human scale.

Attempts to write the history of education from learners' perspectives further illustrate the complex relation between the historian's
point of view and historical research. Note that Cremin's definition of
education encourages such attempts. The goal is to transcend the intentions of teachers and other educators, and perhaps the institutional
boundaries of education as well, in order to assess learning outcomes
and give voice to "the inarticulate." Despite apparent difficulties,
there have been impressive gains in historical research on child-rearing practices, the family, the life of the college student, inmates of
reformatories, and the effects of pedagogy and teacher attitudes.[21]
Through census data, biographical research, street directories, and
such sources as municipal voter registries and school records,
historians can on occasion reconstruct literacy levels and mobility patterns and assess their correlations with identifiable educational experiences. They can make judgments about the forms and extent of
practical intelligence in a particular time or place by examining the
kinds of work people performed, the content of popular literature,
and the dominant modes of social interaction.[22]

The fundamental difficulty in such research is locating valid sources
that speak from within the learner's world. Short of that, there are
risks that an elitist history of education will be supplanted by a new
determinism wherein learners are viewed, if only tacitly, as passive
recipients. Entering the learner's world through sources and records

reflecting their own experiences not only helps assess actual educational practices and outcomes; it also presents fresh perspectives on the learning process. Education, after all, is more than imposition, that is, something done to someone. At some point and by a chemistry not always clear, learners may join the process as active participants, singularly altering it. Perhaps in education, as in voting behavior, people can act in what they perceive to be their own interests.[23] A history of education that avoids depicting learners as mere victims or consumers can include careful analyses of the politics of education, that is, who controls or influences it and to what extent, who is accountable for its outcomes, and who can change or redirect it. Required, too, is consideration of qualitative data on the relation of education to the ways people experience and express meaning, hope, and failure. Biographical research can be of assistance, and, as Maxine Greene has argued, among the most readily available and instructive sources are literature and the arts.[24]

Whatever educational theory or philosophy historians adopt, they find themselves contending with education's elusiveness. It attaches to some experiences but not others. Not all schools prove to be educational, and some are miseducative. There are agencies that intend to promote specified learning, but do not; others enable education accidentally. As idea or intellectual vision, education remains larger and more complex than any single agency or institutional form. It would seem, therefore, that education cannot be reduced to schooling, training, or the accumulation of credentials. Strictly speaking, educational theory or philosophy does not educate. That assignment falls to particular historical forms and processes that can offer actual, rather than hypothetical or illusory, educational opportunities. Greene suggests that these complexities constitute education's paradox, its essential power. They also point to its fundamental connection with policy. As process or institution, education takes particular forms. It acquires goals, rationales, participants, and something akin to evaluation criteria—matters mediated through formal or informal policy.

In the American context, the relation of education to policy is more precise. By the end of the eighteenth century, formal education had been identified as a nation-building strategy. Its possible intrinsic value received little attention relative to the social benefits expected to accrue from the education of citizens. The benefits contained contradictory elements. On one hand, there was talk about education as a means of preparing people for self-government and of freeing them from European attachments and sectional loyalties. On the other hand, there were suggestions that education represented a way to pacify the masses. Both points of view acknowledged that education was needed to promote the national welfare. This double-minded vision—education for public liberation and public control—constitutes a continuing thread in the nation's history. It accounts for the fact that, in the United States, education, at least in part, is a matter of public policy.

PUBLIC POLICY AND HISTORY

David Tyack illustrates the relation between American education and public policy in *The One Best System*.[25] A major contribution, this book synthesizes a wealth of research literature, brings to bear the panoply of urban-related variables in analyzing the history of city schools, and offers a framework for comparing school systems that maintains intact their unique features. Tyack characterizes the book as "an interpretive history," thus serving notice of its critical content and perspective. Actually, it encompasses several perspectives, most notably those not typically found in traditional histories of American education: female teachers, black parents and students, ethnic school administrators, and immigrant parents and their offspring. This history is not peopled with caricatures of heroes and villains, controllers and victims, and it is not inspirational. Without apology, Tyack focuses intentionally on public schools. In an institutionalized society such as the United States, he argues, schools offer reference points in analyzing the interactions of institutions and in marking social development, and, in this country, the latter involves accounting for urbanization. More fundamentally, Tyack insists on characterizing public schools as educational. Despite failure, inadequacy, and even bad faith, they represent a vast delivery system for learning opportunity. Because no other American institution holds that potential, the goals, organization, accessibility, and outcomes of schools represent both educational phenomena and public policy issues.

The One Best System also illustrates intentionally the relation of public policy and history, a relatively new but widely shared emphasis among historians of education. The recent works of such historians as Freeman Butts, Lawrence Cremin, Carl Kaestle, and Michael B. Katz indicate the depth of their interest in policy.[26] On one level, the focus is substantive, as revealed in research on the history of various educational policies. In addition, the relevance of historical research to contemporary policymaking is endorsed explicitly. Concern with policy issues is evident in earlier works by Butts, Cremin, and Tyack, and, indeed, in the research and writings of some nineteenth- and early twentieth-century historians of education as well. The shift is primarily one of emphasis and reflects growing appreciation for the structural character and connections of social and educational problems.

The major issues in American society and in American education during the past two decades can be traced to similar sources: racial injustice, cold war colonialism, war protest, urban decay, poverty, scarcity of resources, misuse of authority and law, unemployment, and inflation. The list should be longer, but these examples serve to indicate the range and depth of the social dysfunctions and controversies that marked the 1960s and 1970s. Some clearly were more fundamental than others. In addition, significant changes were witnessed in the rising expectations of minorities and working-class people, the heightened consciousness of purpose and meaning among women and racial and ethnic groups, the structure of the family, sexual mores, urban demography, technology, and the pervasiveness of communications media. Again, the list is illustrative only. The controversies and changes have proved to be unresponsive to piecemeal or programmatic approaches, suggesting the necessity of more fundamental alterations in the goals and structure of society. Confidence in that insight, which is neither radical nor conservative in origin, can be detected throughout the political spectrum, for it has given rise to the search for policy solutions to social and educational problems. Widespread interest in policy and policymaking is evident among academic scholars, particularly social scientists. Among historians of American education, it stems both from concern with current issues and the expanded research field within which they work. In the 1970s, if not before, no fancy footwork is required for educational historians to be socially relevant. It comes with the territory.

Involvement in policy research reflects and strengthens the expanded field of educational history. It invites inquiry into not only the history of selected policies, for example, compulsory school attendance, but also the history of agencies which operate at some distance from educational institutions but nonetheless influence programs and policies to varying degrees. State departments of education, the U.S. Office of Education, and the National Institute of Education represent obvious examples. The effects on educational practice of professional organizations, accreditation agencies, national testing services, large corporations, and labor unions further illustrate the potential for policy-oriented research in educational history.

Such research rarely can proceed along traditional lines. It is rigorously interdisciplinary. Narrative may be subsumed within a topical analysis. Goals and intentions are weighed against results that in turn can be taken as bases for speculation about unpublished objectives. Policy statements issued by an agency are examined in the context of the agency's organization and budget in order to determine the extent to which public pronouncements disclose or conceal actual priorities. Policies can be formal or informal, manifest or latent, and careful detection may be required to characterize them accurately. Measured in terms of their effects, formal policy may prove to be less potent than informal policy. One of the tasks of policy research is to ascertain whether that is indeed the case. Quantitative analysis is clearly useful in assessing policy outcomes, but couching results in human terms is likely to require documentary and oral sources as well. For example, reconstructing the intent of educational enactments involves analysis of legislative voting patterns, which can be quantified in the case of recorded votes. But there are other matters to be examined: preceding debates, voice votes, party affiliation, cloakroom compromises, and legislators' relations with their constituents. All of these may be stages in the process leading to the passage of a bill. The most influential determinants of legislative intent may not be immediately obvious or clearly susceptible to quantification. Other examples come to mind. Policy research typically requires penetrating the inner reaches of a bureaucracy. That alone may constitute an insurmountable barrier. If accomplished, other difficulties arise. Middle-echelon career bureaucrats tend to play instrumental roles in formal and informal policymaking, but they may not be highly visible within the organization. How is the historian to locate such significant actors and assess their influence? Research on bureaucratic personnel, including biographical study, would seem to be required, but sources may be scarce, examination of data tedious, and the story, in terms of interest value, underwhelming. Of greater historical significance, although equally difficult to produce, are assessments of the effects of

federal educational policies and programs on communities and individuals in the late nineteenth and early twentieth centuries. Such
research requires bringing multiple focuses to bear on relevant actions
in Congress, presidential initiatives, court decisions, and the work of
several federal agencies, including some no longer in operation. Yet
none of these sources speaks directly to the question of local effect. For
research in that direction, the sources are scattered and the empirical
data not always reliable, both of which hamper the important task of
comparing policy outcomes in various settings and among different
segments of the population.

In one noteworthy respect policy research in educational history
departs from recent trends in the field. Inquiry tends to be particularized and typically employs the case study method, but, as in the case of
federal or state policy, it may not be focused on local educational
practices and programs. On the contrary, historians who adopt a
policy orientation confront the possibility that rigorous analysis of
public education in Chicago might, for example, require devoting
considerable attention to distant agencies and influences. In other
respects, policy research in the history of education builds on the revisionist tradition developed over the past two decades. It ranges far beyond schools, utilizes quantitative and nonquantitive methods and
sources, and necessarily adopts a critical posture in analyzing the
educational past. It may also seek to influence contemporary policy.

Short of possible effects on policymaking, history contributes directly to the study of educational policy. Best characterized as a developing interdiscipline, the policy sciences in general remain conceptually
parochial. Analytic models that allow systematic comparisons across
national and cultural boundaries are rare.[27] As a rule, usable theory is
borrowed from one or more of the social sciences, which adds yet
another dimension to the parochialism of policy research. Thus, one
finds American welfare policy and British social policy, which, as the
late Richard Titmuss lamented, is distinct from British economic
policy.[28] Finally, there is the matter of limited objectivity in the policy
sciences. Far from being ideologically free, policy research proceeds
from value commitments. Such bias, in combination with rigorous
analysis of policy objectives and outcomes, represented for Titmuss a
major strength, "providing us with an ideological framework which
may stimulate us to ask the significant questions and expose the
significant choices."[29] An innovative theorist who taught at the Lon-

don School of Economics, Titmuss viewed the policy sciences as an applied research field. Its aim was not merely to study policy but to promote social change through policy formation. The policy sciences contribute to the process directly by clarifying and extending the range of
choices. That expectation optimistically assumes at least a consultative relation between policymakers and policy scientists.

Similar optimism can be detected when David Tyack discusses the
relevance of educational history to policy:

> We stand at a point in time when we need to examine those educational institutions
> and values we have taken for granted. We need to turn facts into puzzles in order to
> perceive alternatives both in the past and in the present. The way we understand that
> past profoundly shapes how we make choices today.[30]

In short, the contributions of history to educational policy must be
presumed and insisted upon.

There is, first and obviously, the introduction of a longitudinal
dimension that facilitates the assessment of policy outcomes. Linear
studies of particular policy issues hold some interest but a more significant contribution is the analysis of such developments within broader
social and cultural contexts. The range of policy options at selected
points in the past can be reconstructed and grounds established for
speculating about the outcomes of rejected possibilities. As a related
resource, research literature on the history of education in various national and cultural settings enables comparative policy studies. Finally, and perhaps least susceptible to fine measurement, there is the contribution of educational history—a humanities-related field—to
policy study—a research area dominated by the social and behavioral
sciences. Supplementing empirical data with qualitative assessments,
history can bring to policy research the humanizing resources available in memory, ideas, values, and traditions that join with grander
economic, social, and political developments in shaping educational
policies and determining their effects on people. History also can be
useful in understanding the extent to which policy and policymaking
are influenced by inertia, the weight of established practice, familiar
ideas, and traditional approaches to problem solving. Within an interdisciplinary approach, history can liberate policy study from
presentism.

But it is futile to claim too much. There is a noticeable gap separating policy research from policymaking.[31] Isolated from each other,
the former is blunted by lack of import, while the latter, at least from

the standpoint of scholars, falls prey to special interests. The fact is that policy represents an effective response to systemic social problems only under certain conditions. It may, as Titmuss argued, promote social change and even structural redistributions of power and resources. Depending on who makes it and their objectives, it may also move in opposite directions. Policy can serve as a facade for the status quo as easily as an instrument for change. And policymaking can become a routine and ritualistic reaffirmation of established goals and values and acceptable responses to social dysfunctions. Such potentialities explain in part Cremin's characterization of the policy orientation as Whiggish.[32] History enters policy study and policymaking with similar limitations. Perceptions of the past, which provide negligible leverage within the political process, may reflect nothing more resourceful than self-serving rationales for business as usual.

These general considerations have direct application to educational policy and its relation to history and historiography. The Whiggish and anti-Whiggish strands in the history of American education offer two general but starkly distinct perceptions of the past.[33] One lays a foundation for the ratification of established educational goals and institutions and the values they reflect. The other encourages critical reassessment and fresh policy departures. Alone or in combination, each can be appropriate and useful in policy study, depending upon the issue being confronted and its context. In either case, the contributions to policymaking remain at best indirect. The potential for history may take subtly complex forms, as historian David Donald has observed to his colleagues, a warning that applies with particular force to historians of American education.[34] The nation's present, he finds, is so radically different from previous eras that its people may be well advised to sever connections. The proposed role for history becomes, ironically, helping people to appreciate the irrelevance of the past, the need to reconceptualize their problems, and the likelihood that solutions will come slowly. It is a limited assignment serving to remind historians that the quality and persuasiveness of their work hold consequences for others and extend into the future.

NOTES

Warren: **A Past for the Present**

1. Among the first and most scholarly treatments of such criticisms is Lawrence A. Cremin, *The Wonderful World of Ellwood Patterson Cubberley: An Essay on the*

Historiography of American Education (New York: Bureau of Publications, Teachers College, Columbia University, 1965). See also Richard J. Storr, "The Role of Education in American History: A Memorandum," *Harvard Educational Review* 46 (August 1976): 331-354.

2. Carl F. Kaestle, "Conflict and Consensus Revisited: Notes toward a Reinterpretation of American Educational History," *Harvard Educational Review* 46 (August 1976): 390-396; reprinted in Chapter 7 of this volume.

3. Arthur Schlesinger, Jr., "America: Experiment or Destiny?" *American Historical Review* 82 (June 1977): 505.

4. M. I. Finley, "'Progress' in Historiography," *Daedalus* 106 (Summer 1977): 132.

5. *Ibid.*, 126.

6. See, e.g., Bernard A. Weisberger, "The Dark and Bloody Ground of Reconstruction Historiography," *Journal of Southern History* 25 (November 1959): 427-447; David H. Donald, *The Politics of Reconstruction, 1863-1867* (Baton Rouge: Louisiana State University Press, 1965); and Robert Kelley, "Ideology and Political Culture from Jefferson to Nixon," *American Historical Review* 82 (June 1977): 531-562, esp. 544-547 and notes. See also responses to Kelley's paper by Ronald P. Formisano and Willie Lee Rose in "Comments," *ibid.*, 568-582.

7. The most thoroughly documented critical assessment of radical revisionist historiography, including historical interpretations by several nonhistorians, is Diane Ravitch, "The Revisionists Revised: Studies in the Historiography of American Education," *Proceedings of the National Academy of Education* 4 (1977): 1-84. Also, Charles A. Tesconi, Jr., "Review of *Reason and Rhetoric*," *Teachers College Record* 78 (February 1977): 383-391.

8. Ravitch, "The Revisionists Revised," 2-5; and Sol Cohen, "The History of the History of American Education, 1900-1976: The Uses of the Past," *Harvard Educational Review* 46 (August 1976): 298-330. For recent comment by Cremin, see Lawrence A. Cremin, *Traditions of American Education* (New York: Basic Books, 1977), 131-134.

9. See esp. Michael B. Katz, *Class, Bureaucracy, and Schools: The Illusion of Educational Change in America*, expanded ed. (New York: Praeger Publishers, 1975). Cremin dates the beginning of the later revisionism with the publication of Michael B. Katz, *The Irony of Early School Reform: Educational Innovation in Mid-Nineteenth Century Massachusetts* (Cambridge, Mass.: Harvard University Press, 1968). See Cremin, *Traditions of American Education*, 131.

10. R. Freeman Butts, "The Public School: Assaults on a Great Idea," *Nation* (April 30, 1973): 553-560.

11. See *id.*, *Public Education in the United States: From Revolution to Reform, 1776-1976* (New York: Holt, Rinehart and Winston, Inc., 1978); Cremin, *Traditions of American Education*, 132; and Merle Curti, *The Social Ideas of American Educators* (New York: Charles Scribner's Sons, 1935).

12. Katz discusses the limited utility of metatheories and quantitative analysis in interdisciplinary approaches to the history of higher education in Michael B. Katz, "Review of *The University in Society: I, Oxford and Cambridge from the Fourteenth to the Early Nineteenth Century; II, Europe, Scotland, and the United States from*

the Sixteenth to the Twentieth Century," Journal of Interdisciplinary History 7 (Autumn 1976): 319-322.

13. Lawrence A. Cremin, *American Education: The Colonial Experience, 1607-1783* (New York: Harper and Row, 1970), xiii.

14. *Ibid.,* xi.

15. Lawrence A. Cremin, "Public Education and the Education of the Public," *Teachers College Record* 77 (September 1975): 5; reprinted in Chapter 2 of this volume. For an elaboration of his 1975 John Dewey Lecture, see *id., Public Education* (New York: Basic Books, 1976).

16. See the bibliographic essay in Cremin, *Traditions of American Education,* 131-163. A thorough survey of recent work in the field, with an excellent bibliography, is Geraldine Joncich Clifford, "Education: Its History and Historiography," *Review of Research in Education* 4 (1976): 210-267.

17. See esp. Maxine Greene, "Identities and Contours: An Approach to Educational History," *Educational Researcher* 3 (April 1973): 5-10; reprinted in Chapter 7 of this volume.

18. Kelley, "Ideology and Political Culture from Jefferson to Nixon," 531-562. Also, responses to Kelley's paper by Geoffrey Blodgett and Formisano in "Comments," *American Historical Review* 82 (June 1977): 563-577.

19. A general history of twentieth-century developments is Margaret Szasz, *Education and the American Indian: The Road to Self-Determination, 1928-1973* (Albuquerque: University of New Mexico Press, 1974). Cremin cautions historians to note Indians' educational contributions to white settlers, especially during the colonial period, and the education available to both general groups through "the experience of culture contact." See Cremin, *Traditions of American Education,* 4-5. For a brief, provocative survey of white efforts to "educate" Native Americans, see Diane Ravitch, "On the History of Minority Group Education in the United States," *Teachers College Record* 78 (December 1976): 213-228; reprinted in Chapter 5 of this volume.

20. A deliberately "overenthusiastic" study of indigenous Indian education, using anthropological tools and resources, is George A. Pettitt, "Primitive Education in North America," *University of California Publications in American Archeology and Ethnography* 43 (No. 1, 1946): 1-182. For a fictionalized depiction of indigenous Indian education and culture contact, see Edwin Corle, *Fig Tree John* (New York: Pocket Books, 1972; originally published in 1935).

21. Clifford, "Education: Its History and Historiography," 219-243.

22. See, for example, Daniel Calhoun, *The Intelligence of a People* (Princeton, N.J.: Princeton University Press, 1973); and esp. Cremin, *Traditions of American Education,* 134-163.

23. For observations on "a new determinism" in analyses of ethnic voting patterns, see Rose, "Comments," *American Historical Review* 82 (June 1977): 580.

24. See, for example, Greene, "Identities and Contours."

25. David B. Tyack, *The One Best System: A History of American Urban Education* (Cambridge, Mass.: Harvard University Press, 1974).

26. See, for example, Butts, *Public Education in the United States;* Cremin, *Public Education;* Carl F. Kaestle, *The Evolution of an Urban School System: New York*

City, 1750-1850 (Cambridge, Mass.: Harvard University Press, 1973); and Katz, *Class, Bureaucracy, and Schools.*

27. For an analysis of one aspect of the policy field, see Richard M. Titmuss, *Social Policy: An Introduction* (New York: Pantheon Books, 1974). See also Philip W. Semas, "How Influential Is Sociology?" *Chronicle of Higher Education* (September 19, 1977): 4.

28. Titmuss, *Social Policy,* 20, 60-74.

29. *Ibid.,* 136.

30. Tyack, *The One Best System,* 4.

31. Semas, "How Influential Is Sociology?" 4.

32. Cremin, *Traditions in American Education,* 132.

33. *Ibid.,* and Clifford, "Education: Its History and Historiography," 215-218.

34. David Herbert Donald, "Personal View: The Past Is Irrelevant," *Chicago Daily News* (September 19, 1977): 15.

TWO

More than Schooling

Public Education and the Education of the Public, by
Lawrence A. Cremin

History of Education as a Field of Study: An Essay on the Recent
Historiography of American Education, by   *Sol Cohen*

Expanding the history of American education beyond an earlier
emphasis on schooling has encouraged research on a broad range of
topics and issues. It has also resulted in more sophisticated analyses of
school history through interdisciplinary and case study methods.
Lawrence Cremin has played a major role in these developments.
Through his own research, he has been instrumental in establishing
the extended perimeter of the field and in clarifying its relation to
other specialties within general history. His contribution to this
chapter illustrates that he has also been influential in reconceptualiz-
ing education as process and institution, its complex social and
cultural relationships, and the pivotal themes and episodes in its
history. Consider the possibilities, for example, when historians approach two basic questions afresh: What constitutes formal education
(or, more narrowly, what constitutes a curriculum)? Where, besides
schools, does one look for public education? Cremin discusses such
questions and the relation between history, education, and public
policy more fully in the expanded version of his John Dewey Lecture
(*Public Education* [New York: Basic Books, 1976]).

Sol Cohen traces recent developments in the history of education in
an interpretive overview of the field's history since the early 1950s. His

article documents the rich variety of research literature produced during this period and comments on the major disagreements over interpretation and methodology that have surfaced among historians of education. Cohen's contributions to psychohistory lend authority to his discussion of the utility of psychoanalytic concepts within education history.

Public Education and the Education of the Public

Lawrence A. Cremin

. . . I had the pleasure of knowing John Dewey during the last few years of his life and of talking with him on any number of occasions. I shall never forget the first time I met him, when he was ninety. We had a mutual friend in Sing-nan Fen, who had translated Dewey's works in China and had then come to the United States to study philosophy of education and in the process had come to know Dewey. . . . Fen asked me quite unexpectedly one evening whether I would be willing to deliver a package for him to the Dewey apartment on my way home, and I said of course I would. . . . I . . . rang the bell and Mrs. Dewey came to the door and graciously accepted the package and asked whether I would like to meet Professor Dewey. I said it would be a privilege and was promptly ushered into the study, where Dewey was pecking away at an ancient typewriter, using two fingers. He looked up, smiled, greeted me warmly, said he was working on an article dealing with the improvement in his concept of interaction that the term "transaction" had made possible, and then asked quite bluntly, "What do you think, Mr. Cremin?" It was one of those occasions when the lips move but the words have trouble coming out. The words did come, and . . . we had a lively conversation for about a half hour, in

Reprinted, with permission, from *Teachers College Record* 77 (September 1975), 1-12. This selection is adapted from the John Dewey Lecture delivered at the annual meeting of the John Dewey Society in Chicago in 1975. The formulations have been developed in the course of a larger research project on the history of American education that has been generously supported by the Carnegie Corporation of New York.

which at the age of twenty-three I was treated as an absolute equal. As I said, I shall never forget it.

Most of my other opportunities to talk with Professor Dewey came at the Old Shanghai Restaurant . . . . Dr. and Mrs. Dewey . . . would dine frequently at the Shanghai on Sunday evenings. Fen was often with them, and through Fen's invitations I came to join them. I must tell you that whatever the emphasis on the social and the communal in Dewey's writing, it was rampant individualism in that Chinese restaurant, and I may be the only person living who learned to use chopsticks fighting over fried rice with John Dewey.

I could go on, but I shall not. Permit me, instead, to turn to . . . three matters: first, I would like to point to a fundamental problem in the progressive theory of education, namely, the positing of a polarity between school and society that does not sufficiently particularize the educational situation as it actually exists; second, I would like to propose a revision of the progressive theory that I believe details the situation more effectively; and, third, I would like to suggest some implications of that revision for public policymaking in education.

. . . *The fundamental problem of the polarity.* One can locate it in John Dewey's *Democracy and Education,* which is, of course, the classic statement of the progressive theory. Recall Dewey's argument in the early sections of the work. The most notable distinction between living beings and inanimate things, he tells us, is that living beings maintain themselves by renewal. Among human beings, that renewal takes place through a process of cultural transmission, which Dewey refers to as "education in its broadest sense." Education in its broadest sense is a process that is continuous, ubiquitous, pervasive, and all-powerful—indeed, so powerful that Dewey draws the moral that the only way in which adults can consciously control the kind of education children get is by controlling the environment in which they act, think, and feel.[1]

Then, in a crucial leap, Dewey goes on to tell us that there is a marked difference between the education everyone gets simply from living with others and the deliberate education offered by the school. In the ordinary course of living, education is *incidental*; in schooling, education is *intentional.* In developing the argument, Dewey takes the familiar early twentieth-century tack of going back to the origins of institutions in some primordial state of society. The family, he tells us, began in the desire to gratify appetites and secure the perpetuity of a line. Religious associations, he continues, began in the desire to ward off evil influences and obtain the favor of supreme powers. And work began in the simple enslavement of one human being to another. Any education that might have derived from participation in these institutions, he points out, was at best incidental. And, indeed, he tells us by way of illustration that savage groups have no special devices or materials or institutions for teaching the young, with the exception of initiation ceremonies. For the most part, they depend on the kind of incidental learning that derives from shared activity.[2]

As civilization advances, however, life becomes more complicated, and much of what adults do is so complex that simple participation no longer suffices for the transmission of culture. At this point, Dewey suggests, intentional agencies, called schools, and explicit materials, called studies, come into being. And the task of transmitting particular aspects of life is delegated to a special group of people called teachers. Dewey is careful to point out that schools are an important means for transmitting culture, but only one means among many, and, when compared with other agencies, a relatively superficial means. Nevertheless, schools are the only means adults really have at their disposal for going systematically and deliberately about the education of the young.[3]

Once this leap is made, it is decisive in Dewey's argument. Though Dewey returns at a number of places to what he calls the "social environment," the remainder of the book is not about families or churches or work, but rather about schools. Dewey's theory of education is ultimately a theory of school and society. And while Dewey was primarily concerned with reconciling the dualism between school and society, I would stress the fact that he may have created the theoretical polarity in order to effect the reconciliation. To say this is in no way to deny that the schools of Dewey's time were abstruse, formalistic, and in need of reconciliation with society. It is rather to suggest that Dewey may ultimately have been victimized by the very polarity he set out to reconcile.[4]

That polarity had prodigious consequences for the discussion of education and politics during the 1920s and 1930s. We can see it in the two quite different arguments put forward within the progressive camp during the early years of the Depression. On the one hand, George S. Counts asked, "Dare the school build a new social order?" and called upon teachers forthrightly to indoctrinate children in the

values of democratic socialism as their contribution to the development of a reconstructed American society. To Counts's argument,
however, Dewey replied that, whether or not teachers dared build a
new social order in that particular way or some other, they probably
could not. In a modern industrial society, with its multiplicity of
political and educative agencies, the school could never be the main
determinant of political, intellectual, or moral change. The best the
school could do would be to form the understanding and the dispositions necessary for movement toward a changed social order.[5]

On the other hand, the group that prepared *The Educational Frontier,* of which Dewey was a member, went in the opposite direction.
Far from daring the school to build a new social order, they despaired
of the school making any appreciable difference whatever until the
larger social ambience within which the school carried on its work had
been fundamentally altered. Hence, Robert Bruce Raup called upon
teachers to enter the political lists and struggle for a better life in order
to create a more hospitable and productive world in which to educate.
"When the type of character desired by the school is so dependent for
support upon conditions in the whole culture," Raup maintained,
"and this support is not forthcoming, the educator's responsibility
moves out into society to agitate and to work for that support." Here
too, however, though Dewey was a working member of the yearbook
committee, he demurred, contending that his advocacy of educators
assisting in the development of a changed social order was in no way
an advocacy of the school throwing itself into the political arena and
taking the side of some particular party there.[6]

Now my interest is only incidentally in locating Dewey with respect
to the problem I have posed. It is primarily in explicating the problem
itself. For, in the last analysis, the Progressives ended up on the horns
of a dilemma: either they could politicize the school, remaining
dubious about their efforts since the school was so powerless, or they
could abandon the school and enter the political lists, seeking
gradually or cataclysmically to change the entire social ambience in
which youngsters came of age. Dewey revealed the dilemma beautifully in an address . . . to a conference on early childhood education at
Teachers College in the spring of 1933. The address began with one of
Dewey's great aphorisms: "The most Utopian thing about Utopia is
that there are no schools at all." Education in Utopia, Dewey went on
to say, is carried out without benefit of schools, since children learn

what they have to know in informal association with the adults who direct their activity. So far, so good. But Dewey did not go on from that point to describe a Utopian society whose values were so pervasive and whose institutions were so cohesive as to form the young through the very process of living. Rather, he went on to describe a society in which there were schools, but essentially activity schools of the sort Dewey and his daughter Evelyn had written about in *Schools of To-Morrow*. In 1933 Dewey was still trying to reconcile the dualism between school and society, but he was for all intents and purposes the victim of his own theoretical polarity. And, indeed, that polarity persists right down to the present time. We see it in the ambivalence of the educational reform movement of the 1960s, with its free-school proponents on the one side and its de-school proponents on the other. And we see it also—and in a more dangerous form perhaps—in the vast pendulum swing of American opinion during the 1970s, from a centurylong overreliance on schooling as a general instrument of social aspiration to a period of widespread disenchantment with schooling. Whether or not we like Dewey and the Progressives, we are heirs to their formulations, and the irony is that an age that has all but forgotten Dewey is still governed by his analytical categories.[7]

. . . *A revised version of the progressive theory.* . . . The crucial point at which Dewey went awry, it seems to me, is the point in his discussion of incidental versus intentional education where he dwelled on the origins of institutions rather than their functions. What matter that the family may have *begun* in the desire to gratify appetites and secure the perpetuation of a line? What matter that religious associations may have *begun* in the desire to ward off evil influences and secure the favor of supreme powers? What matter that work may have *begun* in enslavement to others? For one thing, we cannot really know how they began; for another, the question of origins may not be central to the argument. The important fact is that family life does educate, religious life does educate, and work does educate; and, what is more, the education of all three realms is as intentional as the education of the school, though in different ways and in different measures.

Every family has a curriculum, which it teaches quite deliberately and systematically over time. Every church and synagogue has a curriculum, which it teaches deliberately and systematically over time—the Old and New Testaments, after all, are among our oldest curricula, and so are the Missal and the Mass, and so is the Book of Common Prayer. And every employer has a curriculum, which he teaches deliberately and systematically over time, and the curriculum includes not only the technical skills of typing or welding or reaping or teaching but also the social skills of carrying out those activities in concert with others on given time schedules and according to established expectations and routines. One can go on to point out that libraries have curricula, museums have curricula, boy scout troops have curricula, and day-care centers have curricula, and, most important, perhaps, radio and television stations have curricula—and by these curricula I refer not only to programs labeled educational but also to news broadcasts and documentaries (which presumably inform), to commercials (which teach people to want), and to soap operas (which reinforce common myths and values).

To specify this range of institutions is to save us from the Deweyan polarity of all life being broadly educative and overwhelmingly powerful and the school being intentionally educative but not very powerful at all. Rather, we have a theory of education in which each of the major educative agencies performs a mediative role with respect to the others and with respect to society at large. The family mediates the culture, and it also mediates the ways in which religious organizations, television broadcasters, schools, and employers mediate the culture. Families not only engage deliberately and systematically in the teaching of knowledge, values, attitudes, skills, and sensibilities, they also screen and interpret the teaching of churches, synagogues, television broadcasters, and employers. One can go on and work out all the permutations and combinations. What is more, these various institutions mediate the culture in a variety of pedagogical styles—think of the differences between what Jerome Bruner has called *enactive* education, *ikonic* education, and *symbolic* education, and the different combinations of these styles that pertain in different situations at different times. Further, these various institutions mediate the culture via different technologies for the recording, sharing, and distributing of symbols. In effect, they define the terms of effective participation and growth in the society. Remaining within the broad Deweyan context, we can posit a new formulation: the theory of education becomes the theory of the relation of various educative interactions and institutions to one another and to the society at large.[8]

. . . *Implications of this analysis for policymaking in education.* I would put forward three assertions: first, that we have to think *comprehensively* about education; second, that we have to think *rela-*

tionally about education; and, third, that we have to think *publicly* about education. Let me take each of these . . . in turn.

. . . We have traditionally assumed in the United States that the public school for more than a century created and recreated the American public, virtually singlehandedly, and endowed that public with its unique capability of working cooperatively on social problems, despite its ethnic, racial, religious, and class heterogeneity. The assumption, of course, is not without foundation. The public school has labored mightily over the years to nurture certain common values and commitments and to teach the skills by which a vastly variegated society can resolve its conflicts peacefully rather than by the methods of guerrilla warfare. Indeed, the public school has actually come to symbolize the quest for community in American society. But the public school has never functioned alone or in isolation. Where it has succeeded, it has functioned as part of a large configuration of institutions, including families, churches, Sunday schools, and reform schools, committed to essentially complementary values. When the configuration has disintegrated, however, as it has from time to time in our larger cities, and when the centrifugal forces of heterogeneity have overbalanced the centrifugal forces of community, the public school has been less successful. My assertion is not the powerlessness of public schooling—far from it—but rather the limitations of public schooling. And the moral is simple: The public school ought never to take the entire credit for the educational accomplishments of the public, and it ought never to be assigned the entire blame.

. . . The public is educated by many institutions, some of them public and some of them private, and . . . public schools are only one among several important public institutions that educate the public. There are, after all, public libraries, public museums, public television, and public work projects, the most pervasive, perhaps, being the military services. Other societies, of course, have used quite different agencies to educate the public. The Soviet Union, for example, has used the Komsomol, a network of youth organizations, as an important instrument of public education, while the People's Republic of China has used communes in public factories and on public farms in similar fashion. And the Indians, the Australians, and the Venezuelans have used public radio to teach the skills of literacy in areas too remote for schools.

A kind of obverse of these propositions is the recognition that *all* educational transactions have both private and public consequences. Family nurture that encourages independence, church teaching that condemns family planning, television news programs that dramatize the human consequences of military ventures—these are but a few examples of private educative efforts with profound public impact.

In sum, then, to think *comprehensively* about education, we must consider policies with respect to a wide variety of institutions that educate, not only schools and colleges, but libraries, museums, daycare centers, radio and television stations, offices, factories, and farms. To be concerned solely with schools in the kind of educational world we are living in today is to have a kind of fortress mentality in contending with a very fluid and dynamic situation. Education must be looked at whole, across the entire life span, and in all the situations and institutions in which it occurs. Obviously, public policy will not touch and ought not to touch every situation with equal intensity— that only happens in totalitarian societies, and even in totalitarian societies it never happens quite as efficaciously as the leaders would prefer. Indeed, there are some situations which public policy will not touch at all. But it must consider each so that wise choices can be made as to where to invest what effort to achieve which goals with respect to which clienteles. The United States Congress already does this when it decides to allocate so many dollars to children's television rather than schooling, and, incidentally, in dealing with children's television it inevitably affects the family. And local communities already do this when they decide in a period of budgetary stringency to close a public library rather than a public school. I would only insist that the range of possibilities be understood far more explicitly than it has been in the past and that public authorities approach these questions of allocation rationally rather than whimsically, and with a full awareness of educational consequences.

. . . Second, we must think *relationally.* To do this means . . . to be aware of the problem of allocation of financial and human resources, as indicated above, and of resultant educational outcomes. And it means . . . that, wherever an effort goes forward in education, it must go forward not in isolation from other educative institutions but in relation to them. From the vantage point of the school, this is a significant point. Given the thrust of my argument, I am occasionally accused of downgrading the school and being uninterested in schoolteachers. Nothing could be farther from the truth. I am interested . . . in making schools and schoolteachers more effective. And they will not be more effective until they become aware of and actually engage these other educators.

In some subject areas, of course, the school originates much of what it teaches. Mathematics is an example. In mathematics, the student learns much of what he needs to learn for the first time in the classroom (though with the new mathematics series now being produced for television by the Education Development Center, that may become less and less true). But in other realms, in languages and literature, for example, or in social studies or hygiene, or the arts, or the domain of values and morals, the child has his first learning and possibly his most persuasive learning earlier and elsewhere. In these realms, it may be that the best the school can do is engage the instruction of the other educators and seek to strengthen or complement or correct or neutralize or countereducate, or, most importantly, perhaps, try to develop in students an awareness of the other educators and an ability themselves to deal with them.

What I have argued with respect to the school also goes for the other educators. For day-care workers, pastors, editors of children's encyclopedias, and directors of senior citizen's centers, the message is the same: Whatever is done, to be effective, must be done with an awareness of what has gone on and what is going on elsewhere. Incidentally, the principle has special relevance for evaluation and accountability because whatever judgment is made of any particular educational program must always be made in light of what is going on elsewhere that affects that program. This, to me, is the real message of James Coleman's study of equal educational opportunity, not that the school is powerless but that the family is powerful. What often happens is the same thing that happens when negative numbers are added to positive numbers: An immense contribution by the school is frequently reflected in a comparatively modest showing on an achievement scale, since with respect to the understanding or behavior being measured by the achievement scale, the child started out not at ground zero but with a deficit, at least as defined by the scale. Or, conversely, as is frequently the case with highly selective institutions, a very modest contribution by the school is reflected in an admirable showing on an achievement scale, since the child has already learned elsewhere a good deal of whatever it is the scale is measuring.

. . . By thinking *publicly*, I mean several things. To begin, it means we must be aware that public thinking about education and public policymaking for education goes on at a variety of levels and in a variety of places. It goes forward at the local, state, regional, federal, and international levels, and it proceeds in legislatures, in the courts, in executive agencies, and in private and quasi-public civic organizations. The intense political struggles this past year in Boston, and Kanawha County, West Virginia, are excellent examples, as is the battle to get the Federal Communications Commission to adopt more stringent rules for the governance of children's television. What's more, the growing reliance on the courts during the past quarter century to develop policies through the definition, assertion, and claim of certain social and educational rights is also profoundly relevant. It is an oft repeated truism that the courts have been our most influential agencies of educational policymaking since World War II. But, as John Coons recently pointed out in a discussion at Teachers College, courts tend to stress our differences: They tend to affirm the rights of individuals or groups to dissent from agreed upon policies. Legislatures, on the other hand, tend to deal with the definition and advancement of that which is common. And hence the growing recourse to the courts in matters of educational policy is fraught with significance for substance as well as procedure. And it is fraught with significance for the policy itself. As my former teacher Henry Steele Commager, certainly second to none in his insistent espousal of the cause of civil liberties, pointed out some years ago in a discussion of *Majority Rule and Minority Rights,* recourse to the courts, particularly in the realm of constitutional law, is an immensely powerful tool in a democratic society for the achievement of short-term goals, especially with respect to the redress of civil and political inequity. But recourse to the courts short-circuits certain processes vital to a democratic society. There is, after all, little opportunity for appeal once the court of last resort has handed down its ruling, and there is precious little political education for the public in appellate proceedings. This is not to say that the Warren court and the Burger court have not tried at many points to educate the public with respect to the bearing of the Constitution on education. It is only to argue, with Commager, that the legislative process and the public debate surrounding it is a surer and more fundamental long-range educator of the public than the judicial process.[9]

I should add quite explicitly at this point that nothing here should be taken as a criticism of the political outcomes of recourse to the federal and state courts, from *Brown* in 1954, to *Serrano* in 1971 and *Robinson* in 1973, to *Goss* in 1975. It is merely to argue that the process of public education resulting from court decisions is very different from the process that leads to the enactment and implementation of legislation. And the current turmoil in Boston, the failure of the legislatures of California and New Jersey to accomplish the mandated reforms of their respective state systems of school finance, and the puzzlement that has followed in the wake of the more recent *Goss* ruling on the rights of pupils are illustrative of this fact.[10]

The distinction between the politics of the courts and the politics of legislatures brings me to my final point, namely, that, given the range and variety of institutions that educate the public, some of them public, some of them quasi-public, and some of them private, simplistic notions of "public control" become untenable. Control, after all, varies in character and intensity from the kind of direct supervision one sees in the management of public school systems or public libraries, to the kind of regulation exercised over the television industry by the Federal Communications Commission, to the kind of influence tax policy exerts on the size and structure of families, and hence on the character of familial education. And if one looks at the power of the educative agencies farthest removed from the public reach, one is led not to deny the need for effective public regulation of public schools, public libraries, and public television, but rather to affirm the need for public discussion in the realms beyond the reach of direct public control. And hence we are thrown, inevitably, back to the politics of persuasion and to the public dialogue about educational means and ends that is the essence of the politics of persuasion.

We live in an age that affirms individuality and plurality, and, given what governments, including democratic governments, have done with their power in our time, one can understand and sympathize with the attractiveness of such affirmations. Yet, if Dewey taught us anything, it was that the public good is something more than the sum total of private goods, and that a viable community is more than a collection of groups, each occupying its own turf and each doing its own thing. Indeed, *Democracy and Education* is as much a work of social theory as it is of educational theory, and Dewey's own position is strikingly clear: There must be ample room in a democratic society for a healthy individualism and a healthy pluralism, but that individualism and that pluralism must also partake of a continuing quest for community. In fact, individuality itself is only liberated and fully realized as the individual interacts with an ever-widening variety of communities. Recall Dewey's classic paragraph:

A democracy is more than a form of government; it is primarily a mode of associated living, of conjoint communicated experience. The extension in space of the number of individuals who participate in an interest so that each has to refer his own action to that of others, and to consider the action of others to give point and direction to his own, is equivalent to the breaking down of those barriers of class, race, and national territory which kept men from perceiving the full import of their activity. These more numerous and more varied points of contact denote a greater diversity of stimuli to which an individual has to respond; they consequently put a premium on variation in his action. They secure a liberation of powers which remain suppressed as long as the incitations to action are partial, as they must be in a group which in its exclusiveness shuts out many interests.[11]

How do we achieve the educational balance between individualism and community suggested in this formulation? I have a very simple starting point, to which I think there is no alternative: We talk. The proper education of the public and indeed the proper creation of publics will not go forward in our society until we undertake anew a great public dialogue about education. In fact, I would maintain that the questions we need to raise about education are among the most important questions that can be raised in our society, particularly at this juncture in its history. What knowledge should "we the people" hold in common? What values? What skills? What sensibilities? When we ask such questions, we are getting at the heart of the kind of society we want to live in and the kind of society we want our children to live in. We are getting at the heart of the kind of public we would like to bring into being and the qualities we would like that public to display. We are getting at the heart of the kind of community we need for our multifarious individualities to flourish.

Two thousand years ago, Aristotle wrote that when we educate we aim at the good life; and, since men and women disagree in their notions of a good life, they will disagree in their notions of education. It's as true today as it was two thousand years ago. Obviously, men and women of good will are going to disagree about education. What is important about public education is that we work through to certain agreements about values and policies. We do not simply Balkanize the world; we also decide on common ground. We do that in the public schools, in public libraries, and over certain programs on public television because we have a notion of the kind of society our children are going to grow up in and live in. It is not that we are going to do away with different life-styles and different beliefs or with the educational institutions — both public and private — that keep those different life-styles and beliefs alive. It is that we must practice those different life-styles and beliefs within a common framework of mutual respect and understanding. So often in recent years we have cast the choice as one between a full-blown and segregationist ethnicity on the one hand and some plastic, lowest-common-denominator community on the other. I would reject both in favor of new modes of thought that permit — nay, encourage — maximum variation within certain common policies. I think we have the models in the alternative programs that have grown up in our contemporary public schools, public libraries, and public television systems, and I think we should develop, share, and publicize those models. In the last analysis, the most important dimension of the politics of education is the business of debating and defining the various forms those models might take and the various curricula they might teach. Moreover, the public debate itself over what knowledge, what values, what skills, and what sensibilities we might want to nurture in the young and how we might want to nurture them is more important than the particular decisions we happen to arrive at during any given time. For the debate itself educates, and that education will affect the entire educational apparatus of the society and therefore the principal apparatus for creating the public.

My conclusions, of course, are vintage Dewey. You may recall that, in the pedagogical creed he wrote for *The School Journal* in 1897, he argued that "education is the fundamental method of social progress and reform" and that "all reforms which rest simply upon the enactment of law, or the threatening of certain penalties, or upon changes in mechanic or outward arrangements, are transitory and futile." In the last analysis, the fundamental mode of politics in a democratic society is education, and it is in *that* way over all others that the educator is ultimately projected into politics. You will recognize here the ancient prophetic role, which Dewey himself had in mind when he wrote in 1897 that the teacher is always "the prophet of the true God" and "the usherer in of the true kingdom of God." The millennialist tone of these phrases has always left me a bit uncomfortable, but the insight is nonetheless profound. Prophecy: in its root meaning, the calling of a people to their noblest traditions and aspirations. Prophecy, I would submit, is the essential public function of the educator in a democratic society.[12]

History of Education as a Field of Study: An Essay on Recent Historiography of American Education

Sol Cohen

It was our firm belief that the imperfect knowledge of [the history of education] has affected adversely the planning of curricula, the formulation of policy, and the administration of educational agencies in the present crisis of American education.

Fund for the Advancement of Education,
The Role of Education in American History (1957)

Since it was introduced as a specialty in American teacher training institutions at the turn of the century, the history of education as a field of study has constantly had to justify its "function" in the professional program.[1] From the beginning historians of education have had to counter the skepticism of their colleagues in schools or departments of education. But in the mid-1950s, the history of education encountered a new challenge — that from the departmental historians, from colleagues in university or college departments of history. By then there was a rather large literature in the area, but too much of it was parochial, anachronistic, and out of touch with main currents of scholarship. This was the gist of four important essays that broke new ground in the mid-1950s and early 1960s: The Fund for the Advancement of Education's *The Role of Education in American History,* Bernard Bailyn's *Education in the Forming of American Society,* Wilson Smith's "The New Historian of American Education," and Lawrence A. Cremin's *The Wonderful World of Ellwood Patterson Cubberley.*[2] These essays help to construct a platform from which to survey the history of American education as a field of study during the past quarter century.

In 1951 the Ford Foundation established the Fund for the Advancement of Education, and it became a major agent of change in American education during the 1950s and 1960s, before it ceased to exist in 1965. It distributed more than $70 million and sponsored such well-publicized innovations as team teaching and Master of Arts in

Teaching (MAT) programs.[3] Less well-known are the Fund's efforts to encourage the study of the history of American education.

Under the personal direction of its president, Clarence H. Faust, the Fund began in 1954 to explore with a group of leading American historians the possibility of providing funds for research into the role of education in American history. It was made pointedly clear that no member of the group, which included Arthur Schlesinger, Sr., Paul Buck, Richard Storr, Merle Curti, Samuel Eliot Morison, Richard Hofstadter, Bernard Bailyn, and Ralph Gabriel, was a "specialist" in the history of American education. No member of the group was on the faculty of a school or college or department of education, although several had written books on aspects of the history of American education. There was general agreement among the members that American education was a sadly neglected field of historical inquiry and teaching, and that, relative to its importance in the development of American society, the history of education had been "shamefully neglected by American historians." A second meeting was held in May 1956 at which time the group organized itself into the Committee on the Role of Education in American History, and, with a small appropriation from the Fund, began work on a call to American historians, a call that appeared in the spring of 1957 in the form of a bulletin entitled *The Role of Education in American History*. The committee announced that financial assistance was available for those members of college or university history departments, faculty or students, who desired to devote themselves to close monographic study of the role of education, formal and informal, in American history. The committee appealed for a "new" history of American education that would break from particularized and institutional history and concern itself, instead, with the broader subject of the impact of education upon American society.

For us, what is significant is that the Fund deliberately excluded "specialists" in the history of American education from its conferences and from its offers of financial assistance. Why the slur? Part of the answer lay in the general mood of hostility toward the profession of education that characterized foundations and liberal arts faculties in America in the middle and late 1950s. The other part of the answer may be found in Bernard Bailyn's *Education in the Forming of American Society: Needs and Opportunities for Study*, a study sponsored by the Fund and one of the most important results of the Fund's

efforts to stimulate interest in the history of American education on
the part of the academic or departmental historians. In his seminal
essay, Bailyn, a junior member of the history faculty of Harvard at
that time, brought together two papers: the first, a lengthy critique of
American educational historiography; the second, a provocative revisionist interpretation of colonial educational history. The first essay is
the one that concerns us. At a time of deep public concern over the
schools, Bailyn observed, "the role of education in American history is
obscure. We have almost no historical leverage on the problems of
American education." Why? It was because turn-of-the-century
"educational missionaries" like Ellwood Cubberley and Paul Monroe,
who taught the history of education and wrote the most influential
textbooks, especially Cubberley's *Public Education in the United
States* (1919), viewed the subject not as an aspect of American history
writ large, but rather as a device to dignify and inspire a newly self-
conscious profession. As a consequence, the history of American
education as a field of study developed in almost total isolation from
the major influences of twentieth-century historiography. Because
Cubberly and Monroe and their followers wrote history with an eye for
contemporary relevance, distortions were inevitable. Bailyn condemned their foreshortening, their wrenching of events from historical
context, their persistent anachronism. To these writers the past was
simply the present writ small. Uninterested in the past except as the
"seedbed" of present issues, "they lost the understanding of origins and
of growth which history alone can provide." Because they restricted
their accounts to formal institutions of schooling, they lost the capacity to see education in its full context. As a corrective to this myopic
point of view, Bailyn urged, in a widely quoted dictum, that historians
think of education "not only as formal pedagogy but as the entire process by which a culture transmits itself across the generations."[4]

Wilson Smith, a professor of history at Johns Hopkins University,
continued Bailyn's critique of American educational historiography.
Two traits, according to Smith, would distinguish the new historian of
education from his predecessors: his use of broader historical
references and his wider, more humanistic professional commitment.
The new historian of education would look beyond the vocational
training goals and the limited professional outlook of an older generation of teachers and writers concerned with the history of education.
His goals would perhaps be simply satisfying his own curiosity and

communicating his findings about the past. The history of education would be "functional" as a "servant of intellect and disciplined thinking."[5] Smith had another opportunity to expound on the "new history of education" as a respondent to Bailyn during a conference held at the school of education at Johns Hopkins University. What Bailyn had done, explained Smith, with a degree of hyperbolic overkill, was to "rescue the tired, almost lifeless, figure of the history of education from the waters of professional self-centeredness and doctrinaire presentation. He has brought the figure to the shoreline of historiographical respectability. And he has revived it with a sense of the fullness of history and with the excitement of a newly liberated outlook." Smith called upon the new historian of American education to "exchange the guild piety of his predecessors for the humanistic pieties of the modern man of arts and letters."[6]

Lawrence Cremin of Teachers College, Columbia University, put the finishing touch on the emerging portrait of the "old" versus the "new" historiography of American education in 1965 in his *The Wonderful World of Ellwood Patterson Cubberley.* In *The Wonderful World,* Cubberley is reconvicted of the sins of anachronism, parochialism, evangelism, and isolation from the mainstream of American historiography. Cubberley's *Public Education in the United States* is characterized as inspirational, institutional, instrumental, and enormously influential: "The work is still read . . . has influenced a vast literature . . . to the most recent scholarly text in American history."[7] While acknowledging Cubberley's service to the profession of education, Cremin went on to assert that the Cubberley school of historiography had helped to produce a generation of American schoolmen unable to comprehend, much less contend with, the great educational controversies that beset America in the decades following World War II. Cremin also closed his essay with a call for a "new" history of American education, one closely allied with social and cultural history. His *The Transformation of the School: Progressivism in American Education, 1876-1957,* which won the Bancroft Prize, exemplified just such a history.

The Committee on the Role of Education in American History ran out of money in 1965, and was terminated by the Fund in 1966. It was one of the more successful of the Fund's projects, greatly stimulating the study of the history of education among departmental historians. What is more important, though it was not intended this way, the committee and Bailyn had enormous influence among historians of education on faculties in the schools of education. What a liberating influence to be encouraged: to see education "in its elaborate, intricate involvements with the rest of society." Bailyn's dictum lent encouragement to all historians of education who were anxious to integrate the study of educational history with all that seemed vital in the social sciences. It gave important leverage to younger, more adventurous spirits struggling against the somnambulant old guard in departments of education throughout the country. *Education in the Forming of American Society* was to become the manifesto of the new history of education.

In the 1960s a new generation of historians of education, including David Tyack, Michael Katz, Charles Strickland, Charles Burgess, Clarence Karier, Vincent Lannie, Geraldine Joncich Clifford, John Calam, Marvin Lazerson, Jonathan Messerli, Douglas Sloan, Robert L. McClintock, Barbara Finkelstein, and Patricia A. Graham, came into the field to join R. Freeman Butts, Gordon Lee, Raymond Callahan, Robert L. McCaul, Edward L. Krug, Merle Borrowman, and Cremin. They have been followed by another, equally gifted class of historians, many of them enticed to the promise of research in the history of education by Lawrence Stone at the Shelby Cullom Davis Center for Historical Studies at Princeton University, of which he is director. This group would include Sheldon Rothblatt, James Axtell, Carl Kaestle, James McLachlan, Robert L. Church, and James Selwyn Troen, among others. Thanks especially to the spade work of Cremin, Borrowman, Tyack, and Timothy Smith, historians of education could, in the late 1960s, find journals like the *American Quarterly,* the *Harvard Educational Review,* the *Journal of American History,* and the *American Historical Review* open to them. Under the leadership first of Henry Perkinson and later Paul Mattingly, the *History of Education Quarterly* attracted the work of scholars here and abroad, regardless of their institutional affiliation. The annual meetings of the History of Education Society (HES) and Division F of the American Educational Research Association (AERA) were and are still well attended. There are flourishing sections of HES on the East Coast, in the Midwest, in the South, and on the Pacific Coast. HES is able now to publish a *Newsletter* and to offer prizes for excellence in historical writing, among them the Henry Barnard Prize and the History of Education Society Award. In just a little more than a decade, the vision of Bailyn, Smith, and Cremin that there be a "new history of education," tough-minded, humanistic in character, broadly conceived, and closely allied with the fields of social and intellectual history, has come true. The work in the field has great range and liveliness. There has been an impressive output that has greatly enriched the historiography of education.[8]

Within the past decade, historians of education have begun to study the political and social conditions of the school's existence and the presuppositions concerning it. They have begun to ask new sorts of questions, questions having to do with power and control, with strategies, stakes, interests. Further, historians of American education are now not only asking new questions, different questions, tough-minded questions of the data of educational history; they are also bringing to their work an awareness of the racial, ethnic, and religious conflict that permeates American history. In the past decade some of the discipline's more venturesome practitioners, especially Tyack and Katz, have even demonstrated how methods and insights borrowed from the social sciences can provide significant new approaches to the history of education.[9]

The new historians of American education, whether on education faculties or history faculties, have ceased writing about the public school system as if it were unequivocally progressive and historically inevitable. Their writing has sought not to instill professional pride in school personnel, but, rather, to analyze institutional adaptation to social change, and to emphasize the relation of pedagogical ideas and practices to social, economic, and political contexts.[10] The older style in the historiography of American education was one of attachment to the idea of the public school. There was a consensus, a shared loyalty, a commitment to the public school system. The new historians of American education are largely emancipated from inherited loyalties concerning public schools and school reforms and school reformers. The departure from orthodoxy is represented by their critical attitude toward many of the educational crusaders and educational crusades of the past. For example, Tyack sees the efforts of American school reformers in the early national period as aimed at using the schools to inculcate a patriotic homogeneity. Messerli portrays Franklin with at least one wart—xenophobic where German immigrants to Pennsylvania were concerned. Especially have new approaches to the common school movement led to fresh and even startling conclusions.

Taylor points out that in the South the common school was erected as the buttress of regional orthodoxy rather than the palladium of the republic. Fishlow questions whether there was a common school "crusade" in the 1830s and 1840s.[11] But Katz, in his enormously influential *The Irony of Early School Reform,* questions the very premises of the whole common school movement, concluding that it served the interests of a minority at the expense of the majority.

Nor are later reform movements faring better. Through his study of E. L. Thorndike, Karier is beginning to unravel the tangle of elitist practices and egalitarian promises that characterize much of American education, while Strickland and Burgess have done the same through their study of G. Stanley Hall. Callahan has critically examined school administrators as an interest group. There are even the beginnings of a less pious and more critical approach to Dewey.[12] More recently, a revisionist movement has, as we see below, emphasized social control and imposition as basic features of the American public school system.

Since the early 1960s, the history of American education as a field of study in the United States has been in a productive state of disarray. Cubberley's interpretation has been discredited, but no reformulation has replaced it. We find ourselves lacking a systematic interpretation acceptable to any large number of educational historians. Cremin is proceeding from perhaps the broadest view of education. Cremin defines education "as the deliberate, systematic, and sustained effort to transmit or evoke knowledge, attitudes, values, skills, and sensibilities." Cremin's definition projects him far beyond schools and colleges to the multiplicity of individuals, groups, organizations, and institutions that educate, to "configurations of education" which may be complementary, consonant, or dissonant.[13] Thus, in his magisterial *American Education: The Colonial Experience* he considers the multiple and changing relations between families, churches, and schools, and other paradigmatic colonial "configurations of education."[14] To Butts, "civilization building and the modernization process" provide the framework for his reinterpretation of the history of education.[15] Clifford calls for a new synthesis that places the "neglected constituents, the school patrons," at the center of the story—a "people-centered institutional history that deals, in significant and sensitive ways, with students, parents, school board members, as well as teachers—warts and all." Finkelstein calls for a new synthesis that places children at the center; for her it is in the "primal relationships between parents and children, between teachers and students, between children and their books, and children and the streets that the history of education has proceeded." Then Neil Sutherland has suggested: "Since debate and conflict about the pathological often lay bare the unstated norms, our first centers of attention should be on children and families in trouble." The focus here would be on "special" educational institutions like houses of refuge, reform schools, orphanages, juvenile courts, and so forth.[16]

Many relatively new or hitherto overlooked subjects, or subjects which American educational historians had taken for granted, have recently been given unexpected historical dimensions.[17] Biography is flourishing.[18] The history of the family and of child rearing in America, long a gaping lacuna in our knowledge, has become a high-priority field. For example, James Axtelle, John Demos, and Barbara Finkelstein have persuasively illustrated the possibilities for educational history when views of the child and the history of the family are imaginatively joined to the story of the schools.[19] Daniel Calhoun sees great value in studying the city itself as educator. The urban setting, he maintains, may have far greater educational effects than urban schools. Does investment in schooling, he queries, do as much to change the mentality of people as investment in the more general facilities "that help make urban life quick, close, and specialized?"[20] It is perhaps fair, at this point, to remember ancient Athens and the educative functions then ascribed to that great city.

Calhoun's discussion of the role of the city as teacher invites speculation regarding urban family life as teacher, especially in the education of minority groups. For example, is religion the critical variable in school success, or is it prior urban experience, or is it what goes on in urban schools? What was the attitude of educators toward the education of immigrants from Southern and Eastern Europe who poured into our cities in the early stages of urbanization and industrialization? And, in turn, what was the attitude of immigrants toward the school in America? Timothy Smith portrays a broad social consensus among newcomers and native Americans in his discussion of immigrant social aspirations and American education. The value system of the immigrants, he asserts, centered on their aspirations for success and respectability through education—goals consonant with the reigning

Protestant ethic. These aspirations "account for the immense success of the public school system, particularly at the secondary level, in drawing the mass of working-class children into its embrace."[21] A quite different assessment of the relationship between the American educational system and the children of the immigrants has been advanced by Michael Olneck and Marvin Lazerson. While Scandinavian, British, German, and Russian-Jewish youngsters tended to be as successful in school as those of native parentage, the children of non-Jewish Central and Southern European immigrants experienced much higher rates of failure. On every index of educational attainment, children from these nationalities fared much worse than the others. Recognizing the influence of religious and cultural differences on motivation and aptitude, Olneck and Lazerson suggest that the problem may have been the unwillingness or inability of public education to recognize the legitimacy of working-class and immigrant cultures.[22]

Although the history of education as a discipline coincides with the rise of the city, historians of education have only recently arrived at the study of urban education. Even the Fund for the Advancement of Education's *Education and American History* (New York, 1965) ignored the history of urban education while recommending as a new point of departure "the building of communities on the frontier." The literature in what we can call the history of urban education is scarcely a decade old. Sol Cohen's *Progressives and Urban School Reform* is less concerned with "urban" than with "progressives."[23] But in 1969 Michael Katz organized a symposium on urban education for Division F (History and Historiography of Education) of the AERA.[24] At about the same time, stimulated by the "urban crisis" and the urgent needs of educational policymakers, a flurry of books and articles on the political and organizational aspects of urban education appeared. Then, in the early 1970s, a proliferation of articles appeared in new journals like *Urban Education* and *Education and Urban Society,* as well as in the *History of Education Quarterly.* More recently there have been some splendid books: Marvin Lazerson, *Origins of the Urban School: Public Education in Massachusetts, 1870-1915;* Stanley K. Schultz, *The Culture Factory: Boston Public Schools, 1789-1960;* Carl F. Kaestle, *The Evolution of an Urban School System: New York City, 1750-1850,* Selwyn K. Troen, *The Public and the Schools: Shaping the St. Louis System, 1838-1920;* and the most ambitious of the lot, David B. Tyack's, *The One Best System: A History of American Ur-*

ban Education. Mention should also be made of a solid account of the politics and governance of urban schooling in America: Diane Ravitch, *The Great School Wars: New York City, 1805-1973.*

Despite this renaissance in the history of American education, there are still many opportunities awaiting historians. For example, we now know something about private boarding schools, but we still know little about the Catholic parochial school system.[25] The Catholic schools played a crucial role in helping many newcomers adjust to the city. Other denominations also operate schools, but Catholic schools comprise nine-tenths of all private school education in America. The size of the Catholic system alone should make it a matter of pressing historical concern.

American historians have neglected the writings of foreign observers of American education, writings that provide a rich store of information and insights into American schools.[26] (As Tocqueville puts it, "The majority lives in the perpetual utterance of self-applause, and there are certain truths which the Americans can learn only from strangers. . . .") In fact, although all Western nations have had their own variety of such common historical experiences as immigration, urbanization, industrialization, and racial or religious conflict, Americans still neglect the comparative approach to American educational history. Without comparative data, the full analysis and evaluation of the school's impact on American society is impossible. Not only has American educational history neglected any international or comparative approach; it has also slighted American regionalism. As far as most historians of education are concerned, the American West might be uninhabited: no Indians, Mexican-Americans, Japanese, Chinese, or Negroes; no cities like Los Angeles, San Francisco, or Seattle; no schools. No region of the United States has been so neglected by historians of education as that west of the Rockies.

Today the American Negro is no longer the "invisible man," but on the regional level there is only one major work, Henry Allen Bullock's *A History of Negro Education in the South: From 1619 to the Present.* There is still much to learn about the education of minorities in general, however, and much remains to be done. We need to know a great deal more about the recruitment and training of the educational establishment with reference to the inclusion or exclusion of minority group members. We need studies depicting the role of minority group members as teachers, administrators, local school board members, and professors of education. We have no persuasive analysis of what attitudes toward minorities were conveyed in the classroom. Detailed examinations are needed of the history of particular school districts, not only those with statistically significant numbers of minority students but also those with very few. We need studies of the attempts of minority parents to use the courts to obtain equal educational access for their children at the same time that they were setting up private schools to ensure that the children received some sort of education. The entire crisis of American urban education was racial in its inception. Yet, why it was that the public school was chosen as the arena to fight the battle over segregation-integration is still unclear.[27]

What might be called the "conservative" tradition in American education still awaits its historian. The history of women's education has to be moved into the mainstream of American educational historiography. Finally, though progress has been made, historical research on the American family is still in an early stage. Little is known about the interaction between changes in the family and changes in the structure of education. Did changes in family structure make schools increasingly important agencies of socialization, or did pressures outside the family, from government or from social and religious institutions, provide the impetus for this shift in educational responsibilities? How has submission to the discipline of the school altered the experience of childhood and affected adult behavior? Only in the last few years have such questions begun to receive the attention they merit.[28]

Finally, historians of education have been slow to make any real use of depth psychology in their work. We largely neglect motive, latent or unintended meanings, the "irrational," the "unconscious." Erikson writes that psychoanalysis is, so to speak, at home on the geological surface as well as in the descending shafts. In biography, few of us get below the surface to the core. It might prove fruitful, for example, to ask some fresh questions, especially questions concerning the relation between private life and public act; idealization and debunking have to give way to more full-bodied portraits. It might be fruitful to raise questions concerning the latent or "unconscious" functions of educational practices, principles, and institutions. There has been considerable interest lately on the impact of Freud and psychoanalysis on American life and culture. But little is known as yet of the influence of psychoanalytic concepts on education. The interface between psychoanalysis and education dates back to the first decade of the twentieth century and the earliest meetings of the Vienna Psychoanalytic Society; child psychoanalysis and "psychoanalytic pedagogy" developed together on the Continent in the 1920s and 1930s. Psychoanalysis had considerable influence on progressive education both in Europe and here in those decades; yet there are no comparative studies of progressive education.

The present situation and future prospects for the history of education seem brighter than ever. But the newer tendencies in American educational history are not without their pitfalls. Thus, social science and behavioral science concepts—status anxiety, identity crisis, symbolism, ideology, social class, motivation, socialization—though they produce new and helpful interpretations, will have to be used with caution. And broadening the scope of educational history to include its interrelations with "the rest of society," as Bailyn has urged, may prove as barren as the old, narrow, institutional history. This approach opens up new perspectives, but it also tends to deify "society." Indeed, Laurence Veysey recommends eliminating the concept of "society" from the historian's thinking. This would serve to bring into sharper focus "the myriad competing groups, factions, and individuals who in fact form the stuff of any society."[29]

More disquieting than any other recent development has been the emergence of a radical revisionist school of educational historians: Michael B. Katz, Clarence Karier, Joel Spring, Paul Violas, and, to some extent, David Tyack, among others.[30] The radical revisionists emerged on the American scene at the end of the 1960s. The sources of their dissatisfaction—the war in Vietnam, the oppression of our black population, the blighting of our cities, the lawlessness of our politics—were the same as those which produced alienation and rebelliousness throughout American society in the late 1960s and early 1970s. They were greatly influenced by the New Left movement in politics and social thought, as well as by social scientists like James Coleman and Christopher Jencks; social and educational critics like Paul Goodman, Ivan Illich, and Theodore Roszak; racial economists like Martin Carnoy and Samuel Bowles; and revisionist general historians like James Weinstein and Gabriel Kolko.

Clarence Karier finds "the present educational system heavily racist and designed to protect class interest." For Katz, the most influential of the revisionists, what is "basic" to American public education is this: it is now and always has been "conservative, racist, and bureaucratic." For Tyack, "the public schools have rarely taught the children of the poor effectively — and this failure has been *systematic,* not idiosyncratic [italics mine]." The schools possess no redeeming features. "Racism" is "integral not incidental, to the very structure of public education." The radical revisionists are repelled by American society. Like other supporters of the New Left, their thinking is permeated with contempt for the prevailing middle-class values, outrage against the inequalities of American life, revulsion against a society grown increasingly corrupt, and revolt against remote, impersonal bureaucracies and institutions that are impervious to human needs. As Karier puts it, "We live . . . in a fundamentally racist, materialistic society which, through a process of rewards and punishments, cultivates the quest for status, power and wealth in such a way so as to use people and institutions effectively to protect vested interests." And reform will not do. Reform is anathema to the revisionists. What is required is fundamental reconstruction of American society and American schools. According to Katz, "at this point in history any reform worthy of the name must begin with a redistribution of power and resources. That is the only way in which to change the patterns of control and inaccessible organizational structures that dominate American life. It is the only way in which to make education, and other social institutions as well, serve new purposes."

To the radical revisionists the function of the history of education as a field of study is to serve the cause of social reconstruction. Cubberley and Monroe and their contemporaries and students have to be discredited, and the immediate older generation of historians of education as well. Thus, not only is liberalism finished, so is "liberal" history, that history represented by Bailyn and Cremin, all dated and "irrelevant." The revisionists write history with an "acute awareness of contemporary social crises." For Karier, the "ultimate test" of the essays in *Roots of Crisis* will be "how well they in fact connect with and add meaning to our present world." For Katz, the significance of a "new" history of education depends on how it "links up with, and contributes to, the larger critical, contemporary reappraisal of American life and institutions."

There are many reasons for revision in history: the discovery of new source materials; the impact of new theories, new methods, new academic disciplines; the asking of new or different kinds of questions of the historical data. Of course, someone must interpret our era to our contemporaries, but there is still a need for detachment, balance, judiciousness, and reasoned historical judgment. The radical revisionists are seemingly unaware of the sociologists' difficulties in establishing meanings for the concept of social control. Without a comparative perspective, their standard for criticism approaches some romantic ideal of a preindustrial arcadia. The questions the radical revisionists put to the evidence are so loaded that they can be pretty sure at the beginning what answer they will emerge with at the end. There is a finality and rationality about their history that terribly oversimplifies the ambiguities, incompleteness, and irrationality of historical events. They give us a picture of the past out of which the present simply could not have grown.[31] "There is no more need for romance," Walt Whitman insisted nearly a century ago. "Let facts and history be properly told."

Katz has observed that history can serve reform by "emancipating it from dependency upon an idealized past." If one of the tasks of the historian is to undo denials and myths and idealizations, then the place of the radical revisionists in the history of American education is secure. We will never again be able to look at education in the same way. Their work permitted us to think heterodox thoughts, forced us to face our responsibilities regarding social and political issues. There has recently been a healthy demythologizing of the history of American education. Historians of education are calling into question stereotyped notions of the words "reform" and "progressive" and are thinking in terms of the "irony" of school reform. Most historians of education are now ready to examine the public schools as instruments of social control, giving due regard to their possibly restrictive and coercive functions, and they are willing to disclose phenomena long hidden by official pieties, for example, the maltreatment of immigrants and ethnic groups, the discriminatory treatment of women and minority groups, the connection between schools and politics and between education and social stratification. Most important, the radical revisionists have roused fresh interest in the history of American education.

Historians in teachers colleges, or on school or department of education faculties in the United States, have always worked under a particular strain. They are caught up in the conflict between what may be called the "two cultures" of the school of education. They carry commitments both to history and to the professional program. Their loyalties are claimed by the demands of both past and present. They are caught, as the late Richard Hofstadter put it in a slightly different context, between "their desire to count in the world and their desire to understand it." Their passion for understanding points up their commitment to detachment, neutrality, objectivity. But the urgency of present problems points in another direction, plays upon their desire to get out of history some lessons that will serve the needs of the time. There is the danger of tendentiousness, of entanglement in partisan commitments. But there is another danger. There is a great need for historical understanding of the problems currently besetting America in the field of education, a great need for historical leverage in dealing with the problems of American education. If historians of American education evade such problems, professional educators and laymen alike will turn elsewhere for answers, and we may qualify for Tolstoy's definition of the historians of his own day — deaf men replying to questions that nobody asked them.

NOTES

Cremin: **Public Education and the Education of the Public**

1. John Dewey, *Democracy and Education* (New York: Macmillan, 1916), 3.
2. *Ibid.*, 7-8.
3. *Ibid.*, 8-9.
4. *Ibid.*, esp. 12-27.
5. George S. Counts, *Dare the School Build a New Social Order?* (New York: John Day Co., 1932); John Dewey, "Education and Social Change," *The Social Frontier* 3 (May 1937): 237; *id.*, "Can Education Share in Social Reconstruction?"*ibid.*, 1 (October 1934): 11-12.
6. William H. Kilpatrick, ed., *The Educational Frontier* (New York: D. Appleton-Century Co., 1933), 100; Dewey, "Education and Social Change," 236.
7. Dewey's remarks were excerpted in the *New York Times*, April 23, 1933, under the heading "Dewey Outlines Utopian Schools." I am indebted to Dr. Jo Ann Boydston, director of the Center for Dewey Studies at Southern Illinois University, for this reference.
8. Jerome S. Bruner, *The Relevance of Education* (New York: W. W. Norton, 1971), 7-8; David R. Olson, *Cognitive Development: The Child's Acquisition of Diagonality* (New York: Academic Press, 1970), 193-197; *Media and Symbols: The Forms of Expression, Communication, and Education,* ed. David R. Olson, Seventy-third Yearbook of the National Society for the Study of Education, Part I (Chicago: University of Chicago Press, 1974), Chaps. 1, 6; Lawrence A. Cremin, "Notes toward

a Theory of Education," in *Notes on Education*, No. 1 (New York: Institute of Philosophy and Politics of Education, Teachers College, Columbia University, June 1973), 4-6; and *id.*, "Further Notes toward a Theory of Education," *ibid.*, No. 4 (March 1974), 1-6.

9. Henry Steele Commager, *Majority Rule and Minority Rights* (New York: Oxford University Press, 1943), Chap. 2.

10. *Brown* v. *Board of Education*, 347 U.S. 483 (1964); *Serrano* v. *Priest*, Cal., 487 P. 2d 1241 (1971); *Robinson* v. *Cahill*, 62 N.J. 473 (1973); *Goss* v. *Lopez*, 42 L.Ed. 2d 725 (1975).

11. Dewey, *Democracy and Education*, 101.

12. *Dewey on Education*, ed. Martin S. Dworkin (New York: Teachers College Press, 1959), 30, 32.

Cohen: History of Education as a Field of Study

1. For elaboration, see Sol Cohen, "The History of the History of American Education, 1900-1976: The Uses of the Past," *Harvard Educational Review* 46 (August 1976): 298-330.

2. Fund for the Advancement of Education, *The Role of Education in American History* (New York: Fund for the Advancement of Education, 1957); Bernard Bailyn, *Education in the Forming of American Society: Needs and Opportunities for Study* (Chapel Hill, N.C.: University of North Carolina Press, 1960); Wilson Smith, "The New Historian of American Education," *Harvard Educational Review* 31 (Spring 1961): 136-143; Lawrence A. Cremin, *The Wonderful World of Ellwood Patterson Cubberley: An Essay in the Historiography of American Education* (New York: Bureau of Publications, Teachers College, Columbia University, 1965).

3. Paul Woodring, *Investment in Innovation: An Historical Appraisal of the Fund for the Advancement of Education* (Boston: Little, Brown, 1970), 166-167.

4. Bailyn, *Education in the Forming of American Society*, 14.

5. Smith, "New Historian of American Education," 142.

6. Bernard Bailyn, "Education as a Discipline: Some Historical Notes," in *The Discipline of Education*, ed. John Walton and James L. Kuethe (Madison: University of Wisconsin Press, 1965), Chap. 6; Wilson Smith, "Comments on Bailyn's 'Education as a Discipline,' " in *Discipline of Education*, ed. Walton and Kuethe, 139-140.

7. Cremin, *Wonderful World of Ellwood Patterson Cubberley*, 2.

8. There are comprehensive summaries on the recent historiography of the field in Douglas Sloan, "Historiography and the History of Education," *Review of Research in Education* I (1973): 239-248; Robert L. Church, "History of Education as a Field of Study," *Encyclopedia of Education* 4 (1971): 415-424; and Sol Cohen, "New Perspectives in the History of American Education, 1960-1970," *History of Education* 2 (January 1973): 79-96.

9. See esp. David B. Tyack, *The One Best System: A History of American Urban Education* (Cambridge, Mass.: Harvard University Press, 1974); and Michael B. Katz, *The Irony of Early School Reform: Educational Innovation in Mid-Nineteenth Century Massachusetts* (Cambridge, Mass.: Harvard University Press, 1968).

10. For example, see Berenice Fisher, *Industrial Education: American Ideals and Institutions* (Madison: University of Wisconsin Press, 1967); Ruth Elson, *Guardians of*

Tradition: American Schoolbooks of the Nineteenth Century (Lincoln: University of Nebraska Press, 1964); and Edward A. Krug, *The Shaping of the American High School, 1920-1941* (Madison: University of Wisconsin Press, 1972).

11. David B. Tyack, "Forming the National Character," *Harvard Educational Review* 36 (Fall 1966): 29-41; Jonathan Messerli, "Benjamin Franklin: Colonial and Cosmopolitan Educator," *British Journal of Educational Studies* 16 (February 1968): 43-59; William R. Taylor, "Toward a Definition of Orthodoxy: The Patrician Santa and the Common Schools," *Harvard Educational Review* 36 (Fall 1966): 412-426; Albert Fishlow, "The American Common Revival: Fact or Fancy?" in *Industrialization in Two Systems: Essays in Honor of Alexander Gerschenkron,* ed. Henry Rosovsky (New York: Columbia University Press, 1966), 40-67.

12. Clarence J. Karier, "Elite Views on American Education," *Journal of Contemporary History* 2 (July 1967): 149-163; *Health, Growth, and Heredity: G. Stanley Hall on Natural Education,* ed. Charles E. Strickland and Charles Burgess (New York: Teachers College Press, 1965); Raymond Callahan, *Education and the Cult of Efficiency* (Chicago: University of Chicago Press, 1962); Frederic Lilge, "John Dewey in Retrospect: An American Reconsideration," *British Journal of Educational Studies* 8 (May 1960): 99-111. See also the *History of Education Quarterly* 15 (Spring 1975). The entire issue is devoted to "John Dewey Revisited."

13. Lawrence A. Cremin, "Further Notes toward a Theory of Education," *Notes on Education* 4 (1974): 1.

14. *Id., American Education: The Colonial Experience 1607-1783* (New York: Harper and Brothers, 1970). See also *id., Traditions of American Education* (New York: Basic Books, 1976).

15. R. Freeman Butts, "Civilization-Building and the Modernization Process: A Framework for the Reinterpretation of the History of Education," *History of Education Quarterly* 7 (Summer 1967): 147-174.

16. Geraldine J. Clifford, "Saints, Sinners, and People: A Position Paper on the Historiography of American Education," *ibid.,* 15 (Fall 1975): 257-268; Barbara J. Finkelstein, "Choose Your Bias Carefully: Textbooks in the History of American Education," *Educational Studies* 5 (Winter 1974-75): 214; Neil Sutherland, "The Urban Child," *History of Education Quarterly* 9 (Fall 1969): 305-311.

17. For example, William Edward Eaton, *The American Federation of Teachers, 1916-1961: A History of the Movement* (Carbondale: Southern Illinois University Press, 1975); Donald R. Warren, *To Enforce Education: A History of the Founding Years of the United States Office of Education* (Detroit, Mich.: Wayne State University Press, 1974).

18. For example, Theta H. Wolf, *Alfred Binet* (Chicago: University of Chicago Press, 1973); Harlan Lane, *The Wild Boy of Aveyron* (Cambridge, Mass.: Harvard University Press, 1976); Rita Kramer, *Maria Montessori: A Biography* (New York: G. P. Putnam's Sons, 1976); George Dykhuizen, *The Life and Mind of John Dewey* (Carbondale: Southern Illinois University Press, 1973); Geraldine Joncich, *The Sane Positivist: A Biography of Edward L. Thorndike* (Middletown, Conn.: Wesleyan University Press, 1968); Dorothy Ross, *G. Stanley Hall: The Psychologist as Prophet* (Chicago: University of Chicago Press, 1972); and Jack K. Campbell, *Colonel Francis W. Parker: The Children's Crusader* (New York: Teachers College Press, 1967).

19. John Demos, *A Little Commonwealth: Family Life in Plymouth Colony* (London: Oxford University Press, 1970); James Axtelle, *The School upon a Hill: Education and Society in Colonial New England* (New Haven, Conn.: Yale University Press, 1974).

20. Daniel Calhoun, "The City as Teacher: Historical Problems," *History of Education Quarterly* 9 (Fall 1969): 312-325. See also *id., The Intelligence of a People* (Princeton, N.J.: Princeton University Press, 1973).

21. Timothy L. Smith, "Immigrant Social Aspirations and American Education, 1880-1930," *American Quarterly* 21 (Fall 1969): 543. See also *id.*, "Native Blacks and Foreign Whites: Varying Responses to Educational Opportunity in America, 1880-1950," in *Perspectives in American History,* Volume 6, ed. Donald Fleming and Bernard Bailyn (Cambridge, Mass.: Charles Warren Center for Studies in American History, 1972), 309-332.

22. Michael Olneck and Marvin Lazerson, "The School Achievement of Immigrant Children, 1900-1930," *History of Education Quarterly* 14 (Winter 1974): 453-482 (reprinted in Chapter 5 of the present volume). See also David K. Cohen, "Immigrants and the Schools," *Review of Educational Research* 40 (Winter 1970): 13-27. And, in general, see Diane C. Ravitch, "On the History of Minority Group Education in the United States," *Teachers College Record* 78 (December 1976): 1-29.

23. Sol Cohen, *Progressives and Urban School Reform* (New York: Teachers College Press, 1964).

24. The papers, with an introduction by Michael Katz, were subsequently published in *History of Education Quarterly* 9 (Fall 1969).

25. Two important works on Catholic education, however, are Vincent P. Lannie, "Church and School Triumphant: The Sources of American Catholic Educational Historiography," *ibid.,* 16 (Summer 1976): 131-145; and James W. Sanders, *The Education of an Urban Minority: Catholics in Chicago, 1833-1965* (New York: Oxford University Press, 1977).

26. See *American Education in Foreign Perspectives,* ed. Stewart E. Fraser (New York: John Wiley and Sons, 1969). See also William W. Brickman, "An Historical Survey of Foreign Writings on American Educational History," *Paedagogica Historica* 2 (No. 1, 1962): 5-21.

27. Richard Kluger, *Simple Justice: The History of Brown v. Board of Education and Black America's Struggle for Equality* (New York: Knopf, 1976).

28. John E. Talbott, "The History of Education," *Daedalus* 100 (Winter 1971): 142.

29. Laurence R. Veysey, "Toward a New Direction in Educational History: Prospect and Retrospect," *History of Education Quarterly* 9 (Fall 1969): 343-359.

30. See the following by Michael B. Katz: *Class, Bureaucracy, and Schools: The Illusion of Educational Change in America* (New York: Praeger, 1975); *School Reform: Past and Present* (Boston: Little, Brown, 1971); and *Education in American History: Readings in the Social Issues* (New York: Praeger, 1973). See also *Shaping the American Educational State, 1900 to the Present,* ed. Clarence J. Karier (New York: Free Press, 1975); Clarence Karier, Paul Violas, and Joel Spring, *Roots of Crisis: American Education in the 20th Century* (Chicago: Rand McNally, 1973); and Joel H. Spring, *Education and the Rise of the Corporate State* (Boston: Beacon Press, 1974), and Tyack, *One Best System.*

31. There is a large literature critical of the radical revisionists. Perhaps the most interesting are R. Freeman Butts, "Public Education and Political Community," *History of Education Quarterly* 14 (Summer 1974): 165-184 (reprinted in Chapter 3 of this volume); Merle L. Borrowman, "Studies in the History of American Education," *Review of Education* 1 (1975): 56-66; Maxine Greene, "Identities and Contours: An Approach to Educational History," *Educational Researcher* 2 (April 1973): 5-17 (reprinted in Chapter 7 of this volume); and Wayne J. Urban, "Some Historiographical Problems in Revisionist Educational History: Review of *Roots of Crisis*," *American Educational Research Journal* 12 (Summer 1975): 337-350. Most comprehensive is Diane Ravitch, "The Revisionists Revised: Studies in the Historiography of American Education," *Proceedings of the National Academy of Education* 4 (1977): 1-84.

THREE

Looking and Finding

Ways of Seeing: An Essay on the History of Compulsory Schooling, by *David B. Tyack*

Public Education and Political Community, by   *R. Freeman Butts*

What historians of American education find through their research is determined not only by where they look for evidence but also by their assumptions and perspectives. That a variety of viewpoints informs the work of contemporary educational historians has already been made abundantly clear in Sol Cohen's essay. Some historians argue that, because such bias is inevitable, it should be stated explicitly. Such an approach has the advantage of candor and sharpens the debate over differing interpretations of the educational past. These benefits are strengthened substantially when historians are equally explicit in revealing data that contradict or cannot be explained by their hypotheses and theories.

David Tyack's essay, at the beginning of this chapter, analyzes the usefulness and limitations of theories of interpretation in educational history. Along the way, he offers a "prospective historiography" intended to aid historians in avoiding reductionism, the form of simplification that shrinks evidence to fit a thesis. In comparing approaches to the history of compulsory schooling, Tyack also speaks to the relation of history and policy. He tends to follow his own advice. Tyack's latest book, *The One Best System: A History of American Urban Education* (Cambridge, Mass.: Harvard University Press, 1974)

gives voice to a variety of perspectives on the history of urban education, while contributing directly to the analysis of fundamental questions of educational policy.

With the advantage of a distinguished career in the field, R.
Freeman Butts interprets recent developments in the history and
historiography of American education from the perspective of a long-
term direct participant. His support for recent advances in the field is
evident, and, one might add, remarkable, given his continued advocacy of two cardinal tenets. For Butts, the school occupies center
stage in the history of education, however broadly defined. He insists,
too, on viewing the school conceptually and historically as a political
institution that has contributed significantly to social growth and
change. For a systematic and comprehensive treatment of these
perspectives, readers will want to consult Butts's most recent work,
*Public Education in the United States: From Revolution to Reform,
1776-1976* (New York: Holt, Rinehart and Winston, Inc., 1978).

Ways of Seeing: An Essay on the History of Compulsory Schooling

David B. Tyack

I should warn you that what you are about to read is not a bullet-
proof, airtight, unsinkable monograph. It is an *essay* in the root sense
of the word: a trial of some ideas. Kenneth Burke wrote that "a way of
seeing is always a way of not seeing."[1] In our specialized age people are
taught and paid to have tunnel vision — and such specialization has
many benefits. Socialization within the academic disciplines focuses
inquiry: economists explain events in economic terms, sociologists in
sociological ways, psychologists by their own theories. Splintering even
occurs within fields; Freudians and behaviorists, for example, see the
world through quite different lenses.[2]

Historians tend to be eclectic more often than people in other
disciplines, but they often make their reputations by developing a

Reprinted, with permission, from *Harvard Educational Review* 46 (August 1976),
355-389. Copyright © 1976 by President and Fellows of Harvard College.

single line of argument. The frontier was the major shaping force in American history, Turner tells us. Status anxiety is the key to the progressive leaders, Hofstadter argues. Economic interests are the figure in the historical carpet, Beard claims. Other historians make their reputations by attacking Turner, Hofstadter, or Beard.[3] And so it goes.

Historiography normally is retrospective, telling us in what diverse ways scholars have explained events like the American Civil War. What I propose to do here is a kind of prospective historiography. I am impressed with the value of explicitly stated theories of interpretation but also struck by the value of discovering anomalies which any one theory does not explain. Thus, it seems useful to entertain alternative modes of explanation as a way of avoiding the reductionism that selects evidence to fit a particular thesis. Using different lenses to view the same phenomenon may seem irresponsibly playful to a true believer in any one interpretation, but at least it offers the possibility of self-correction without undue damage to an author's self-esteem.[4]

The topic of compulsory schooling lends itself to sharply different valuations, as the cartoons in Figures 3-1 and 3-2 suggest. Earlier students of compulsion, like Forest Ensign and Ellwood Cubberley, regarded universal attendance as necessary for social progress and portrayed the passage and implementation of compulsory laws as the product of noble leaders playing their role in a long evolution of democracy.[5] Standing firmly on "the structure of civilization," as in Figure 3-1, leaders used the mechanism of schooling to raise "American Social and Economic Life." In recent years radical critics have offered a quite different view of compulsory schooling. Figure 3-2 visually represents some of the elements of this revised interpretation. The school offers different and unequal treatments based on the race, sex, and class of incoming students. Compartmentalized internally, it produces a segmented labor force incapable of perceiving common interest. Rather than liberating the individual, the school programs him or her so as to guarantee the profits of the invisible rulers of the system. The school is thus an imposition that dehumanizes the student and perpetuates social stratification.[6] Such differing valuations as these necessarily influence explanatory frameworks and policy discussion.

In this intentionally open-ended essay, I first sketch what I take to be the phenomena of compulsory schooling that the theories should explain. Then I examine two sets of interpretations, political and economic, which I find initially plausible. Some of the explanations are

Figure 3-1

Source: Edgar Mendenhall, *The City School Board Member and His Task* (Pittsburgh, Kans.: College Inn Books, 1929), frontispiece; reprinted with permission.

Figure 3-2

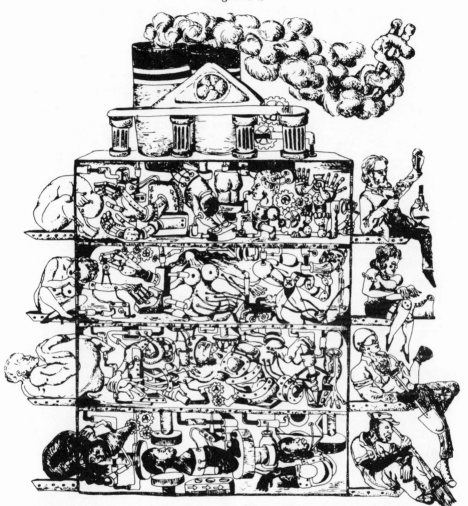

Source: Diane Lasch, *Leviathan* 1 (No. 3, June 1969): 12; reprinted with permission.

complementary, some contradictory; some explain certain events well but not others. Although each discussion is brief, I have tried to state the theories fairly, believing it not very useful to shoot down interpretations like ducks in a shooting gallery, only to bring out the *right* one (mine) at the end. But naturally I have interpretive preferences. Therefore, I intend to indicate what I see as flaws in the theories and anomalies they may not explain. In my conclusion, I do not attempt to reconcile the various interpretations in any definitive way, but instead suggest what we can learn from such comparative explorations.

WHAT NEEDS TO BE EXPLAINED?

At this point in my reading, I see two major phases in the history of compulsory school attendance in the United States. During the first, which lasted from [the] mid-nineteenth century to about 1890, Americans built a broad base of elementary schooling which attracted ever-growing numbers of children. Most states passed compulsory attendance legislation during these years, but generally these laws were unenforced and probably unenforceable. The notion of compulsion appears to have aroused ideological dispute at this time, but few persons paid serious attention to the organizational apparatus necessary to compel students into classrooms. Therefore, this phase might be called the *symbolic* stage. The second phase, beginning shortly before the turn of the twentieth century, might be called the *bureaucratic* stage. During this era of American education, school systems grew in size and complexity, new techniques of bureaucratic control emerged, ideological conflict over compulsion diminished, strong laws were passed, and school officials developed sophisticated techniques to bring truants into schools. By the 1920s and 1930s increasing numbers of states were requiring youth to attend high school, and by the 1950s secondary school attendance had become so customary that school-leavers were routinely seen as "dropouts."[7]

Even before the common school crusade of the mid-nineteenth century and before any compulsory laws, Americans were probably in the vanguard in literacy and mass schooling among the peoples of the world. Although methods of support and control of schools were heterogeneous in most communities before 1830, enrollment rates and literacy were very high—at least among whites. Public school advocates persuaded Americans to translate their generalized faith in education into support of a particular institution, the common school. Between 1850 and 1890 public expenditures for schools jumped from about $7 million to $147 million. Funds spent on public schools increased from 47 percent of total educational expenditures to 79 percent during those years.[8] Table 3-1 indicates both the high initial commitment to schooling and the gradual increase in attendance and decline in illiteracy.[9]

Educational statistics and data on literacy during the nineteenth

Table 3-1

Selected educational statistics for the United States, 1840-1890

Selected statistic	1840	1850	1860	1870	1880	1890
Enrollment rates of persons aged 5-19, in percentage (a)	37	42	49	60	58	64
Percentage of enrolled pupils attending daily (b)	—	—	—	59	62	64
Average length of school term, in days (b)	—	—	—	132	130	134
Percentage of population 10 years and older illiterate (c)	25-30	23	20	20	17	13

Sources: (a) John K. Folger and Charles B. Nam, *Education of the American Population* (Washington, D.C.: Government Printing Office, 1967), Chaps 1, 4; (b) W. Vance Grant and C. George Lind, *Digest of Educational Statistics,* 1974 ed. (Washington, D.C.: Government Printing Office, 1975), 34; (c) Folger and Nam, *Education of the American Population,* 113-114.

century are notoriously unreliable, but Table 3-1 at least suggests the magnitude of change. The aggregated national data, however, mask very important variations in attendance and literacy by region (the South lagged far behind the rest of the nation); by ethnicity (commonly forbidden to read under slavery, blacks were about 90 percent illiterate in 1870; and foreign-born adult whites were considerably less literate than native-born); and by other factors such as social class and urban or rural residence. Furthermore, the use of the broad age range of five to nineteen (common for both census and Office of Education statistics) hides variations in attendance at different age levels in different kinds of communities. In the industrial states, for example, children tended to start school earlier and to leave earlier than in farm states. In a census sample of both kinds of states, however, eight or nine out of ten children attended school from [age] ten to fourteen. Finally, the percentages obscured the magnitude of the sevenfold absolute growth in enrollment from 1840 to 1890; in the latter year, over fourteen million children were in school. By the close of the nineteenth century the typical child could expect to attend school for five years, according to United States Commissioner of Education William T. Harris; Harris and many others regarded this as a triumph, and indeed by then the United States led the world in its provision for mass education.[10]

These changes in attendance and literacy before roughly 1890 took place with minimal coercion by the states—despite the fact that by then twenty-seven legislatures had passed compulsory attendance laws. A survey in 1889 revealed that in all but a handful of states and individual cities the laws were dead letters. Indeed, in several cases state superintendents of education said the responsible local officials did not even know that there was such legislation.[11] Educators were often ambivalent about enforcement of compulsory attendance laws. Often they did not want the unwilling pupils whom coercion would bring into classrooms. In many communities, especially big cities, schools did not have enough seats even for children who wanted to go to school. And many citizens regarded compulsion as an un-American invasion of parental rights. Except in a few states like Connecticut and Massachusetts, provisions for enforcement were quite inadequate.[12]

Phase two of the history of compulsory schooling, the bureaucratic stage, built on the base of achievement laid down during the symbolic stage. The basically simple structure of the common school became much more elaborate, however, and mass education came to encompass the secondary school as well, as indicated by Table 3-2.

Public attitudes toward compulsory schooling appeared to become more positive in the years after 1890. This was true even in the South, which had previously resisted such legislation. States passed new laws with provisions for effective enforcement, including requirements for censuses to determine how many children there were, attendance officers, elaborate "pupil accounting," and often state financing of schools in proportion to average daily attendance. Age limits were gradually extended upwards, especially under the impact of the labor surplus in the Depression, until by the mid-1930s youths were typically required to attend school until age sixteen.

Early in the century the great majority of teenagers in school were lumped in the upper grades of the elementary school as a result of the frequent practice of forcing children to repeat grades. In the 1920s and 1930s, however, the practice of "social promotion"—that is, keeping age groups together—took hold, and the percentage of teenagers in high schools increased sharply. The increasing numbers of children compelled to attend schools, in turn, helped to transform the structure and curriculum of schooling. Of course, there were still many children

Table 3-2

Selected educational statistics for the United States, 1900-1950

Selected statistic	1900	1910	1920	1930	1940	1950
Enrollment rates of persons aged 5-19, in percentage (a)	72	74	78	82	84	83
Percentage of enrolled pupils attending daily (a)	69	72	75	83	87	89
Percentage of total enrollment in high schools (a)	3	5	10	17	26	23
High school graduates as percentage of population 17 years old (b)	6	9	17	29	51	59
Percentage of population 10 years and older illiterate (c)	11	8	6	4	3	3
Estimates of educational attainment, in years (d)	—	8.1	8.2	8.4	8.6	9.3

Sources: (a) Grant and Lind, *Digest of Educational Statistics*, 34; (b) U.S. Bureau of the Census, *Historical Statistics of the United States: Colonial Times to 1957* (Washington, D.C.: Government Printing Office, 1960), 207; (c) Folger and Nam, *Education of the American Population*, 114; (d) *ibid.*, 132.

who escaped the net of the truant officer, many who were denied equality of educational opportunity: an estimated two million children aged six to fifteen were not in any school in 1940. But during the twentieth century universal elementary and secondary schooling gradually was accepted as a common goal and approached a common reality.[13]

Over the long perspective of the last century and a half, both phases of compulsory school attendance may be seen as part of significant shifts in the functions of families and the status of children and youth. Households in American industrial cities became more like units of consumption than of production. Indeed, Frank Musgrove contends that the passage of compulsory school legislation in England "finally signalized the triumph of public over private influences as formative in social life and individual development; in particular, it tardily recognized the obsolescence of the educative family, its inadequacy in modern society in child care and training."[14] Advocates of compulsory schooling often argued that families—or at least some families, like those of the poor or foreign-born—were failing to carry out their traditional functions of moral and vocational training. Immigrant children in crowded cities, reformers complained, were leading disorderly lives, schooled by the street and their peers more than by Christian nurture in the home. Much of the drive for compulsory schooling reflected an animus against parents considered incompetent to train their children. Often combining fear of social unrest with humanitarian zeal, reformers used the powers of the state to intervene in families and to create alternative institutions of socialization.

Laws compelling school attendance were only part of an elaborate and massive tranformation in the legal and social rules governing children.[15] Children and youth came to be seen as individuals with categorical needs: as patients requiring specialized medical care; as "delinquents" needing particular treatment in the courts; and as students deserving elaborately differentiated schooling. Specific adults came to be designated as responsible for aiding parents in the complex tasks of child care: teachers, truant officers, counselors, scout leaders, and pediatricians, for example—not to mention Captain Kangaroo. Formerly regarded as a central function of the family, education came finally to be regarded as synonymous with schooling. The common query "Why aren't you in school?" signified that attendance in school had become the normal career of the young.[16]

POLITICAL DIMENSIONS OF COMPULSORY ATTENDANCE

Only government can compel parents to send their children to school. In legally compelling school attendance, the democratic state not only coerces behavior but also legitimizes majority values, as Michael S. Katz has argued.[17] Thus, sooner or later, any historian investigating compulsory school attendance logically needs to attend to political processes.

In recent years, however, few historians of American education have paid close attention either to the politics of control of schools or to the nature of political socialization in schools. Echoing Horace Mann's concern for social cohesion as well as social justice, R. Freeman Butts [see below] has suggested that both radical historians (stressing imposition by economic elites) and "culturist" historians (broadening the definition of education to include all "habitats of knowledge") have somewhat neglected the political functions of public schooling in both national and international contexts—what he calls civism.[18] Such neglect did not characterize much of the earlier work in the history of education, which, like writings in other branches of history, had a marked political and indeed nationalistic flavor. Among political sociologists, the emergence of new nations has also aroused interest in the political construction of education.

I begin, then, with an examination of a broad interpretive framework which stresses education as a means of incorporating people into a nation-state and legitimizing the status of "citizen" and "leader." After noting difficulties in relating these notions to the loosely organized political system of the United States, I proceed to a rather different form of analysis—namely, one which seeks to interpret the passage of compulsory schooling laws as a species of ethnocultural conflict. This explanation appears to fit phase one far better than phase two. To interpret phase two, I draw upon what one historian has called "the organization synthesis," an approach that seeks to explain political and social changes during the progressive era in terms of the growing importance of large-scale bureaucratic organizations and the attempt to resolve political issues by administrative means.

The Political Construction of Education

It is natural in the Watergate era to agree with Dr. Johnson that "patriotism is the last refuge of the scoundrel" and to suspect that nationalistic rhetoric about schooling disguises real motives. Yet I am struck by the range of ideology and class among persons in the United States who justified compulsory public education on explicitly political grounds. If the patriots were scoundrels, there were many of them in assorted walks of life. Moreover, nationalism has been associated with compulsory attendance not in the United States alone but also in European nations during the nineteenth century and in scores of developing nations today. In 1951 UNESCO sponsored a series of monographs on compulsory education around the globe; the organization assumed that all United Nations members agreed on "the general principle of the necessity of instituting systems of compulsory, free and universal education in all countries."[19]

How can one construe the political construction of education? Why does schooling seem so important to the modern state? In their essay, "Education and Political Development," John W. Meyer and Richard

Rubinson have argued that modern national educational systems in effect create and legitimate citizens. New nations are commonly composed of families and individuals who identify with regions, religions, ethnic groups, tribes, or interest groups. Such persons rarely think of themselves as either participants in or subjects of the state. Indeed, the whole notion of universal citizenship might seem to them fanciful and implausible. Meyer and Rubinson argue that the central political purpose of universal education is precisely to create citizens and legitimize the state. Families in potentially divisive subgroups turn over their children to state schools to learn a common language, a national history, and an ideology that incorporates them as citizens into the broader entity called the state. The point is not that this new compulsory political socialization is actually successful in accomplishing its cognitive or effective tasks, but simply that the institutional process is designed to create a new category of personnel — citizens. Similarly, advanced education may create and legitimate elites. People who formerly ruled by hereditary right or other kinds of ascriptive privilege may still wield power, but the rituals of higher state education turn them into legitimate "civil servants." As states expand their control over new sectors of society, state schooling gives an apparently rational and modern justification for new social rules that replace the older ones based on regional, ethnic, religious, or family loyalties. By these means, education helps to institutionalize the authority of the state.[20]

It is a complicated argument. Let me illustrate with historical examples from American, French, and Prussian experience. After the American Revolution, numerous theorists like Thomas Jefferson, Benjamin Rush, and Noah Webster argued that without a transformed educational system the old prerevolutionary attitudes and relationships would prevail in the new nation. Rush said that a new, uniform state system should turn children into "republican machines." Webster called for an "Association of American Patriots for the Formation of an American Character," strove to promote uniformity of language, and wrote a "Federal Catechism" to teach republican principles to school children. Jefferson wanted to create state primary schools to make loyal citizens of the young. In addition, many early theorists wanted a national university to prepare and legitimate elites for leadership.[21] Similarly, French writers on education after the 1789 Revolution advocated a universal state system that would teach all French citizens to read and would give them pride in their country's history and political institutions. In both cases education was regarded as an instrument deliberately used to create a new status, to turn people with diverse loyalties into citizens of a new entity—the republican state.

The use of schooling as a means of incorporating people into the nation-state was not limited to liberal regimes, however. Compulsory schooling also served militant nationalism in conservative Prussia during the nineteenth century by attaching people to the centralized and corporate state. Victor Cousin observed in his report on Prussian education that the parental duty to send children to school "is so national, so rooted in all the legal and moral habits of the country, that it is expressed by a single word, *Schulpflichtigkeit* [school duty, or school obligation]. It corresponds to another word, similarly formed and similarly sanctioned by public opinion, *Dienstpflichtigkeit* [service obligation, that is, military service]."[22]

To some degree the political construction of education I have sketched here does fit the development of compulsory schooling in the United States. As mentioned above, postrevolutionary writers on education stressed the need to use schools to transform colonials into citizens. Repeating their arguments, Horace Mann contended that common schools would imbue the rising generation with traits of character and loyalties required for self-government. Waves of immigration intensified concern over the incorporation of new groups into the polity. For a time the federal government took an active interest in schooling ex-slaves so that they, too, might become proper citizens like their foreign-born fellow compatriots.[23] The national government even used schooling as a way to shape people conquered in war into the predetermined mold of republican citizenship: witness the fate of native American children torn from their parents and sent to boarding schools, the dispatch of American teachers to Puerto Rico and the Philippines after the Spanish-American war, and the attempts to democratize Germany and Japan after World War II.[24] Even the Japanese-Americans "relocated" during World War II were subjected to deliberate resocialization in the camps' public schools.[25]

Clearly, Americans had enormous faith in the power of schooling to transform all kinds of people—even "enemies"—into citizens. The process of entry into the status of citizenship was rather like baptism; like the sprinkling of water on the head of a child in an approved church, schooling was a ritual process that acquired political significance because people believed in it. Characteristically, Americans intensified their attempts at political socialization in schools whenever they perceived a weakening of loyalties (as in World War I), or an infusion of strangers (as in peak times of immigration), or a spreading of subversive ideas (whether by Jesuits or Wobblies or Communists). Interest in compulsory attendance seems to correlate well with such periods of concern.[26]

There are problems, however, with applying this conception of the political construction of education to the United States. The ideas of the revolutionary theorists were not put into practice in their lifetime, for example. One could argue that early Americans learned to be citizens by participating in public life rather than by schooling and, indeed, that they had in effect been American "citizens" even before the Revolution. Before the common school crusade, educational institutions tended to reflect differences of religion, ethnicity, and social class — precisely the sorts of competing loyalties presumably detrimental to national unification. Furthermore, in the federated network of local, state, and national governments, it was by no means clear what "the state" really was. Although many advocates of compulsion turned to Prussia for evidence of how the state could incorporate the young into schools for the public good, opposition to centralization of state power was strong throughout the nineteenth century. The ritualized patriotism of Fourth of July orations and school textbooks was popular, but actual attempts to coerce parents to send their children to school were often seen as un-American and no business of the state. Prussian concepts of duty to the state sharply contrasted with nineteenth-century American beliefs in individualism and laissez-faire government. Different groups in American society tended to express different points of view about using the state to reinforce certain values and to sanction others.[27] I will explore this point in the next section on ethnocultural politics.

During most of the nineteenth century, the apparatus of federal and state control of education was exceedingly weak. Although leaders from Horace Mann forward talked of the virtues of centralization and standardization in state systems, state departments of education were miniscule and had few powers. In 1890 the median size of state departments of education, including the superintendent, was two persons. At that time there was one state education official in the United States for every one hundred thousand pupils. One pedagogical czar with the effective sanctions and rewards might have controlled such masses, but state departments of education prior to the turn of the twentieth century rarely had strong or even clear-cut powers.[28] Federal control was even weaker, although some reformers dreamed of massive federal aid and extended powers for the Office of Education. In effect, the United States Commissioner of Education was a glorified collector of statistics — and often ineffectual even in that role. An individual like Henry Barnard or William T. Harris might lend intellectual authority to the position, but the Office itself probably had trivial influence on American schools.[29] De facto, most control of schools lay with local school boards.

So the theory of the political construction of education is powerfully suggestive, but the American historical experience raises certain anomalies. Most Americans during the early national period apparently felt no need to legitimize citizenship through formal state schooling, although that idea began to take hold by [the] mid-nineteenth century. Until the end of the century there was considerable opposition to centralized state power, both in theory and in practice. Thus it is difficult to envisage the state during either period as legitimizing individuals as citizens through education or effectively extending its jurisdiction into other parts of society like the family.

Much of this changed in the era beginning roughly in 1890, as the notion of the state as an agency of social and economic reform and control took hold and an "organizational revolution" began. Thus it seems useful to supplement the broad theory of the political construction of education with two other interpretations that give a more focused perspective on the two phases of compulsion.

Ethnocultural Politics in Compulsory School Legislation during the Nineteenth Century

During the nineteenth century Americans differed significantly in their views of citizenship and the legitimate domain of state action, including compulsory attendance legislation. A number of interpreters of the political contests of the period have argued that these cleavages followed ethnic and religious lines. In a perceptive essay on this ethnocultural school of interpretation, James Wright notes that these historians dissent from both the economic class conflict model of Charles Beard and the consensus model that emerged after World War II. The ethnocultural historians, he says, do not argue.

. . . a simplistic model in which war heelers appeal to ethnic, religious, or racial prejudices and loyalties in order to divert attention from "real" economic issues. Rather,
the real issues of politics have been those most significant relative to life style and
values: prohibition, public funding or control of sectarian schools, sabbatarian laws,
woman suffrage, and efforts to hasten or retard ethnic assimilation.[30]

Richard Jensen points out that religious congregations, often
divided along ethnic lines, were very important in shaping political attitudes and behavior in the Midwest. Such sectarian groups provided
not only contrasting world views but also face-to-face communities
that reinforced them. Like Paul Kleppner, Jensen has identified two
primary religious persuasions that directly influenced political expression. One was represented by the pietistic sects—groups like the Bap-
tists and Methodists that had experienced great growth as a result of
the evangelical awakenings of the century—which tended to reject
church hierarchy and ritual and insist that right belief should result in
upright behavior. Seeing sin in the world, as represented by breaking
the Sabbath or drinking alcohol, for example, the pietists sought to
change society and thereby, as Kleppner explains, "to *conserve* their
value system and to restore the norms it preserved." The liturgicals, by
contrast, believed that salvation came from right belief and from the
preservation of the particular orthodoxies represented in the creeds
and sacraments of the church. Liturgicals like Roman Catholics and
Lutherans of certain synods tended to see morality as the preserve not
of the state but of the church, the family, and the parochial school.
According to both Kleppner and Jensen, the Republican Party tended
to attract the pietists, the Democratic Party the liturgicals. By and
large, the Republicans supported a "crusading moralism" for a single
standard of behavior, while the Democrats spoke for a "counter-
crusading pluralism."[31]

These politically important religious distinctions cut across ethnic
lines. Although old-stock Americans tended to be pietistic and
Republican, the Irish Catholics to be liturgical and Democratic, for
example, other ethnic groups, like the Germans, split into different
camps. *The* immigrant vote was a fiction based on nativistic fear; can-
ny politicans knew better. Furthermore, this kind of status-group
politics needs to be distinguished from the theory of the politics of
status anxiety or status discrepancy that was advanced by political
scientists and by Richard Hofstadter in the 1950s. Status groups assert-
ing themselves through the political process during the nineteenth

century rarely saw themselves on the skids socially. Rather than regarding ethnocultural politics as in some sense pathological, it is quite as accurate to describe it as the positive assertion of groups that believed in their own values and life styles and sought to extend their group boundaries and influence.[32]

The politics of "crusading moralism" and "counter-crusading pluralism" often focused on issues like temperance or Sabbath observance and frequently resulted in blue laws, which, like dead letter compulsory attendance legislation, were often more symbolic assertions than implementable decisions. Republican politicians often winked at breaches of the laws where it was politically astute to do so. It was one thing to enforce prohibition in a town where the only public drinker was the town Democrat, and quite another to do so in German wards of Milwaukee. Laws which stamped the pietistic foot and said "Be like me" might satisfy symbolically without alienating dissenters by active enforcement.[33]

Were nineteenth-century compulsory school attendance laws of that character largely passed by Republican pietists? I don't know, but the hypothesis seems worth testing by evidence, perhaps by the political composition of the state legislatures that passed such laws and by values expressed in textbooks. For now, the interpretation seems plausible. Evangelical ministers were at the forefront of the common-school crusade as the frontier moved westward, and ministers like Josiah Strong saw the school as a bulwark of the evangelical campaign to save the cities. Public schooling was widely publicized as the creation of "our Puritan, New England forefathers." Pietists saw themselves not as an interest group but as representatives of true American values. People who wanted compulsory attendance laws were presumably already sending their children to school; by branding the nonconforming parent as illegal or deviant, they thereby strengthened the norms of their own group (the explanation follows what can be called the tongue-clucking theory of the function of crime).[34]

Much of the rhetoric of compulsory schooling lends itself to this ethnocultural interpretation and further refines the theory of the political construction of education. In 1891 superintendents in the National Education Association (NEA) passed a resolution favoring compulsory education. The resolution's preamble stated that "in our free Republic the State is merely the expression of the people's will, and not an external governmental force." The NEA statement sounds quite different than the notion of a strong central state creating citizens through schooling, as in the view explored above. Why then, did the state have to compel citizens to send their children to school? Because compulsion created liberty.[35]

The assumptions behind this Orwellian paradox become more clear when one reads accounts of the discussions of compulsion which took place that year in the National Council of Education, the prestigious think tank of the NEA. A committee had just reported to the Council that the idle and vicious were filling the jails of the nation, corrupt men were getting the ballot, and "foreign influence has begun a system of colonization with a purpose of preserving foreign languages and traditions and proportionately of destroying distinctive Americanism. It has made alliance with religion. . . ." The committee was really saying that there were two classes of citizens, us and them. Said an educator in the audience: "The report assumes that when the people established this government they had a certain standard of intelligence and morality; and that an intelligent and moral people will conform to the requirements of good citizenship." Things have changed, he observed: "People have come here who are not entitled to freedom in the same sense as those who established this government." The question was whether to raise these inferior newcomers to the standards of the Anglo-Saxon forefathers or to "lower this idea of intelligence and morality to the standard of that class" of new immigrants from southern and eastern Europe. Republican liberty depended on a homogeneity of virtue and knowledge that only compulsion could create in the new generation. Almost without exception native-born and Protestant, NEA leaders in the nineteenth century took naturally to the notion that real citizens were those who fit the pietist mold.[36]

In 1871, in a speech on the "New Departure of the Republican Party," Republican Senator Henry Wilson linked compulsory schooling to nativist and Protestant principles. Pointing out that the Fifteenth Amendment had expanded suffrage to include blacks and that unrestricted immigration was flooding the nation with millions "from Europe with all the disqualifications of their early training," he argued for an educational system that would transform "the emigrant, the freedman, and the operative" into proper citizens in accord with the "desirable traits of New England and the American character."[37] An editorial in the *Catholic World* promptly attacked Wilson for wanting compulsory schooling to mold all "into one homogeneous people, after what may be called the New England Evangelical type. Neither his politics nor his philanthropy can tolerate any diversity of ranks, conditions, race, belief, or worship."[38]

Evidence of ethnic and religious bias abounds in the arguments about compulsory schooling throughout the nineteenth century. In the 1920s bias surfaced again in Oregon when the Ku Klux Klan and its allies passed a law that sought to outlaw private schooling. Two compulsory schooling laws in Illinois and in Wisconsin in 1889 aroused fierce opposition from liturgical groups, especially German Catholics and Lutherans, because of their provisions that private schools teach in the English language and that they be approved by boards of public education. In both states Democrats derided the laws as instances of Republican paternalism and hostility to pluralism; defeated Republicans learned to disavow spokesmen who believed that extremism in defense of virtue is no vice. After the disastrous votes in 1892, one Republican wrote to a friend that "defeat was inevitable. The school law did it—a silly, sentimental and damned useless abstraction, foisted upon us by a self-righteous demagogue."[39] Both Kleppner and Jensen see these contests over compulsory instruction in English as classic examples of ethnocultural politics.[40]

These Illinois and Wisconsin conflicts may, however, be exceptional cases; other states passed similar laws requiring English-language instruction and state accreditation without such contests erupting. It is possible that there was bipartisan support for the ineffectual state laws passed before 1890 and that widespread belief in public education made consensus politics the wisest course. The South, which lagged in compulsory legislation, had few immigrants and few Catholics; its population was native-born and evangelical with a vengeance. How well does an ethnocultural hypothesis fit the South? Is the educational politics of race substantially different from white ethnocultural politics? Only careful state-by-state analysis can test the theory that ethnocultural politics was a key factor in compulsory attendance legislation during the nineteenth century. But where there is the smoke of ethnocultural rhetoric, it is plausible to seek political fires.[41]

In any case, the high point of ethnocultural politics of compulsory education was probably the nineteenth century. The assumption persisted into the twentieth century that there were real citizens—those with the right heredity and principles—who needed to shape others to their own image. But at the turn of the century attention shifted to efficient organizational means for compelling school attendance.

FROM POLITICS TO ADMINISTRATION:
AN ORGANIZATIONAL INTERPRETATION

Despite some notable exceptions, open ethnocultural strife in school politics appears to have subsided during phase two of compulsory attendance. Many of the decisions that once had been made in the give-and-take of pluralistic politics now shifted to administrators within the system. At the turn of the century a powerful and largely successful movement centralized control of city schools in small boards of education elected at large rather than by ward. Furthermore, state departments of education grew in size and influence and led in the consolidation of rural schools and the enforcement of uniform educational standards. Advocates of these new forms of governance argued that education should be taken out of politics and that most decisions were best made by experts. Government by administrative experts was, of course, a form of politics under another name: decisions about who got what in the public allocation of scarce resources were simply shifted to a new arena. The line between public and private organizations became blurred as proponents of centralization urged that school systems adopt the corporate model of governance. As decision-making power shifted to superintendents and their staffs, the number of specialists and administrators ballooned. School systems grew in size, added tiers of officials, and became segmented into functional division: elementary, junior high, and high schools; vocational programs of several kinds; classes for the handicapped; counseling services; research and testing bureaus; and many other departments.[42]

The new provisions for compulsory schooling reflected these bureaucratic technologies. In city schools, in particular, large attendance departments were divided into supervisors, field workers, and clerks. Attendance experts developed the school census, elaborate forms for reporting attendance, manuals on "child accounting," and civil service requirements for employment. By 1911 attendance officers were numerous and self-conscious enough to start their own national professional organization. Schools developed not only new ways of finding children and getting them into school, but also new institutions or programs to cope with the unwilling students whom truant officers brought to their doors: parental schools, daylong truant schools, disciplinary classes, ungraded classes, and a host of specialized curricular tracks. Local officials gathered data by the file full to aid in planning a rational expansion and functional specialization of the schools. Doctoral dissertations and other "scientific" studies analyzed existing patterns of attendance and promoted the new methods.[43]

Surely one can find examples of these new techniques and institutional adaptations prior to phase two, but what I find striking is the very rapid increase in the machinery of compulsion and the structural differentiation of the schools in the years after 1890. A new method of inquiry called "educational science" helped educators to gather and process information so that they could not only describe quantitatively what was going on in schools, but also forecast and plan. In national organizations these new functional specialists shared ideas and strategies of change. Older local perspectives gradually gave way to more cosmopolitan ways of thinking. The new hierarchical, differentiated bureaucracies seemed to many to be a superb instrument for continuous adaptation of the schools to diverse social conditions and needs. Theoretically at least, issues of religion or ethnicity were irrelevant to decisionmaking in such bureaucracies, as were parochial tastes or local prejudices.[44]

Samuel Hays sees the rise of large-scale organizations and functional groups as characteristic of many sectors of American society during the twentieth century. He points out that the new technical systems defined what were problems and used particular means for solving them. "Reason, science, and technology are not inert processes by which men discover, communicate, and apply facts disinterestedly and without passion, but means through which, through systems, some men organize and control the lives of other men according to their particular conceptions as to what is preferable." He argues that the rapid growth of empirical inquiry — normally called "science" — has enabled people in organizations to plan future courses of action. This differentiates these new technical systems from earlier bureaucracies. Not only did these new methods change decisionmaking within organizations, but functional specialists like educators, engineers, or doctors banded together in organizations to influence the larger environment collectively as interest groups.[45]

How does this vision of organizational change help explain the enactment and implementation of compulsory schooling? John Higham has observed that "the distinctive feature of the period from 1898 to 1918 is not the preeminence of democratic ideals or of bureaucratic techniques, but rather a fertile amalgamation of the two.

An extraordinary quickening of ideology occurred in the very midst of a dazzling elaboration of technical systems."[46] Robert Wiebe, likewise, sees the essence of progressivism as "the ambition of the new middle class to fulfill its destiny through bureaucratic means."[47] Thus, one might interpret the passage of child labor legislation and effective compulsory attendance laws as the work of functional groups and national reform associations that combined ideological commitment with bureaucratic sophistication. These groups knew how to create enforcement systems that would actually work, and they followed up on their results. Active in this way were such groups as educators (who increasingly came to the forefront in compulsory schooling campaigns), labor unions, the National Child Labor Committee, and elite educational associations (like the Philadelphia Public Education Association) with cosmopolitan connections and outlooks.[48]

In his essay, "The Emerging Organizational Synthesis in Modern American History," Louis Galambos says that historians of this persuasion believe

. . . that some of the most (if not the single most) important changes which have taken place in modern America have centered about a shift from small-scale, informal, locally or regionally oriented groups to large-scale, national, formal organizations . . . characterized by a bureaucratic structure of authority. This shift in organization cuts across the traditional boundaries of political, economic, and social history.[49]

This interpretation has called attention to the fact that large-scale organizations deeply influence the lives of most Americans, and to a degree it has explained how. There is somewhat less agreement among historians as to why this shift has taken place or how to assess the human consequences. Most historians would agree that the rise of complex organizations relates in some fashion to new technology, new forms of empirical inquiry, and institutional innovations designed to cope with size and scope of functions. Economic historians like Thomas Cochran, Alfred Chandler, and Fritz Redlich have described how business firms changed from small, local enterprises (often owned and run by a single family) to vast and diversified multitier bureaucracies in order to cope with problems of growth of markets, complexity of production, and widening spans of control.[50] Raymond Callahan and others have shown how educational administrators consciously emulated these new business corporations.[51]

Although the new organizational approach in history may provide a useful focus for the study of compulsory attendance, especially in the years after 1890, the interpretation is not without flaws. It may not be sound to generalize urban experience to the educational system as a whole; bureaucratization was probably neither rapid nor systemic throughout American schools, but gradual and spreading from certain centers like drops of gas on water. The conceptualization of an organizational revolution is also somewhat rudimentary at this point, leading to the same dangers of misplaced concreteness one finds in the use of concepts like "modernization" and "urbanization." It is very important not to portray this kind of organizational change as an inevitable process. Some people helped to plan the changes and benefited from them, others did not; some results were intended, others were not. Schools are rarely so politically neutral as they portray themselves. One virtue of the economic interpretations to which we now turn is that they provide models of behavior that help to explain the interests or motivations of people who acted collectively in organizations.[52]

TWO ECONOMIC INTERPRETATIONS OF SCHOOL ATTENDANCE

It is misleading, of course, to attempt to separate economic interpretations too sharply from political ones. In the three variants of political models sketched above, issues of economic class are present even where, as in ethnocultural conflict, they may not be salient. Both of the economic interpretations I examine also involve political action. Not surprisingly, however, economic historians tend to focus on economic variables, and it is useful to see how far this kind of analysis carries us in interpreting school attendance.

Two contrasting views seem most relevant: human-capital theory and a Marxian model. Both have precursors in nineteenth-century educational thought, but both have received closest scholarly attention during the last generation. Both are related to political interpretations in the broad sense in which Thomas Cochran says that the economic order shaped the political order: "On the fundamental level the goals and values of a business-oriented culture established the rules of the game: how men were expected to act, what they strove for, and what qualities or achievements were rewarded."[53] Naturally, economic interpretations may differ in what they take to be the basic driving forces in historical events, and such is the case in the two models I explore.

Human Capital Theory and School Attendance

Mary Jean Bowman has described the notion of investment in human beings "as something of a revolution in economic thought." The notion of investigating the connection between resources spent on increasing the competence of workers and increased productivity and earnings was not entirely new, of course, but experience after World War II showed that "physical capital worked its miracles only in lands where there were many qualified men who knew how to use it (the Marshall Plan countries and Japan)." Economists interested in economic growth then began to analyze the effects of "human capital" on development and discovered that education appeared to have considerable explanatory power.[54]

Work on investment in human beings moved from general studies of the contribution of schooling to economic growth in whole societies to analyses of the rates of return of formal education to individuals. Economists treated the microdecisionmaking of individuals or families about schooling as a form of rational cost-benefit analysis. They developed increasingly sophisticated ways to estimate rates of return on investment in education by including not only the direct costs of schooling but also the value of foregone earnings and the costs of maintaining students as dependents. Albert Fishlow, for example, has calculated that during the nineteenth century the "opportunity costs" paid by parents about equalled the sums paid by the public to support all levels of the educational system. Despite disagreements over specific rates of return, most economists agree that schooling does have significant impact on growth and earnings.[55]

Although economists have only recently honed the theory of human investment, similar notions have been current in educational circles for a long time. An idea circulating among educators for over a century has been that schooling created economic benefits for the society as a whole through greater productivity and for individuals through greater earnings. The first influential advocate of this view in the United States was Horace Mann, Secretary of the Board of Education of Massachusetts, who devoted his *Fifth Annual Report* in 1842 chiefly to this theme. In his report Mann presented an economic justification for greater investment in schooling, but his arguments were soon picked up as justification for compulsory school attendance. As Maris Vinovskis has observed, Mann actually preferred to advocate education by noneconomic arguments—the role of schools in moral or civic development, for example. But in his fifth year as Secretary, when his work was under political attack in the legislature and when a depression was forcing government to retrench, Mann decided that the time had come to show thrifty Yankees that education was a good investment. He argued that education not only produced good character and multiplied knowledge "but that it is also the most prolific parent of material riches." As proof he adduced the replies of businessmen to his questionnaire asking about the differences between educated and uneducated workers. What his study lacked in objectivity and scientific rigor it made up in evangelical enthusiasm; Mann concluded that money spent on primary schooling gave an aggregate rate of return to society of about 50 percent. He claimed that education enabled people to become rational decisionmakers by "comprehending the connections of a long train of events and seeing the end from the beginning." In addition to instilling this orientation toward the future—perhaps of most benefit to entrepreneurs—schooling made workers punctual, industrious, frugal, and too rational to cause trouble for their employers.[56]

Although Mann's evidence was largely impressionistic, his questionnaire highly biased, and his conclusions suspect for those reasons, his report was welcome ammunition to school reformers across the country. The New York legislature printed and distributed eighteen thousand copies; Boston businessmen applauded him for proving that the common school was not only "a nursery of souls, but a mine of riches"; and a leading educator said in 1863 that Mann's report probably did "more than all other publications written within the past twenty-five years to convince capitalists of the value of elementary instruction as a means of increasing the value of labor."[57] In 1870 the United States Commissioner of Education surveyed employers and workingmen and reported results similar to those of Mann.[58] A committee of the United States Senate which took testimony on "the relations between labor and capital" in the mid-1880s found that businessmen and employees across the nation tended to agree that schooling increases the productivity and predictability of workers.[59] So fixed had this view become by the twentieth century—reflecting dozens of rate-of-return studies at the turn of the century—that a high school debaters' manual on compulsory schooling listed these as standard arguments for the affirmative:

Education is the only guarantee of the prosperity of every individual in the State.
Education will pay in dollars and cents.

The education of the State and the wealth of the State bear a constant ratio one increasing with the other.[60]

As human capital theory has developed in recent years, economists
have applied models of decision theory to the development of compulsory schooling in the nineteenth century. Generally they have
focused upon individuals or their families and assumed that they make
rational calculations of their presumed future benefits. For example,
in their essay "Compulsory Schooling Legislation: An Economic
Analysis of Law and Social Change in the Nineteenth Century,"
William Landes and Lewis Solmon adopted as their "theory of the
determinants of schooling levels" the model that an individual "would
maximize his wealth by investing in schooling until the marginal rate
of return equaled marginal cost (expressed as an interest rate)."[61]
They found that in 1880 there was a higher investment in schooling in
states that had compulsory attendance laws than in those that did not.
But by also examining levels of schooling in 1870, when only two states
had laws, they discovered that the states which passed laws during the
1870s had already achieved high levels of investment in public education prior to enactment of compulsory legislation. They concluded
that compulsory education laws did not much influence the supply
and demand curves and were

. . . not the cause of the higher schooling levels observed in 1880 in states with laws.
Instead, these laws appear merely to have formalized what was already an observed
fact; namely, that the vast majority of school-age persons had already been obtaining
a level of schooling equal to or greater than what was to be later specified by statute.[62]

In other words, the legislation merely applauded the decisions of
families who had concluded that schooling paid off for their children.
But this does not explain why parents had to be forced by law to send
children to school. In another article, Solmon admits that variation in
state support for schooling "might reflect politics rather than individual market decisions, but even these are worked out in the
'political market place' and presumably reflect the tastes of the
'typical' individual."[63]

Why, then, pass the laws? Landes and Solmon argue that on the demand side, educators wanted "legislation that compels persons to purchase their product" (the laws did appear to increase the number of
days the schools were open); and law may have had external benefits

"to members of the community since it is a way of giving formal recognition to the community's achievement in committing more resources to schooling."[64] With regard to supply, since schooling was already widely available and most parents were sending their children anyway, the cost of passing the laws was minimal in light of the presumed gains.

Albert Fishlow reaches similar conclusions in his study of investment in education during the nineteenth century. He notes a rapid rise of spending on human capital in the industrialized nations of the United States, England, France, and Germany. But in contrast with the key role of the central state in Europe, Fishlow says, American investment arose from a local consensus on the value of education: "Under such circumstances, the educational commitment was a matter of course from parents to children rather than from community to schools."[65] Most parents, he argues, made the calculation that education was worth the price, both in public outlays and in private opportunity costs. But there were some families that did not make this decision, and Fishlow argues that "the entire history of compulsory-schooling legislation and of child-labor legislation is usefully viewed as social intervention to prevent present opportunity costs from having weight in the educational decision."[66]

The actual opportunity costs differed sharply between rural and urban communities and between richer and poorer families. Schools in farm areas could adjust the academic calendar to match the need for child labor in agriculture, thus nearly eliminating the need to forego the earnings of children. In cities, by contrast, work opportunities were generally not seasonal, and compulsory attendance effectively barred children from adding substantially to family income. In addition, the poor did not have the same opportunity to invest in their children as did middle- and upper-income families, since they could not generally borrow capital against their children's presumed higher future income. Thus, the very large private contribution to schooling through the opportunity costs was a source of major educational inequality — one recognized, incidentally, by truant officers, judges, and other officials who confronted the problems of compulsory attendance firsthand.[67]

How convincing is the human investment paradigm in explaining the history of school attendance? On the surface it appears to require quite a stretch of the imagination to envisage families actually making the complex calculations of future benefit embodied in some of the models of economists. But, as Mary Jean Bowman writes, "the economist is not concerned, as is the psychologist, with explaining individual behavior per se. If people behave as if they were economically rational, that is quite enough, provided we are dealing with multiple decision units."[68] The decisionmaking model is of course a conscious simplification, omitting factors of public welfare or intrinsic pleasure that probably do affect choice. If one defines as voluntary that school attendance which is unconstrained by law (in the absence of law, or beyond legally required years, or in communities where laws were unpublicized or unenforced), it does appear that voluntary attendance was influenced in part by the prospect of future economic advantage, for families always had competing demands on their incomes. And the evidence is quite convincing that compulsory laws were passed in states where most citizens were already investing in schooling up to the point required by law. A powerful recurring argument for compulsion was that taxpayers could realize the full return on their large investment only if free schooling reached all the children; the presumption was that children who were out of school needed education the most and would become an economic burden to the community if left uneducated. Hence, there was a social benefit in investing in all children as human capital. Thus far the human capital theory seems fruitful.

The kind of decisionmaking assumed by this theory requires, I believe, at least some awareness of the economic benefits of education. Did nineteenth-century Americans, in fact, link schooling with economic success? In this century we have become accustomed to thinking of schools as sorters, as institutions that help to determine the occupational destiny of students. Increasingly, not only the professions but many other jobs as well have come to require educational credentials or prescribed levels of schooling even for entry-level positions.[69] Not only is this screening function of schools embodied in specific institutional arrangements, like high school counseling programs, but it has also become common knowledge in the population at large. In 1973, 76 percent of respondents in a Gallup poll said they thought education was "extremely important" to "one's future success."[70]

There is little evidence, however, that citizens in the nineteenth century thought this way about schooling. Rhetoric about the purposes of education emphasized socialization for civic responsibility and moral character far more than as an investment in personal economic advancement. Indeed, there is some counterevidence that businessmen, for one group, were actually hostile to the notion of education beyond the confines of the common school.[71] The arguments of Horace Mann and his early successors stressed not so much individual earnings as aggregate productivity and the workmanlike traits such as reliability and punctuality. The most influential spokesmen for nineteenth-century educators — people like William T. Harris — did stress a general socialization for work, but they tended to see success as the result of later behavior in the marketplace. Harris estimated that, as late as 1898, the average person attended school for only five years. Out of one hundred students in all levels of education, ninety-five were in elementary, four were in secondary, and only one was in higher education.[72] Furthermore, family incomes were much lower in the nineteenth century than in mid-twentieth, and the structure of the labor force was far different. The percentage of the population engaged in agriculture dropped from 37.5 in 1900 to 6.3 in 1960, while the percentage in white-collar occupations rose from 17.6 to 43.5 in those years.[73] It is likely, then, that motives other than future rate of return on educational investments in individuals were more significant during the nineteenth century than in the twentieth. The microdecisionmaking paradigm in human capital better explains our more recent history, when disposable family income has substantially risen, when parents are better educated and more capable of calculating future benefits, and when schooling has become far more important in sorting people into occupational niches.[74]

A Marxian Analysis

"We are led to reject the individual choice model as the basis for a theory of the supply of educational services," Samuel Bowles and Herbert Gintis have written.

The model is not wrong — individuals and families do make choices, and may even make educational choices roughly as described by the human capital theorists. We reject the individual choice framework because it is so superficial as to be virtually irrelevant to the task of understanding why we have the kinds of schools and the amount of schooling that we do.[75]

Why superficial? Because the individual choice model provides only a partial interpretation of production, treats the firm "as a black box," and offers no useful insight into the basic question of how the capitalist class structure has been reproduced. The perpetuation of great inequalities of wealth and income over the past century and the development of schools as social institutions have not resulted simply from an aggregation of individual choices, Bowles and Gintis argue; rather, schooling has served to perpetuate the hierarchical social relations of capitalist production. In their view, society is not a marketplace of individuals maximizing their advantages but a class structure in which power is unequally divided. It may appear that the American educational system has developed in accord with "the relatively uncoordinated 'investment' decisions of individuals and groups as mediated by local school boards," but in actuality these "pluralistic" accommodations have taken place in response to changes in production "governed by the pursuit of profit and privilege by those elements of the capitalist class which dominate the dynamic sectors of the economy." By setting boundaries of decision — establishing the rules of the game — the capitalist class determines the range of acceptable choice in a manner that strengthens and legitimizes its position.[76]

Bowles and Gintis are primarily interested in the consequences of the system of schooling rather than in the conscious motives of elites or school leaders. The important question is whether the outcomes of formal education have supported capitalism — for example, through differential training of workers and employers in ways that maintain the social division of labor. From this point of view, if Mann were a saint and yet his system of education perpetuated injustice because it supported exploitative relations of production, then the case for radical change would be all the stronger.

In developing their model of economic and educational change, Gintis and Bowles do not treat compulsory attendance in detail, but one can easily extrapolate an interpretation of compulsion from their theory. Their explanation has two major components. First, they account for educational reform periods, which shaped ideology and structure, as accommodations to contradictions engendered by capital accumulation and the incorporation of new groups into the wage-labor force. Second, they seek to demonstrate how the educational system has served capitalist objectives of achieving technical efficiency, control, and legitimacy.

"The capitalist economy and bicycle riding have this in common," they argue: "forward motion is essential to stability." As capital accumulates and new workers are drawn into expanded enterprises, potential conflict arises. Bowles and Gintis say that the contradictions inherent in this process gave rise to the common school movement during the mid-nineteenth century, a time of labor militancy as the wage-labor force expanded and inequality increased. Such contradictions, they believe, also gave rise to the progressive movement at the turn of the twentieth century—a period of conflict between big business and big labor. Social discord stemmed from the integration of immigrant and rural labor into the industrial system. During these times, they argue, workers demanded more education, and "progressive elements in the capitalist class" acceded to the demands only insofar as they could adapt the school to their own purposes. Bowles and Gintis see educational development, then, "as an outcome of class conflict, not class domination." Workers won schooling for their children, but by controlling decisionmaking in education and "suppressing anti-capitalist alternatives," the ruling class maintained the social relations of production while ameliorating conditions and dampening conflict. In this view, schooling has been a crucial tool for perpetuating the capitalist system amid rapid economic change. Periodically, when the schools ceased to correspond with the structure of production, major shifts in the scope and structure of education took place, dominated in the final analysis by the class that set the agendas of decision.[77]

How did schools meet the capitalist objectives of technical efficiency, control, and legitimacy? Gintis and Bowles claim that the social relations of the school closely matched the needs of the hierarchical relations of production. The school prepared individuals differentially—in skills, traits of personality, credentials, self-concepts, and behavior—for performance in different roles in the economic hierarchy. This differentiation was congruent with social definitions of race, sex, and class. Thus, for example, when structures of production were relatively simple, schools concentrated on such qualities as punctuality, obedience to authority, and willingness to work for extrinsic rewards—all of which were useful in shaping a disciplined labor force for industry or commerce. As economic organizations became larger and more complex and the labor force increasingly segmented in level and function, schooling in turn grew more differentiated. This segmentation, coupled with differential treatment based on race and sex, helped to splinter employees into separate groups and to blind them to their common interest as workers. Schooling increasingly selected those who would get the good jobs; the rhetoric of equality of opportunity through education rationalized unequal incomes and status and legitimized the system. "The predominant economic function of schools," Bowles and Gintis observe, was "not the production or identification of cognitive abilities but the accreditation of future workers as well as the selection and generation of noncognitive personality attributes rewarded by the economic system."[78] As the work of different classes differed, so did the pattern of socialization in schools.

Just as Mann prefigured some of the human capital theory, earlier Marxian theorists anticipated some of the Bowles-Gintis model, but they tended to see the laboring class as a more continuously active agent in educational change and capitalists as more hostile to public education. In 1883, for example, Adolph Douai, as a representative of the Socialistic Labor Party of the United States, presented a Marxist perspective on schooling to the United States Senate committee on the relations between labor and capital.[79] Half a century later, in the midst of the Great Depression, Rex David wrote a Marxian pamphlet on *Schools and the Crisis*.[80] Both strongly urged the creation of free and compulsory education for all young people; both stressed the opposition of capitalists to expanded educational opportunity; both saw teachers and other intellectual workers mostly as servants of vested interests but believed that educators could become an important means of spreading the light for socialism. For them, as for a number of progressive labor historians, the working class was normally the dominant part of the coalition pushing for equality, and the ruling class was frequently hostile.

The interpretation of these earlier Marxists differs in emphasis from but does not directly contradict the Bowles-Gintis theory of educational change. Bowles and Gintis develop a more explicit model of how an apparently liberal educational system played a crucial part in reproducing unequal distribution of wealth and hierarchical relations of production. They further argue that owners and employers were not part of an undifferentiated group of capitalists but that the schooling reforms were engineered by those who controlled the leading sectors of the economy — exemplified by the corporate leaders at the turn of the century who sought to stabilize and rationalize the economy and supporting social institutions.[81]

Bowles and Gintis offer a general model of capitalist education rather than a specific interpretation of compulsory attendance. Thus, what follows is my own extrapolation from their writing. Since they say that the "impetus for educational reform and expansion was provided by the growing class consciousness and political militancy of working people," presumably worker groups were advocates of universal attendance, perhaps aided by "progressive elements in the capitalist class." According to the theory that entry of new groups into the wage-labor force prompted demands for education, one might predict that the compulsory education laws would appear first where the wage-labor force was growing most rapidly. At the same time, the ineffectiveness of these laws during the nineteenth century might be interpreted in part as a sign of ambivalence toward universal education among capitalists themselves (some might have preferred cheap child labor to the labor of schooled youth or adults, for example). On the other hand, phase two, the period of effective laws and increasing bureaucratization, might reflect growing capitalist consensus on the value of differentiated schooling in producing a segmented labor force for increasingly complex social relations of production. Indeed, the correspondence of the structure and processes of the schools with those of the work place is precisely the point of the analysis; changes in the latter drive the former.[82]

The Marxian model sketched here is to a degree congruent with both the general theory of the political construction of education and the organizational synthesis. It suggests, however, that the capitalist class, as the ruling class, defines the production of citizens through education according to its own interests in the political economy. It adds to the organizational synthesis an explanation of why the large organization became dominant: capitalists had concentrated their ownership and power. It does not deny the choice model of human capital theory, but it declares that the choices have been set within a capitalist zone of tolerance; further, it adds the notions of class conflict and reproduction of social structure.

The Bowles-Gintis analysis addresses important questions and poses a clear, explicit model. In my view, however, this kind of class analysis does not sufficiently explain the motive force of religious and ethnic differences in political and social life, especially within the working class. It tends to downplay important variations among employers' attitudes toward child labor and the different forms of education. The older Marxist view here has some substance; as Thomas Cochran and others have documented, many businessmen were opposed to extension of educational opportunity. The wage-labor hypothesis does not help us to understand widespread provision of schooling and numerous compulsory-schooling laws in communities and states in which the family farm was the predominant mode of production. As class analysis becomes further refined, however, it promises to add much to our understanding of both the continuities in social structure and the dynamics of economic and educational change.[83]

CONCLUSION

So what does one learn from exploring alternative ways of seeing compulsory schooling? Should one simply add them all together, like the observations of the blind men feeling an elephant, and say that the reality is in fact accessible only through multiple modes of analysis, that each mode is helpful but partial? Do some explanations fit only a particular time or place? To what degree are the interpretations mutually exclusive, and to what degree do they overlap? How might one test the assumptions and assertions of each by empirical investigation? Would any kind of factual testing be likely to change the mind of a person committed to a particular way of seeing or to a particular purpose?

The different kinds of interpretations do call attention to different actors, motives, and evidence, and in this sense one could say that the historian interested in all the phenomena of compulsory schooling might simply add together the various sets of observations. Those arguing for the political construction of education emphasize the role of the state and stress the importance of incorporating a hetero-geneous populace into a unified state citizenry. The ethnocultural in-terpretation posits religious-ethnic differences as a motive force in political actions. The organizational synthesis stresses the role of the new middle class in changing the nature of American life through the creation of large organizations that dominate political and economic activities. Human capital theorists focus on the family as a decision unit in calculating the costs and benefits of schooling. Finally, the Marxists see class struggle as the source of the dialectic that produces historical change. Each interpretation, in turn, directs attention to certain kinds of evidence which can confirm or disprove its assertions of causation: growth of new state rules and apparatus, religious differ-ences expressed in political conflict, the rise of large organizations and related ideologies, the individual and social rates of return on school-ing, and changes in the social relations of production and of schooling.[84]

There are problems with simple additive eclecticism, however. Some interpretations do fit certain times and places better than others, as we have seen. More fundamentally, the models deal with social reality in quite different levels: the individual or the family, the ethnocultural group, the large organization, and the structure of political or economic power in the society as a whole. Scholars advancing such interpretations often have quite different conceptions of what drives social change and, hence, quite different notions of appropriate policy. Some may concentrate on changing the individual, others on improving the functioning of organizations, and still others on radically restructuring the society. Ultimately, one is likely to adopt a framework of interpretation that matches one's perception of reality and purpose in writing, and thus simple eclecticism may lead to blurring of vision and confusion of purpose.

To argue that one should not mix interpretations promiscuously does not mean that it is unwise to confront alternative conceptualizations or to attempt to integrate them into a more complex understanding of social reality. This, in turn, may make historians more conscious of the ways in which theories and empirical research interact with one another, so that an anomalous piece of evidence may call a theory into question and a new mode of explanation may be generated.[85] One of my purposes in this essay has been to extend the boundaries of discussion about the history of American education. I have become convinced that much of the recent work in the field — my own included — has used causal models too implicitly. It has also tended to constrict the range of value judgments. Was schooling "imposed" by elites on an unwilling working class, for example, or was John Dewey a servant of corporate capitalism? Entertaining explicit alternative models and probing their value assumptions may help historians to gain a more complex and accurate perception of the past and a greater awareness of the ambiguous relationship between outcome and intent — both of the actors in history and of the historians who attempt to recreate their lives.[86]

Public Education and
Political Community

R. Freeman Butts

For some fifteen years we have been busily engaged in revising the history of American education. It is now time to gain some perspective on the revisionist movements as we look ahead to see what shape the historiography of education should take in the next fifteen years.

The first time I really became conscious of a revisionist movement in the writing of history was in Urbana, Illinois, where I was attending, if my memory serves correctly, my first convention of the American Historical Association. It was in December 1933 when I was a third-year graduate student at the University of Wisconsin. I was, of course, awed by the thought that I was actually rubbing elbows with some of the great historians of the day. I was especially enchanted by the rousing presidential address given by none other than the doyen of American historians, Charles A. Beard. His address, entitled "Written History as an Act of Faith," undoubtedly had an abiding effect on me. I was fascinated by the assurance of the man as well as by his eloquence and charisma:

. . . It [history] is thought about past actuality, instructed and delineated by history as record and knowledge — record and knowledge authenticated by criticism and ordered with the help of scientific method. This is the final, positive, inescapable definition.[1]

But even Charlie Beard could not for long convince his colleagues that he had settled their problems for all time. In fact he was destined to provoke so much discussion and argument that *his* revisionism became the object of successive waves of revisionism that are still flowing and ebbing on the historiographical shores. In the 1920s and 1930s Beard and his fellow "New Historians" were busily revising the scientific historians who, in John Higham's terms, made up the first generation of professional historians brought up on German models of institutional history.

Reprinted, with permission, from *History of Education Quarterly* 14 (Summer 1974), 14, 165-183. This was an invited address to Division F (History and Historiography) of the American Educational Research Association at its annual meeting in Chicago, April 1974.

And no sooner had Beard, Turner, Robinson, Parrington, Becker, and other "progressive" historians of the second generation come to dominate the profession with their themes of conflict between the few and the many and their commitments to reform, egalitarianism, and collectivist democracy, but their successors, the third generation of professional historians in the 1950s, began to soft-pedal the conflict themes in favor of consensus themes and to reassert a kind of revival of scientific history in order to rescue history from the present-mindedness of Beard and the progressives. And then, of course, the New Left historians of the 1960s began to revive the conflict motifs of the progressives and to reassert a social reformism that the more conservative consensus historians of the 1950s and early 1960s had largely eschewed.

What all this means is that for virtually the entire life of professional history in this country, just about 100 years, we have witnessed wave upon wave of revisionism, and the fashions and moods have changed ever more rapidly since 1950. All this is to confirm, it seems to me, that Beard did have an inescapable element in his definition of written history, albeit not final or absolute, that is, that history is contemporary thought about the past:

. . . every written history . . . is a selection and arrangement of facts, of recorded fragments of past actuality. And the selection and arrangement of facts . . . is an act of choice, conviction, and interpretation respecting values, is an act of thought.[2]

The historian who writes history, therefore, consciously or unconsciously performs an act of faith. . . . He is thus in the position of the statesman dealing with public affairs; in writing he acts and in acting he makes choices, large or small, timid or bold, with respect to some conception of the nature of things.[3]

The upshot of his argument?

It is that any selection and arrangement of facts pertaining to any large area of history, either local or world, race or class, is controlled inexorably by the frame of reference in the mind of the selector and arranger. This frame of reference includes things deemed necessary, things deemed possible, and things deemed desirable. It may be large, informed by deep knowledge, and illuminated by wide experience; or it may be small, uninformed, and unilluminated. It may be a grand conception of history or a mere aggregation of confusions.[4]

Now, this was heady stuff for a graduate student, whose history courses, even in that citadel of progressivism at Madison, were mostly couched in the fairly dull, pedantic past-mindedness of German scientism. I gravitated then, and I still do, to the idea that history should have relevance to present-day problems, that the frame of reference of the historian is an important factor in writing history, that conflict is more the stuff of American history than consensus, and that the American experience of the past three hundred years shows major directions of movement rather than simply chaos or cycles.

In any case, I have found it instructive to read again John Higham's volume in 1962 on *The Reconstruction of American History* as his authors looked back upon the revisionism of the 1950s[5] and to compare it with the volume edited in 1973 by William H. Cartwright and Richard L. Watson, Jr., whose authors assess the revisionism of the 1960s.[6] In doing so I was reminded more than once of the succinct definition once made by James R. Hooker, "Revisionism is the conscious effort to rewrite a resented past." And when this resentment takes the form of enhancing one's own personal or professional reputation by downgrading one's predecessors, I recall a comment by Louis B. Wright in the AHA *Newsletter:*

The revisionist may write a book that is proudly acclaimed as a great advance over earlier prejudiced works. Yet too often the revision is merely new prejudice writ large.[7]

All this is by way of putting revisionism into some perspective as seen by one who belongs to both the second and third generations of professional historians and to urge a bit of humility about the "final, positive, inescapable" contributions that each of us is likely to be able to make to the history of education. Of course, we can improve upon our predecessors, but, without them, we would have a harder time improving ourselves. And there are always our successors, who will find it still easier to improve upon us.

Let me say a word about recent revisionism in the history of American education as a prelude to my own suggestions for needed correctives in the future—obviously another case of revision of the revisionists. In the past fifteen years the two major approaches that have received the widest notice have gone off in quite different directions from the common source of their reproach, that once most widely read of all American historians of education and now the most universally rejected, Ellwood P. Cubberley. Cubberley's great fault was, of course, that he painted an unrelieved "pietistic" picture of the "public school triumphant."

The first revisionist mood says in effect that Cubberley was wrong because, fundamentally, schools played only a minor role in the much broader stream of educative functions of American culture. The second mood says that Cubberley was wrong because even though the public schools played a major role, their impact was to miseducate the American people. Between them the revisionists have left a vacuum that urgently needs to be filled.

The first mood, as we all know, was set by Bernard Bailyn's critique published in 1960. He argued that when we think of education "as the entire process by which a culture transmits itself across the generations," we see "schools and universities fade into relative insignificance next to other social agencies."[8] And he cited the family, community, and church as the truly influential educative agencies of colonial America. Building upon this generally intellectual and cultural approach to history, Lawrence A. Cremin has carried forward with some modification its major assumptions into his historiographical writings and into his comprehensive three-volume history of American education:

I have defined education in my recent work as the deliberate, systematic, and sustained effort to transmit or evoke knowledge, attitudes, values, skills, and sensibilities. . . . The definition projects us beyond the schools and colleges to the multiplicity of individuals and institutions that educate — parents, peers, siblings, and friends, as well as families, churches, synagogues, libraries, museums, summer camps, benevolent societies, agricultural fairs, settlement houses, radio stations, and television networks.[9]

The recurrent theme in Cremin's three volumes is a stress upon education as *paideia,* the deliberate pursuit of a cultural ideal, and the total configurations or constellations of educational pursuits of which the "school was only part." Inevitably, the school comes to play a minor role in the story in comparison with the weight of affectionate attention that is given to the pluralism and the wide variety of "the entire range of institutions that educate."[10]

This "culturist" mood is carried forward by Robert McClintock who not only argues that "schools are only one among many agencies of education," but also that we should suspend or revise the compulsory education laws requiring that "the young be inducted into the schooled society."[11] Instead, we should seek alternatives to compulsory schooling, "a better set of provisions by which the community can promote literacy, intellectual skills, and a common culture."[12] In all this, education is to serve personal purposes, not those of commerce or the state.[13]

And Douglas Sloan would go much beyond the usual institutional history of higher education that focuses upon colleges and universities to search among the various "habitats of knowledge" for all the ways that people pursue the higher learning:

. . . centered in many places besides colleges and universities, including such diverse places as circles of writers and free-lancing intellectuals, lay scholarly societies, professional organizations, lyceums, coffee houses, libraries, publishing firms and a variety of religious, political and reform groups.[14]

Now, let me try to be clear about my point in this. It is *not* that the effort to broaden the history of education to include much more than schooling is a wrong thing to do. It is a good thing to do and is a valuable corrective for Cubberley's school-oriented history. My point is that if this approach is carried to its extreme and is not balanced with continued attention to schooling, it will skew our views just as badly as Cubberley did. I believe it tends to lead the profession and the public to underestimate the importance of public education. And I could see this as even more damaging than *over*emphasizing its importance.

To give too little attention to schooling or to public institutions of education in American history can be just as anachronistic as Cubberley was. Entranced as we are by the educational importance of television and the other mass media in the later twentieth century, we should not be misled to underplay the role that public schools and colleges and universities played in the nineteenth and early twentieth centuries. I am impressed by Patricia Graham's insistence that we should not forget the primacy of the public schools in the late nineteenth and twentieth centuries, for they were clearly the most important agencies of education at the time. It is no wonder that Cubberley and Monroe, and other earlier historians concentrated on the schools. This is not to say that Cubberley painted the "final, positive, inescapable" picture.

The second mode of revisionism has set out not only to revise Cubberley but also to revise Cremin and the culturist view which the radical revisionists prefer to condemn as "liberal." This second mood turns Cubberley upside down by arguing that "the public school triumphant" was pretty much a disaster for its major role in miseducating the American people. In contrast to both Cubberley and the culturists, the public schools have been powerful agencies for enforcing the wrong values and attitudes of the dominant economic classes upon the reluctant or defenseless lower classes. The public school movement was not the enlightened, humanitarian crusade that Cubberley and Cremin have pictured it; it was at root a means of social control whereby the native middle classes exerted their dominion over immigrant ethnic groups and, of course, the black and other racial minorities. All in all, there should be no wonder that the public schools are doing such a poor job today; they have always stressed those middle-class values of order, stability, obedience, and patriotism that would induce the lower classes to serve the interests of the upper classes under the guise of the rhetoric of Americanization or efficiency or unity.

Of course, the radical revisionists are not all of one piece and I do not intend so to lump them together; and, since they have attracted much more controversial comment, both from without their ranks and among themselves, I cannot hope to sort out the agreements and the differences among them. I would simply like to make one or two points. My main point is that both the culturists and the radicals have in their different ways contributed to a depreciation, even an under-mining, of the idea of public education in the past as well as in the present. Coming at a time when public education has been subjected to a decade of shrill and angry denunciation by the romantic critics and by the deschoolers as well as by the more measured refrains of the social science investigators of economic inequality, the faith in school-ing and particularly in public schooling is faltering badly — especially in the view of publicists and segments of the profession, if not indeed among that part of the public that knows the public schools best.[15]

Now I am not about to argue that we should overlook contemporary defects and failures and try to restore a confidence in present-day pub-lic schools simply by rewriting the history of public education in the past. But I do think we need to look at the problem as historians who, as Beard said, are in "the position of the statesman dealing with public affairs." Cubberley wrote in the progressive era of the early twentieth century when conflict was seen as a means to steady reform; Cremin wrote his earlier pieces in an era of consensus revisionism in the late 1950s and early 1960s; Michael Katz, Clarence Karier, and their radi-cal colleagues are responding to the urban crises of the late 1960s and the campus unrest surrounding the Vietnam War, civil rights battles, and disenchantment with all forms of academic and economic estab-lishment with which they identify the public schools. Curiously, the "evangelism" of Cubberley which Bailyn and Cremin criticize has had a revival in the moral outrage of the radicals; only now the schoolmen and reformers who were Cubberley's good guys have become Katz's bad guys, while Cremin is charged by Karier, Paul Violas, Joel Spring, and Colin Greer with being no better than Cubberley.

We should take note of the fact that the natural history of revi-sionism is taking its course. Just as the radical revisionists have taken the cultural revisionists to task for not really revising Cubberley, so the radical revisionists have begun to receive assorted licks from *their* critics. From this rostrum last year Maxine Greene charged Katz, Greer, Karier, Violas, and Spring with selective reading of the past, historicism, negativism, and oversimplifying the workings of social control. At the American Educational Studies Association in Denver last October Ronald Goodenow, J. Christopher Eisele, J. Stephen Hazlitt, and others raised a whole series of questions ranging from selective use of evidence to authenticity of documentation and misinterpretation. And for two years running at the Southern History of Education Society meetings in Atlanta Wayne J. Urban undertook very extensive critiques of Katz and the authors of *Roots of Crisis.*

In a long and detailed criticism of Katz's two books in 1972, Urban cites examples of overgeneralization, simplistic definition of ideology, neglect of sociologists' studies of ideology, confusing of categories under the heading of "reformers," not distinguishing among administrators, laymen, and teachers, partiality in attributing true motives to the statements of working-class people but charging rhetorical duplicity to the statements of reformers, ambivalence in the conception and inevitability of bureaucracy, and a simplistic view of classes that ignores ethnicity as a modifier of class.[16] A year later Urban subjected the *Roots of Crisis* to a similar critical analysis.[17]

Now, I cannot sort out and untangle the revisionist networks from Cubberley and Cremin to Katz and Karier, and I do not mean to demean their work. I find it valuable and stimulating for some historians to be putting education into the broader context of cultural and intellectual history and for others to be probing the darker recesses of organized schooling in relation to our institutional past and present. But I am not satisfied that either of these approaches will achieve the kind of history of education we need for the coming decades. The cultural revisionist approach has broadened our view of education, but it underplays the role of schooling and it has developed no very explicit conceptual framework to explain the dynamics of social change or the direction of educational change. On the other hand, the radical revisionist approach does emphasize schooling and does hint at a conceptual framework of social change, but I believe it is too narrowly class oriented to give a fair and persuasive view of the good and the ill that public schooling has wrought.

So I believe we need a history of American education that is neither conservatively defensive and laudatory of the past achievements of public education, nor radically devaluative and pervasively suspicious of the motives of the builders of public education. It should not be viewed simplistically as a crusade by idealistic reformers whose motives were pure, nor as the product of calculating schemers whose real purposes underlying their rhetoric were to protect their vested interests and exert social control over those who were alien to them. It should not be written as apology and celebration, nor as indictment and conviction of the perpetrators.

How then should the future revisionism of the 1970s be viewed? I believe it should consist of four kinds of correctives for the revisionism of the 1950s and 1960s.

First, we need more explicitly formulated conceptual frameworks for our research and writing in the history of American education, frameworks that spell out our theories of the direction of social and educational change. I believe such frameworks should be defined more explicitly than the culturists have done and should be more inclusive and "generous" than that of the radicals.

I agree with Karier's introduction in the *Roots of Crisis* that one's view of the present is closely linked with the past, but I disagree with his narrow, limited, and foreshortened frame. In the past decade I have been looking again at the broad sweep of education as it functioned in some of the major civilizations of mankind, and especially in Western civilization. I cannot agree with the radicals' unrelieved pessimism about the role of education in the United States during the past 100 to 150 years. I believe that a conceptual framework focusing upon the process of modernization in America as a phase of Western civilization since the eighteenth century is the most useful conceptual tool for interpreting American education.

I have elaborated the conception of modernization in my recent book, *The Education of the West,* but I am not yet satisfied with the application of the framework to America and I expect to devote much of my time to it in the coming years. I cannot begin to outline here the schema I have developed so far, but I am convinced that we will achieve a more satisfactory interpretation of the history of American education if we see it as an essential phase of the major directions of social change summed up in the term modernization.

By modernization I mean the accelerating interaction of several long-term trends that increasingly distinguish modern from traditional societies from the sixteenth and seventeenth centuries to the present. Those that are especially important for the direction that education has taken are: the mobilizing and centralizing power of the nation-state (a matter of large-scale political organization); rural transformation and industrial urbanization (a matter of the use of inanimate power and increasing social and economic differentiation); the secularization and technicalization of knowledge (a matter of special expertise); imperialism and colonialism (a matter of the missionizing fervor); increasing popular participation in public affairs (a matter of equality); the search for religious and cultural pluralism (a matter of freedom); the drive for racial and ethnic integration (a matter of justice); the widespread faith in popular education (a matter of individual and social efficacy or achievement).[18] The interaction of these often divergent trends, especially the twin drives to pluralism and to integration, has resulted in chronic tensions and cleavages over the control and practice of education. To single out one of these factors, such as industrial urbanization, to explain what happened to education at any particular time and place is to miss the complicated and subtle interplay of these several ingredients which can only be separated for purposes of discussion.

As I was coming to this frame of reference during the 1960s, largely through my concern with the broader history of Western education and its impact upon the societies of Africa, Asia, and Latin America, I found to my gratification that a few American historians were beginning to arrive at similar conclusions for American history in general. A dissatisfaction with both the earlier progressive and the more recent consensus and radical frames has led to the search for a new overarching frame. In his paper on American historiography in the 1960s written in honor of Merle Curti on his retirement at Madison in 1968, John Higham beautifully characterized the mood of this search:

. . . we have today no unifying theme which assigns a direction to American history and commands any wide acceptance among those who write it. Nothing in the current situation of the historian more seriously compromises his civic function and influence.

. . . Men need a unifying vision of who they are and where they are going. That kind of vision establishes both a goal for the future and a synthesizing perspective upon the past. Without it, a fully human life is impossible.

. . . That *some* general scheme of historical meaning will emerge from the present confusion can scarcely be doubted, however. We may also be confident that an effective scheme will transcend the limits of a scientific hypothesis. It will partake as well of myth and ideology.[19]

As if in answer to this search I find several historians turning to the theme of modernization. I take three examples that span the earlier as well as the later periods of American history. Richard D. Brown found the theme appropriate to his studies of personality in the colonial period and early nineteenth century:

As a general synthesis it has the advantage of permitting the cross-cultural, cross-chronological comparisons which are crucial for testing virtually any general hypothesis . . . the concept of modernization, with its emphasis on historical processes . . . is one framework that makes the issue of American uniqueness a testable hypothesis rather than an article of faith.[20]

In his recent studies of working classes in the nineteenth and early twentieth century, Herbert C. Gutman finds different responses and tensions arising as successive waves of people reared in premodern societies of rural, agrarian, and village cultures migrate to America in its preindustrial stage (1815-1843), in its rapidly industrializing stage (1843-1893), and in its mature industrial stage (1893-1919).[21] Viewing the role of public education as a phase of the different stages of American modernization would broaden the purely class-oriented history of education and picture the educational reformers rather more as members of a new professional middle class who saw themselves as modernizers of premodern immigrants than simply as nativist oppressors imposing their superior culture upon unwilling and inferior alien immigrants.

And, finally, Robert H. Wiebe makes the theme of modernization the key to the progressive era in the early twentieth century:

The fundamental issue at stake in the history of the progressive era is modernization, and around this issue a profound change in scholarship is occurring. . . .

Behind these investigations is a compelling sense that something big was abroad in the land around 1900, that some fundamental shift was underway during the progressive years, and it is this feeling which has elevated modernization — the term that best captures its essence — to the place of primacy.

As elusive as it is important, *modern* is a conceptual expression of our present, an attempt to abstract from our society those critical characteristics that distinguish not merely today from yesterday or the United States from Ghana but one way of life, one quality of culture, from some other. Modernization is the process creating this present.[22]

If we can do for the history of American education what is being called for by Brown, Gutman, and Wiebe, we may be able to enhance the "civic function and influence" which Higham feels is so seriously compromised among historians generally.

My second corrective for recent revisionism has to do with the need for a thoroughgoing reexamination of the role of organized schooling in social change. We need a new well-rounded synthesis of the role of public education to replace the Cubberley synthesis. I do not believe that the cultural revisionists are giving it to us, and I agree with Carl Kaestle that we are not getting it from the radical revisionists:

. . . What we need and do not yet have is a new synthesis that will account for the school as a focal point of idealism as well as self-interest, an institution at once the object of public scrutiny and public ignorance, an institution that evolves more by mundane accretion than dramatic reform and yet continually arouses herculean efforts and exaggerated expectations. Most of all, we need a synthesis that abjures the premise that the American school has been an unequivocal failure, for such a premise — like the earlier presumption of success — precludes the explanation of change over time.[23]

I believe that the time is ripe for a new focus upon the institutional history of education so that we do not again become isolated from a major trend within general historiography itself. John Higham views the new institutional history as "one of the most vigorous aspects of American historiography."[24] Robert Wiebe finds a similar vitality with regard to the progressive years.[25]

In fact, educational historians may very well be in the lead in the new institutional history. Some of you here today are producing the building blocks for what I hope will be a well-rounded synthesis of public schooling that will take into account the whole range of modernization trends and their interactions upon one another.

David Tyack's impressive study of the organizational revolution in American education has shown the way toward a general interpretive framework for the history of urban education.[26] As Tyack so well displays in his work, "institutional history" need not be "house history," but can be "broad and multi-faceted."

Several other studies have shown that the histories of particular localities can also deal with a wide range of the modernizing forces I have mentioned and do it in the framework of the institutional history of public schools. Notable here are the histories of schooling in New York City by Carl F. Kaestle and Diane Ravitch, in Boston by Stanley K. Schultz, in St. Louis by Selwyn K. Troen, and of four systems in different sections of the country by Patricia A. Graham.[27]

There are numerous wide-ranging studies like those of the Office of Education by Donald R. Warren[28] and the history of school boards in fourteen large cities by Joseph M. Cronin.[29] And I am sure that there are many, many more in the works. The result, I hope, will be a soundly based, inclusive conceptual framework for the history of American public schooling that will not only satisfy the most rigorous canons of historical scholarship, but will assist policymakers and opinionmakers to develop a responsible and creative role for American education in the postmodern era of the nation's third century. Such a conception would be the best antidote for a microscopic empiricism in historical research as well as for a narrow ideological revisionism. But we will need to weave these separate studies together into an overall synthesis. We will need to put it all together.

My third corrective for latter-day revisionism will come as no surprise to those of you who know what I have been up to in the past dozen years. I believe that we must be much more sedulous in viewing the history of American education in comparative and international perspective as a phase of the modernization of Western civilization. Western education is an interlinking network showing common characteristics as well as significant differences. I have spelled out this theme in considerable length in my recent book and in a number of articles. I come to this theme not only because of the need to recognize the networking of modernization in all its phases, including the educational, but also because of the significant movements in historiography since the 1950s that stress comparative history and an interconnected world history. I need only mention such diverse proponents for this view as C. Vann Woodward, C. E. Black, William H. McNeill, Robert R. Palmer, John K. Fairbank, and John Higham.

I believe we have been too long too negligent in this field. Of course, the history of American education has taken account of European influences from the founding of the colonies through the eighteenth and nineteenth centuries, but by and large the truly comparative approach to the history of American education has not been highlighted either by historians of American education or by comparative educators. The radical revisionists seem to pay little or no attention to the international perspective, and, while Cremin acknowledges its importance in his historiographical monographs, it is yet to be seen how great or integral a part it will play in his forthcoming volumes.

The groundwork is being laid for the comparative and international approach if we will but take advantage of it. Stewart Fraser and

William W. Brickman have made available valuable documentary sources for the nineteenth century[30] and Stewart Fraser for the twentieth century.[31] But we now need rigorous comparative analyses of the various stages of modernization in the several Western and non-Western countries. For example, it would be fascinating to compare what Kaestle found in New York, or Schultz in Boston, or Katz or Lazerson in Massachusetts with Brian Simon's study of reform efforts of [the] middle class and [the] working class in England,[32] or with the theoretical proposals of social conflict marked by domination and assertion as formulated by Vaughan and Archer in their comparative studies of France and England in the early nineteenth century.[33] Similarly, we might gain useful perspective on the radical revisionist view of mid- and late-nineteenth- and twentieth-century American education by comparisons with Shipman's study of modernization and education in England and Japan,[34] with the study by Marius B. Jansen and Lawrence Stone of modernization in Japan and England,[35] with Brian Simon's study of education and the labor movement in England,[36] or with John Talbott's study of politics and reform in France between the [world] wars.[37] The list could be much longer and I believe the rewards still greater from such undertakings.

Each one of the major aspects of modernization that I have mentioned could become the focal point of historical studies to see what light they throw on the peculiar and distinctive role of education in the United States in comparison with other societies as they struggled to achieve nation-statehood, popular participation, industrial urbanization, secularization of knowledge, religious and cultural pluralism, racial and ethnic integration, or the "civilizing mission." For example, we could gain some perspective now on that pioneer comparative study of citizenship education undertaken by prominent political scientists in the late 1920s, headed by Charles E. Merriam.[38] We will need to relate those studies of nine countries to such recent studies by Almond and Verba on the civic culture,[39] by Byron G. Massialas and his colleagues on political attitudes and political knowledge,[40] and Judith Torney's most recent studies of civic education in ten countries as part of the International Educational Achievement project.[41]

We are developing a good deal of evidence concerning political socialization in the 1960s and 1970s to which we might relate the benchmark study of civic education in the 1920s — and if possible somehow discover ways to reexamine the historical role of education in nation building from the eighteenth century forward. We have had relatively little attention to this subject since the works on nationalism and education by Edward H. Reisner and Isaac L. Kandel in the 1930s. And far too little with respect to the United States itself or to the outward reach of American education as it exerted influence upon education and modernization in Latin America, Africa, and Asia, whether through the civilizing mission, imperialist expansion, technical assistance, or genuinely cooperative programs of international education. I am confident we could gain insights about the essence of our educational history at home by becoming more aware of our history in other lands.

I think, finally, that we need in the coming decade to give special attention to the history of the role of organized public education in building political community in the United States. I do not need to recite to you what Robert Hutchins has termed the "overkill" in attacks upon public education during the past decade. I have drawn attention to this in a series of articles during the past year.[42] The constant downbeat of romantic critics about the horrors perpetrated by public schools upon innocent children; the upswing of effort by religious groups to get public funds; the volatile feelings about busing to overcome segregation; the social scientists' dictum that public schools do not reduce inequality or really make much difference in social change at all; the heightening of group feelings among racial and ethnic groups in their search for maintaining or reasserting particularist identities; the revulsion against any kind of authoritative establishmentarianism symbolized by compulsory attendance laws or credentialling; the contests over community versus professional control—these and many more specifics have transformed the siren call of "alternatives" into a bullhorn of nonnegotiable demands.

In all this uproar of particularism we have nearly forgotten the principal, original reason for moving America to a system of education that would be public in purpose, public in access, public in control, and public in support, namely, to help create and maintain a democratic political community in a society made up of diverse ethnic, religious, and cultural groups. The revolutionary generation stressed the importance of a system that would promote republican ideals, knowledge, attitudes, and behaviors. In the past few years we have heard little about the positive political goals of public education in the midst of our preoccupation with the problems of politics and education. And our two main revisionist movements have been strangely silent on this issue, one tending to praise the virtues of diversity and pluralism and voluntarism, and the other to condemn the evils of a monolithic, monopolistic, bureaucratic system reared in the past and dominating the present.

I am fully aware of the suspicions of, not to say the revulsions against, using the schools for patriotism, propaganda, partisanship, or politicization of right or left or middle. These fears have had recurrent justifications as a result of excesses in World War I, World War II, and Vietnam. But I believe it is time that we faced once again, and much more candidly and factually, the historical underpinnings of political purpose of public education. Surely, the reevaluations of public morality in government that we are now going through make the reexamination of public education more urgent than ever. And, as far as I can see, few educators are taking the matter very seriously.

The several national commissions on educational policy recently at work (President's Science Advisory Committee, USOE Panel, Kettering, and Carnegie) have had precious little to say about the political purposes of education. The economists and sociologists have been hung up on matters of income, inequality, and class; the psychologists with genetics and achievement. True, the political scientists and a few anthropologists have begun seriously to study contemporary and comparative political socialization as well as politics and education, but the historical dimension also urgently needs attention. The original idea of American public education drew upon the Western stock of Enlightenment ideas which assumed that public education had primarily a political purpose in the modernization process. We need to reexamine what has happened to that idea during the past two hundred years.

I believe that we must look again at our history to see what the public schools did do and did not do, what they did well and what they did ill for the building of political community in a society composed of diverse peoples divided along religious, linguistic, racial, ethnic, economic, cultural, and social-class lines and in a world of nations that were rapidly modernizing their political systems, agriculture, industry, urban centers, science, technology, and secular styles of life. To what degree has American public education succeeded and to what degree has it failed in this political function?

By political community I refer to those persisting sets of relationships that bind together the members of a society as they undertake to conduct their common affairs through a shared political system. In the United States the political community is symbolized in the term "We the People" who represent the ultimate authority in the political system. What makes a diverse people into a "we" are the common moral commitments and the shared sense of distinctive identity and cohesion that are essential for building, maintaining, and improving the basic political structure as well as the day-to-day processes of governmental decisionmaking. I am especially concerned with the role that education plays in forming the codes of behavior, the common frames of knowledge, belief, and value that characterize the overall political community and the basic political structures (often called the regime) through which the community operates. The political community is thus to be distinguished from those other types of communities whose binding relationships are based upon religion, kinship, race, ethnicity, language, culture, nature, social or economic class, intellectual interest, scholarly knowledge, military power, or revolutionary violence. The tensions and cleavages arising from the conflicting loyalties and contending interests of these other kinds of communities make the building of political community a particularly difficult and demanding task.

All modern political communities have developed some form of public education as an aspect of their community-building process. In a democratic and libertarian political community, education professes to promote the maximum freedom for the individual and to honor social and cultural diversity among the other communities as well as to build the cohesion and unity essential for a viable polity. The political goal of education is thus to prepare the individual to be able to play his part in the structures and processes of his political community by acquiring the understanding, attitudes, and commitments necessary for making deliberate choices among real alternatives and to do this upon the basis of disciplined thought and solid and reliable knowledge, upon what Lyman Bryson called "significant truth rather than plausible falsehood or beguiling half-truth."

In attempting to socialize the younger generation to the political culture and recruit persons to perform the tasks required for the orderly and effective conduct of the political system, education is caught up in the contests between the goals of social cohesion versus cultural pluralism, assimilation versus ethnicity, religious values versus secular morality, equality of opportunity versus economic individualism, egalitarianism versus intellectual hierarchy, complex bureaucracy versus creative professionalism, social justice versus racial or class separatism, civil liberty versus national security, and national interest versus international comity.

This then is the setting in which we need to direct attention to the history of the political role of public schooling: a neglect by revisionist historians so far, a growing body of contemporary research in political socialization and political culture that may provide new insights into the history of the role that the schools played in the past, and the desperate need for new insights into the basic moral and educational underpinnings of our entire political system. I agree with Senator James L. Buckley's eloquent and tortured statement of March 19, 1974, in which he said:

The Watergate affair can no longer be thought of as a troublesome episode such as occurs from time to time in the political history of every country. . . . Watergate has expanded on a scale that has plunged our country into what historians call a "crisis of the regime." . . . A crisis of the regime is a disorder, a trauma, involving every tissue of the nation, conspicuously including its moral and spiritual dimensions . . . .

I speak of the spreading cynicism about those in public life and about the political process itself. I speak of the pervasive and undeniable sense of frustration and impotence that has become the dominant political mood in the nation. I speak of a perception of corruption that has effectively destroyed the President's ability to speak from a position of moral leadership. And I speak of the widespread conviction that Watergate and all that it has brought in its wake has done unique and perhaps irrevocable damage to our entire system of government.[43]

As educators and as historians we must now strive as never before to throw light upon the political role of American education. I agree with Donald Warren's assessment that the public school in origin was a political idea of great importance. Despite its failures and threats of fearsome control over nonconformity and cultural diversity, we need to recognize that it is still a great idea providing "a splendid and liberating vision of a nation sustained by enlightened citizens and leaders" and remains worth salvaging.[44] I am impressed too with Charles Tesconi's intriguing point that the fragmentation of society and privatization of the individual which marked advanced industrial society makes the individual more susceptible to social control by corporate life rather than less and that the calls for greater diversity and pluralism and alternatives will thus raise the individual's susceptibility to accepting more social control through further fragmentation. Since affiliation and commitment to stable and enduring institutions are necessary to the well-being of individuals, we need more public schooling, not less.[45]

I am convinced that we thus need to look as hard as we can at the successes and failures of public education in building a sense of civism appropriate to the goals of a libertarian political community in the United States over the past two hundred years. We will need to summon all the imaginative historiographical resources we can muster to this task. The political scientists and sociologists can interview present students and teachers about the development of their political attitudes, but it will be much more difficult to discover how and what sentiments, commitments, and political virtues the schools were responsible for in the past.

Right now, I think that the development of a strengthened civic morality and political integrity is the first order of business for America, and the development of an appropriate civic education is the first order of business for American education. And integral to both is a renewed vision, if you please a *re*vision, of the historic public purposes of American education. If I may paraphrase John Higham in the quotation I cited earlier: "We have today no unifying theme which assigns a direction to the history of American education and commands any wide acceptance among those who write it. Nothing in the current situation of the historian of education more seriously compromises his civic function and influence." And again, "Historians of education need a unifying vision of who they are and where they are going. That kind of vision establishes both a goal for the future and a synthesizing perspective upon the past. Without it a fully educative life is impossible."

So we come to the epitome of my theme . . . :

The Progress of the Pilgrim Called Historian

Once upon a time, 'way back in the Progressive Era, Historian was content to follow Evangelist Cubberley's Pietistic history of American education.

But this progressive enthusiasm was destroyed in the turmoils following the wars of the world.

So Historian left the City of Destruction in search of new historical truth in the Celestial City. As he was struggling up the Hill of Difficulty he was met by two contending Revisionists.

Cultural Revisionist urged him to replace his Pietistic history of education with a Paideia-istic *history of American education. So Historian followed this path for awhile, but he found that while it brought him to the multifarious educative agencies of House Beautiful, Vanity Fair, Bypath Meadow, and the Land of Beulah, there were too few schools from which he could learn about the true history of education.*

So Historian returned to the main path of schooling and turned into the lane urged upon him by Radical Revisionist, but he found that this lane of Iconoclastic *history of education only led him into the Slough of Despond and the Valley of Humiliation, and he ended up in the Doubting Castle of Giant Despair.*

Just when it looked as if Historian would be eternally condemned to one of these "alternatives," he met up with a third Revisionist who urged upon him a Modernizing *history of American education to replace the Pietistic, and Paideia-istic, and the Iconoclastic histories. Modernizing Revisionist promised to synthesize the sentiments of Interpreter, Faithful, and Hopeful with the empirical and scientific facts of modern (not to say quantitative) history.*

And just when it seemed that Pilgrim Historian was finally to reach the City on the Hill, there appeared in the distance still another Revisionist who warned that modernization with its warring national sovereignties, crumbling cities, rival group loyalties, and environmental pollution would not enable Historian to surmount safely the River of Death. Thus, in the nick of time, Ecumenical Revisionist at last was about to bring Historian to the final, positive, inescapable truth in which the history of American education would find its place in a world-wide history of education befitting the emerging postmodern City of the Ecumene.

NOTES

Tyack: **Ways of Seeing**

1. Kenneth Burke, *Permanence and Change* (New York: New Republic, 1935), 70.
2. Everett C. Hughes, *Men and Their Work* (Glencoe, Ill.: Free Press, 1958).
3. *The State of American History,* ed. Herbert Bass (Chicago: Quadrangle Books, 1970).
4. *American History and the Social Sciences,* ed. Edward N. Saveth (New York: Free Press, 1964).
5. Forest C. Ensign, *Compulsory School Attendance and Child Labor* (Iowa City: Athens Press, 1921); Ellwood P. Cubberley, *Changing Conceptions of Education* (Boston: Houghton Mifflin, 1909).

6. A sampling of radical views can be found in writings of Paul Goodman, Ivan Illich, Michael Katz, and Samuel Bowles and Herbert Gintis. (The last two are discussed in the "Marxian Analysis" section, below.)

7. For a more detailed explication of this phrasing, see my study *The One Best System: A History of American Urban Education* (Cambridge, Mass.: Harvard University Press, 1974).

8. Albert Fishlow, "Levels of Nineteenth-Century American Investment in Education," *Journal of Economic History* 26 (December 1966): 418-436; *id.*, "The American Common School Revival: Fact or Fancy?" in *Industrialism in Two Systems: Essays in Honor of Alexander Gerschenkron,* ed. Henry Rosovsky (New York: Wiley, 1966), 40-67.

9. John K. Folger and Charles B. Nam, *Education of the American Population* (Washington, D.C.: Government Printing Office, 1967), Chaps. 1, 4; W. Vance Grant and C. George Lind, *Digest of Educational Statistics,* 1974 ed. (Washington, D.C.: Government Printing Office, 1975).

10. Folger and Nam, *Education of the American Population,* 25, 3, 211-268; William T. Harris, "Elementary Education," in *Monographs on Education in the United States,* ed. Nicholas M. Butler (Albany, N.Y.: J. B. Lyon, 1900), 79-139.

11. U.S. Commissioner of Education, "Compulsory Attendance Laws in the United States," *Report for 1888-1889,* I (Washington, D.C.: Government Printing Office, 1889), Chap. 18.

12. Mary J. Herrick, *The Chicago Schools: A Social and Political History* (Beverly Hills, Calif.: Sage, 1971), 58; John D. Philbrick, *City School Systems in the United States,* U.S. Bureau of Education, Circular of Information, No. 1 (Washington, D.C.: Government Printing Office, 1885), 154-155.

13. U.S. Bureau of the Census, *Historical Statistics of the United States: Colonial Times to 1957* (Washington, D.C.: Government Printing Office, 1960), 207, 215; John K. Norton and Eugene S. Lawler, *Unfinished Business in American Education: An Inventory of Public School Expenditures in the United States* (Washington, D.C.: American Council on Education, 1946); Newton Edwards, *Equal Educational Opportunity for Youth* (Washington, D.C.: American Council on Education, 1939), 152.

14. Frank Musgrove, "The Decline of the Educative Family," *Universities Quarterly* 14 (September 1960): 377.

15. John W. Meyer and Joane P. Nale, "The Changing Status of Childhood," paper presented at the annual meeting of the Society for the Study of Social Problems, San Francisco, Calif., 1975.

16. *Children and Youth in America: A Documentary History,* ed. Robert H. Bremner, Volumes I and II (Cambridge, Mass.: Harvard University Press, 1970-71).

17. Michael S. Katz, "The Concepts of Compulsory Education and Compulsory Schooling: A Philosophical Inquiry," unpub. diss., Stanford University, 1974.

18. R. Freeman Butts, "Public Education and Political Community," *History of Education Quarterly* 14 (Summer 1974): 165-183. This article is reprinted as part of this chapter.

19. Australian National Commission for UNESCO, *Compulsory Education in Australia* (Paris: UNESCO, 1951), Preface.

20. John W. Meyer and Richard Rubinson, "Education and Political Development," in *Review of Research in Education,* III, ed. Fred Kerlinger (Itasca, Ill.: F. E. Peacock, 1975), 134-162.

21. David Tyack, *Turning Points in American Educational History* (Waltham, Mass.: Blaisdell, 1967), 83-119.

22. Victor Cousin, as quoted in Edward Reisner, *Nationalism and Education since 1789: A Social and Political History of Modern Education* (New York: Macmillan, 1922), 134, Chap. 2.

23. William Edward Burghardt DuBois, *Black Reconstruction in America: An Essay toward a History of the Part Which Black Folk Played in the Attempt to Reconstruct Democracy in America, 1860-1880* (Cleveland, Ohio: World Pub., 1964), 637-669.

24. John Morgan Oates, *Schoolbooks and Krags: The United States Army in the Philippines, 1898-1902* (Westport, Conn.: Greenwood Press, 1973).

25. Charles Wollenberg, *All Deliberate Speed: Segregation and Exclusion in California Schools, 1855-1975* (Berkeley, Calif.: University of California Press, 1976), Chap. 3.

26. Howard K. Beale, *A History of Freedom of Teaching in American Schools* (New York: Charles Scribner's Sons, 1941); John W. Meyer, "Theories of the Effects of Education on Civil Participation in Developing Societies," unpub. paper, Department of Sociology, Stanford University, May 1972.

27. Merle Curti, *The Roots of American Loyalty* (New York: Columbia University Press, 1946).

28. Department of Superintendence, National Education Association, *Educational Leadership: Progress and Possibilities* (Washington, D.C.: NEA, 1933), 246, Chap. 11.

29. Donald Warren, *To Enforce Education: A History of the Founding Years of the United States Office of Education* (Detroit: Wayne State University Press, 1974).

30. James E. Wright, "The Ethnocultural Model of Voting: A Behavioral and Historical Critique," *American Behavioral Scientist* 16 (May 1973): 655.

31. Richard Jensen, *The Winning of the Midwest: Social and Political Conflict, 1888-1896* (Chicago: University of Chicago Press, 1971), 63-66, xv; Paul Kleppner, *The Cross of Culture: A Social Analysis of Midwestern Politics, 1850-1900* (New York: Free Press, 1970), 71-74.

32. John W. Meyer and James G. Roth, "A Reinterpretation of American Status Politics," *Pacific Sociological Review* 13 (Spring 1970): 95-102; Joseph R. Gusfield, *Symbolic Crusade: Status Politics and the American Temperance Movement* (Urbana, Ill.: University of Illinois Press, 1963), Chaps. 1, 6, 7.

33. Jensen, *The Winning of the Midwest,* 122.

34. Timothy L. Smith, "Protestant Schooling and American Nationality, 1800-1850," *Journal of American History* 53 (March 1967): 679-695; David B. Tyack, "Onward Christian Soldiers: Religion in the American Common School," in *History and Education,* ed. Paul Nash (New York: Random House, 1970), 212-255.

35. J. K. Richards, *Compulsory Education in Ohio: Brief for Defendant in Error in the Supreme Court of Ohio, Patrick F. Quigley v. The State of Ohio* (Columbus, Ohio: Westbote, 1892), 23.

36. National Education Association, *Journal of Addresses and Proceedings,* 1891 (Topeka: Kansas Publishing House, 1891), 295-298, 393-403.

37. Henry Wilson, "New Departure of the Republican Party," *Atlantic Monthly* 27 (January 1871): 111-114.

38. "Unification and Education," *Catholic World* 13 (April 1871): 3-4; John Whitney Evans, "Catholics and the Blair Education Bill," *Catholic Historical Review* 46 (October 1960): 273-298.

39. Jensen, *The Winning of the Midwest,* 122, 129.

40. Kleppner, *The Cross of Culture,* 169-170.

41. Horace Mann Bond has given us a brilliant analysis of how the politics of race mixed with the politics of competing economic groups in his *Negro Education in Alabama: A Study in Cotton and Steel* (Washington, D.C.: Associated Publishers, 1939).

42. Marvin Lazerson, *Origins of the Urban Public School: Public Education in Massachusetts, 1870-1915* (Cambridge, Mass.: Harvard University Press, 1971), Chaps. 5-9; Joseph M. Cronin, *The Control of Urban Schools: Perspectives on the Power of Educational Reformers* (New York: Free Press, 1973).

43. Frank V. Bermejo, *The School Attendance Service in American Cities* (Menasha, Wis.: George Banta Publishing Co., 1924).

44. Tyack, *The One Best System,* Pt. 4.

45. Samuel Hays, "The New Organizational Society," in *Building the Organizational Society: Essays on Associational Activity in Modern America,* ed. Jerry Israel (New York: Free Press, 1972), 2-3, 6-8.

46. John Higham, "Hanging Together: Divergent Unities in American History," *Journal of American History* 61 (June 1974): 24.

47. Robert Wiebe, *The Search for Order, 1877-1920* (New York: Hill and Wang, 1967), 166.

48. Walter Trattner, *Crusade for the Children: A History of the National Child Labor Committee and Child Labor Reform in America* (Chicago: Quadrangle Books, 1970).

49. Louis Galambos, "The Emerging Organizational Synthesis in Modern American History," *Business History Review* 44 (Autumn 1970): 280.

50. Thomas C. Cochran, *Business in American Life: A History* (New York: McGraw-Hill, 1972), Chaps. 9, 16; Alfred D. Chandler, Jr., and Fritz Redlich, "Recent Developments in American Business Administration and Their Conceptualization," *Business History Review* 35 (Spring 1961): 1-31.

51. Raymond E. Callahan, *Education and the Cult of Efficiency* (Chicago: University of Chicago Press, 1962).

52. For some of these criticisms of the "organizational synthesis," I am indebted to Wayne Hobson's unpublished manuscript, "Social Change and the Organizational Society," Stanford University, 1975.

53. Cochran, *Business in American Life,* 304.

54. Mary Jean Bowman, "The Human Investment Revolution in Economic Thought," *Sociology of Education* 39 (Spring 1966): 113, 117; Barry R. Chiswick, "Minimum Schooling Legislation and the Cross-sectional Distribution of Income," *Economic Journal* 79 (September 1969): 495-507.

55. Bowman, "The Human Investment Revolution," 118-119; Fishlow, "Levels of Nineteenth-Century Investment," 426; Marc Blaug, *An Introduction to the Economics of Education* (London: Penguin, 1972), Chaps. 1-3.

56. Maris Vinovskis, "Horace Mann on the Economic Productivity of Education," *New England Quarterly* 43 (December 1970): 562, 550-571.

57. *Ibid.*, 570.

58. U.S. Commissioner of Education, *Report for 1870* (Washington, D.C.: Government Printing Office, 1870), 447-467.

59. U.S. Senate, *Report of the Committee of the Senate upon the Relations between Labor and Capital and Testimony Taken by the Committee* (Washington, D.C.: Government Printing Office, 1885), II, 789-790, 795-796; IV, 504-505, 729-730.

60. "Selected Arguments, Bibliographies, etc., for the Use of the Virginia High School and Athletic League," ed. John S. Patton, *University of Virginia Record, Extension Series,* 1 (1915): 103-104.

61. William M. Landes and Lewis C. Solmon, "Compulsory Schooling Legislation: An Economic Analysis of Law and Social Change in the Nineteenth Century," *Journal of Economic History* 32 (March 1972): 58-59.

62. *Ibid.*, 77-78.

63. Lewis Solmon, "Opportunity Costs and Models of Schooling in the Nineteenth Century," *Southern Economic Journal* 37 (July 1970): 72.

64. Landes and Solmon, "Compulsory Schooling Legislation," 87-88.

65. Fishlow, "Levels of Nineteenth-Century Investment," 435-436.

66. *Ibid.*, 427.

67. *Ibid.*, 426; Solmon, "Opportunity Costs and Models of Schooling," 120.

68. Bowman, "The Human Investment Revolution," 120.

69. Ivar E. Berg, *Education and Jobs: The Great Training Robbery* (New York: Praeger, 1970).

70. *The Gallup Polls of Attitudes toward Education, 1969-1973,* ed. Stanley Elam (Bloomington, Ind.: Phi Delta Kappa, 1973), 169.

71. Irwin Wyllie, *The Self-made Man in America* (New Brunswick, N.J.: Rutgers University Press, 1954), Chap. 3; Cochran, *Business in American Life,* 174-176.

72. Harris, "Elementary Education," 3-4, 54; Selwyn Troen, *The Public and the Schools: Shaping the St. Louis System, 1838-1920* (Columbia, Mo.: University of Missouri Press, 1975), Chap. 6.

73. U.S. Bureau of the Census, *Historical Statistics of the United States* (Washington, D.C.: Government Printing Office [1960]), 67-78.

74. In "Education and the Corporate Order," *Socialist Revolution* 2 (1972): 61, David K. Cohen and Marvin Lazerson point out that the "tendency to use market criteria in evaluating education flowered around the turn of the century." For a survey of such studies, see A. Caswell Ellis, "The Money Value of Education," in U.S. Bureau of Education, *Bulletin No. 22* (Washington, D.C.: Government Printing Office, 1917).

75. Samuel Bowles and Herbert Gintis, "The Problem with Human Capital Theory—A Marxian Critique," *American Economic Review* 65 (May 1975): 78.

76. *Ibid.*, 75.

77. Samuel Bowles and Herbert Gintis, "Capitalism and Education in the United States," *Socialist Revolution* 5 (No. 3, 1975): 111, 116-118.

78. *Id.*, "The Contradictions of Liberal Educational Reform," in *Work, Technology, and Education,* ed. Walter Feinberg and Henry Rosemont, Jr. (Urbana:

University of Illinois Press, 1975), 124, 133. I have cited these essays by Bowles and Gintis because the more complete version of their analysis was not available at the time of writing. Now, see *Schooling in Capitalist America: Educational Reform and the Contradictions of Economic Life* (New York: Basic Books, 1976), esp. Chaps. 2, 4, 5, 7, and 9.

79. Douai's testimony is in U.S. Senate, *Report on Labor and Capital,* II, 702-743.

80. Rex David, *Schools and the Crisis* (New York: Labor Research Associates, 1934).

81. Bowles and Gintis, "The Contradictions of Liberal Educational Reform."

82. Bowles and Gintis, "Capitalism," 118, 126-133.

83. On ethnic and religious dimensions to school politics, see Troen, *Public and the Schools,* Chaps. 2-4; Diane Ravitch, *The Great School Wars, New York City, 1805-1973: A History of the Public Schools as Battlefield of Social Change* (New York: Basic Books, 1974), Chaps. 3-7. As Solmon and Fishlow indicate (see n. 67, above), enrollments in rural schools in many parts of the nation were higher than in industrialized areas; almost two-thirds of the states that passed compulsory schooling legislation prior to 1890 were overwhelmingly rural in the distribution of population.

84. Charles M. Dollar and Richard J. Jensen, *Historian's Guide to Statistics* (New York: Holt, Rinehart and Winston, 1971), Chaps. 1-2.

85. Martin Rein, *Social Science and Public Policy* (London: Penguin, 1976); Henry Levin, "Education, Life Changes, and the Courts: The Role of Social Science Evidence," *Law and Contemporary Problems* 39 (No. 2, 1975): 217-240.

86. Robert K. Merton, "The Bearing of Sociological Theory on Empirical Research," and "The Bearing of Empirical Research on Sociological Theory," in *Readings in the Philosophy of the Social Sciences,* ed. May Brodbeck (New York: Macmillan, 1968), 465-485.

Butts: **Public Education and Political Community**

1. Charles A. Beard, "Written History as an Act of Faith," *American Historical Review* 39 (January 1934): 219.

2. *Ibid.,* 220.

3. *Ibid.,* 226.

4. *Ibid.,* 227.

5. *The Reconstruction of American History,* ed. John Higham (New York: Harper Torchbooks, 1962).

6. *The Reinterpretation of American History and Culture,* ed. William H. Cartwright and Richard L. Watson, Jr. (Washington, D.C.: National Council for the Social Studies, 1973).

7. American Historical Association, *Newsletter* (June 1965): 28.

8. Bernard Bailyn, *Education in the Forming of American Society: Needs and Opportunities for Study* (Chapel Hill, N.C.: University of North Carolina Press, 1960), 14.

9. Lawrence A. Cremin, "Notes toward a Theory of Education," in *Notes on Education,* No. 1 (New York: Institute of Philosophy and Politics of Education, Teachers College, Columbia University, June 1973), 4.

10. *Id., American Education: Some Notes toward a New History* (Bloomington, Ind., 1972), 15.

11. Robert McClintock, "Universal Voluntary Study," *The Center Magazine* (January-February 1973): 24.

12. *Ibid.,* 27.

13. Robert McClintock, "Some Thoughts on 'Permanent Education,' " in *Notes on Education,* No. 3 (New York: Institute of Philosophy and Politics of Education, Teachers College, Columbia University, December 1973), unpaged.

14. Douglas Sloan, "New Perspectives on the Higher Learning in America," *ibid.,* No. 1 (1973), 6.

15. See R. Freeman Butts, "Public Education and the Public Faith," *Educational Quest* 18 (Spring 1974).

16. Wayne J. Urban, "A Critique of Michael Katz," paper presented to the Southern History of Education Society, Atlanta, Georgia, October 21, 1972.

17. *Id.,* "Revisionists and Liberals: A Critique of *Roots of Crisis,*" paper presented to the Southern History of Education Society, Atlanta, Georgia, November 16, 1973.

18. R. Freeman Butts, *The Education of the West: A Formative Chapter in the History of Civilization* (New York: McGraw-Hill Book Co., 1973), Chaps. 9, 12, and 13.

19. John Higham, *Writing American History: Essays on Modern Scholarship* (Bloomington, Ind.: Indiana University Press, 1970), 173-174.

20. Richard D. Brown, "Modernization and the Modern Personality in Early America, 1600-1865: A Sketch of a Synthesis," *Journal of Interdisciplinary History* (Winter 1972): 228.

21. Herbert C. Gutman, "Work, Culture, and Society in Industrializing America, 1815-1919," *American Historical Review* 78 (June 1973): 531-588.

22. Robert H. Wiebe, "The Progressive Years, 1900-1917," in *The Reinterpretation of American History and Culture,* ed. Cartwright and Watson, 425-426.

23. Carl F. Kaestle, "Social Reform and the Urban School," *History of Education Quarterly* 12 (Summer 1972): 217.

24. Higham, *Writing American History,* 161.

25. Wiebe, "The Progressive Years," 431-439.

26. David B. Tyack, *The One Best System: A History of American Urban Education* (Cambridge, Mass.: Harvard University Press, 1974). This volume is an enlarged version of *From Village School to Urban System,* Project No. 0-0809, Department of Health, Education, and Welfare, Office of Education, September 1, 1972.

27. Carl F. Kaestle, *The Evolution of an Urban School System: New York City 1750-1850* (Cambridge, Mass.: Harvard University Press, 1973); Diane Ravitch, *The Great School Wars, New York City, 1805-1973: A History of the Public Schools as Battlefield of Social Change* (New York: Basic Books, 1974); Stanley K. Schultz, *The Culture Factory: Boston Public Schools, 1789-1860* (New York: Oxford University Press, 1973); Selwyn K. Troen, *The Public and the Schools: Shaping the St. Louis System, 1838-1920* (Columbia: University of Missouri Press, 1975); Patricia A. Graham, *Community and Class in American Education, 1865-1918* (New York: John Wiley, 1974).

28. Donald R. Warren, *To Enforce Education: A History of the Founding Years of the United States Office of Education* (Detroit, Mich.: Wayne State University Press, 1974).

29. Joseph M. Cronin, *The Control of Urban Schools: Perspectives on the Power of Educational Reformers* (New York: Free Press, 1973).

30. *A History of International and Comparative Education: Nineteenth Century Documents,* ed. Stewart E. Fraser and William W. Brickman (Glenview, Ill.: Scott Foresman, 1968).

31. *American Education in Foreign Perspectives,* ed. Stewart E. Fraser (New York: John Wiley, 1969).

32. Brian Simon, *Studies in the History of Education, 1780-1870* (London: Lawrence and Wishart, 1960).

33. Michalina Vaughan and Margaret Scotford Archer, *Social Conflict and Educational Change in England and France, 1789-1849* (Cambridge, Eng.: Cambridge University Press, 1971).

34. M. D. Shipman, *Education and Modernisation* (London: Faber and Faber, 1971).

35. Marius B. Jansen and Lawrence Stone, "Education and Modernization in Japan and England," *Comparative Studies in Society and History* 9 (January 1967): 208-232.

36. Brian Simon, *Education and the Labour Movement* (London: Lawrence and Wishart, 1965).

37. John E. Talbott, *The Politics of Educational Reform in France, 1918-1940* (Princeton, N.J.: Princeton University Press, 1969).

38. Charles E. Merriam, *The Making of Citizens* (Chicago: University of Chicago Press, 1931; reprint ed., New York: Teachers College, Columbia University, 1966).

39. Gabriel A. Almond and Sidney Verba, *The Civic Culture: Political Attitudes and Democracy in Five Nations* (Princeton, N.J.: Princeton University Press, 1963).

40. *Political Youth, Traditional Schools: National and International Perspectives,* ed. Byron G. Massialas (Englewood Cliffs, N.J.: Prentice-Hall, 1972).

41. Russell F. Farnen, Abraham N. Oppenheim, and Judith V. Torney, *Civic Education in Ten Countries* (New York: John Wiley, 1975).

42. See R. Freeman Butts, "The Public School: Assaults on a Great Idea," *The Nation* 216 (April 30, 1973): 553-560; see also *id.,* "The Public Purpose of the Public School," *Teachers College Record* 75 (December 1973): 207-221, and "Public Education and the Public Faith."

43. *New York Times,* March 20, 1974, 29.

44. Donald R. Warren, "Public School as Political Idea," paper presented at the annual meeting of the American Educational Studies Association, Denver, Colorado, October 1973.

45. Charles A. Tesconi, Jr., "Schooling and the Privatization of Experience," *ibid.*

FOUR

Sometimes Upward:
School Reform and Social Class

Review of Michael B. Katz, *The Irony of Early School Reform,* by *Neil Harris*

Social Reform and the Urban School: An Essay Review of Michael B. Katz, *Class, Bureaucracy, and Schools* and *School Reform;* David J. Rothman, *The Discovery of the Asylum;* and Marvin Lazerson, *Origins of Urban Education,* by   *Carl F. Kaestle*

Reflecting concepts and techniques borrowed principally from sociology, social-class analyses related to the history of American education establish correlations between schooling variables and economic and status mobility. A related line of inquiry focuses on the social-class attitudes and preferences of school reformers. In the hands of unskilled historians with axes of their own to grind, such research can merely produce stereotypes, an unenlightening catalog of heroes and villains. Executed with care, it provides a basis for interpreting evidence on historical mobility. It can also contribute to the consideration of institutional organizations as mediators between social change and social structure and as modes and inhibitors of educational innovation. Where evidence of class bias is found in the rationales for reforms and in formal or informal educational policy, grounds are established for investigating the extent of institutionalized discrimination and the likelihood of social-class differences in schooling outcomes.

117

The relation between school reform and social class has received considerable attention in recent research on the history of American education. The following essays by Neil Harris and Carl Kaestle review examples of this literature, focusing on the work of Michael Katz. It is generally agreed that Katz's first book, *The Irony of Early School Reform,* initiated a critical revision of American educational history, as Harris predicted it would in 1969. Harris's assessment continues to hold interest not only because it offers a thorough analysis of what proved to be an important work but also because it antedates the wave of revisionism that followed the publication of Katz's book. Focused more broadly on social reform, Kaestle's essay reviews subsequent works by Katz and Marvin Lazerson, which examine aspects of educational change and school reform, and a monograph by David Rothman on the history of "asylums" in the United States.

Review of *The Irony of Early School Reform*

Neil Harris

What do we do with reformers? As a group they have proven to be both fascinating and maddeningly elusive. Their stance toward the social order tends to be complex and ambivalent. Lacking the clarity of reactionaries and revolutionaries, they are totally committed neither to the old way of doing things, nor to a new order which is meant to overturn and purify. Their intentions generally outstrip their achievements, and their reputations are often more imposing than their actual accomplishments. Yet in almost every period of American history, as Jeffersonians, Jacksonian Democrats, abolitionists, populists, progressives, New Dealers, temperance crusaders, muckrakers, suffragettes, some variety of the reform temperament has exerted a primary force on the political, social, and intellectual life of the nation.

Reprinted, with permission, from *Harvard Educational Review* 39 (Spring 1969), 383-389. Copyright © 1969 by President and Fellows of Harvard College. The volume reviewed was Michael B. Katz, *The Irony of Early School Reform: Educational Innovation in Mid-Nineteenth Century Massachusetts* (Cambridge, Mass.: Harvard University Press, 1968).

Historians have always been fascinated by the dynamics of American reform movements. At one time such movements were seen simply as testimony to the inherent progressivism and pluralism of American life, to its institutional elasticity and intellectual tolerance. But the place of reformers in the last twenty years of our historiography has grown much less secure. Some of the most provocative and influential works in recent historical literature have been critical of the crusades of the past, attempting to expose the shortcomings of the reformers' intentions or the hidden springs of their energies. Enriched by the research of contemporary sociologists, psychologists, political scientists, and social anthropologists, and fortified by such older masters as Freud, Marx, Weber, and Durkheim, the most recent generation of American historians has begun the reexamination of transformations once taken to be benevolent and foreordained. Richard Hofstadter, David Donald, Stanley Elkins, Christopher Lasch, and Gabriel Kolko figure largely in this literature, and they have focused on a wide range of Americans who sought to modify political and economic institutions.

Status anxieties, identity crises, power conflicts, and symbolic uses apparently affected not only political reformers, but the creators of art, entertainment, newspapers, prisons, universities, and libraries, the whole spectrum of cultural and philanthropic apparatus. Since novel institutions require money, energy, and a rhetoric of justification, their founders cast themselves in the role of reformers, attempting to fulfill cultural strategies which turn out to be less bland and benevolent than they appear. A concern with disguised meanings and hidden allusions is not new to American scholars. It is almost half a century since the work of Constance Rourke, Lewis Mumford, and Richard Chase first appeared. Since then, historians such as Henry Nash Smith, R. W. B. Lewis, Charles Sanford, William R. Taylor, and Kenneth Lynn, to name but a few, have explored some of the ideological commitments which lay behind the construction of our art forms. What is new, however, is the application of their insights to institutions and movements, as well as to individual artists. Gerald Grob, George M. Fredrickson, Albert V. McLean, Jr., David Lewis, and others have been concerned not with the great masters of the past, or the politically influential, but with less-known architects of hospitals and asylums, philanthropies, vaudeville, and prisons. These historians have broadened the study of institutional change to include the analysis of the specific terms of debate, the choices made, the human effects of innovation.

These two streams in our historiography—the new, severe critique of political reformers, and the uncovering of cultural strategies behind institution founding—have been brought together and applied to the history of American education in a suggestive book by Michael Katz. Combining a view of Jacksonian America as a period of considerable tension and anxiety with some careful studies of several educational controversies, he has written what amounts to a revisionist view of the school reformers. The motives as well as the aims of the reformers, Katz suggests, were not as disinterested or as benevolent as earlier generations believed. The reformers who promoted the new public school expansion, he insists, did not seek to widen the educational base in the interest of equalizing opportunity and increasing mobility. Instead, their efforts reflected a desire to shape and channel an increasingly chaotic environment. Their pleas for public high schools were pleas for new instruments of social control which would restore the unities and social connections destroyed by urbanization and industrialism.

It was not the poor, the underprivileged, the working classes who were most anxious to expand public education. Instead, it was promoters of new industries, well-to-do merchants and professionals, and master artisans who supported public school reform. Attracted by the promise and repelled by the reality of the new society produced by factory and slum, they sought to institutionalize their concern with maintaining their values in the face of change and to educate their own children with public funds. In Beverly and Groton, the two places Katz studies in detail, the working classes formed the core of opposition to the new public high schools. Unable to afford the luxury of placing children there, often geographically separated from the new institutions, and anxious about increased taxation, lower-income groups fought the establishment of the new schools.

In the debates over the establishment of high schools in Massachusetts, in the bitter quarrels among teachers concerning techniques and prerogatives in the new educational bureaucracies, and in the development of reform schools and other penal institutions (the three main subjects of [his] book), Katz discerns special interests and contradictory goals at work. Reforms, consolidations, rationalizations, changes in teaching methods and curriculum, came about by imposition, not request, and reflected similar techniques employed by the new industrialists. "Schoolmen, like industrialists," Katz remarks, "sought to increase the 'marginal productivity' of labor through training, feminization, innovation, and reorganization" (p. 60). Few of the educators pushing the innovations had any true insight into the ambiguities of their position. The school improvements they sought would only speed the expansion of the urban-industrial environment which they blamed as the source for vice, crime, and immorality. Education, as conceived by the reformers, Katz contends, would only add to the number of "company men" at large, increase the efficiency of the business system, and promote the time and work disciplines which had become necessary. Inevitably, the reformers failed to accomplish their larger humanistic goals, and merely froze educational philosophies and bureaucracies into programs distant from the real needs and aspirations of workingmen. With one eye on the current resentment of urban parents to professional schoolmen, Katz suggests that the early nineteenth-century reformers worked too fast and too hard. "Educational reform and innovation represented the imposition by social leaders of schooling upon a reluctant, uncomprehending, skeptical, and sometimes . . . hostile citizenry. School committees hoped to serve their own ends and the ends of the status-seeking parents that supported them. . . . In making the urban school, educational promoters of the mid-nineteenth century fostered an estrangement between the school and the working-class community that has persisted to become one of the greatest challenges to reformers of our own time" (p. 112).

The attempt to write the history of educational reform more critically and apply the techniques and insights of scholars in other fields is most valuable. Katz has illuminated the complexity and double-edged character of many of the innovations in a well-written and clearly organized narrative. The computerized findings, which occupy a fifty-page appendix, represent an exhaustive try at recovering some of the specific interests and variables which entered into school debates and attempt to correlate a community's ambitions with its real level of prosperity and economic development. School expansion was indeed a product of the strains of industrialization, and many of the conclusions Katz offers are immensely useful and original.

But the book as a whole must be treated with some caution, for it is obvious that it will have great influence on future works and it contains a number of severe shortcomings. These relate, first, to the kinds of evidence presented to support the arguments; second, to the general tone of some of Katz's observations; and, finally, to the overall thesis.

Concerning the evidence, it is, despite the mass of statistics presented, often uneven and one-sided. The rhetoric of the school reformers receives much attention, and Katz illuminates its authoritarian and self-interested character. But the opposition, except in the votes of various town meetings, is largely silent. Resentment of the reform campaigns was apparently rarely expressed verbally. The causes of this resentment, particularly in the high school controversy, must therefore be imputed from the demographic data, which are frequently too skimpy to be fully satisfying.

Moreover, the statistical evidence provided does not always support the conclusions reached. For example, Katz insists that the struggle over retention of a high school in Beverly was largely a battle between the middle and working classes: the latter objecting to taxation for schools which would not benefit their children; the former supporting the new institutions as a means of retaining or enhancing status in the growing complexities of the business world. Katz admits that other variables, such as the presence or lack of school-age children in some families and location of residence, were important. But class lines, he argues, were most crucial. It is true that the wealthy and established were most favorable to the high school in Beverly. Almost all professionals, public employees, gentlemen, and sea captains supported it. But the votes of other groups are more ambiguous. For example, [of] those whose total estate was less than $1,000 (the poorest people in the town), 54 were in favor of the high school [and] 94 were opposed. This hardly reflects the total resentment Katz implies. The crucial vote was that of the town's shoemakers, who were opposed to the school almost three to one. The vote was taken in 1860, just at the time of a massive strike, and Katz has to turn to neighboring Lynn, and pull out pieces of strike rhetoric, to support his argument. The attempt is imaginative but unconvincing. The aspects of the strike which Katz isolates as most critical to the school controversy in Beverly rest on only a few quotations, rather loosely interpreted.

Moreover, even if the voting figures are accepted as representing basic interests, the categories are not precise. What, for example, did it mean to be an artisan in Beverly in 1860? At one point Katz suggests that artisans were fairly well-to-do, often with apprentices working under them, but at another point he refers to "poor artisans." The occupational and status classifications are not described in enough detail to satisfy the burdens the argument places on them.

In other places the use of evidence is even more questionable. Katz devotes a number of pages to the town of Lawrence, a planned textile center, to indicate the inadequacy of reformer intentions. Lawrence, which had been planned to promote virtue in the controlled environment [in order] to counter the ugly charges that industry inevitably brought with it the squalor and deprivation it fostered in Europe, quickly degenerated into a center of crime, truancy, idleness, and unemployment. "Despite the best educational system a group of informed Massachusetts citizens could devise, Lawrence was a city characterized by discord, immorality, and proverty" (p. 110). In five years the place had changed from "a model town" to "a Primary School of Vice."

But in the study of Lawrence, the careful statistical underpinning present in other portions of the book disappears entirely. We are treated to a highly subjective (and perhaps exaggerated) view of the town's difficulties and crime rates. Lawrence newspaper editorials are used to demonstrate that "the immorality and blackguardism exhibited upon our public streets" was especially acute in that city, although practically every city's journals featured such comments through the nineteenth century. No comparison is made with other towns of the same size or character, no suggestion is made that the planned community was any better or any worse off than other sites in Massachusetts or Rhode Island where employers and city fathers took less interest in the intellectual or moral welfare of the citizenry. The Lawrence reformers may indeed have failed ultimately, but, in order to gauge the degree of their failure, the town's condition should be placed in a statistical frame as carefully worked out as that provided for the Beverly school dispute.

Other evidence suffers from the failure to provide certain necessary explanations or to fill information gaps. Little is said about the precise kinds and levels of taxes which supported schools. Exactly what it meant, in monetary terms, for various groups within the community to erect a high school is never specified. Moreover, although we discover that reformers planned schools that workers' children did not attend, not much is said about the number of parochial schools; the percentage among unskilled laborers of Roman Catholics (who were generally hostile to the public school system); and the difficulty of attracting Catholics to any school system administered, at best, in a nonsectarian, and, at worst, in an aggressively Protestant manner. Religious commitments may have been an effective bar to the success of any public school system in the mid-nineteenth century. To blame the reformers for the failure of public schools to take root among the working classes, as Katz does, seems a little unfair without further discussion.

Finally, some of the evidence, along with some of the arguments, appears contradictory. The Beverly fight, Katz argues, was a clear case of ideological opposition. But in Groton the dispute was simply one of power. Those living in Groton Junction, far from the proposed high school site, fought its establishment. Those in the vicinity favored it. Groton quarrels between central boards and local districts also reveal no ideological bases, but simply a desire for control and patronage. If Beverly and Groton represent the varieties of educational warfare, then this warfare was more various, less defined, less ideological than the book indicates. If ideology was irrelevant in one place, and the struggle was simply one for power, there is little reason to pay attention to the rhetoric employed. But if the ideology behind the high school reflected more than simple self-interest and involved comprehensive visions of a different social order, then the fight involved not just power, but ultimate intentions, ends, images of the future as well.

These problems of evidence and argumentation, however, are in some ways less disturbing than the book's tone. Certainly historians are entitled to a reasonable amount of polemicism in trying to state their argument more effectively and reverse a prevailing historiographic trend. Overargument is not always a vice. But this hardly justifies describing as a "paranoiac response" a relatively mild verbal attack on Cyrus Pierce for his having criticized the public schools. "The educationists responded with fury," Katz tells us, and he supports this view by quoting statements like: "We ought not to be told that for thirty years we have been doing the public an injury, by a defective system of education," and "There must be some mistake" (p. 158). Such statements are evidences of disagreement, not of fury.

There are other exaggerations. Charles Storrow, the first mayor of Lawrence and an advocate of high schools, reveals "a curious mixture of benevolence and hunger for power." The school committees "excoriated the working-class parents." Moral education was "a kind of intellectual totalitarianism." Katz's use of these phrases, despite his pious warnings that reformers should not be judged by standards of cultural relativism which have evolved since their day, indicates an acerbity which weakens the effec·iveness of the whole argument.

The presentist tone of the book, however, is related to its overall thesis, and this is, of course, the most critical issue. Educational innovation in the early nineteenth century and the processes of professionalization did possess many ironies, and Katz is justified in pointing them out. But all historical intentions, both reform and revolutionary, can be shown to involve ironies. After reading the denunciation of the reformers, one is left asking what alternative schemes were possible or proposed. On this, Katz is somewhat vague. "We have still to see a movement driven by a desire to bring joy and delight to the life of the individual, to enrich experience solely for the purpose of making life more full and lovely," he notes, commenting on both nineteenth-century and contemporary urban educational schemes (p. 214). But this kind of observation does not help very much. A historian with different biases could find statements in the writings of Horace Mann and some of his followers, indicating that they also were seeking to enrich experience and increase pleasure. All depends on the meaning attached to words like "delight" and "experience."

The one alternative Katz offers in the book seems inadequate given these larger aims. In Part II, "The Uses of Pedagogy," Katz shrewdly and imaginatively outlines some of the perils of professionalism, and the sterilities which enlarged bureaucracies invariably bring with them. The reformers, in many ways, were not much better than the rigid disciplinarians they replaced. But the account of the debate between Mann's forces and the old-line educators is a strange one. Terming the innovators "soft-line educators," Katz describes their effort to substitute internal for external restraints, to emphasize learning through models, and to abolish memorization, rote repetition, student passivity, and harsh discipline. The changes certainly had psychic costs. The opponents, the older entrenched group, however, reveal a much harsher and less compassionate tone. The old schoolmasters insisted that "kindness cannot supply the place of authority, nor gratitude that of submission." Implicit "obedience to rightful authority must be inculcated and enforced upon children as the very germ of all good order in future society." Anyone permitting deviation from docility was dangerous, "sapping the foundations of social order," "Children," said one hard-line educator in scornfully describing Mann's scheme, "were to be led along by the cords of love."

Yet this group of hard-liners, whose statements seem incredibly rigid and authoritarian, is put forward by Katz to prove that an intelligent alternative to Mann's reforms existed. If the "reformers of the time had no other choice," Katz admits, "then the criticism might be excessively moralistic or simply irrelevant" (p. 149). But the hard-liners, he insists, provided such a choice. They were "a vocal and articulate group" arguing for "more slowly paced educational development," wanting change "to come through community action," sensing that "professionalization and centralization would, to a large extent, cut off the school from the community" (p. 149). After some thirty pages describing the era's educational controversies, this description of the old-line educators seems bizarre. The quotations Katz produces simply do not come close to supporting it.

The reasons for this discrepancy may lie in a confusion of categories. The older masters certainly wished to retain local control over schools and opposed centralization, but this program was far different from the "creative freedom" Katz seeks as part of his educational design. In the mid-nineteenth century popular control, particularly by those already sending their children to the public schools, was probably further away from a joyous curriculum than Mann's proposals. No statement can be definitive here, but Katz's assumption that community control and creative freedom would have been synonymous is unproven. The older masters might have delayed the rise of self-serving bureaucracies, but it is equally probable that the schools they envisioned would have continued to be the monotonous, irrelevant, and constraining institutions which the innovators opposed. Local control meant stern discipline, and Mann's schemes still seem more personally liberating. The alternative to reform, so crucial to Katz's argument, is thus never really presented.

In the end, then, this book remains curiously unsatisfying. It is obviously the work of a highly imaginative and innovative scholar, and rests on careful and elaborate research. It is filled with interesting suggestions and intelligent observations. But the individual chapters do not add up to a convincing overall argument. Irony is not what one ends up with in history; it is what one begins with. In his zeal to expose the inadequacies of the Panglossian school of educational historians, Katz runs the risk of substituting one kind of teleology for another. Instead of a recitation of the glories of American educational history and its progressive triumphs, we are now given a jeremiad lamenting its inevitable failures and inherent illogicalities. This kind of argument should be transcended, and it is only fair to note that while *The Irony of Early School Reform* does not manage the job on its own, it could well be the basis for works that do.

Social Reform and the Urban School:
An Essay Review

Carl F. Kaestle

The growth of American educational historiography has been stunted. While American political history underwent a major revision at the hands of the progressive historians, writers of our educational history, with a few notable exceptions, continued in the Whiggish tradition of Ellwood P. Cubberley. Because of its isolation from other historical work, this field was relatively unaffected by the progressives' paradigmatic reformulation of American history. During the past decade this isolation has been much reduced, and several sophisticated books that escape easy categorization have appeared in educational history. Now, furthermore, nearly sixty years after Charles Beard wrote about the self-interest and class conflict embodied in our political institutions, the history of American education seems destined to have its own progressive phase.

The progressive historians, like their colleagues in law, journalism, and literature, attempted to expose the hard realities of life hidden behind abstract ideals of justice, democracy, and opportunity. Where Bancroft had seen the gradual perfection of American institutions, Beard saw a series of recurring confrontations in which the interests of the common man lost out to those of the ruling elite. Both views of the American past displayed that equation of past and present that Herbert Butterfield has called "foreshortening" and that we generally label "presentism." While the Whigs' version was optimistic and laudatory, however, the progressives' view was pessimistic and alienated.

Although it displays imagination and originality, Michael Katz's recent work in educational history is reminiscent of the progressive assault on a complacent Whig tradition. In his influential book, *The*

Reprinted, with permission, from *History of Education Quarterly* 12 (Summer 1972), 211-228. The essay reviewed Michael B. Katz, *Class, Bureaucracy, and Schools: The Illusion of Educational Change in America* (New York: Praeger Publishers, 1971); *School Reform: Past and Present*, ed. Michael B. Katz (Boston: Little, Brown and Company, 1971); David J. Rothman, *The Discovery of the Asylum: Social Order and Disorder in the New Republic* (Boston: Little, Brown and Company, 1971); and Marvin Lazerson, *Origins of Urban Education: Public Education in Massachusetts, 1870-1915* (Cambridge, Mass.: Harvard University Press, 1971).

Irony of Early School Reform, . . . he asserted that popular education did not result from "democracy, rationalism, and humanitarianism," but rather from the desire of the middle class and the professional educators to saddle the general community with a school system that would serve their particular interests. In his latest book, *Class, Bureaucracy, and Schools,* Professor Katz has broadened that interpretation to cover both the nineteenth and twentieth centuries, providing us with a fascinating, lucid, and provocative manifesto of the new critical revision of educational history. Although the book is based primarily on previously published essays, it nonetheless displays a coherence and readability that will make it popular among college students and laymen. The comparison between antebellum, progressive, and current school reform, suggested in *The Irony of Early School Reform,* is here reasserted, and the didactic intent is frankly admitted. One purpose of the book is "to proclaim and to account for the illusion of educational change in America" (p. xv).

Earlier historians have seen the development of free, compulsory, public schooling as the bulwark of democracy, the key mechanism of opportunity and national greatness; Katz sees it as an engine of conformity, a means of maintaining the status quo, and an index of national failure. The Whiggish historians of education, as described in the famous historiographical essays of Bernard Bailyn and Lawrence Cremin, saw the mission of the educational historian as inspirational—to inculcate loyalty and support for the public school system; Katz and others of the new persuasion see the historian's proper role as cautionary—to expose the hidden purposes and invidious consequences of public schooling. While both views have strong ties to the present, they are polar opposites normatively.

Nevertheless, Katz's work does not represent simply an ideological reversal read backwards in time, nor are his books simply a replay of progressive insights applied to educational history, despite the analogy I have made; for Katz's work displays wide-ranging research, an admirable knowledge of sociology and statistics, and—reflecting one of the more hopeful trends in recent American history—a penchant for making his analytical framework explicit. *Class, Bureaucracy, and Schools* is a good example of this latter trend. Responding to the anticipated charge of presentism, the author asserts, "I have chosen to make manifest my questions and my concern . . . the time for methodological unconsciousness within history has ended" (p. xxv). In the

introduction Katz faces directly such questions as: Were there alternatives to the bureaucratic structure that emerged in the nineteenth century? (Yes.) Was the adoption of the bureaucratic structure inevitable?(No.) . . . Is that bureaucratic structure independent of class bias?
(No.) The analytical explicitness continues in the three chapters that
follow. The first chapter examines alternative models of school organization in the early nineteenth century; the second chapter traces the
adoption of bureaucratic characteristics, as defined by Carl Friedrich,
in the Boston school system between 1850 and 1876; and the third
chapter asserts a parallel between antebellum, progressive, and recent
reform movements in order to explain the schools' persistent failure to
change. The second chapter, which shows how later reformers were
frustrated when they tried to undo the bureaucracy earlier reformers
had wrought, was originally published in the *History of Education
Quarterly* (Summer 1968 and Fall 1968) and is familiar to many
readers. I shall therefore concentrate on the more recent first and
third [chapters].

Professor Katz's alternative models for educational organization in
the early nineteenth century are labeled paternalistic voluntarism,
democratic localism, corporate voluntarism, and incipient bureaucracy. The first is illustrated by early charitable organizations like the
New York Public School Society, the second by advocates of pluralism
like Governor Seward's Secretary of State, John Spencer, as well as
rural local control advocates. The third model, corporate voluntarism, is exemplified by promoters of academies and independent colleges, and the fourth, incipient bureaucracy, triumphed in the organization of our centralized public school systems. This triumph, Katz
rightly asserts, has obscured the seriousness with which the other
models were considered as viable alternatives at the time.

The idea of a taxonomy of alternative organizational schemes is
not, in itself, new. Cubberley described the "pauper school idea," the
"voluntary system," "the transition academy," and the "state control
idea," among others.[1] But Katz's recasting of the alternatives does
serve to escape the bias that made Cubberley see the rejected schemes
simply as preludes or impediments to the inevitable and desirable
triumph of centralized public systems. Katz provides a different normative framework for understanding such episodes as the high school-
academy controversy, or Bishop Hughes's fight to obtain government
funds for Catholic schools. Gradually, schemes of organization that

had served localities' and minorities' particular schooling goals gave way as the imperatives of an urban, industrial society impelled schoolmen to create centralized school bureaucracies.

As conceptual molds into which we can pour the complexity of educational history, however, Katz's four models have some faults. Their status is not quite clear. Professor Katz says they are not ideal types but that each existed in pure form in reality. Unfortunately, the "paradigm" examples suffer from impurities. The New York Public School Society, presented as pure paternalistic voluntarism, displayed incipient bureaucracy from the state. The Lancasterian system, contrary to Katz's judgment, was a vehicle for interschool as well as intraschool standardization, and by 1842, when the society was curtailed, its citywide system displayed most of the bureaucratic characteristics Katz emphasizes in his Boston study. The two models in this case, then are not alternatives but perhaps stages, and even then it is impossible to define where one ends and the other begins. Also, the terms used to define the models are not of the same order and are therefore not mutually exclusive. For example, "paternalistic voluntarism" (for example, a charity school society) was usually corporate, and "corporate voluntarism" (for example, an academy) could just as easily be paternalistic. One adjective has to do with attitude, the other with organization.

The remaining model, democratic localism, was a genuine alternative, but it lacks coherence as a single force. Localism was not an educational philosophy but a set of arguments used by very different groups operating on different assumptions. Katz recognizes this difficulty, especially later in the book in his discussion of localism today (pp. 139-40), but in his nineteenth-century analysis he still tends to champion a position taken as easily by the bigot and the pennypincher as by the tolerant pluralist. It is difficult to see how, if you advocate localism "at its best," you can avoid also getting it "at its worst" (pp. 20-21. Despite these flaws in the specific models, their premise, that "organization mediated between social change and social structure" (p. 54), is valid, and further refinement of this approach may prove fruitful.

The relationship between bureaucratic organization and the schools' class and cultural biases plays an extremely important role in Katz's analysis, both of school history and of the present dilemma. The conformism and ethnic prejudices of early schoolmen are among the important themes emerging from the present reexamination of the "common" school, and Katz accurately describes the relationship of these biases to the allegedly neutral bureaucracy when he says, "Cultural homogenization played counterpoint to administrative rationality" (p. 39). The structure and procedures of the emerging bureaucracy militated against diversity, reinforcing the schoolmen's effort to create homogeneity among the increasingly fractionalized population. But Katz goes further than this to claim that racism (meaning class and cultural bias) and antisexuality are "integral, not incidental, to the very structure of public education" (p. 40), that is, as I understand it, they are not merely historically associated, and reinforcing, but inherently connected. This raises the most serious question of the book, one of great import for present reform as well as for historical analysis. If racism, class bias, and repressive morality are "integral" to the system, there is no possible reform *of* the system; as Katz argues, nothing but a radical restructuring will have any effect. If the premise is true, these ugly features of urban school bureaucracies were not only inevitable, but they are ineradicable. This presents a bleak prospect to those who advocate reform within the system.

As prophecy, this connection may prove correct, and I think the bleak outlook is justified; but, in analytical terms, the logic of the connection is questionable. One can argue—and for the moment I shall—that people, not bureaucracies, are racist (or are motivated by class interest or support a repressive morality). Racism is not inherent in "the system," but is stubbornly and sadly stamped on the national character, and thus becomes expressed by institutions. Therefore, in the unlikely event that the bureaucratic structure were overthrown, the problems would persist in whatever new structures were created. The best organization might be Mark Hopkins on one end of a log with a student on the other, but the personal contact won't do the student much good if his Mark Hopkins turns out to be a bigot and a prude. This is not to imply that the structure of school organization is neutral, or that structural reform is irrelevant, but that structure per se is not the main impediment to freeing the system from racism and class bias. At any rate, the system won't change until people's attitudes change. Most people are not disposed toward radical school reform precisely because most people support, in varying degrees, the conservative purposes of the system. This is an "uncomfortable piece of reality" which Professor Katz faces in his discussion of the present (p. 193), but which does not come through strongly in his historical analysis.

The "notes" toward a history of twentieth-century reform that constitute [the third chapter] of *Class, Bureaucracy, and Schools* were foreshadowed by the conclusion of *The Irony of Early School Reform*. Progressive educational reform is seen as a basically middle-class conservative movement that shared the anti-immigrant bias and desire for social control of antebellum school reform. The progressive movement was thus doomed before it started; it would not challenge the status quo in any fundamental way, and its legacy in actual practice is more accurately seen in the testing-measurement-placement fetish of our schools, which serves the status quo, than in any liberated individualism or increased dignity of the child. There is much evidence for this interpretation of the "darker side" of the progressives. The viewpoint is bolstered by the unpublished work of Clarence Karier and paralled by that of Gabriel Kolko and James Weinstein on political progressivism. Katz's chapter is a skeletal preview of the thorough reversal of judgment on progressive education that seems forthcoming in educational history's neo-progressive phase. It is, however, more fragmentary than his interpretation of nineteenth-century developments and runs an even greater risk of presentism.

One problem in dealing with progressive education, if the phrase is taken to mean all educational innovation from 1890 through the 1920s, is the bewildering variety of programs and philosophies. The liberating, conformist, individualizing, and bureaucratizing tendencies set loose in these years make almost any interpretation possible if you look at the right group of people and statements. This leads one to vote with Peter Filene to "tear off the familiar label" and recognize the ambiguity and variety of the period.[2] But beyond this, a few of the problems with the Katz-Karier trend in analyzing the early progressives, especially John Dewey and Jane Addams, are, first, in substituting the notion "conformist" values where they would have used "cooperative" values (for example, p. 119), a considerable shift of connotation, and second, in implying that educators and social commentators of the early twentieth century should have been able to foresee what we in 1972 can see: the tremendous toll wreaked by technology on the privacy and integrity of the individual. In Katz's brief analysis the failings of the progressive movement are persuasively argued, and the legacy of what the reformers did and left undone is assessed with much truth and no joy. But the generous impulses, the tolerance, and the strenuous efforts at reform that many of the so-called progressive educators displayed are undervalued. Also, once again, there is the problem of consensus. The fact that truly innovative, progressive schools succeeded only in enclaves like the avant-garde community of Greenwich Village and not in the Lynds's Middletown is only further witness that the failure of reform arose from its rejection by the schools' constituents and not by their governors alone.[3]

Katz has attempted a new synthesis of American educational history, in sharp contrast to the previously regnant tradition, a synthesis informed by current disillusionment with the schools, supported by a great deal of evidence from the past, and illuminating some unpleasant truths about our educational history. As a manifesto of a new point of view, with didactic intent, *Class, Bureaucracy, and Schools* does not strive for balance, and it will produce much controversy. More important, like the early work of the progressive historians, the revisionist viewpoint in educational history should generate much detailed research that will confirm or modify the general interpretive framework. We know very little for example, about who went to the public schools, especially in nineteenth-century cities, what effect schooling had on status and occupation, what attitudes were held by the immigrants and native working class toward the schools, and many other issues. The great value of the revisionist viewpoint is that its confirmation or rebuttal forces us to look at new questions and new data. To bring my analogy with the progressive historians to its foregone conclusion, I suspect that when we have reaped the benefit of further research, we shall find that Michael Katz's formulation has reduced the complexity of history unduly.

Ellwood Cubberley's general interpretation of public school development has been discredited, but no successful reformulation has taken its place. It is always easier to destroy an interpretation than to create one, and the energy with which educational historians have recently attacked the Cubberley tradition has somewhat impeded sophisticated reformulation. Also, the generally accepted verdict of failure in today's urban schools has increased the tendency simply to seek the roots of failure in the past. What we need and do not yet have is a new synthesis that will account for the school as the focal point of idealism as well as self-interest, an institution at once the object of public scrutiny and public ignorance, an institution that evolves more by mundane accretion than dramatic reform and yet continually arouses herculean efforts and exaggerated expectations. Most of all, we need a synthesis that abjures the premise that the American school has been an unequivocal failure, for such a premise—like the earlier presumption of success—precludes the explanation of change over time.

Professor Katz's *School Reform: Past and Present,* a collection of documents, complements *Class, Bureaucracy, and Schools.* Although the book contains relatively little editorial comment for a collection of this sort, the selection of documents flows from the analysis of the past seen in Katz's essays. In his words, "By juxtaposing primary-source material from the nineteenth century with selections from the mid-twentieth century, it attempts to suggest continuities between the way public education began and the way in which it exists today" (p. 1). Here, then, are Henry Barnard and James B. Conant, Horace Mann and Bruno Bettelheim, Orestes Brownson and Marilyn Gittell, all making similar points about urban schooling. A number of important parallels are demonstrated. Schoolmen faced with recurrently perceived urban crises have persistently turned to "infant" or "preschool" education of the slum child, insisted on more and more compulsory education, and maintained that schooling reduces crime and poverty. They have devised pedagogies that would help children internalize the values deemed necessary for modern industrial society. Although urban reformers have characteristically supported environmental theories that seem to underline the dignity and potential of the individual, they have nevertheless assumed that minority-group children must be assimilated by the dominant culture. Finally, despite periodic critiques, reformers have found no way to escape bureaucratic forms of organization in urban schooling.

In his introduction, Katz warns that "the context of apparently similar activities in past and present has altered so radically" that history cannot provide predictions. "Historical analogies can be useful, indeed, but they are subtle, delicate, and intricate undertakings" (p. 2). Yet *School Reform: Past and Present,* like all such collections, loses the historical contexts of the documents and thereby loses the subtlety and intricacy of the parallels. The thrust of the book is to show that American public education is now and has always been "conservative, racist, and bureaucratic" (p. 3). It does not provide the novice with an opportunity to construct his own interpretation, nor is it intended to. The book illustrates a point of view, a timely one, and it does that well, particularly if one also reads *Class, Bureaucracy, and Schools* to confront the arguments in detail.

This point of view contains a heavy weight of truth. There is continuity in the history of our public school systems. To a depressing degree, the present is like the past. The similarities may be more important to us as citizens and educators than the differences, because they teach us what prodigious and imaginative efforts will be required to overcome the inertia of the urban school and the inhumanity of seemingly neutral procedures. As historians, however, we need to know fully as much about the differences between the past and the present. The historian of reform must deal with both continuity and change. Some reform efforts are cyclical, as Michael Katz emphasizes. Others, however, are linear and create permanent changes. One of the conceptual tasks for the historian is to distinguish between these cyclical and linear developments.

The history of American social reform, with its two prominent surges of energy in the antebellum and progressive periods, is particularly amenable to a cyclical interpretation. From the present perspective, in the apparently waning years of a third period of reform, the historian is all the more prone to historical relativism in an attempt to explain the persistent failure of reform in schools and other institutions. The dangers must not put us off, however, for it is possible to argue, without making any metahistorical claims, that the morphology of reform movements indeed impels a cyclical development that, if not inevitable, is made very likely by the inherent difficulties of institutional change.

First, there is a cycle of expectations. Reform literature typically begins with stinging exposés that decry the shameful state of an institution, then moves to utopian programs that promise a total solution of the problem or even the reformation of the whole society. This generates high expectations within the movement and among the public. Once new institutional schemes are launched, there is some feedback. The reformation of the clients is charted, applauded, and disputed. The problem may be alleviated but does not disappear. The exaggerated claims of those who initiated the reform cannot be met, and disillusionment results.

Second, there is a cycle of personnel. In many reform movements the initial impetus has been provided by the talented amateur. Once the movement takes on an institutional shape, however, there is a need

for full-time staff and for the training and certification of new workers. The resulting professionalization leads to expertise and efficiency,
some real and some illusory, but also to insularity and often to medi-
ocrity, contributing to the downtrend in the reform cycle.

Third, there is an accompanying cycle of support. The public will
often allocate extraordinary financial resources in the early stages of
institutional reform, but as public enthusiasm and professional optimism dwindle, support in terms of resources per client tends to diminish. Overcrowded facilities and inadequate staff make humane treatment, flexibility, personal attention, and sophisticated reflection—all
envisaged by the initial reformers—impossible. This leads to poor
results and a vicious circle of further diminished resources.

Fourth, there is a cycle of ideology. The sociology of knowledge applies strikingly to the theories that support reform programs. Of
course there is, in the development of theoretical and empirical
knowledge about the causes of deviance and poverty, some portion
which is linear and cumulative, that is, which adds to a long-standing
corpus of accepted knowledge. But, to a great extent, prevailing
theories parallel the cycles of reform. Although environmental and
hereditarian explanations coexist at almost all times, environmental-
ism thrives during the optimistic uptrend and genetic explanations
during the pessimistic downtrend of reform cycles. One variant of this
phenomenon is the shift from psychological to somatic explanations of
insanity that paralleled the shift from humane to custodial treatment
in asylums. This parallel is not a necessary one; future linear developments (for example, an effective organic cure for schizophrenia)
might herald a momentous reform of treatment. Nevertheless, the
connection between particular theories and cycles of reform has been
strong historically.

Despite the similarities between reform movements, the context is
never quite the same, the tools of reform are never quite the same, and
neither the clients nor their problems are ever quite the same. Beneath
the apparent circularity lie linear developments that have transformed
both our social problems and our approaches to them. In the past,
linear theories of history often equated change, over the long run, with
positive progress. But linear developments that are neutral or evil are
equally obvious in an age of atomic bombs and exhausted natural
resources; and some linear developments, in contrast with cyclical
developments, appear relatively permanent. The dilemma of the

reformer, given these two dimensions of change, is, first, how to sustain reform enthusiasm and avoid cyclical degeneration and, second, how to reverse undesirable and seemingly irreversible linear trends like excessive bureaucratization and professionalization. The historian of reform must also be sensitive to both kinds of development, for both exist in history and both help illumine where we stand today. Each of the books under review here is pertinent to that effort.

David J. Rothman's *The Discovery of the Asylum* describes the most important linear development in the American response to deviance: the shift from noninstitutional to institutional solutions. Rothman contrasts the colonial response to crime, poverty, and insanity with that of Jacksonian Americans, and he examines the development of prisons, juvenile asylums, mental hospitals, and almshouses, those places that Erving Goffman has aptly labeled "total institutions." The result is a book of broad sweep, full of important insights, the best general treatment of the subject yet written. Although Rothman does not deal with schools, which are not, technically, total institutions, there are many parallels that will interest students of educational history.

In colonial America, institutions were places of "last resort." Insane asylums and juvenile asylums did not exist, almshouses and workhouses were limited to larger towns, prisons were generally places for detention until trial, not for punishment, and none of these, moreover, was looked to for the reformation of deviants. The insane, the poor, and the unruly were left in families, and, if they had no proper family, they were assigned to one or placed in institutions that were run as much like families as possible. The regimentation, isolation, and distinctive architecture of later institutions were unknown.

In the early decades of the nineteenth century, however, poverty, crime, and insanity became more obvious, more threatening, and less taken for granted. The young republic seemed imperiled by industrialization, acquisitiveness, and diversity, while at the same time the Calvinist explanations of unavoidable poverty and divinely ordained insanity were breaking down. The Enlightenment promised infinite improvement and demanded rational solutions to social problems. The doctrine of original sin waned, and men looked to their deteriorating environment for the causes of deviance. The institution builders of Jacksonian America sought to recreate, artificially, the simple, coherent, stable environment of colonial times. Their institutions would not only reform the criminal, the insane, the poor, and the delinquent, but would serve as a model of the well-ordered society. Those who were deviant only represented the most clear-cut symptoms of a whole society that was splintering. Thus an Ohio prison chaplain wrote, "Could we all be put on prison fare, for the space of two or three generations, the world would ultimately be the better for it" (p. 84). Because these institutions were considered an improved environment over the outside world, and because they were for rehabilitation and not punishment, the question of the clients' rights did not arise. This led to committals without due process and in the case of juveniles justified the indeterminate sentence, a legacy only recently challenged.

Although the impulse was nostalgic, the creations of these reformers were fundamentally new. The ethos of the asylum was "regimentation, punctuality, and precision," which, as Rothman points out, was more characteristic of the developing industrial ideology than of any previous rural life-style. "This was the new world offered the insane. They were among the first of their countrymen to experience it" (p. 154). Thus, although Rothman concludes that the asylums failed both at reforming their inmates and at reforming the whole society, there is a sense, perhaps a perverse sense, in which they achieved their second goal: these asylums were prototypes, both of later total institutions, and, as the values of punctuality, routine, and discipline were diffused, of the noncustodial institutions Americans faced in an increasingly organized society.

This is the long-term, or linear, dimension of the story. In the short run, however, the asylum builders experienced the cyclical problems I have described above: shifts in expectations, personnel, resources, and ideology. Insane asylums became primarily custodial, prisons became primarily punitive, and juvenile asylums turned into little prisons. Designed to reform the larger society, these institutions became fortresses set off from it, dumping grounds for undesirables. By 1850 their architectural identity had been standardized; as Rothman quips, "An outsider would have no doubt that he was looking upon an institution. His only difficulty would be in recognizing which one it was" (p. 227).

The antebellum urban school shared in this metamorphosis. Schools, which in the colonial period had looked like other houses, by 1850 looked like other institutions. Other aspects of their development are similar to the asylums. The urban elementary school of the antebellum period was a regimented organization designed to teach order, sobriety, frugality, and industry to children, especially the children of the poor and the immigrants, who were considered deviants from the native, middle-class culture. School promoters saw the nonschool environment of the children in negative terms, and it was hoped that the school would be a model for the larger society; indeed, unlike the asylums, the schools sent their clients home every night and hoped that they would influence their parents. Schools also shared with asylums a shift from reform intent to custodial function, though here the shift is more subtle than in the total institutions.

Schools, like asylums, were part of a general trend, the institutionalization and rationalization of reform efforts designed to solve social problems that, in an earlier and simpler society, had been handled in an ad hoc manner through personal contacts. Although Rothman does not emphasize the process, income stratification, residential segregation, and cultural diversity had estranged the governing and working classes. Institutions were interposed for face-to-face contact. The upper class "is not much disposed to go to the lower places in society," said Walter Channing in 1843. "If it attempts to aid Pauperism, it does so by delegation" (p. 174.) Rothman's book describes more than custodial institutions, then. It describes a general process in society of which the asylum was an emblem.

As a description of what happened, Professor Rothman's book is fresh, clear, and gracefully written. The transformation to incarceration is established persuasively. As an explanation of why it happened, however, the book is less satisfactory. One problem has to do with his rejection of urban explanations, another with his slighting of the early national period, and a third with his assertion of American uniqueness.

In his introduction (pp. xvi-xvii) Rothman rejects an urban social control explanation, partly because rural areas adopted the same institutions, partly because the social control argument seems to be simplistic, economic determinism, and partly because twentieth-century America, highly urbanized, has turned somewhat away from the asylum as a solution to social problems. The argument that towns and rural areas adopted the same institutions will not do, for we are trying to account for their genesis, not their diffusion. The argument that urban America has turned away from incarceration (and indeed it has not done so very substantially) proves little, for the reason might be that we have finally discovered that these institutions do not work,

something their founders did not know. Professor Rothman throws out
the baby with the bath. We all know that we must avoid "urbanization" as a vague first cause. William Diamond's article on this problem is now thirty years old and is still being reprinted in undergraduate anthologies.[4] However, the rejection in toto of urban causes
eliminates specific causal factors along with artificial constructs.
Rothman relies instead on a national level of analysis, utilizing exhor-
tatory addresses and social commentary. These are perfectly legitimate; Americans were worried in general about acquisitiveness, social
mobility, and the pace of life. But one misses in these pages the central
problems facing anxious reformers in the burgeoning coastal cities,
who, as Rothman reminds us (pp. xiii, 209), led in the creation of asylums. Residential segregation on class and ethnic lines, an urban phenomenon, led to increasing reliance on institutional solutions to deviance. Street crime, and especially massive juvenile vagrancy, led to
increased pressure for custodial institutions. Even more important,
one of the crucial suppositions of the asylum builders—that incarceration was a favor rather than an imposition—was based largely on the
obvious and frightening deterioration of the urban environment. In
the end, Rothman's rejection of urban explanations is incompatible
with the central theme of the book. The passing of the colonial world
of personal, stable relationships, which led to the creation of asylums,
is intimately connected to the concentration of population in nineteenth-century cities. One need not argue that causes were uniquely or
deterministically urban in order to argue that they were characteristically so.

Related to this problem is Professor Rothman's treatment of immigration. We hear nothing of immigrants in relation to crime and poverty until the end of the book when he wants to explain the institutional shift from rehabilitation to custody. "Beginning in the 1850's,
outsider and immigrant—in the person of the Irish—became increasingly synonymous" (p. 254). Again and again he emphasizes class and
ethnic differences as the most important cause of change after 1850:
"the swelling number of foreign-born not only rendered the ideas of
moral treatment obsolete, but gave a new pertinence to a custodial
operation" (p. 283; see also 285, 292). That the shift from rehabilitation to custody was reinforced—or, as Rothman would have it,
caused—by the increasing percentage of ethnic minorities among the
institutions' clients is a theme already established by Gerald Grob in

The State and the Mentally Ill.[5] But Rothman, eschewing class and ethnic explanations before 1850 only to make them preeminent after 1850, exaggerates the theme. The asylums' inmates were predominantly lower class from the start; therefore cultural alienation and disdain existed between the governors and the clients all along. More important, immigration was significant long before 1850. The identification of crime and poverty with immigrants begins in New York City as early as the 1790s, and the virulent nativism of the 1840s was based on long-standing economic and religious antipathies. Immigration was therefore an important factor not only in the degeneration of the institutions but in their establishment as well. Ethnic and class divisions helped propel the shift from noninstitutional to institutional solutions.

Professor Rothman makes another contrast too stark when he compares the early national period with the 1820s and 1830s. The great surge of asylum building occurred in the third and fourth decades of the century, and he accepts the traditional periodization of antebellum reform. Although his major contrast, between colonial and Jacksonian America, is very useful, the decades from 1790 to 1820, sandwiched between, are treated perfunctorily. Rothman also slights the English and continental background of American reform thought. The two faults are related, for only when we study reform in the early national period in some detail, a task that awaits future scholars, will the connections from Phillipe Pinel, William Tuke, Patrick Colquhoun, John Howard, and others to American institutions become clear. Further work on the social attitudes of such Americans as Benjamin Rush, Thomas Eddy, and Noah Webster will, I think, show the evolution of reform thought to have been more gradual, and the debt to European reformers greater, than Rothman asserts.

Other readers will find further objections on specific points. For example, the parallel analysis does not fit almshouses as well as other asylums. Many kinds of outdoor relief continued and expanded, and the almshouse never became the "first resort" in attempting to solve poverty. Also, Rothman will raise some hackles in his rejection of religious motives; he may be correct, but the argument (pp. 75-76) is insufficient. That the crisis was more than a religious crisis (as John Thomas implies) does not mean that the response to the crisis was not shaped by religion; and the fact that the specifically religious organizations (on which Timothy Smith concentrated) did little beyond Bible distribution does not speak at all to the religious motives of men in nominally nonreligious organizations.[6]

The numerous problems raised by Professor Rothman's book illustrate how sweeping and ambitious his analysis is. While probing its weaknesses, we should also be grateful for the clarity and brevity of this book. Even if all the objections are valid, they do not, in my opinion, shake the central thesis of the book, which is why its publication is of such importance to everyone interested in the American response to social problems. Institutionalization, bureaucratization, and professionalization are the most important linear developments in American reform history, and Professor Rothman has made a major contribution in his analysis of one of the earliest and most fundamental transformations in this history.

Linear developments in history can be presented in two ways, often not as distinct as historians claim they are: as constant, gradual processes, such as "modernization," or as compact transformations located in time, like an "industrial revolution," a "bureaucratic revolution," or the "discovery of the asylum." Historians, at the risk of some distortion, tend to prefer the revolution—or its milder cousin, the "watershed"—both for its dramatic quality and for the way in which it clarifies essential differences between two adjacent periods in history. Of course, some linear developments actually do occur at a faster rate than others, but the dangers of telescoping by the historian must be kept in mind. Such a dilemma is presented by the *Gemeinschaft-Gesellschaft* schema formulated by Ferdinand Tönnies and often applied to American history. *Gemeinschaft* started turning into *Gesellschaft* shortly after the Pilgrims landed at Plymouth Rock, much to the dismay of William Bradford; yet there are some ways in which the concepts apply . . . to the period 1880 to 1920, the period for which they have been so ably popularized by Robert Wiebe in *The Search for Order*.[7] The creation of national economic markets and transportation systems, increased immigration, industrialization, and urbanization, and the assumption of power by larger and larger organizations not only broke down the autonomy of the "island communities" that had characterized America but caused a . . . crisis in the cities. With the perils of "watershed" history in mind, as well as the preceding discussion of cyclical and linear developments in reform, let us examine a book that applies Wiebe's general interpretive framework to urban education in the same period, Marvin Lazerson's *Origins of the Urban School: Public Education in Massachusetts, 1870-1915.*

The increasing transiency, poverty, and diversity of urban schoolchildren had rendered the school's program largely ineffective and irrevelant by the late nineteenth century. Because social leaders perceived the poor urban family as an insufficient or downright pernicious moral influence, there was great pressure on the schools to restore orderly social virtues in the community. Once the nineteenth-century drive to get all the children into the schools began to succeed substantially, schoolmen had to figure out what to do with them. This prompted a period of basic reconsideration and restructuring of programs. Some of these pressures, however, were not as new as Professor Lazerson implies. Whereas Michael Katz emphasizes cyclical development and slights linear change, Lazerson emphasizes uniqueness in his period, overlooking some precedents. He covers his bases in the introduction, explaining that "little of this was entirely novel," but that only after 1870 did public schooling affect "the mass of Americans" (p. xiv). Yet he claims to be talking about the "origins" and not the diffusion of urban public school practice, and asserts that in this period "our school system was established" (p. xv). Here he exaggerates, for many of the urban problems of the late nineteenth century were long standing, and the echoes of antebellum urban reform, though unacknowledged, are numerous in this book. The nostalgia of school reformers for an earlier, simpler time, as Lazerson admits (p. 25n), was not new, nor was their antagonism for the home environment of the child. The notion that the poor are failing their children, which Professor Lazerson calls a "dominant theme of the era" (p. 32), has been a dominant theme in all urban school reform. The assertion that kindergarten enthusiasts discovered "the importance of the early years" (p. 41) overlooks much antebellum rhetoric on the subject and, specifically, the infant school movement imported from England in the 1820s. Other minor points remind one of the cyclical nature of urban school reform and lead to the conclusion that Lazerson's theme is better described by the phrase "reconstruction" of the urban school (p. 30) than by the title of the book.

After the precedents are noted, however, much remains that was genuinely new. Through studies of the kindergarten and manual training movements in Massachusetts, Lazerson demonstrates that in this period school reformers moved from an attempt to reform the society through the schools to an attempt to fit the schoolchild for his place in the society, and, most important, that in the process the school moved from a common curriculum to a differentiated curriculum, a momentous and seemingly irreversible linear development in the history of American education. Thus the watershed is divided into two subperiods: the first, roughly to 1900, when reformers tried to change social attitudes and conditions, and the second, 1900-1915, when they turned to adjusting the child to the existing system.

Early kindergarten enthusiasts shared the settlement workers' ambivalence toward the poor and the immigrant. Their disdain could lead them to statements like, "let us take the little child in the future from its possibly ignorant, filthy, careless mother as soon as it can walk" (p. 49). Yet they believed that the parents would be influenced by the habits their children learned at kindergarten, and to further that connection they set up visitation programs and mothers' clubs that occupied the teachers' afternoons. As the independent kindergartens run by philanthropists were incorporated into the school system, however (another version of the cycle from amateur to professional), they lost their reform thrust. Originally related to the problems of the community, they became related to the demands of the school. Concern for economy soon eliminated the teachers' involvement with the parents, and the kindergarten became an adjunct to first grade.

At first, manual education, like the kindergarten, was aimed at the inculcation of community values, not the occupational preparation of the child. Early woodworking programs were symbolic, not productive; they were designed to teach the wealthy as well as the poor the dignity of manual labor. But eventually the increasing diversity of pupils and demands for relevance in the school program subverted this common school concept and led to a differentiated curriculum. Lazerson devotes the greater part of his book to this shift "from the principles of work to the teaching of trades" (p. 132). Frank Leavitt, professor of industrial education at the University of Chicago, was prophetic when he wrote that industrial education "frankly recognizes that all cannot have and do not need the same education. . . . It means a thorough revision of our school system. . . " (p. 134). Lazerson traces this revision of program and philosophy with skill. He describes in detail the famous Douglas Commission report, which marked the shift to specific vocational training, and the ideas of State Commissioner of

Education David Snedden, the noted advocate of early differentiation.

This shift left the schools with the immense philosophical problem of who would decide what particular program suited each child. The answer, of course, was the expert educator, and the desire to make these decisions in seemingly impartial ways led to the emphasis on testing and the rise of the guidance counselor. Although these educators seemed generally unaware of the problem of self-fulfilling prophecy in the tracking of students, they did realize that differentiated programs demanded a new definition of equal educational opportunity. Snedden's response to that challenge is one of the ugly legacies of the period: "equality of opportunity can only be secured by recognition of differences which theoretically individual, may nevertheless, for practical purposes, be regarded as characterizing distinguishable groups of children" (pp. 200-201).

Lazerson's detailed attention to this theme makes his book a welcome addition to the literature on the early progressive period in education. Interestingly, he ignores the term; the work "progressive" appears nowhere in the book, although many familiar themes associated with progressive education occurred in Massachusetts. This eliminates the messy problem of definition and leaves the author free to ponder the causes and consequences of particular programs. However, he also ignores developments outside Massachusetts. This leaves the reader curious as to whether Massachusetts educators were unaffected by John Dewey's writings, for example, or by the report of the Committee of Ten. If so, it is a matter of some interest and deserves comment; if not, Lazerson's Massachusetts men are made to seem more isolated than they were. These sins of omission, however, if they are sins, do not detract from the value of the book.

Lazerson's analysis of Massachusetts education illustrates once again that the cyclical uptrend and downtrend in reform constitute more than simply the rise and fall of ideas destined to recur later in parallel form. Rather, the cycle is one in which initial goals degenerate and are transformed into different goals that may become permanently implemented in institutions. Linear developments, the residue of recurring reform cycles, often represent a distorted but recognizable version of original solutions. Thus, the demand that the school relate to life found institutional expression in a tracking system based largely on social-class origins (Lazerson, p. 201). Thus, too, the notion that asylums provided a superior environment led to the equation of incarceration and reform, which masked the shift to mere custody (Rothman, p. 238).

Reforms in America have sprung not simply from a desire for order or from the threat to the community from deviance and poverty, but also from a genuine recognition of injustice and from empathy with the plight of the ill, the exploited, and the outsider. However, the pressures of demographic growth, industrialization, and technology have tended to push institutions into implementing programs that reflect aggregate values, like security and productivity, rather than individualistic values, like personal integrity and self-discovery. The challenge of the reformer is to find ways to promote and sustain these individualistic values on a broad scale, which means, at least until some utopia arrives, that they must be compatible with the basic imperatives of a mass society. History shows us the strong tendency for aggregate values to prevail, both in short-run cycles of reform and in the long-run developments of our institutions. But history does not teach us how to escape the process.

NOTES

Kaestle: **School Reform and the Urban School**

1. Ellwood P. Cubberley, *The History of Education* (Boston: Houghton Mifflin Co., 1920), 615-616, 679, 696, 711.

2. Peter G. Filene, "An Obituary for 'The Progressive Movement,' " *American Quarterly* 22 (Spring 1970): 34.

3. See Robert S. Lynd and Helen Merrell Lynd, *Middletown in Transition: A Study in Cultural Conflicts* (New York: Harcourt Brace, 1937), Chap. 6. Caroline F. Ware *(Greenwich Village, 1920-1930* [Boston: Houghton Mifflin Co., 1935], Chap. 11) describes the rejection of liberal Progressive practices by the public school staff and parents of Greenwich Village. They were more like Middletowners than Ware's "Villagers."

4. William Diamond, "On the Dangers of an Urban Interpretation of History," in *Historiography and Urbanization: Essays in American History in Honor of W. Stull Holt,* ed. Eric F. Goldman (Baltimore, Md.: Johns Hopkins University Press, 1941), 67-108.

5. Gerald N. Grob, *The State and the Mentally Ill: A History of Worcester State Hospital in Massachusetts, 1830-1920* (Chapel Hill: University of North Carolina Press, 1966), 136-142, 165-186.

6. John L. Thomas, "Romantic Reform in America, 1815-1865," *American Quarterly* 17 (Winter 1965): 656-681; Timothy L. Smith, *Revivalism and Social Reform in Mid-Nineteenth Century America* (New York: Abingdon Press, 1957).

7. Ferdinand Tönnies, *Community and Society (Gemeinschaft und Gesellschaft)*, tr. and ed. Charles P. Loomis (East Lansing: Michigan State University Press, 1957); Robert H. Wiebe, *The Search for Order, 1877-1920* (New York: Hill and Wang, 1967).

FIVE

Strangers at Home: Schooling, Exclusion, and Acculturation

On the History of Minority Group Education in the United States, by *Diane Ravitch*

The School Achievement of Immigrant Children: 1900-1930, by *Michael R. Olneck* and *Marvin Lazerson*

Success and Failure in Adult Education: The Immigrant Experience, 1914-1924, by *Maxine S. Seller*

The social benefits expected to accrue from formal education in the United States required inclusive public schooling opportunities, for strategic if not humanitarian reasons. Unless all young people had access to them, the schools clearly could not fulfill their assigned roles in promoting national community through common moral training and what came to be known as political socialization. The latter included literacy as a necessary precondition for effective citizenship. Support for compulsory school attendance legislation, which gained momentum during the second half of the nineteenth century, reflected not only a desire to postpone the entrance of teenagers into the job market but also a recognition of the schools' more general contributions to domestic well-being. Reality fell short of the ideal. Patterns of exclusion from school emerged, some of which remain effective. Detecting and assessing direct exclusion and its consequences are relatively easy matters. De facto exclusion, however, can take subtle forms. Consider the welcome experienced by Catholic children in public schools which

149

routinely employed the King James Version of the Bible in religious exercises and history textbooks with decidedly anti-Roman interpreta- tions of the Reformation. Consider immigrant children who learned in school to disparage the cultural traditions and language of their parents. Such forms of exclusion occurred. What is more difficult is establishing the extent to which they were systemic. More complex still is the task of assessing their impact. As David Tyack has argued, such research helps to reconstruct what may well be the central theme in American educational history. Given the rationale for public educa- tion in the United States, assessing the treatment of minorities in schools illuminates profoundly their overall effectiveness.

In the first essay in this chapter, Diane Ravitch interprets the unique developments and complexities within the educational history of selected minority groups and comments on the difficulty of general- izing from these experiences. Michael Olneck and Marvin Lazerson caution against making generalizations that do not take into account local variations in the school achievement of children, even when they represent the same immigrant group. In addition to empirical data, they utilize cultural and ethnographic sources to interpret the differ- ing school experiences of Southern Italians and Russian Jews. Maxine Seller's article compares the successes and failures of school-based ed- ucational programs for immigrant adults and the formal and informal education made available within immigrant communities. The education of women is notably missing from this chapter. Jill Conway's article in Chapter Seven actually serves a dual purpose. Her discussion of the education of women in the United States provides perspective for future historiography, but it also speaks to the question of exclusion in schools.

On the History of Minority Group Education in the United States

Diane Ravitch

Because of the heterogeneous character of the American popula- tion, the education of minority groups is a controversial subject — one

Reprinted, with permission, from *Teachers College Record* 78 (December 1976), 213-228.

which is frequently politicized by those who study it. Educational historians have tended to interpret this issue in accordance with their own political and social orientation. The dominant perspective, until the past decade, was that the American public schools were the highest realization of the democratic ideal, that they provided equal opportunity to all and rapid mobility to the deserving. This view, even at its most popular, never received universal assent; such distinguished historians as George Counts and Merle Curti criticized it vigorously. In recent years, this idealistic and optimistic vision has been dethroned by a barrage of criticism, and a new construct has been raised up in its place. The new interpretation holds that public schooling has been a capitalist tool of indoctrination, that it has been purposefully used to stamp out cultural diversity, and that it has been slyly (or brutally) imposed on unwilling masses by arrogant reformers.

Whereas the old concept was oversimplified in its optimism, the new concept — which permeates the work of contemporary New Left historians of education — is oversimplified in its cynicism. The former too easily proclaimed the inevitable triumph of democracy, equality, and opportunity; the latter too glibly perceives oppression, indoctrination, and conspiratorial behavior.[1]

Both interpretations are highly ideological, the one intent on proving the success of American education, the other intent on proving its failure. And it is not surprising that researchers with ideological blinders tend to find what they seek, to confirm what they previously believed. Today there are few adherents to the success theory. For a variety of reasons — the despair which followed the political assassinations of the Kennedy brothers and Martin Luther King, the anger which flowed from urban riots and the Vietnam War, and the cynicism which followed the Watergate disclosures — the failure theory of the radical revisionists is strongly in the ascendancy.

None of us is entirely free from a value orientation, but I submit that a dispassionate effort to see the broad spectrum of minority group education in American history leads to the conclusion that neither of these interpretations is adequate, that both are clichés that mislead rather than enlighten. As general interpretations, they are both distortions of history.

It is not that the truth lies in the middle, somewhere between optimism and cynicism, but that it is too complicated to be explained by simplistic slogans. Not every minority group is or was similar; some did not want to be assimilated, but others did. Each group must be studied separately, within the context of its own interests and with due consideration of the historical situation.

Just to consider the types of minorities in American history is to have some sense of the problems and responses that have characterized educational efforts. There have been racial minorities, religious minorities, linguistic minorities, and national minorities. Each has had its own educational needs, which have been met or not met in different ways; it is historically unjustified to assert that all have been crushed by their education into a homogeneous, deracinated mass.

When each group is looked at on its own terms, several important points emerge. First, most groups are not monolithic; it is fallacious to speak of the views of *all* Catholics or Poles or blacks or any other group. Second, the way a particular group was treated differed, sometimes dramatically, from one time period to another. Third, even within the same time period, a particular group often encountered inconsistent policies in different locales. Fourth, not all education of minorities took place in public schools; further, the decision to respect the right of minority groups to maintain private schools was itself public policy. Fifth, the current emphasis on oppression of minority groups is usually lacking cross-national perspective; Americanization through schooling, even at its most assimilationist, was more benign than the physical elimination of those who are different (which has occurred in some countries with minority populations).[2]

HOW SHOULD A NATION SCHOOL ITS PEOPLE?

For most of the United States's existence, there has been no national policy of education. Communities and states devised their own arrangements for schooling, free of any pressure from the federal government. While there were many variations, there were two basic approaches: One was the common school, open to all children in the community (though "all children" was often defined as "all white children") and supported at least in part by public funds; the other approach was state subsidy of private schools. Various communities experimented with the latter approach (sometimes in combination with common schools). Some states sponsored private academies; some cities granted public funds to private philanthropic societies to educate poor children. New York City, during the first quarter of the nineteenth century, directly funded nearly a dozen church schools.[3]

The New England common school, originally set up by the Protestant leadership for its own educational purposes in the seventeenth century, was secularized during the eighteenth century, and by 1826 was hailed as the quintessential American common school by Massachusetts school reformer James G. Carter. The common school was not merely a good and useful way of providing schooling; in Carter's view, it was America's example "to the civilized world," a school supported by all members of the community for the instruction of "all classes of the community—the high, the low, the rich, and the poor."[4] And this common school was more than just a school. It was a form of egalitarian social action because it promised to eliminate factitious distinctions and to guard against the formation of an aristocratic class by democratizing knowledge. That the common school was an agency of social and political reform was widely popularized in the late 1830s and 1840s by Horace Mann.

However, the common school itself was not the invention of zealous reformers like Carter, Mann, and Henry Barnard. Most communities outside the South moved spontaneously toward some variant of common schooling, not for ideological reasons, but because it seemed to be the most practical way of setting up schools. Horace Mann and his generation of reformers may have been the articulators, rather than the initiators, of a trend that was already well grounded. Interest in public schooling can be found in many cities and states in the first quarter of the nineteenth century; Albert Fishlow has documented a high level of school enrollment which predated the flowering of the common school movement. In Wisconsin, still a frontier region in the early nineteenth century, community-sponsored schools were organized which became the forerunners of a state system of common schools. As early as 1818, the Virginia state legislature, by a single vote, failed to establish a state school system. Even without the New Englanders' ideology, state-supported common schools were under consideration or in rudimentary form in many states.[5]

During the second half of the nineteenth century, public schools were firmly established throughout the country; the New England ideology, which asserted that the survival of the American republic was dependent on the common schools, became commonplace. The ideology seems to have been more a selling point for public support than an article of faith, however. If Americans really believed that their nation's institutions and freedom depended on the strength of the common schools, they would have prohibited nonpublic education. But Americans apparently respected freedom of choice more

than the common school ideology, for private schools abounded.
Many minorities took full advantage of the freedom to maintain their
own schools, and there were Catholic schools, Jewish schools, German
schools, French schools, Polish schools, and numerous other schools
run by benevolent agencies and small sects.

While there were bitter struggles over subsidizing Catholic schools,
the right of nonpublic institutions to exist was never seriously in
jeopardy until the 1920s. An initiative measure . . . narrowly adopted
by the voters of Oregon in 1922 require[d] parents to send their
children to public schools. The bill, the sponsors of which included the
Ku Klux Klan, reflected the superpatriotism of the postwar period.
The purpose of the measure, aimed especially at immigrants and
Catholics, was to forcibly Americanize all children by putting them into the same public classrooms. David Tyack has described how the
Klan publicists employed a twisted version of the common school ideal
to argue "that the public school should mix children of all the
people — all ethnic groups, all economic classes — in order to produce
social solidarity. . . ." Klan spokesmen did not recognize the irony of
their advocacy of social, racial, and economic integration. The attorney for Oregon used traditional egalitarian rhetoric to maintain
that "the great danger overshadowing all others which confront the
American people is the danger of class hatred. History will
demonstrate the fact that it is the rock upon which many a republic
has been broken, and I don't know any better way to fortify the next
generation against that insidious poison than to require that the poor
and the rich, the people of all classes and distinction, and of all different religious beliefs, shall meet in the common schools, which are
the great American melting pot. . . ."[6]

Happily for the nonpublic schools of America, the United States
Supreme Court in 1925 declared Oregon's law unconstitutional and
held it to be an unreasonable interference with the liberty of parents to
direct their children's education. The state does not have the power,
wrote the court in *Pierce* v. *Society of Sisters,* "to standardize its children by forcing them to accept instruction from public teachers only."[7]

AFTER WORLD WAR I

The period during and after World War I was characterized by
heightened patriotism, xenophobia, and fear of subversion by un-
American elements. After years of partial restrictions, immigration

was finally reduced to a trickle, and educators turned their attention to "Americanizing" the nation's large immigrant population. In many public schools, Americanization took the form of citizenship instruction and literacy classes for all ages; it invariably meant a strong emphasis on patriotic exercises and the teaching of idealized American history and hero tales.

There is little evidence that immigrants were spiritually destroyed by these kinds of Americanization efforts. Those historians who infer that they were apparently see the immigrants as easily intimidated. To be sure, Americanization efforts were frequently crude and chauvinistic, and many an immigrant child was made to feel ashamed of his family's speech and customs. But to understand this process solely as a one-way relationship between victim and oppressor is to miss an interesting aspect of American history. Many immigrants had a strong sense of the value of their own heritage. Jane Addams recalled lecturing Greek immigrants on the glories of America's past; when she was done, one of her audience remarked, quietly but assuredly, that his own Greek ancestors were better than her Anglo-Saxon forebears.[8] While imbibing the public and private Americanization programs, the immigrants participated in a vigorous cultural life which flourished among those groups that wished to preserve ties to their heritage and to their compatriots from the old country. German[s], Irish[men], Italians, Slavs, Jews, Finns, Hungarians, Greeks, Poles, and others had ethnic associations, their own press, and a broad range of communal activities.

A remarkable fact, which is rarely noted by historians bent on proving the cultural rapacity of Americanization programs, is that immigrant groups themselves were frequently sponsors of Americanization. Timothy L. Smith has documented an immigrant thirst for education which is sharply at variance with the radical historians' image of coerced and brutalized immigrants. Smith points out that the night school movement was started by immigrant associations, then adopted by public school agencies. Early parochial schools "stressed the learning of English quite as much as the preservation of Old World culture." Far from fighting to withdraw to ethnic enclaves, immigrants "realized that to learn to speak and read English was to make their investment of time, expense, and emotion gilt-edged. The earliest volumes of virtually any Slavic newspaper published by religious or secular organizations in America carried lessons in English, announced the publication of simple dictionaries or grammars, and exhorted readers to learn the new tongue as a means of getting and holding a better job." But their self-Americanization was not necessarily at the expense of their cultural values; Slovaks, Greeks, Hungarians, Serbs, Roumanians, and Russians sent their children to public schools, but also "insisted upon frequent and sometimes daily attendance at the church for catechetical instruction, precisely as Orthodox Jewish parents sent their youngsters from public schools to the synagogue in the late afternoon or on Sunday."[9]

Similarly, Mordecai Soltes's study of the Yiddish press describes it as "an Americanizing agency." At the time of World War I, there were five Yiddish-language newspapers with a circulation of half a million readers. These newspapers consistently supported the public schools as well as supplementary religious instruction. The Yiddish press, wrote Soltes, "actively cooperates with the civic and patriotic purposes of the school." To assume today that immigrants who accepted and furthered Americanization had been indoctrinated is to credit the immigrants with little intelligence or self-interest. It is more likely that they took from Americanization programs what they wanted and ignored what they did not want.[10]

The ugly side of the postwar Americanization crusade stemmed from intense anti-German feelings, which caused most states to adopt laws restricting foreign-language instruction in both public and private schools. Many states required English as the basic language of instruction (there were foreign language schools where English was rarely spoken). Some states, like Nebraska, went further; in 1919 it prohibited the teaching of any modern language in the first eight grades of all public and nonpublic schools. When a parochial school teacher in Nebraska was convicted of teaching German, he carried his appeal to the Supreme Court. In *Meyer* v. *Nebraska* (1923), without questioning the state's power to require English instruction, the Supreme Court overturned Nebraska's law and reaffirmed the teacher's right to teach and the parent's right to engage a teacher without state interference. Similarly, when Americanizers passed a law in Hawaii to force the use of English as the exclusive language of instruction in Japanese private schools, the Japanese went to court and won.[11]

What tends to be overlooked in focusing on the efforts to suppress diversity is the remarkable diversity that did exist in many public and private schools. Private foreign-language schools were established by Germans, Poles, French Canadians, Czechs, Norwegians, Dutch,

Lithuanians, Jews, Japanese, Koreans, and Chinese, among others. Bilingual programs could be found in many nineteenth-century public schools, particularly in the Midwest, where there were large islands of Germans, and in the Far West, where both California and New Mexico had Spanish bilingual schools. Baltimore and Indianapolis had German bilingual school systems during the nineteenth century, and Cincinnati had a strong German bilingual program from 1840 until 1917.[12]

Heinz Kloss, a German scholar of national minority laws, has found American policy towards its non-English-speaking minorities to be remarkably tolerant. Americans have the right to use their mother tongue at home and in public; the right to establish private cultural, economic, and social institutions in which their mother tongue is spoken; the right to cultivate their mother tongue in private schools — which are not only tolerated but granted a state charter of tax-exempt status. Kloss does not agree with those radical historians who argue that the homogeneity of the American people is the result of persistently coercive educational efforts to strip minorities of their differences. He holds that,

. . . the non-English ethnic groups in the United States of America were Anglicized not because of nationality laws which were unfavorable towards their languages but in spite of nationality laws favorable to them. Not by legal provisions and measures of authorities, not by the state did the nationalities become assimilated, but by the absorbing power of the unusually highly developed American society. The nationalities could be given as many opportunities as possible to retain their identity, yet the achievements of the Anglo-American society and the possibilities for individual achievements and advancements which this society offered were so attractive that the descendants of the "aliens" sooner or later voluntarily integrated themselves into this society.[13]

In much the same vein, Joshua Fishman attributes the rapid absorption of non-English-speaking minorities to the openness of American society, not to educational coercion. Noting that American nationalism has always been "nonethnic" in character, Fishman writes that "there was no apparent logical opposition between the ethnicity of incoming immigrants and the ideology of America. Individually and collectively immigrants could accept the latter without consciously denying the former. However, once they accepted the goals and values of Americans, the immigrants were already on the road to accepting their life-styles, their customs, and their language."[14]

Assimilation was facilitated, if Kloss and Fishman are correct, by *lack* of oppression. Specific instances of discrimination against foreign children have usually been traced to the attitudes of teachers, an Anglocentric curriculum, and a generalized American disparagement of Old World cultures. More often than not, this discrimination was sporadic rather than systematic. Had it been more substantive and more threatening, it would probably have impeded assimilation by raising immigrant self-consciousness and resistance.

THE CASE OF THE AMERICAN INDIAN

Where educational oppression of a minority was blatant and purposeful, as in the case of the American Indian, the policy was a disaster which neither educated nor assimilated. Through most of American history, missionaries and government officials took it as their duty to civilize and Christianize the Indians; usually this meant that Indian culture and language and folkways had to be eliminated. While some were weaned away from "the blanket," as the saying went, most simply developed a strong internal resistance to the new behavior. Forced efforts at assimilation tended to produce precisely the opposite of what was intended.[15]

Christian missionaries tried to bring white civilization to the Indians throughout the colonial period. In the mission schools, Indian children were given English names, haircuts, and baths; they learned to sit at benches and to use knives and forks. Missionaries strove to teach them the work ethic; they wanted the Indians to take up farming and to appreciate the value of private property. Though there were some successes for the missionaries, they were time and again frustrated by the Indians' cultural stubbornness. To the chagrin of the missionaries, many Indians never ceased to doubt the superiority or at least equality of their own values.[16]

From 1778 until 1871 the federal government signed treaties with Indian tribes in which the Indians ceded land and the government pledged various public services, such as education and medical care. In 1802 and 1819 Congress appropriated funds to promote "civilization among the aborigines." This money, commonly called the "civilization fund," was apportioned among missionary organizations which cooperated with government agents. Government policy during the nineteenth century was to push the Indians farther and farther west, forcibly when necessary, to satisfy the expanding American nation's hunger for land. Education policy was an adjunct of the government's land policy: By civilizing the Indians and turning them from hunters to farmers, it was hoped that their need for land would diminish.

Most missionary schools favored bilingual instruction using Indian languages, but after the Civil War the federal government began to insist on faster assimilation. A government report in 1868 urged the establishment of Indian schools with compulsory attendance where "their barbarous dialects would be blotted out and the English language substituted." After the treaty period ended in 1871, the government began to displace the bilingual mission schools with government schools where only English was spoken. The establishment of these schools also caused the elimination of many Indian-initiated schools. The Cherokees, in particular, had created their own school system, which sent graduates to Eastern colleges; further, they published a bilingual newspaper using a Cherokee alphabet devised by a member of the tribe in 1821. Schools were also run by Choctaws, Creeks, and Seminoles.[17]

In the 1870s, with several Indian tribes making their last stand in ferocious battles, the federal government launched a new educational program designed to extirpate Indian culture. The model for the new system was the Carlisle Indian School in Pennsylvania, a boarding school founded in 1879:

The school was run in a rigid military fashion, with heavy emphasis on rustic vocational education. The goal was to provide a maximum of rapid coercive assimilation into white society. It was designed to separate a child from his reservation and family, strip him of his tribal lore and mores, force the complete abandonment of his native language, and prepare him in such a way that he would never return to his people.... The children were usually kept in boarding school for 8 years during which time they were not permitted to see their parents or relatives.[18]

The founder of Carlisle, General R. H. Pratt, had a slogan: "Get the Indian away from the reservation into civilization, and when you get him there, keep him." By 1886 no federal funds went to any school where Indian children were instructed in any language other than English.[19]

The federal government, relying on the Carlisle philosophy, provided both day schools and boarding schools, emphasizing the latter. It should be noted, however, that many Indian children were not in federal schools but in state-run public schools and in mission schools. In the early 1920s, before there had been any serious criticism of the

Carlisle approach, there were as many Indian children in public schools as in federal schools.

Not until 1926 did government officials begin to question the effectiveness of their Indian education policies. For one thing, the 1920 census revealed that Indian illiteracy was a shocking 36 percent, as compared to 6 percent for the population as a whole. The Secretary of the Interior commissioned a study of government's Indian policies by the Institute for Governmental Research (later called the Brookings Institution). This study, called the Meriam report for its director, Lewis Meriam, had a dramatic effect on the assumptions that undergirded government policy.

Published in 1928, the Meriam report was a sharp repudiation of the policies of the previous half century. It urged the government to renounce coercive assimilation and, in its stead, to "respect the rights of the Indian . . . as a human being living in a free country," to recognize "the good in the economic and social life of the Indians in their religion and ethics," and to seek "to develop it and build on it rather than to crush out all that is Indian." The report criticized the emphasis on boarding schools, where nearly 40 percent of Indian children were enrolled. Many of these schools were overcrowded, poorly maintained, and "grossly inadequate." But the worst indictment was that they separated the Indian child from his family and community, "where he belongs."[20]

The Meriam report embodied pluralistic ideas whose time had come; its recommendations became guideposts during the New Deal era under the leadership of John Collier, Commissioner of Indian Affairs from 1933 until 1945. Congress passed an act in 1934 to strengthen tribal self-government, and Collier launched a program of cultural freedom for the Indians. For the first time, the Bureau of Indian Affairs repudiated coercive assimilationism and emphasized bilingualism, native teachers, adult education, and preservation of the Indians' cultural heritage. In 1933 the federal schools were still overwhelmingly boarding schools; by 1943 most federal schools had become day schools.

During most of Collier's tenure, his innovative approaches were under attack by Congress, which grew increasingly suspicious of Collier's emphasis on Indian culture and deemphasis of assimilation. With a resurgence of superpatriotism, congressional pressure finally forced a reversal of federal policy and a return to the boarding school approach in the 1950s. Appropriately, the Commissioner of Indian Affairs appointed in 1950 to revive this policy was Dillon S. Myer, who had supervised the relocation of thousands of Japanese-Americans during World War II.

Coercive assimilation was again repudiated in the 1960s, at first tentatively during the Kennedy years, then decisively during the Johnson administration. Both the Economic Opportunity Act of 1964 and the Elementary and Secondary Education Act of 1965 gave impetus to policies based on respect for the rights of Indian parents and Indian communities; furthermore, they set into motion political forces within the Indian communities that will make any future reversion extremely improbable. The implicit trends received official recognition by President Johnson in 1968, when he urged that the highest priority be given to improving Indian education and transferring the control of Indian schools to Indians.[21]

The story of Indian education in the United States illustrates the variability of the historical experience — even when it is that of a clearly oppressed group. It is a history that most nearly fits the radical concept of education as a tool of coercion and imposition. Yet to read it only from that perspective would be to miss a number of intriguing divergences. The very substantial shift to pluralistic policies in the late 1920s and then again in the 1960s underlines the struggle between opposing philosophies and the differentness of time periods. The existence of a Cherokee school system in the nineteenth century suggests that Indians themselves were not necessarily hostile to schooling — as the radical analysts would have it — but to cultural suppression. It further suggests that a policy of cultural respect, in this as in other instances, might have stimulated Indian educational efforts and, ultimately, Indian assimilation on terms set by Indians.

BLACK EDUCATION

The case of black educational history, like that of other minority groups, also defies the simplistic labels of ideologists, but for different reasons. Whereas government policy attempted to force the assimilation and deethnicization of the Indians, it explicitly sought to prevent the assimilation of blacks. Whereas the cultural aspirations of European immigrant groups were at least tolerated and frequently encouraged, those of blacks were ignored, or, worse, mocked. The vicious doctrine of white supremacy was used to justify social and economic repression of blacks, in both the North and the South.

And here, too, broad generalizations tend to oversimplify and distort a complicated picture. Those radical historians who speak assuredly of education as a tool of oppression fail to account for the slaveholders' deadly fear of education. "Believing that slaves could not be enlightened without developing in them a longing for liberty," the slave states one after another adopted laws prohibiting the education of slaves. Some states, viewing ignorance as the best social control, expelled free Negroes because they might have access to abolitionist literature and spread the contagion of insurrection to illiterate blacks. To salve their Christian consciences, some planters encouraged verbal religious instruction for their slaves.[22]

To portray blacks solely as victims locked into illiteracy is to overlook the tenacious struggle of countless individual blacks to filch an education even within the slave system. Some slaves developed personal relationships with their masters and, as house servants, acquired literacy; some plantations, for their own internal purposes, trained slaves as artisans, carpenters, blacksmiths, weavers, and tailors. Both Woodson and Bullock have found numerous accounts of slaves whose zeal for learning could not be denied, no matter how many laws were passed.[23]

Another source of education in the antebellum South was mission schools. They were available to only a few blacks, principally those who were favored household servants and those who were free. (The number of free blacks in the South was not insignificant: Bullock holds that it grew from 32,523 in 1790 to 258,346 in 1860.) Despite the state laws, courageous blacks and whites maintained clandestine schools for blacks.[24]

These educational opportunities, limited though they were, provided what Bullock has called "a hidden passage" within the institution of slavery—one which permitted the development of a potential middle class. Far from having schooling imposed on them by arrogant reformers, blacks resorted to extraordinary means to obtain an education that state law denied them. Indeed, some former slaves who had by stealth and iron-willed persistence acquired literacy while in bondage became highly effective spokesmen for the abolitionist movement in the North.

Blacks in the antebellum North, usually a small minority, were generally either confined to segregated schools or excluded from public schools altogether. Many colored schools had been opened by philanthropists at a time when the only free schools were pauper schools. Consequently, when common schools were introduced the idea of racial segregation was already commonplace in many cities. New Jersey was unusual in that it never practiced legal segregation. Most northern and western states, for varying periods and in various communities, maintained racially segregated schools. In at least two instances (Boston and Hartford), separate schools were instituted at the request of the black population,[25] largely because of the desire to protect black children from white hostility.

After the Civil War, the Freedmen's Bureau was responsible for providing southern blacks with education. A network of schools run by benevolent societies, missionaries, and the Freedmen's Bureau sprang into existence, staffed mostly by northern teachers, many of them trained in New England colleges and fired with Christian zeal. The curricula in the mission schools, which reflected the New England bias of their teachers, stressed liberal arts rather than practical education. Many of them taught classical languages, which southern whites thought absurd. Senator John C. Calhoun of South Carolina had once said that he would be willing to believe in the possibility of black equality if ever he met a black who could parse a Latin verb or write the Greek alphabet. According to Horace Mann Bond, this oft-quoted remark was frequently cited in the autobiographical accounts of college-educated blacks of the first free generation. In Bond's view, the New Englanders' faith in liberal education was eventually justified: "Based on the academic successes of first, second, and even third generation descendants of the students of the early mission schools, available evidence suggests that these institutions provided for Southern Negroes some of the most effective educational institutions the world has ever known."[26]

Southerners complained that the Yankee schoolteachers imposed their ideals and aspirations on their Negro students, but there is abundant evidence that the newly freed blacks eagerly sought the formal schooling so long denied them. Furthermore, those blacks who were delegates to state constitutional conventions in the South took a positive attitude towards the spread of public schooling. Echoing the sentiments of common school reformers of an earlier generation, black representatives argued for compulsory schooling and for schools that would be open to all, without regard to race. Despite enormous political and financial obstacles, public school systems began to operate during Reconstruction, and Negroes responded enthusiastically.[27]

The end of Reconstruction and the abandonment of southern blacks by the federal government coincided with the onset of a series of civil rights reversals in the Supreme Court, the impact of which was to erode the Negro's constitutional protection and to sanction the system of segregation that the South fashioned to supplant slavery. The political enfeeblement of the black population, achieved by intimidation after Reconstruction, was written into law across the South in the two decades after 1890; loss of the ballot through such devices as poll taxes and literacy tests assured the Negro's political impotence. A disenfranchised people could have no influence in the shaping of educational policy, no voice when school funds were unfairly apportioned. It was a classical vicious circle: Illiteracy was the justification given for excluding blacks from the polls (though equally illiterate whites could vote by grace of grandfather clauses); their exclusion left them powerless to contest for educational facilities with which to remedy their illiteracy.

Just as General Pratt's Carlisle Indian School became the model for Indian education, General S. C. Armstrong's Hampton Normal and Agricultural Institute became the southern model for Negro education (actually, Pratt was following the Hampton example when he established Carlisle). Founded in 1868, Hampton embodied Armstrong's view about the special educational needs of the Negro race: Armstrong championed industrial education, not only to make the black an efficient worker but to improve his moral character. His most influential disciple was Booker T. Washington, who opened Tuskegee Institute in 1881; as an educator, Washington came to symbolize the idea that blacks required a special education, one that equipped them to adjust to their place in a caste system. The Hampton-Tuskegee idea was applauded by the white South as an appropriate education for blacks; it quickly found favor with influential white philanthropists, who seized on the chance to aid black education without offending white southern sensibilities. Critics of this emphasis on industrial education included not only W. E. B. Dubois but also W. T. Harris, the United States Commissioner of Education, who argued forcefully on behalf of liberal education for blacks.[28]

What guaranteed the predominance of the Hampton-Tuskegee

model was the political impotence of blacks. As late as 1889, according to Bullock, there was little difference between white and black schools in the apportionment of funds, the length of the school term, or teachers' salaries; but with the legal disenfranchisement of blacks in the 1890s discrimination grew. The industrial education idea provided a convenient excuse for spending less on black schools and teachers, since industrial education was supposedly simpler and cheaper than the traditional schooling given to whites. But historians today do not know with any certainty to what extent black schools in the South adopted, rejected, or combined industrial and academic education. What is needed is a painstaking investigation of individual schools, which is unlikely to occur so long as historians consider the question of black educational history to be a settled one.

It is rare to discover an exploration of black successes such as Horace Mann Bond's *Black American Scholars,* a study of the family background and schooling of black recipients of the doctoral degree in the period 1957-1962. Bond identifies certain remarkable black families whose educational aspirations and achievements have been repeated across several generations. He locates black high schools that produced unusual numbers of scholars. Foremost among these was the M Street School (later called the Paul Laurence Dunbar High School) in Washington, D.C. Founded in 1870, the school consistently symbolized academic excellence. Its teachers were graduates of the nation's best colleges, its curriculum was college preparatory, its standards were high, and its graduates went to top colleges. Dunbar graduates received more doctorates than any other black high school in the period studied by Bond. Bond singled out other urban schools from which doctoral recipients had graduated, like the Frederick Douglass High School in Baltimore and the McDonough 25 High School in New Orleans. Certain black schools in small towns produced unusual numbers of doctorates in relation to their size. Some of these schools were former mission schools with high academic standards; others were located in towns where there were one or more black families with strong educational backgrounds or where there was even a single black educator who inspired young people to go to college. There was no evident explanation for the Wayne County Training School in Jesup, Georgia, which had the highest ratio of doctorates to graduates of any black school in the country. Three of its graduates received doctorates between 1957 and 1962, though its typical graduating class was only 14. The point about these black schools in the South is not that they were good, but that we know so little about them; and the more we are tied to the familiar labels applied to black educational history, the less we are inclined to try to reconstruct what was actually happening in individual schools.

The number of black doctorates was small, and the barriers blocking their academic paths were high. Their success is a tribute to them, not to the racist system that they overcame. Yet, it is noteworthy that the system made their success extremely difficult but not impossible. Blacks were more often oppressed by the education that they did not receive than by the education that they did receive.

Another fresh approach to black educational history is embodied in Vincent P. Franklin's "The Education of Black Philadelphia: A History of Race Relations and Education in a Northern City, 1900-1950," a recent doctoral dissertation [completed] at the University of Chicago. Franklin critically examines the education of blacks in Philadelphia within a broad social, economic, and political context. A lesser historian would have been content merely to document white racism in school policies. Franklin, however, analyzes the energetic response of black Philadelphians to the school system, and, in particular, their struggle to change repugnant policies. His illustration of indigenous community education programs, both formal and informal, creates a sense of a community that was determined to maintain its dignity and its cultural heritage.

BLACK EDUCATION SINCE 1954

In the twenty-two years since state-enforced school segregation was ruled unconstitutional, the education of blacks has been as varied from one school to the next and from one city to the next as it is for other groups. Most whites and blacks are uncertain about the best education for blacks, surely as uncertain as they are about the best education for whites. At different times and in different communities, some have advocated the pursuit of excellence in black education, which others have attacked as elitism; some have advocated egalitarian educational policies, which others have attacked as catering to the lowest common denominator; some have advocated racial integration as a first principle, which others have attacked as mindless assimilationism; some have advocated black control of black schools, which others have attacked as naive separatism. A large part of the uncertainty about the right direction for the education of blacks is the confusion of educational and social issues. It is not clear today whether the major problem is how to raise the educational level of the black population or how to bring about full racial integration. At the time of the *Brown* decision, racial integration appeared to be synonymous with quality education—that to achieve one was to achieve the other. There is mounting evidence that this is not necessarily so, but there remain many who believe that racial integration is an end in itself, not a means.

To the extent that a governmental policy has developed towards black education in the years since 1954, it embodies the view of the integration movement that all-black schools are inherently inferior. This derives from the statement in *Brown* that "separate educational facilities are inherently unequal." At first it seemed that separate educational facilities were unequal because the state had set them aside for blacks and compelled blacks to attend them; it now seems that such facilities are unequal because only blacks attend them.

The shift in meaning is subtle but significant, for it suggests that stigma is attached not just to the illegal act of segregation but to the concentration of blacks themselves. "Real" integration is taken to mean that no school has a black majority. To effect this, the courts have been asked and have ordered the dispersion of black pupils throughout school districts, or in some instances across traditional district lines. If such a policy emanated from the government, it might appear to be a policy of cultural homogenization since one of its purposes is to break up black concentrations.

This trend toward dispersion of blacks as an educational and social strategy is a development of the last decade, and it is unique in the history of minority group education. Other groups have asked to be let alone, either in public or in private schools; or to have governmental support for the promotion of their own cultures; or to be given the same treatment as other groups and access to the same facilities. At times, blacks have asked for some or all of these approaches. Only in the past decade have black organizations asked, as a matter of right, that the children of their racial group be dispersed among the majority population.

SOME CONCLUSIONS

This brief attempt at synthesizing the experiences of a broad variety
of minority groups has necessarily condensed the lives and experiences
of millions of diverse people into a short essay. To try to do so in a
sense violates the point I have been urging about the complexity of
each group's experience. What I have hoped to do is to rescue the
topic from an ideological bog and to argue for investigations which go
beyond the radical homilies of the 1960s. Some of the conclusions I
draw are as follows: In a free society with a free press, education liber-
ates more often than it oppresses. In such a society, ignorance and illiteracy are the most dangerous instruments of social control. Advocates
of schooling had mixed motives, which were more good than bad.
Every individual and every group should have the freedom to decide
whether to assimilate into the general population. Political powerlessness is a precondition to educational discrimination. Different
members of different groups have different educational goals at different times and in different places. In historiographical terms, this
essay is a plea for less assertion and more documentation, less ideological posturing and more mining of source materials.

Until late in the nineteenth century, this nation was considered by
its majority to be a white Protestant country; at some time near the
turn of the century, it became a white Christian country; after World
War II, it was a white man's country. During the past several years it
has become a multiethnic, multiracial country intensely aware of differences of every kind, a country in which almost everyone thinks of
himself or herself as a member of a minority group. Having once been
a society in which differences were shunned, accents studiously un-
learned, and foreignness somewhat suspect, the United States has become a nation where people are seeking out their long-forgotten roots,
learning ancestral languages, celebrating the traditions that their
fathers (and mothers) rejected.

This very celebration of our differences may signal the relative un-
importance of those differences. Joshua Fishman, writing about language groups, wrote that ethnic group schools teach *about* ethnicity,
whereas authentic ethnicity consists of *living* ethnically: "In the
school, ethnicity became self-conscious. It was something to be
'studied,' 'valued,' 'appreciated,' and 'believed in.' It became a 'cause.'
As it was raised to the level of ideology, belief system, national symbol-

ism, or selective sentimentality it also ceased being ethnic in the original and authentic sense." Thus, Italians and Poles and Irishmen and
Jews can march in each others' parades; their daughters and sons can
and do intermarry without causing any family rupture. Relations between blacks and whites have not reached that point, though inter-
racial contacts at all levels have increased steadily over the past
generation.[29]

But what do we want? Do we want cultures that differ significantly
from each other, or do we want cultures that differ in name and history only? Do we want schooling that accentuates awareness of cultural
differences or do we want schooling that minimizes them? Do we want
ethnicity to persist or do we want it to slip away unobtrusively? It is this
very ambivalence about the value of ethnicity and pluralism that pre-
vents our educational patterns from having a single guiding principle.

To study the history of the education of minority groups is to become aware of the inappropriateness of applying sweeping ideological
labels to the diverse experiences of all minorities. What is needed is
more nuance and more discernment, not less. The task for historians
of education today is to set aside tendentious generalizations and to
search for a sense of once-living people with once-vital aspirations, for
the cultures within which they lived, and for the processes by which
they were educated.

The School Achievement of Immigrant Children: 1900-1930

Michael R. Olneck
Marvin Lazerson

Public schooling has held a central place in the mythologies
celebrating the assimilation of immigrants into American life. It is no
surprise, then, to find that the historiography of schooling and immigration has been characterized by a good deal of polemic and a
paucity of data. Depending upon their political persuasions, scholars

Reprinted, with permission, from *History of Education Quarterly* 14 (Winter 1974),
453-482.

have either described the schools as an immense success in providing opportunities or as reactionary institutions designed to perpetuate the existing class order.[1]

Scholars have also tended to concentrate on "the immigrant experience," and to neglect differences between nationality groups. While the popular imagination has been dominated by the idea of the melting pot, professional scholarship has tended to focus on the themes of alienation and disorientation.[2] We feel that the tendencies to characterize the history of immigrants and schools in these monolithic fashions have seriously obscured complex and varied patterns of experience, and have prevented historians from pursuing the kinds of comparative analyses which such patterns demand. While we cannot offer a full treatment of all the questions which might be asked about immigrants and schools, we hope that the data and analyses presented here will direct attention to where it properly belongs: the dimensions, sources, and consequences of differential patterns of adaptation to American institutions.[3]

The issue which we treat is limited, but it is a beginning point of an effort to understand the roles schools played in assimilating immigrants into American culture, and in offering them avenues toward economic mobility. We are concerned here with the school achievement of immigrant children compared to the achievement of children of native, white Americans, and with variations in school achievement between different nationality groups.[4]

The data which we draw on come from a variety of sources, all of them inadequate in some serious respects. We are limited in the measures of achievement that are available, in the accuracy of reports on . . . school performance and the socioeconomic characteristics of specific groups, and in the susceptibility of the data to combination and analysis. These limitations must be borne in mind throughout. They mean that, despite any appearances of exactitude, whatever calculations or manipulations we have made, the data give only approximations and orders of magnitude. We believe, however, that the data we report and try to explain suggest important conclusions about patterns of immigrant adaptation which might otherwise by ignored in the absence of "hard" data.

What follows is first a comparison of the children of the foreign-born to the children of white, native-born parents on measures of school attendance and school continuance during the first thirty years of this century. Then the performance of specific nationality groups compared to one another and to the children of native whites is analyzed on the basis of continuance, completion, and retardation rates, and on the basis of sex ratios at the secondary level. The last sections consider in detail two specific nationality groups: Southern Italians and Russian Jews. An effort is made to account for the differences between these two groups in school performance by considering the effects of nationality differences in parental length of residence in the United States, home language, age at school entrance, standardized test scores, and occupational and income levels. The inadequacies of differences on these measures to account fully for Italian-Jewish differences on school performance lead us to suggest the continuing importance of varying cultural factors for shaping the responses of these immigrant groups to the schools. We turn to these factors in the final section.

IMMIGRANT CHILDREN AND CHILDREN OF NATIVE WHITES

During the first three decades of the twentieth century, the younger children of immigrants were as likely to be in school as children of native-born whites. At older age levels, however, they neither attended nor completed school in the same proportions as children of native whites. Throughout the schooling process, they were more likely to drop out when legally permitted, though the trend after 1920 was for most children to stay in school longer. These findings suggest that, while attendance in elementary school was roughly similar for immigrants and nonimmigrants, rates of progress through school varied. Nevertheless, the differences between native-born and immigrant were not large, and they were especially small for immigrant children from English-speaking homes. Only at the point of high school entrance did substantial disparities become evident.

Table 5-1 shows the national attendance rates for children of native whites, native-born children of foreign or mixed parents, and for foreign-born children in 1910, 1920, and 1930.

Table 5-1 tells us what proportion of children of a given age were in school at a particular time. But since children of the same age were not necessarily in the same grade, Table 5-1 cannot be used to make quantitative comparisons about educational attainment, though it is a safe inference that as attendance became more equal so did eventual attainment. This issue of the relationship between age and grade fig-

Table 5-1

**Percentage of children attending school in United States
by age and parentage, 1910, 1920, 1930**

Date	Background	Age group			
		7-13	14-15	16-17	18-20
1910	Native white of native white parents	88	80	51	20
	Native of foreign or mixed parents	93	74	37	12
	Foreign-born	87	59	18	5
1920	Native white of native white parents	92	84	49	18
	Native of foreign or mixed parents	94	78	35	19
	Foreign-born	84	67	24	7
1930	Native white of native white parents	96	90	61	24
	Native of foreign or mixed parents	98	91	54	12
	Foreign-born	98	93	52	16

Source: U.S. Bureau of the Census, *Abstract of the Fifteenth Census of the United States* (Washington, 1933), 261; see also T. J. Woofter, Jr., *Races and Ethnic Groups in American Life* (New York: McGraw-Hill Book Co., 1933), 166.

ured prominently in the educational debates of the early twentieth century. In city after city, researchers and administrators found that large numbers of elementary pupils were not in the grade considered normal for their age level, a condition universally defined as "retardation."[5] Using as a measure children two or more years behind their normal grade level, the U.S. Commission on Immigration found high proportions of children retarded in twelve major cities in 1908. But the Commission also found only five percent more of the children of immigrants were behind than children of native whites. Immigrant children from English-language nationalities were virtually equal to children of native whites in school progress, and only 7 percent more of the children from foreign-language-speaking nationalities were behind than were those of native whites (Table 5-2).

Within individual cities, the picture is more complicated. Promotion practices varied from city to city, so that the proportion of all students that were retarded shows a wide range. In the largest cities, especially, immigrants were progressing at close to the same rate as children of the native born. In only five cities was the gap between those children and immigrant children greater than 15 percent of the city's overall retardation rate. Indeed, immigrant school progress was actually more equal to the progress of children of native whites than Table 5-2 indicates. Immigrant children tended to enter school at a

Table 5-2

Percentage of ten-, eleven-, and twelve-year-olds "retarded" in school progress
in 1908, by parentage and city

| | | Foreign | | |
City	Native white	English-language groups	Non-English-language groups	All foreign
Twelve cities	41	40	47	46
Eleven cities (excludes New York)	42	37	48	46
Boston	11	14	20	17
Buffalo	18	19	37	33
Chicago	36	40	45	44
Cincinnati	40	47	46	46
Cleveland	30	34	43	42
Detroit	38	43	52	49
Newark	54	58	65	64
New York	41	46	46	46
Philadelphia	52	54	61	59
Pittsburgh	55	63	63	63
Providence	25	29	45	39
St. Louis	62	65	67	67

Source: U.S. Immigration Commission, Reports (Washington, D.C.: Government Printing Office, 1911), Vols. 30-35, calculated from city-by-city tables on retardation.

later age than did children of native whites, and since late entrants were classified as retarded even where they were making normal progress through school, some portion of the apparent gap between the two groups was due to disproportionate late entrance among immigrants. There is some indication that almost all of the gap could be due to this factor.

This becomes clear when the Immigration Commission *Summary* data for children over age eight in a selected subsample are reanalyzed. When foreign-language-group children are assumed to have the same proportion of normal age entrants as children of native whites, the difference in retardation falls from 15 percent to 2 percent.[6] This result suggests that the gap of only 6 percent between immigrant children of foreign-language nationalities and children of native whites observed in the dozen major cities would be considerably reduced if age of entrance could be taken into account.

It would be possible, of course, for retardation rates of groups to have been similar, and for the groups to have differed on other

Table 5-3

Approximate percentage of eighth graders beginning high school
and percentage of ninth graders reaching senior year,
by parentage, 1908

City	Parentage	Ratio of ninth graders to eighth graders	Ratio of twelfth graders to ninth graders
Boston	Native white	71	23
	Foreign	54	13
Chicago	Native white	57	25
	Foreign	37	20
New York	Native white	54	20
	Foreign	34	17
Philadelphia	Native white	56	21
	Foreign	50	23
St. Louis	Native white	56	24
	Foreign	41	32

Source: Calculated from U.S. Immigration Commission, *Reports,* Vol. 33, 190-193, 564-568; Vol. 34, 624-628.

measures of school progress. One measure for which we can draw ten-tative conclusions is the proportion of students completing grammar school. In the Immigration Commission data, children with foreign-born parents were only slightly less likely to have attended eighth grade, providing they had attended seventh grade.[7] This finding rein-forces our sense that the progress immigrant children made in the lower grades was little different from the progress that children of native whites made.

At the point of high school entrance, however, sharper disparities become evident, though they were not consistent across cities. Perhaps these disparities resulted from the proportion of school-age population drawn from the immigrant communities or from the varying ethnic composition of the foreign-born population. In three of five major cities in 1908, we found the proportion of eighth graders beginning high school was around 10 percent higher for children of native whites than for immigrant children (Table 5-3). Having begun high school, however, the immigrant child in New York and Chicago had about the same chance of reaching the senior year as did a child of native white parents. In Boston, where a substantially higher proportion of all pupils continued on to the ninth grade, this was not the case. There the proportion of children of native whites who began ninth grade and reached twelfth grade exceeded the proportion of similar children with foreign parents by 10 percent. In Philadelphia, the disparity at the point of high school entrance was trivial, and in both Philadelphia and St. Louis high school persistence slightly favored children of immigrants.

When we thus compare children of foreign parentage to those of native-born parents during the early part of this century, it seems clear that the former were somewhat more disadvantaged on such measures as school attendance, age-grade retardation, high school entry, and high school completion. The differences, however, were negligible for the elementary years and were not particularly striking once children entered high school. The line of demarcation appears to have been between completion of grammar school and high school entry.

SCHOOL PROGRESS AND NATIONALITY GROUPS

Comparisons between children of the foreign-born and children of native, white Americans are important because they permit some generalizations about the degree and manner in which the immigrants responded to the schools. But such comparisons can also be misleading. For example, finding that immigrant school progress at the elementary level was about equal to the progress of children of native whites suggests that adaptation to the public school was proceeding uniformly. That immigrants were also less likely to begin high school suggests that there was some uniform influence which prevented them from taking advantage of the public secondary schools. The problem with such conclusions, however, is that they obscure a more basic finding: there was no single immigrant experience in the schools. Nationality groups varied substantially on such measures as elementary school retardation, grammar school continuance, high school entrance, continuance, and completion, and in the ratio of males to females in high school.

The evidence to support these contentions is striking. Data compiled on elementary school retardation reveal a few immigrant groups at less than the average of children of native whites, and some groups with unusually high rates of retardation. Table 5-4 shows the percent of ten- through twelve-year-olds who were two or more years over-age for grade level in three major cities in 1908.

Table 5-4

Percentage of ten-, eleven-, and twelve-year-old "retarded" in school progress in 1908, by nationality group and city

Father's birth	Boston	Chicago	New York
Native white	11(.64)[a]	36(.74)	41(.85)
Native black	24(1.39)	64(1.31)	72(1.49)
English	15(.87)	41(.84)	45(.93)
Swedish	12(.70)	30(.61)	36(.75)
German	12(.70)	41(.84)	33(.68)
Irish	13(.75)	45(.92)	49(1.02)
Hebrew-German	06(.35)	36(.74)	33(.68)
Hebrew-Russian	19(1.10)	50(1.02)	46(.95)
Southern Italian	36(2.41)	72(1.47)	69(1.43)
Polish	25(1.44)	74(1.51)	58(1.20)
Average group rate[b]	17	49	48

[a]Ratio of group rate to average group rate.

[b]Arithmetic average of separate group rates. Equivalent to city rate standardized for unequal nationality composition.

Source: U.S. Immigration Commission, *Reports,* Vols. 31 and 33, calculated city-by-city tables on retardation.

Despite certain anomalies in these results (for example, why were German Jews in Boston so advantaged on school progress?), we are most impressed with the consistency of findings across cities. It would be fortunate if we could compare these data to comparable data for subsequent years, separating the children of newcomers from those of long-term residents. We cannot, but what scanty data we do have suggest the persistent impact of nationality background on elementary school progress. For example, the results of a study conducted in New York in 1933 paralleled the findings of the 1908 Immigration Commission. Schools in which Poles and Italians predominated were characterized by retardation rates higher than the city average, while schools in which Germans and Jews predominated were characterized by rates lower than the city average.[8]

We saw earlier that the proportion of seventh graders continuing on to the last grade of grammar school was only slightly greater for children of native whites than for immigrant children. However, grammar school continuance, like elementary retardation, depended to a considerable extent on nationality. For some groups, over 80 percent of the seventh graders continued on to eighth grade, while, for others, the figure was closer to 60 percent. Table 5-5 shows the ratio of

Table 5-5

**Approximate percentage of seventh graders continuing to eighth grade
in Boston, Chicago, and New York, combined,
by nationality, 1908**

Father's birth	Percentage of seventh graders beginning eighth grade
Native white	80
Native black	66
English	82
Swedish	81
German	75
Irish	80
Hebrew-German	82
Hebrew-Russian	74
Southern Italian	58
Polish	62

Source: Calculated from U.S. Immigration Commission, *Reports,* Vol. 31, 190-193, 564-578; Vol. 34, 624-628.

the number of eighth graders to the number of seventh graders in three cities combined in 1908.

Differences between nationality groups were even more pronounced at the secondary level than they were at the elementary level. High school entrance, continuance, and completion varied appreciably from group to group. In 1908 only a minority of grammar school graduates continued on to high school. However, for some groups, close to or more than half of the eighth graders began ninth grade. At the other extreme, for some groups, less than a quarter of the eighth graders began the ninth grade, usually the first year of high school. Table 5-6 shows the ratio of the number of ninth graders to the number of eighth graders in Boston, Chicago, and New York, combined.

Almost 60 percent of the eighth graders with native white parents began high school in these three cities. Almost half of the black, English, Irish, and German-Jewish eighth graders began high school. Around a third of the German, Russian-Jewish, and Swedish eighth graders continued, and slightly under a quarter of the Italians did.

Comparing rates of retardation and rates of continuance, it is clear that a precise relationship did not exist between the two. While high retardation rates were usually followed by low continuance levels, low

Table 5-6

Approximate percentage of grammar school graduates entering high school
in Boston, Chicago, and New York, combined,
by nationality, 1908

Father's birth	Percentage of eighth graders beginning ninth grade
Native white	58
Native black	49
English	47
Swedish	33
German	33
Irish	51
Hebrew-German	46
Hebrew-Russian	35
Southern Italian	23
Polish	—[a]

[a]N less than 200.

Source: Calculated from U.S. Immigration Commission, Reports, Vol. 31, 190-193, 564-568; Vol. 34, 624-628.

retardation rates were not invariably accompanied by high continuance levels. Germans and Swedes did not continue into the ninth grade at the levels expected by their low retardation rates. In part, we believe this is so because retardation studies usually failed to account for age of entrance, and the apparent advantage of some groups might have been inflated due to this factor. Groups that entered school late would appear retarded even if they were progressing at normal rates. This seems to have been the case for Russian Jews. An alternative explanation would focus on the occupational options open to young adolescents. Swedish and German youth might have been attracted away from school by entry into skilled crafts via apprenticeships or family contacts. Our data do not allow us to pursue these possibilities at present.

In the years after 1908, high school attendance rose for everyone. However, nationality groups continued to differ in their rates of attendance. Data which are directly comparable to the Immigration Commission data presented above are not available. However, for at least one city—Cleveland—we can compare the number of students in high school to the number of students in all the elementary grades at two points in time. Table 5-7 indicates that the rate of high school attendance for Germans and Jews almost doubled, while the rate of

Table 5-7

Number of high school students per hundred elementary school students,
by language groups, Cleveland, 1908 and 1916

Language group	1908	1916
English	14	17
German	7	14
Yiddish (Jewish)	5	9
Italian	2	2
Polish	2	3

Source: Calculated from U.S. Immigration Commission, *Reports,* Vol. 31, 780-783;
and Herbert Miller, *The School and the Immigrant* (Cleveland, Ohio: Cleveland
Foundation, 1916), 80-81.
Note: The comparison is not exact because the classification of the later data is by
home language, and so children of foreign parents who used English at the time of the
survey would have been classified with children of native Americans. The comparison
also requires combining the English-speaking nationality groups of 1908 into one
category.

Italians and Poles showed no increase between 1908 and 1916. This
result could be misleading, however, if the age composition of the
Italian and Polish groups was altered by new immigration during
those eight years, while that of the other groups was unchanged.
Though we doubt its effect, out data do not permit checking this
possibility.

We have already seen that children of immigrants were only slightly
less likely than children of native whites to reach their senior year if
they began high school (Table 5-3). But as was the case with entrance,
progress through secondary school was closely tied to nationality.
Table 5-8 summarizes the results of studies of high school progress
from 1908 to 1925.

The results of Table 5-8 cannot be used to make any firm inferences
about the exact proportion of high school students of a given nationality group that completed the four-year course. High school persistence, however, rose over time, so that the proportion of entering
students who finished went from around a fifth in 1908 to closer to a
half in the mid-1920s. It is also clear that only the Poles and the
Italians consistently failed to reach the last two years of high school in
proportions reasonably close to the average. There is some city-by-city
variation among groups. Compared to other nationality groups, the
Irish, for example, were doing considerably less well in Hartford than

Table 5-8

High school progress and nationality, selected studies

New York, Boston, Chicago — 1908		Bridgeport, Conn. — 1922		Hartford, Conn. — 1925	
Father's birth	Ratio of seniors to freshmen	Father's birth	Ratio of seniors to freshmen	Nationality	Ratio of juniors to freshmen
United States		United States	.44	United States	
white	.22	Scandinavian	.37	white	.64
United States		German	.61	Scandinavian	.48
black	.20	Irish	.48	German	.44
English	.20	Russian-Jewish	.51	Irish	.34
Swedish	.18	Italian	.17	Jewish	.80
German	.18	Polish	.15	Italian	.28
Irish	.16			Polish	.24
Hebrew-German	.18				
Hebrew-Russian	.19				
Southern Italian	.08				
Polish	—a				

aN less than 125.

Source: U.S. Immigration Commission, Reports, Vol. 31, 190-193, 564-568; Vol. 34, 624-628; George S. Counts, The Selective Character of American Secondary Education (Chicago: University of Chicago Press,1922), 108; Gustave Feingold, "Intelligence of the First Generation of Immigrant Groups," Journal of Educational Psychology 15 (February 1924).

in Bridgeport. Finally, while the high rate of continuance for Jews in Hartford was exceptional, it does indicate the beginning of a trend in which Jewish educational attainment exceeded that of most other groups.[9]

Another way of viewing the distinctions among nationality groups is by comparing secondary school attendance by sex. If there were no cultural factors that affected attendance in the secondary schools, we would expect that the sex ratios among high school students would be the same from group to group. We would also expect the proportions of males and females among immigrants to be about the same as for native Americans. In fact, the sex ratios among high school students varied substantially from group to group. Table 5-9 shows the number of female high school students per 100 male students for three major cities in 1908, and for Bridgeport High School in 1922.

For most groups, girls were more likely to have been in high school

Table 5-9

Number of female high school students per hundred male students,
by parentage, Boston, Chicago, and New York, combined, 1908;
and Bridgeport, 1922

Boston, Chicago, New York — 1908		Bridgeport, Conn. — 1922	
Father's birth	Females per hundred males	Father's birth	Females per hundred males
Native white	135	United States	134
English	161	British Empire	131
Swedish	131	Scandinavian	116
German	103	German	122
Irish	137	Irish	135
Hebrew-German	107	Russian-Jewish	97
Hebrew-Russian	76	Italian	65
Southern Italian	48	Polish	92
Polish	64		

Source: U.S. Immigration Commission, *Reports,* Vol. 31, 190-193, 564-568; Vol. 34, 624-628; Counts, *Selective Character of American Secondary Education,* 113.

than boys. This was especially true among the Irish, English, and children of native Americans. There is good economic reason why this should have been the case. Employment opportunities for men without high school training were greater than the opportunities for untrained women. Men could take industrial jobs. The sectors of the economy that were growing which were open to women often required preparation in skills. This was true for secretarial and office work and for teaching. In Bridgeport, in 1922, well over three-quarters of the high school girls were enrolled in the commercial and normal tracks. High school attendance did not offer boys the same specific job preparation. For boys, high school was principally the route to college, and that was a route only a small minority of any group would follow.[10]

It thus made more economic sense, at least in the short run, for boys to take jobs and girls to continue on in school. Yet for Russian Jews, Poles, and Southern Italians, the groups we suspect were economically the most impoverished, males predominate over females in high school attendance. In part, we believe this to be the result of cultural attitudes toward the education of the sexes. Russian Jews historically tended to place a high premium on schooling the male child.[11] In the United States, college attendance leading to professional occupational status replaced religious study as the mark of highest success. Russian

Jews were being sent to high school almost exclusively to prepare them for college entrance. In Bridgeport in 1922, for example, 90 percent of the Russian-Jewish boys were in the college or scientific tracks of the high school compared to 75 percent of the males with native-born fathers.[12]

For Italians, male predominance among high school students is probably explained not by a special positive valuation of schooling for boys, but by a strong cultural aversion to sending girls to school. Italian parents felt, more strongly than most, that girls required close parental supervision and that they should be preparing for their future roles as homemakers.[13]

There was, then, no single immigrant experience in the schools. In the absence of statistically reliable and longitudinal studies, our conclusions cannot be precise. Yet it does seem clear that some groups made slower progress through school than others. Some groups were more likely to finish grammar school than others. It also seems evident that going on to and continuing in high school depended to a considerable extent on nationality and that the sex ratio at the secondary level was also related to nationality. Finally, we are struck by the extent to which nationality background continued to influence school achievement over time. This means that group differences in school performance cannot be accounted for solely by differences which existed at the outset of life in the United States. While immigration continually introduced large numbers of people who were beginning the process of assimilation, by the 1920s the school population, particularly the high school population, included large numbers of children whose parents had been in this country for some time. The persistence of nationality differences in the schools over time is strong evidence that groups were adapting to public education at different rates.

RUSSIAN JEWS AND SOUTHERN ITALIANS

A number of characteristics tie Russian Jews and Southern Italians together. Both groups arrived in the United States at roughly the same time (1880-1930), were poor upon arrival, spoke little English, and settled in close proximity to one another along the Eastern seaboard. But Russian Jews and Southern Italians differed in at least two significant ways: on measures of school performance and in their occupational history. Jews arrived in the new world with higher levels of vocational skill and advanced vocationally more rapidly than did Southern

Italians, and they outperformed them in school on measures of retardation and retention, and on standardized tests. The two are related; doing better vocationally was paralleled by better school performance. Yet we will argue that differences in occupational attainment do not fully account for differences in school achievement. Russian Jews and Southern Italians at the same occupational level did not perform equally well in school. Nor are differences in such variables as length of parental residence in the United States, age of school entrance, use of English in the home, and scores on standardized tests sufficient to explain school differences between the two groups. The failure of either occupational level or the other variables to account fully for these differences in school performance leads us to suggest that group cultural values must be taken into account if we are fully to understand school achievement.

In its summary volume on education the Immigration Commission analyzed the effects of a number of variables on elementary school retardation rates.[14] The commission found, for example, that the longer a student's father had resided in the United States, the less likely the student was to have been behind. However, ethnic differences persisted in retardation rates *within* categories of length of father's residence. In the case of Russian Jews and Southern Italians, the gap was greatest for children whose fathers had been here the longest (Table 5-10).

Table 5-10

Percentage retarded by father's length of residence in the United States, pupils over eight years, Immigration Commission summary, 1908

Father's birth	Father's length of residence			
	Less than 5 years	5-9 years	10 or more years	All groups
Hebrew-Russian	75	57	31	41
Southern Italian	82	75	59	63

Source: U.S. Immigration Commission, *Reports,* Vol. 29, 92.

While inferences from cross-sectional data to processes over time are risky, it would appear that longer residence markedly reduced the Russian-Jewish rate of retardation. The Italian rate was also substantially reduced, but not by nearly as much. One way of showing the differential effect of father's length of residence is to ask what would happen to the Southern Italian and Russian-Jewish rates of retardation if both groups had been here equally as long as a third, and particularly long-term group. When the Southern Italians are assigned the same distribution of length of residence as that of the Germans in the sample, their overall rate of retardation falls by only 3 percent, from 63 to 60 percent. The Russian-Jewish rate, however, falls from 44 to 33 percent, a rate equal to the German rate. Compared to at least one other group, then, Southern Italians seem to have been exceptionally immune to the effects of longer residence, while Russian Jews seem to have been quite susceptible.[15]

The later a student entered primary school, the more likely he or she was to have been retarded. This follows, of course, even if the student was making normal progress. In the commission's sample, Russian Jews and Southern Italians were equally likely to have entered school below the age of eight, so virtually none of the Southern Italian–Russian-Jewish difference in elementary retardation could be attributed to differences in age of entrance.[16] Moreover, while the vast majority of both Southern Italians and Russian Jews who entered school at eight years or over were over-age for their grade level in 1908 (92 to 83 percent), only 29 percent of the Russian Jews who entered at ages six or seven were retarded, compared to 55 percent for Southern Italians. When Russian Jews are hypothetically equalized to Germans on age of entrance, their rate of elementary retardation falls by one-fifth; after such equalization, the Southern Italian rate falls by only one-tenth.

A student whose family used English in the home was more likely to have been making normal progress than a student whose home language was not English. Over two-thirds of the Southern Italians in the commission's sample came from homes where English was not used. About half of the Russian Jews came from homes where English was not used.[17] It would be reasonable to expect that the use of English in more Russian-Jewish than Italian homes accounts for a large portion of the difference in retardation rates. However, use of English in the home did not sufficiently affect Italian school progress to explain much of the group difference in retardation. When Southern Italians are assumed to have the same proportion of English-speaking homes as the Russian Jews, their rate of retardation falls by only 3 percent, reducing the gap between the groups by less than one-seventh. In the Immigration Commission data, then, Southern Italian–Russian-Jewish differences in elementary retardation cannot be accounted for by differences [in] language use, age of school entrance, or length of father's residence in the United States.

When we turn to consider the effects of standardized test scores on school performance, we are faced with a number of complicated questions. Should a test score be treated as an outcome like any other measure of school achievement, or should it be treated as a measure of prior ability? To the extent that a test measures acquired cognitive skills, general information, and the ability and willingness to take pencil-and-paper tests, it measures some of the same things that grades and retardation rates measure. Explanations for test score differences could therefore apply as well to school achievement differences. That is, whatever "causes" test score differences probably "causes" school achievement differences. On the other hand, there are ways in which scores can be seen as a "cause" of school performance. If tests measure intellectual ability, and ability is a large cause of grades, then test scores can be said to "cause" school achievement. Moreover, if academic success affects whether or not a student remains in school and if ability affects grades, then test scores can be said to affect school persistence. Finally, teachers might treat students differently depending on their scores. Discriminatory treatment could affect how students feel about school and whether they continue or drop out. With these complications in mind, we will consider the magnitude of Jewish-Italian test score differences, the apparent effect of these differences on school achievement, and the possible sources of group differences on test scores.[18]

In the early part of the century, Italian and Jewish students differed in their performance on standardized tests. The extent of these differences depended upon the tests used and the samples under investigation. Our general impression, based on the few reported studies conducted in the 1920s which separated subjects by nationality, is that Jewish students scored about a half a standard deviation above Italian students.[19] Since the general literature on the relationship between test scores and measures of achievement suggests that less than half the variation in achievement was associated with variation in test scores, we are led to conclude that the advantage Jewish students enjoyed on school performance cannot be attributed solely to their advantage on test scores.[20]

Despite the risks inherent in making inferences from data about differences among individuals to differences between groups, we think that this conclusion is sound. There is a smattering of evidence that bears more directly on the question. In the 1924 study of Hartford High School, ratios between final exam scores and ability scores were calculated for Jewish, Irish, and American students. This controlled for the effect of ability scores on achievement. Jews ranked the highest on this measure of performance. In that same study, the variation in group test scores was not related to the group variation in school retention. Jews scored lower or equal to children of English, Scottish, German, and native white parents, and yet were much more likely to have reached their junior year than were these groups.[21]

Finally, if we combine data from disparate sources, we can estimate the proportion of the difference in Jewish and Italian educational attainment associated with group test score differences. Jencks has estimated the correlation between standardized test score at age eleven and eventual educational attainment as .58.[22] This estimate is based on a number of studies in which the testing occurred during the 1920s, and so applies roughly to the population with which we are concerned.[23] We have concluded that Italian elementary students were about one-half standard deviation below Jewish students on tested ability. This means that if test differences fully accounted for differences in educational attainment, Italians should be .29 standard deviations below Jews on attainment. Duncan and Duncan have reported educational attainment for a national sample of white male workers born between 1898 and 1937, by father's nationality.[24] In the Duncans' sample, a standard deviation on educational attainment was 3.30 years. Therefore, we would expect Jews to exceed Italians in attainment by slightly under a year (0.96 years). In fact, men in that sample whose fathers were born in Russia (and are presumed to be predominantly Jewish) exceeded men whose fathers were born in Italy by 2.08 years. If our estimates are correct, then less than half of the Italian-Jewish difference in educational attainment is associated with differences in test scores.

Differences in scores, however, are still relevant to our present problem. If we can explain why there were differences in group averages on test scores, we may have explained, in part, why there were differences on measures of school performance. Were the differences between Jewish and Italian scores true "nationality" differences? There is considerable evidence, for example, that parental occupational status bore a strong relationship to test scores. If it were also true that parental occupational status and nationality were confounded, we would conclude that at least some part of the apparent differences in test scores was due to group differences on occupational status.

Sorting out nationality from social-class influences is exceedingly complex, in part because few studies have measured simultaneously the effects of ethnicity and parental economic status on school performance. Nonetheless, we do have data on the basis of which to posit some tentative conclusions. Though varying widely in approaches and quality, all studies of the effects of parental occupation on school achievement show considerable differences between children from various backgrounds.[25] We know that parental occupation bore a relationship to high school entry and completion, to tracking and curriculum assignment, and to test scores.[26] This suggests that what appear to have been nationality differences may in fact have been economic differences. This is partially true — social class and school success are related — but we are convinced that group differences in parental occupations and incomes are insufficient to explain group differences in eventual educational attainment. Our reasons become clear when we turn to an analysis of Russian-Jewish and Southern Italian economic and educational attainment.

Jewish and Italian immigrants had very different occupational histories in both Europe and the United States. Between 1899 and 1910, almost two-thirds of the Jewish immigrants reporting Old World occupations identified themselves as skilled laborers; only 14 percent were classified as unskilled laborers.[27] Among immigrants from Southern Italy during the same period, 15 percent reported having had skilled occupations, and 77 percent were classified as laborers. This does not necessarily mean that Jews landed any richer than others. It does mean that Jews were more prepared to enter skilled labor jobs in the United States.

Jews entered the American occupational structure at higher levels than Southern Italians did. Table 5-11 shows the occupational distribution of foreign-born Southern Italians and Russian-Jewish men over age sixteen in seven major cities in 1910.

A third of the Southern Italian immigrants in these cities had become unskilled laborers. Less than 1 percent of the Russian Jews were classified as general laborers. Over half the Jews had become manual producers. The largest proportion of these were in the needle trades, which paid higher wages than other manufacturing pursuits.[28] Almost 30 percent of the Italians were similarly classified, but even when Italians worked in the same occupational category, and even within the clothing industry, they earned less than Jewish workers.[29]

Table 5-11

Occupations of foreign-born Southern Italian and Russian-Jewish
males over age sixteen, in seven cities, 1910

Occupational category	Southern Italian	Russian-Jewish
Professional	01.5	02
Trade	13	34
Transport	09	03
Manufactures and mechanical	29	55
Domestic and personal	09	02.5
General labor	32	00.5
Other	06.5	03

Source: U.S. Immigration Commission, Reports, Vol. 1, 761. The cities were New
York, Chicago, Philadelphia, Boston, Cleveland, Buffalo, and Milwaukee.

Jewish occupational superiority was generally reflected in family incomes higher than those earned by Southern Italian families. Table
5-12 shows the average annual family income in five cities in 1910 for
Russian-Jewish and Southern Italian families.[30]

Table 5-12

Average annual income, by nativity of family head

Nationality	Boston	Chicago	Cleveland	New York	Philadelphia
Hebrew-Russian	$543	647	501	813	434
Southern Italian	534	504	412	688	441

Source: U.S. Immigration Commission, Reports, Vol. 26, 226, 318, 404, 423, 577.

Starting with certain skill advantages, Russian Jews quickly translated these into higher occupational roles and family incomes than
Southern Italians were able to achieve. This strongly suggests that
ethnic differences in school performance may well have been due to
economic differences. However, we are persuaded that economic differences themselves may reflect cultural values, and that the available
data do not support an exclusively "economic" explanation of group
differences on school performance.[31] For example, if income differences accounted for differences in elementary school progress, we
would expect to find that Italian and Jewish rates of retardation were
close to equal in those cities where average incomes were equal, and to
find the largest differences in retardation in those cities where average
incomes were least equal. Instead, we find no apparent relationship

Table 5-13

Jewish and Italian family income differences (1910)
and elementary retardation differences (1908),
pupils aged ten, eleven, and twelve

	Boston	Chicago	Cleveland	New York	Philadelphia
Jewish minus Italian income	$ + 09	+ 143	+ 89	+ 125	− 07
Jewish minus Italian rate of retardation	− 17%	− 22	− 28	− 23	− 25
Jewish and Italian retardation difference as percentage of city retardation rate	100%	50	67	50	42

Source: Calculated from Tables 5-4 and 5-12, above.

between group income differences and differences in rates of elementary retardation. Table 5-13 shows the differences between the average annual family incomes of families headed by foreign-born Russian Jews and Southern Italians, and the differences in rates of retardation, for five cities.

In the two cities where the Jewish income advantage was the greatest, Chicago and New York, Jewish students enjoyed no additional advantage in school progress over what they enjoyed in the other cities. In both Cleveland and Philadelphia, the differences in the proportions of Russian-Jewish and Southern Italian students who were behind were greater than in either Chicago [or] New York. In relative terms, the Italian-Jewish difference in retardation was greatest in Boston, where average family income was virtually equal. There, the difference in retardation of 17 percent represented 100 percent of the city's overall retardation rate. In the Immigration Commission data, then, the advantage of Jewish families had over Italians in earnings does not appear to explain the advantage their children held in elementary school progress.

One should, however, make a distinction between parental occupational status and income. The former appears to have had more to do with school progress than did the latter. In some ways, this makes sense. While we would expect lower incomes to lead to early leaving from school, we would also expect that parental occupations, independent of income level, shape aspirations and motivation. Combining data from Jencks *et al.,* and from the Duncans, as we did earlier with respect to the effect of IQ on attainment, we can estimate the effect of Italian-Jewish differences in father's occupation on group differences in educational attainment. In the Duncans' data, Russian parental occupational status exceeded Italian parental occupational status by .59 standard deviations.[32] Jencks gives the correlation between father's occupation and son's eventual education as .49. If the Jewish-Italian differences in attainment were due only to the effect of the group difference in parental occupation, we would expect Jews to exceed Italians by .29 standard deviations, or 0.96 years. This is less than half of the observed differences in attainment of 2.08 years in the Duncans' sample.

It is also exactly the amount of the difference which we found was associated with the Jewish-Italian difference in test scores. This might suggest that differences in test scores and in average parental occupation together account for almost all of the difference in attainment. However, because there is a relationship between father's occupational and test score, as well as between father's occupational status and educational attainment, and between test score and attainment, this suggestion is wrong. When these joint relationships are taken into account, we find that group differences in test scores and in parental occupation together predict a difference in attainment of 1.39 years.[33] This is substantially less than the observed difference of 2.08 years. While inferences from disparate data are suspect, it would seem that around a third of the difference between Russian-Jewish and Italian males in school attainment is not explained by differences in test scores or father's occupation.

The measures of school performance that we have utilized are related to factors other than ethnicity. Children who entered school on time, had fathers who had been in the United States for some time, and came from homes where English was used were more likely to have been making normal progress in elementary school than were other children. Children with higher parental occupational backgrounds scored higher on standardized tests, and were more likely to have begun, and, if they had begun, to complete high school.

Jews were more favored on most of these factors than were Italians. Jewish students were more likely to have come from homes in which English was used. They scored higher on tests, and they had fathers whose occupational status was higher than the status of Italian fathers. The differences on these factors, however, have not proven sufficiently large to fully explain the magnitude of the differences between the two groups on indexes of school performance. This leads us to conclude that group cultural values substantially affected the school progress and attainment of Russian-Jewish and Southern Italian children. What some of these values were is the focus of our next section.

ETHNIC CULTURE AND SCHOOL PERFORMANCE

Success and persistence in school require certain capacities and competencies. Some are cognitive or intellectual, others attitudinal and behavioral. They include the ability and willingness to obey and to follow the prescribed regimen, responsiveness to the school's reward system, facility with words and abstraction, and the belief that completing school is important. While tied to immediate social and economic circumstances, these capacities and beliefs also reflect differing cultural values based in part on group histories and traditions. What different groups think about learning, schools, and teachers, how they see public institutions in general, their belief in opportunity and confidence in individual effort, and the character of the demands placed on children are not simply the effects of economic level. In the case of European immigrants, they were patterns, evolved in the Old World, which shaped group responses to American institutions and partially conditioned the manner in which groups adapted to American society.

This does not mean that each family or individual embodied all the cultural traits we discuss. Nor are we talking about innate traits or unchangeable characteristics of group behavior. Cultures are sustained and modified by circumstances, but, while almost all groups in America have accepted the dominant value system, the rates and modes of assimilation have differed among groups and for individuals within groups. In our judgment, evidence drawn from anthropological sources, immigrant novels, and sociological studies makes clear that Russian-Jewish culture prepared that group to fare very well in terms of educational success, and that Southern Italian culture was at odds with the demands of formal schooling in America.

Study and learning were highly valued and deeply rooted in Russian-Jewish society. Orthodoxy required the study and learning of the Holy Law, while social practice institutionalized religious imperatives in an extensive system of Jewish schooling. The conduct of Jewish education trained and reinforced habits of mind that stressed mental agility, close attention to the meaning of words, and lively criticism. While few men in the Jewish town or shtetl achieved the highest levels of study, the ideal of learning and scholarship as a principal criterion of social evaluation permeated the Jewish community.

While the shtetl system of schooling was not reproduced in the United States, the traditional respect for learning seems to have been transplanted and turned to secular purposes. An old Yiddish lullaby expressed the twin hopes of Jewish parents for their sons: "My Yankele shall learn the Law/The Law shall baby learn/Great books shall my Yankele write/Much money shall he earn." Learning was therefore both important in its own right and for its use in bringing material success.[34]

High regard for schooling did not necessarily mean that Jews would prepare their children to succeed in the public schools. Had Jews been highly suspicious of American institutions—and their experience in Russia gave reason to be wary of state institutions in a Christian country—they might have sought educational success outside the public system. Instead, they embraced America and enthusiastically entrusted their children to its schools. Most of the literary evidence portrays Jews as "true believers" in American opportunity. Children are told that "in America you can become almost anything you wish—a fireman, a policeman, a mayor, a Congressman," and that this "is a different land we are in now, a better country—the best country on earth. It is not only overflowing with milk and honey, but with opportunities . . . . If you study hard you can make anything you want of yourself."[35]

In addition to Jewish values about schooling and a belief in American opportunity, Jewish parental attitudes and practices encouraged successful school performance. Parental attitudes, like beliefs about opportunity, are tied up with attitudes about the future. The view that the conditions of the present can be improved in the future is a central tenet in Judaism.[36] In concrete terms, placing stock in the future means placing stock in the futures of children. This requires a willingness to make sacrifices for the sake of the child. One such sacrifice is to forego greater immediate economic security in order that a child complete school. A Jewish mother wrote of her dilemma as follows: "If I were to withdraw my son from high school, I could dispense with the salesman, but my motherly love and duty to the child do not permit me to take that step, for he is a very good scholar . . . . I must have his assistance in order to keep my business going and take care of the other children; but at the same time I cannot definitely take him out of school . . . . I lay great hopes on my child."[37] Jewish high school attendance and completion rates early in the century probably exceeded the rates of economically comparable or superior groups because of an atypical willingness on the part of Jewish families to tolerate the economic burdens of keeping their children in school longer.

The other side of the coin of parental duty is pressure on the child to succeed. The literary and the sociological evidence suggest that Jewish children were subjected to high expectations, and to child-rearing practices that demanded early individual mastery. In *Witte Arrives,* Emil thought to himself that "everybody must have an aim in life . . . . Since his father had talked to him about school and opportunities, his aim was 'to make something of himself' as his father had put it, a lawyer a judge or teacher. Certainly he must grasp the opportunities which this country offered." In *Journey to the Dawn,* Moses says "the goyim really are different. Their mothers don't shout at their children as much as Jewish mothers do, and I don't think they care so much if their kids get good marks or bad ones. I mean, they care, but not as much as our mothers."[38]

Studies of parental attitudes, child-rearing practices, and achievement motivation during the 1950s and 1960s support the view of Jewish students as unusually motivated and able to meet the demands of formal schooling. In Kohn's recent study of a national sample of fathers of children aged three to fifteen, fathers of Eastern European-Jewish extraction were more likely than any other group to place a high value on "self-direction" for their children. McClelland in the mid-1950s found Jews to expect a variety of individual masteries at an average age of 6.1 years, lowest for any group in his sample, and markedly lower than the average of 8.2 years for Italian Catholics. Work on achievement suggests a relationship between child-rearing practices that stress independence and mastery and achievement motivation, a finding reinforced by Strodtbeck who found Jews more likely than Italians to hold beliefs in an orderly world, amenable to rational mastery and planning, to be willing to leave home to make one's own way in life, and to prefer individual rather than collective credit for work. These differences, he argued, strongly influenced achievement differences.[39]

Whereas Russian-Jewish culture seemed readily adaptable to the American educational system, Southern Italian culture stood in marked contrast to many of the values associated with school success. Italians of the *contadino* or peasant class from the *Mezzogiorno,* the southern part of Italy, constituted the vast majority of the Italian immigrants in the United States. Residents of impoverished rural hill towns, the cultural patterns which these newcomers brought with them had been conditioned by chronic poverty, a rigid social structure, and by exploitation of frequently absent landlords. Their lives practically untouched by the *Risorgimento,* the unification of Italy in the mid-nineteenth century, the views the *contadini* held about institutions like the state and schools, their responses to authority and officialdom, and their expectations for and demands on their children were initially inimical to successful advancement through America's public schools.[40]

The central and controlling feature of Italian peasant culture was the division of the world into an "us-them" polarity. "Them" were the outsiders—the state, the schools, the official church; even neighbors were considered *forestrere,* strangers. Living in a Southern Italian district during the 1930s, Carlo Levi reported that to the *contadini,* "the State is more distant than heaven and far more of a scourge because it is always against them." "Us" was the family, the blood relatives who stood together depending on one another for sustenance. In a world heavily stacked against the *contadini,* the family was the sole refuge within which trust and loyalty could be cultivated. The family required complete allegiance, viewed the outside world as off limits, and discouraged independence and autonomy [in] its members.[41]

In America, the Italian family's exclusiveness was modified. A peer group society emerged that expanded upon the family structure and extended the boundaries of participation and mobility. However, the central perception of a dichotomized world persisted, and the peer group society continued to restrict its members from pursuing individual goals that would remove them from the groups.[42] The conflicts that emerged in the Italian-American community between expanding one's participation in the world and loyalty to kin and peer group were cogently summarized by William F. Whyte in *Street-Corner Society:*

One of the most cherished democratic beliefs is that our society operates so as to bring intelligence and ability to the top. Clearly, the difference in intelligence and ability does not explain the different corners of Chick and Doc. There must be some other way of explaining why some Cornerville men rise while others remain stationary. . . .

Chick [the college boy] and Doc [the corner boy] also had conflicting attitudes toward social mobility. Chick judged men according to their capacity for advancing themselves. Doc judged them according to their loyalty to their friends and their behavior in their personal relations. . . .

Both the college boy and the corner boy want to get ahead. The difference between them is that the college boy either does not tie himself to a group of close friends or else is willing to sacrifice his friendship with those who do not advance as fast as he does. The corner boy is tied to his group by a network of reciprocal obligations from which he is either unwilling or unable to break away.[43]

In this conflict, most Southern Italian parents were undoubtedly torn; opportunity versus loyalty were not easy choices to make, and most, we suspect, hoped that both could be achieved. Yet as a group Southern Italian parents sought to train their children for family and group membership primarily, and expected that the desire for independence and mobility would be filtered through the family's larger needs. Child rearing was thus dominated by obedience and a philosophy of control: *"i figli si devono domare"* — children must be tamed. Filial obligation, more important than parental obligation, combined with the expectation that the achievements of the children would not exceed those of the parents. An old Southern Italian proverb went, "Stupid and contemptible is he who makes his children better than himself."[44]

These cultural assumptions were reinforced by a negative view of formal schooling. To the Southern Italian peasant, schools were alien institutions maintained by the upper classes at the expense of the *contadini*. In the rigid class structure of Southern Italy education as an agency of upward mobility had little meaning. The adage toward the *contadini* was, "Of what use is school to you anyway? You'll always be a peasant." Few *contadini* children went beyond third grade. School facilities were always in bad repair, while the teachers made little effort to encourage peasant children to pursue their schooling. Nor did formal education receive religious support. Catholicism in Southern Italy was marked by mysticism, the supernatural, and emotional identification with the patron saints. Rarely was the Italian peasant expected to be able to read the prayer book. Knowledge — religious and secular — was based on community folklore not on written texts, to be learned not debated or analyzed.[45]

This background ill-disposed Southern Italian immigrants to respond favorably to American schools. Schooling was seen as a direct challenge to family values and parental control. The dominant concern of many Southern Italian parents seems to have been that the school would indoctrinate their children with ideas antagonistic to the traditional codes of family life. "School education in America, as the southern Italian peasant found it," Leonard Covello observed, "not only had no appeal to him; it was conceived to be an institution demoralizing youth and disorganizing their traditional patterns of family life." Moreover, schooling, especially for adolescents, conflicted with the economic needs and expectations of Southern Italian families. Once old enough to contribute, Italian youth were expected to work.[46]

Southern Italian children may indeed have left school earlier because their families were poorer than others. Certainly the emphasis on the family's economic needs lends credence to this. But had Italian parents seen the world differently, they might have been more willing to tolerate the acute discrimination their children felt in the public schools and the economic disadvantage of continued education, and kept their children in school longer.[47]

CONCLUSION

Our treatment of the role cultural values played in determining the school performance of immigrant groups has been necessarily brief and methodologically limited. We have focused primarily on only two nationality groups, and we have confined our analysis to the experience of the first and second generations before World War II. We have not charted the extent to which, or the reasons why, the impact of ethnic cultures diminished—if [it] did—in the postwar period. We feel, though, that the argument we have made and the data we have presented support the view that immigrant groups were not indistinguishable masses awaiting civic remodeling in the schools. Nor were they merely collections of individuals bound together by common ancestry and present economic plight. In large measure, immigrants acted on group values and preferences in responding to the institutions which touched their lives.

This does not mean that some groups did not want to succeed in America. We believe that the rules of schooling were often insensitive to group differences. Indeed, the growth of parochial schools during the early twentieth century suggests that public educators and their supporters were unwilling to modify in any substantial way their views of the "American way." Nor do our findings lead us to argue that all

groups were free to determine their destinies unhindered by the demands and discriminations of the economic and social system. Nevertheless, within that system there were choices, and the kinds of choices
groups made, their priorities, how they perceived the trade-offs, and
the levels of trauma they experienced were related in large measure to
the ethnic culture they brought with them and reordered in the
American environment. The limits of toleration within that environment is the other half of the picture, one we expect to pursue in further work.

Success and Failure in Adult Education:
The Immigrant Experience,
1914-1924

Maxine S. Seller

In the late nineteenth and early twentieth centuries millions of
Southern and Eastern European immigrants left their homes to enter
a rapidly urbanizing and industrializing United States. Stimulated by
the current interest in the education of minority children, historians in
recent years have explored the public school experiences of the
children of these immigrant communities.[1] But most immigrants were
adults at the time of their arrival. Of the 2,953,000 non-English-
speaking immigrants reported in the census of 1910, there were
2,565,612 over twenty years old, well beyond the limits of compulsory
public education laws.[2] An understanding of the educational experience of these immigrant adults is important, not only to the history of
immigrant communities, but also to the history of adult education in
the United States.

The educational needs of the adult immigrant population were
great. Many came from rural areas such as South Italy, where educational opportunities were few. Members of politically and culturally
oppressed ethnic groups such as the Ukrainians, the Poles, the Lithuanians, and other minorities in the Russian, Turkish, Austro-Hungar-

Delivered at the annual meeting of the American Educational Research Association,
Division F (History and Historiography), held at New York City in 1977.

ian, or German Empires were not allowed to educate their children in their native languages and culture.[3] Thus, many immigrant adults arrived illiterate or semiliterate in even their own languages and unschooled in their own cultural heritage. Others had years of formal education unrelated to the demands of modern industrial life. Many Jewish males who arrived, for example, were educated in traditional Jewish law and literature but ignorant of modern sciences, mathematics, or geography.[4]

Adult immigrants had three different kinds of educational needs. First, most wanted to learn to speak and read English as a tool for earning a living in the new country, and most of those who planned to remain in the United States permanently wanted to learn enough about America to become citizens. Second, many were eager to learn to read and write their native languages, to increase their knowledge of their own national traditions. Such education would compensate for the frustrations of past educational deprivation and enable immigrants to participate more meaningfully in their ethnic communities, often the only focus of social identity available to them in the United States. Finally, many wanted to taste the broader culture — philosophy, science, art, literature, history, politics (the elements of a liberal education) — that had been reserved for a privileged few in their homeland.[5]

These educational needs were met, or not met, in varying degrees. Between 1914 and 1924 professional American educators made a massive effort to provide education for adult immigrants, an effort that had limited impact upon those for whom it was intended. At the same time, immigrant communities provided informal and formal educational opportunities for their own members that were much more widely used. Both efforts are surveyed here, and reasons why the latter were more successful than the former are set forth.

Efforts of the native-born professional to educate the adult immigrant began before 1914. Night schools and settlement houses were active in such endeavors by the closing decade of the nineteenth century. Motivation ranged from an altruistic desire to help the foreign-born adjust and succeed in their new country to an ethnocentric desire to control an unruly lower class and, by "improving" them, to safeguard the American way of life. Between 1914 and 1924, however, fears generated by World War I and by the Russian Revolution increased concern for the education of adult immigrants to a national obsession.

Non-English-speaking and nonnaturalized immigrants, that is, "hyphenated Americans," whether from countries on the "right" side or the "wrong" side during the war, were suddenly feared as being potentially disloyal. Industrial and political fear of wartime sabotage evolved into fear of Bolshevism and added to the frenzied demands that immigrants be educated to protect against treachery and subversion.[6]

The emotional wartime atmosphere produced new hundred-percenters (the name given to fanatical Americanizers) who joined settlement house workers, ministers, and other educators in a massive campaign to get every non-English-speaking or nonnaturalized immigrant into a classroom. Established organizations, such as the North American Civic League for Immigrants, the Immigrants Protective League, the California Commission of Immigration and Housing, the YMCA and the YWCA, local chambers of commerce, and the Daughters of the American Revolution, became more active in their attempts to educate immigrants. New groups such as Frances Keller's Inter-Racial Council and the National Americanization Committee and federal agencies such as the Federal Bureau of Education, the Department of Immigration and Naturalization, the Council of National Defense, and the Committee on Public Information flooded the country with pamphlets, posters, and other materials. State legislatures passed enabling legislation for the formation of night schools throughout the country, and some states required adults whose English was not up to a specified level to attend.[7] Industrialists in Detroit announced that they would not promote or, in some cases, even hire men who were not attending night schools or factory schools.[8] In Buffalo, 20,000 lapel buttons were distributed bearing the caption "I am making Buffalo a Christmas present. Ask me." The Christmas present was the enrollment in high school of one non-English-speaking alien.[9]

The educational activities of night schools, factory schools, churches, and similar organizations varied, but the major thrust between 1914 and 1924, even more than in the earlier years, was English lessons for all. For men, there was training in citizenship (with emphasis upon the virtues of democracy and capitalism), as well as instruction in work habits and safety. Lessons for women stressed hygiene, child care, and American-style cooking and homemaking. The activities and programs of the many private and public Americanization agencies have been capably described by the individuals who organized them and by historians such as Edward George Hartmann,

Robert A. Carlson, Gerd Korman, and Allen Davis.[10] Less well-documented, perhaps, is the critical fact that the programs failed to attract and to hold the people for whom they were intended.

Night schools were the most widespread and widely touted agencies for the education of adult immigrants, yet they failed to reach more than a tiny fraction of their intended audience. In the early 1920s there were about 14 million nonnaturalized immigrants beyond the age of compulsory public schooling. After years of intensive advertising and campaigning on the part of the Americanizers, only 250,000, or less than 2 percent, were attending night school.[11] The results were badly distributed as well as meager. Though men usually had more out-of-school opportunity to learn English than women, there were three times as many men as women enrolled in the night schools.[12] Nor did the states with the greatest need always exert the greatest efforts. New York, first in need, was third in performance; Illinois, sixth in need, was twenty-first in performance; and Wisconsin, eleventh in need, was twenty-seventh in performance.[13]

The rapid expansion of night schools in the early decades of the twentieth century should not obscure their failure to educate the vast majority of immigrants. Most night school students were old-stock Americans or the American-born children of immigrants. In 1915 Buffalo, New York, had a foreign-born population of 118,687 (over half the population of the entire city), of whom 30,000 adults could not speak English and 11,000 could neither read nor write even their native language. Yet, of the 14,316 students enrolled in night school in 1914-1915, fewer than 2,000 were immigrants. In the next few years efforts to enlist the foreign-born in night school intensified, but, as America entered the war, enrollment actually dropped to half of the earlier figure "on account of excessive overtime demanded of the men at the plant." It was at this point that a massive enrollment campaign was launched, using the press, the schools, the churches, the women's clubs, and the business community. The campaign was a failure. Only 120 new immigrants were registered—an increase of about 8 percent.[14]

Other cities shared Buffalo's lack of success. Two years later the number of foreign-born persons over ten years of age who could not speak English exceeded 200,000 in Chicago, the home of the Immigrant Protective League (an active proponent of immigrant education). Only 17,613 people were registered for night school, however, and three years of intensive recruiting made little difference. By 1920 the unnaturalized adult immigrant population of Chicago had grown to nearly 300,000, yet the combined efforts of the city's sixty-five different Americanization agencies reached only 25,000 of those people, including 1,500 men in factory classes and 400 women in mothers' classes.[15] In smaller communities the situation was often worse. In 1925, Toledo, Ohio, reported a total night school enrollment of 247, not all of whom were foreign-born, that included only 17 women.[16]

Meager as these figures are, they are a gross overstatement of the actual numbers of immigrants in night school because the dropout rate was high. In Chicago only 7 percent of the night school pupils attended as many as seventy sessions in an eighty-session term, while almost one out of four attended fewer than twenty sessions.[17] These figures are based on the entire night-class populations; among just the foreign population, they would be worse. Over 80 percent of the immigrant women who entered the highly praised educational program instituted by the California Home Teachers Act of 1914 did not complete the program.[18] This experience was typical, not exceptional. According to John Daniels, author of a Carnegie Corporation study of Americanization, "the great majority of public evening school classes in English and civics for adult immigrants, though they start with a large enrollment, dwindle to small proportions or die out altogether."[19]

Churches, YMCAs, and other private agencies reached even fewer people. Secular settlement houses were sometimes able to reach immigrant women, largely through clubs rather than formal classes, but many women who participated in settlement house programs were native-born or already spoke English fluently. This was not the population the Americanizers hoped to reach. Similar attempts to reach immigrant men were almost always fruitless. According to William E. McLennen, one of the most experienced settlement workers in the country, "the subject of settlement men's clubs and that of Arctic orange groves have this in common, that not only are their data somewhat meager and indefinite, but the evidence at hand appears to show that neither is at present in a conspicuously flourishing condition."[20]

Contemporary observers and later historians have identified many reasons for the failure of American educators to reach the adult immigrant population. Immigrant fatigue,[21] inappropriate materials,[22] inconvenient locations and scheduling,[23] inability of instructors to speak immigrant languages,[24] lack of understanding of immigrant cultures,[25] the condescending, patronizing attitudes of many American educators toward their prospective students,[26] and American refusal to allow immigrants to participate in planning their own educational experiences[27] were major reasons for this massive failure in adult education. There were also religious, ideological, and political factors. Catholic and Jewish immigrants distrusted the educational efforts of Protestant churches and agencies such as the Salvation Army and the YMCA, fearing real or imagined proselytizing. Workers involved in unions or in socialist organizations distrusted Americanization education because they recognized its links to the interests of big business.[28]

It is ironic that the war itself, which had sparked the massive campaign for adult education, also helped to defeat it. The booming industrial wartime economy encouraged immigrants, for patriotic and economic reasons, to spend more hours at work. This left fewer hours and less energy for schooling. Industrialists who tried to make attendance at Americanization classes a prerequisite for employment were defeated by the labor shortage, for workers could find employment elsewhere. Finally, increased involvement with the fate of their native lands during the war heightened many an immigrant's awareness of emotional ties to the Old World. Enthusiastic Americanization campaigns were unpleasantly reminiscent of "Russification," "Magyarization," and other attempts to suppress cherished languages and cultures.[29]

One frequently overlooked reason for the failure of the educational campaign of 1914-1924 was the fact that resources fell far short of rhetoric. In 1917, 1919, and 1920 an economy-minded Congress refused to pass bills appropriating even modest sums for immigrant education. Between 1919 and 1921 many states passed laws permitting, or requiring, local communities to provide such education but usually offering little more than token financial support.[30] Because their resources were limited, local communities hesitated to assume the responsibility. Nor were private agencies necessarily more generous. In 1919 the National Conference on Americanization in Industry expressed its support of Americanization classes in factories — provided that public school systems assumed the responsibility of paying the teachers and that employees attend on their own time, without compensation from the company.[31]

Perhaps the most important reason why these massive educational programs failed to attract and hold their intended audience was because they concentrated almost exclusively upon the teaching of the English language, civics, and the "American way of life." Immigrants wanted knowledge of their native language and heritage, as well as that of America. They were interested in industrial and homemaking education, but they were also interested in learning about the art, philosophy, science, politics, history, literature, and economics.

Immigrant communities succeeded where American educators failed. They provided education planned and executed either by the immigrants themselves or by second-generation members of the communities. Classes were taught in the native language and in ways that did not violate cultural traditions. They were sponsored by and housed in institutions that immigrants knew and trusted—the lodge, the church, the union. The programs developed by the immigrant communities addressed not only "Americanization," but the entire spectrum of an immigrant's cultural and intellectual interests.

The ethnic neighborhood was filled with informal but very effective educational institutions. The Finnish boarding house, the Greek or Armenian coffeehouse, the local candy store, the ubiquitous corner saloon—these and similar gathering places served as informal, natural classrooms where old-timers taught newcomers a few basic English words, how to get a job, where to find help in case of illness or another crisis, what local politician could be relied upon for various services, and which American laws were enforced and which could be broken with impunity. The night school taught American ideals; the saloonkeeper taught American realities. This, in addition to the more convivial atmosphere, explained ability of the latter to attract and hold its audience.

More formal institutions—lodges, athletic societies, nationalist societies, cultural societies, musical and literary circles, political organizations, women's organizations of many kinds, cooperatives, theaters, unions, and churches—provided more formal educational opportunities. Membership was in itself an educational experience. Conducting meetings, participating in elections, serving as officers, planning programs, conferences, and political activities at the local, regional, or national level were all important learning experiences for the foreign-born men and women who participated. Although the individual's dues were usually small, larger organizations handled substantial amounts of money, the management of which provided many lessons in practical economics.

Some immigrant organizations, for example, literary societies and debating societies, were specifically educational in purpose. In many of these organizations the better-educated immigrants shared their knowledge with those less well educated, whether American-born or newly arrived. The Hebrew Literary Society of Philadelphia brought in professors from the local colleges and universities to lecture on religious, political, and scientific subjects, sponsored debates in Yiddish for those who spoke no English, and maintained a library in Hebrew, Yiddish, Russian, German, and English.[32] The Finnish-American Literary Society encouraged its members to write as well as to read.[33]

The Hungarian community in New York City created an institution apparently modeled after the popular American lyceum. The Hungarian Free Lyceum was organized to "further the education and political knowledge" of the Hungarian community and to "acquaint them with American customs and institutions." Here Hungarian-Americans attended lectures in Hungarian or English on topics dealing with their own background, such as "Modern Hungarian Poets" and "Industrial and Social Transformation of Europe;" on American history and geography;and on topics of current interest such as "The Waterfront and Transportation System of Our City," "The Influence of the Press," "Industrial Hazards," and "Problems of the Education of the Future." The Hungarian Free Lyceum attracted members of the community-at-large as well as Hungarian-Americans. It catered to recent immigrants with special lectures on Americanization and naturalization. What is significant is that such lectures came at the end,not at the beginning, of the academic season, after the immigrant audience had been attracted by other kinds of offerings.[34]

Another educational experiment within the immigrant community was "the Polish University," established in Chicago around 1910 and still functioning a decade later. Begun by a group of 50 Polish socialists as an attempt to reach the new immigrant working-class population, its original program consisted of lectures on Polish history and on the problems and future prospects of Poland. Gradually the program expanded to meet more varied educational interests. By 1920 the university had 200 paid subscribers, and its special lectures, held in a public park, attracted as many as 1,000 people at a time. The nature of this university and the reasons for its success are revealed in the following account by one of the founders:

Some Americans think . . . that we immigrants can comprehend only such thoughts as "I see a cat; the cat is black" — as the teachers in the evening schools make grown men repeat. But the minds of most immigrants are not so feeble as that. For the poor man, America is all work-work-work. We believe in work, all right, but we want thought and education to go along with it. So we took up questions about the beginning of things — the creation of the world, the theory of evolution, primitive man, the development of language . . . . All the lectures were in Polish . . . obviously the use of Polish was necessary if such subjects, which are hard enough to grasp, anyway, and which involve many scientific terms and fine shades of meaning, were to be got across to our audiences.

Gradually . . . we came to subjects connected with America and with civic problems. But here we do more than have lectures. We go and see for ourselves how civic agencies work. At different times we have visited most of the public departments and institutions of this city. Every little while we take a week-end excursion to some city — not far away — and see how things are run there . . . .

. . . We Socialists have not tried particularly to spread our propaganda. Less than half of the paying members are socialists, and most of the people who attend the lectures are not. We haven't preached "Americanization," either . . . [but] if what America wants is people who think and act for themselves, then we're *doing* Americanization.[35]

While the Polish University promoted Americanization and naturalization only indirectly, between 1914 and 1924 many immigrant communities formed special organizations, often called "Citizens Clubs," devoted solely to those purposes. The relatively modest community of Brockton, Massachusetts, had an active Lithuanian Citizen's Club of 300 members. Ukrainians in Philadelphia, Portuguese in New Bedford, Syrians in Boston, and other groups organized societies to conduct citizenship classes within their own communities. The activities of such societies were often remarkably successful. An Italian Club in Richmond, Virginia, was instrumental in nationalizing hundreds, so that by 1920 all but a small percentage of the Italian population of the city had become naturalized. A Greek Club in Nashville, Tennessee, experienced similar success.[36]

Organizations formed primarily to serve noneducational purposes often had strong educational components. Fraternal lodges, mutual benefit societies, and athletic and cultural groups were broadly educational, promoting knowledge of the homeland, general education, and Americanization in varying proportions and with varying methods. The Yiddish Workmen's Circle, a national labor-oriented mutual benefit society with 250 locals in New York City alone, sponsored educational lectures, debates, and original as well as classical theater presentations, distributed its own educational materials, and assisted its members with the naturalization process.[37] The largest Italian fraternal order, the Sons of Italy, with 125 lodges in Chicago alone, had special officials called "orators" to give lectures and help members learn English and become naturalized.[38]

The largest immigrant organizations were the National Alliances, many of which combined the functions of mutual benefit societies with the pursuit of nationalist political aims, such as the restoration of the independence of the homeland, and also furthered a wide variety of educational objectives in the United States. These organizations, besides keeping alive the language and history and culture of the homeland, helped members adjust to their new environments. Publications, meetings, schools, lectures, and other educational activities of the nationalist societies reached hundreds of thousands. In 1921 the Polish National Alliance alone had a membership of more than 125,000.[39] Not the least of the educational benefits of the nationalist societies were the lessons in practical American politics that members learned while lobbying for the interests of the homeland.

Women were active in educational programs, both as members of auxiliary organizations and independent groups. For example, the Italian Women's Club of Albuquerque, New Mexico, started an English-language school for its members in 1923.[40] The Lithuanian Women's Alliance in Chicago refused to allow its members to participate in its popular mutual benefit society unless they also participated in its educational program, which included English lessons and homemaking.[41] The first issue of the official magazine of the Ukrainian Women's Alliance contained articles on child care, hygiene, and on the Women's Suffrage Movement, urging women to take a greater interest in politics.[42]

Singing and instrumental music societies also encouraged knowledge of the language and cultural traditions of the homeland. The effect of such organizations was widespread and long lasting; it cut across age and class. Buffalo, New York, had three Polish singing societies involving hundreds of people before the turn of the century. Gymnastic societies such as the German *Turn Verein,* the Bohemian *Sokol,* and the Polish *Falcons* sponsored singing and dramatics, lectures and libraries, as well as gymnastics, and encouraged naturalization and American political activity. The national *Turn Verein* body (with 194 constituent societies, each with up to 450 members) insisted that all its new members be citizens or in the process of becoming citizens.[43]

One of the most important educational institutions in many immigrant communities was the theater. There were hundreds of amateur ethnic theaters throughout the nation. Many were sponsored by cultural or athletic societies, ethnic churches, settlement houses, or unions. Finnish, German, Hungarian, and Jewish workers formed theater groups to educate fellow workers about industrial problems. In large cities the Chinese, German, Italian, Hungarian, and Jewish communities sponsored commercial theaters that performed regularly and went on tour to smaller population centers throughout the country. Chicago had three professional Italian theaters, and the lower East Side of New York had five Jewish theaters.

Many foreign-language theaters were started purely for the purpose of entertaining,[44] but there was also educational value. Every ethnic theater produced the great Italian operas, the German theaters produced works by Schiller and Goethe. When it came to historical dramas, Jewish theatergoers saw plays portraying biblical events, German theatergoers saw productions about Napoleon or Frederick the Great, and Chinese theatergoers witnessed the succession of imperial dynasties. Italian, German, and Yiddish theaters produced not only their own literary classics; there were also translations and adaptations of plays by Molière, Schiller, Tolstoy, Shakespeare, Zola, Ibsen, and Molnár. Many immigrants considered theater such a necessary part of their lives that they would go without meals to save the pennies for a ticket. For immigrants with widely varying degrees of education, from intellectual to illiterate, and for immigrants from every age group and social class, the theater was an important educational experience.[45]

Two institutions that, though they were not intrinsically ethnic, were functionally so in many neighborhoods were the labor movement and the Church. Both were active in immigrant education. Most workers were not unionized, but in specific areas, such as the garment industries of New York City or the stockyards of Chicago, the union proved to be an enormously important educational influence. In unions with mixed ethnic memberships, the mastery of English was stimulated by the immigrant's desire to participate in the business of the union. In the ethnic locals, where business was conducted in Yiddish, Italian, Polish, or another language, union officials encouraged members to learn English and to become naturalized.[46]

Italian- and Jewish-dominated garment unions of New York and New Jersey undertook extensive educational programs that included informal reading rooms, movies, lectures, and plays, as well as formal classes in English, public speaking, economics, history, and literature. The International Ladies' Garment Workers' Union cooperated with the Women's Trade Union League and a number of institutions of higher learning, such as Bryn Mawr College and the University of Wisconsin, to set up summer schools for workingwomen, many of them foreign-born. The curriculum was broad, emphasizing the social sciences and the humanities.[47] The Finnish Socialists, affiliated with the International Workers of the World, operated the Work People's College in Duluth, Minnesota, where young workers, again many of them foreign-born, studied not only labor history, theory, and organizational tactics, but also a broad curriculum of social and physical sciences and the humanities.[48] The numbers who attended labor-sponsored educational programs were not great, but many of those who did attend were profoundly influenced by the experience.

As with the labor movement, the Catholic Church was, in theory, a universal institution. As with the labor movement, the Catholic Church also often found itself an ethnic institution in practice. Churches in ethnic parishes often fostered knowledge of the traditional immigrant language and culture as a method of strengthening religious loyalty. During the early years of Southern and Eastern European immigration, the Catholic Church was cautious in its approach to Americanization, fearing that, if assimilation were too rapid, this would weaken religious ties. Individual parishes did, however, undertake some Americanization programs. In 1914, for example, the Polish church in Chicago sponsored the "King Casimir the Great Polish Citizens Club," which conducted English classes, guided hundreds through the naturalization process, and concerned itself with local civic improvements.[49]

After the United States entered World War I, the Social Action Department of the National Catholic War Council launched the first official nation-wide drive for Americanization under Church auspices.

The Social Action Department prepared a special textbook modeled on the familiar religious catechism. The widely distributed text, entitled *Civics Catechism on the Rights and Duties of American Citizens,* appeared in twelve languages, and each translation was accompanied by the English version. The department also provided local parishes with materials for Americanization classes, including motion pictures (with subtitles in both immigrant languages and English), a guaranteed attraction. Americanization programs were even launched in remote rural or mining areas. Such programs were often successful because the Church was a trusted and familiar institution that recognized and stressed the value of traditional language and culture and was not associated with radical attempts at Americanization. Wherever possible, churches, like labor organizations, used instructors familiar with the language and traditions of the prospective students. In 1921 Italian-speaking lawyers taught a Church-sponsored civics program to 787 Italian immigrants in San Francisco.[50]

Undoubtedly, however, the foreign-language press stands out as the single most influential educational force in the immigrant community. In 1920 the foreign-language press was conservatively estimated to have a circulation of 7,608,407; other estimates ran as high as 10 million.[51] Even the larger estimate fails to suggest the full impact of the ethnic press. Copies were passed from hand to hand and were read aloud in family groups, in taverns, in boardinghouses, and in work places, reaching even the illiterate and the most impoverished.[52]

In urban centers such as New York or Chicago, large immigrant communities supported dozens of papers, while no ethnic group — Lett, Estonian, Wend, Catalan — was so small that it did not have at least one. Ethnic papers were as varied as the communities they served: some local, some national, some organs of churches or various societies, some independent commercial ventures. They were devoted to literary interests, concentrated on humor, or specialized in topics of interest to farmers, musicians, socialists, anarchists, trade unionists, feminists, and others.

The most vital educational function of the foreign-language press was the promotion of literacy. Many immigrants first learned to read their native languages by spelling out the large type and simple words of headlines and advertisements and then moved on to the more complicated features, news, and editorials. Recognizing that much of their public was semiliterate, many editors kept their materials deliberately simple: "Chewed over, as for a baby," said one.[53]

The immigrant press attracted its audiences with materials on the homeland and, more important, news of the immigrant community in America, that is, news about themselves. The better papers kept their readers informed about American life, especially American politics and economics, through skillful coverage of the national news. The socialist press, especially important among Finns, Bohemians, and Jews, organized the news within the ideological framework of the all too familiar struggle for bread. According to sociologist Robert Park, the socialist press made an enormous contribution by giving the common man a point of view from which he could think about the news and his life. "It made the sweatshop an intellectual problem."[54]

The editorial columns kept intellectuals up to date on the controversies of the day, as leaders of various political, economic, and religious factions debated ideology and tactics. Of wider interest were the many practical articles on child care, food, health, and how to obtain citizenship and register to vote. The Ukrainian paper *Svoboda* published feature articles by Julian Chapka on the America legal system and the United States Constitution. Additional education about American life came from advertisement of goods and services and from the "letters to the editor" columns, which gave practical advice on making a living, getting along with family, friends, and employers, and coping with the demands of a new way of life.

Like other immigrant educational institutions, the press presented information on Americanization along with a variety of other educational materials. In the Yiddish press, Abraham Cahan, Abner Tannenbaum, and other journalists introduced their reading public to Darwinism and other scientific ideas and to the science fiction of Jules Verne. A Lithuanian paper introduced its readers to Nietzsche by publishing a translation of *Thus Spoke Zarathustra.* Many ethnic papers featured fiction and poetry, much of which serialized the work of "hack" writers, but they also provided a forum for the works of talented members of the ethnic community and for classic works from the homeland.

The impact of the foreign-language press on the immigrant is even more impressive when one realizes that the experience of reading a newspaper was a new one for most immigrants. Of 312 readers surveyed by a Russian newspaper, only 16 had read newspapers in

Russia. In the United States, Russian immigrants not only became faithful readers of Russian-language publications, but over a quarter also became regular readers of the American press, and two-thirds became regular theatergoers, whereas almost none had attended the theater in Russia. Journalist Mark Villchur, who conducted the survey, concluded:

An interest in the [Russian] press creates an interest in the book, in the theater, and the whole outlook of the Russian in America widens. Not only his own interests and the interests of his family and of his circle become near and dear to him, but also the problems of his country, of the republic in which he resides, and, gradually, of the whole wide world.[55]

Education within the immigrant community was not free of problems. The fact that some organizations made participation in English and citizenship instruction a prerequisite for membership suggests that prospective members were less than enthusiastic about such instruction. The quality of the many classes and countless special lectures offered by the various immigrant organizations ranged from excellent to bad; sometimes there was more enthusiasm than enlightenment.[56] Second-generation ethnic Americans could be as condescending in their efforts to educate more recently arrived countrymen as the most insensitive descendant of the Puritans.[57]

Still, immigrant institutions operating within the immigrant communities were far more successful at adult education between 1914 and 1924 than the official night schools and other Anglo-Saxon Protestant Americanizing agencies. During the same years that Anglo-Saxon America was conducting its intensive and, as already demonstrated, not very successful effort to Americanize immigrants, educational activities within the immigrant communities were expanding rapidly, partly in response to pressure from Anglo-Saxon America and partly to meet internal needs. Political activity in response to reports of oppression in the homelands increased membership in nationalist societies, and, within those societies, the demand for information dealing with the history and culture of the homeland. World War I stimulated circulation of the immigrant press and increased its effectiveness as an agency of mass education.[58] When the war was finally over and long-suppressed Eastern European nations were again independent, immigrants from those lands were faced with the conscious choice of whether to remain in the United States or to return to their birthplace. Many returned, but those who chose to remain in the

United States experienced a new sense of permanent commitment that encouraged the growth of ethnic-sponsored English classes and citizenship programs.[59]

Between 1914 and 1924 the educational programs of immigrant cultural societies and unions enrolled tens of thousands; immigrant social and nationalist organizations enrolled hundreds of thousands, perhaps millions. And immigrant newspapers reached many millions. These numbers are far greater than those reached by Anglo-Saxon Protestant Americanization agencies, and the contacts were more prolonged. Those who read the newspapers, attended the theaters, were members of a church or a union, or loyally supported a variety of ethnic organizations had strong social, ideological, and emotional ties that made them much less likely to drop out of the programs. Immigrant autobiographies attest that the educational impact of the immigrant community was not only quantitatively great; it was also qualitatively intense. The widow of a Jewish immigrant continued his subscription to a Yiddish newspaper after his death, bringing the paper to his grave because it had meant so much to him during his lifetime.[60]

The efforts of American institutions to educate and Americanize immigrants have been well documented. More work needs to be done on the efforts of immigrants, as individuals and as members of communities, to educate and Americanize themselves. Adults who immigrated to the United States were more than passive recipients of American-initiated educational programs; they were also the initiators of important programs of their own. Who initiated the programs within immigrant communities? Why and how were the programs initiated? What effect did the programs have? How were the programs affected by ethnic, class, religious, and sex differences? More intensive study of these and other questions about education and Americanization carried on within immigrant communities may be of use not only to historians of education, but also to those planning adult education programs today.

NOTES

Ravitch: **On the Theory of Minority Group Education in the United States**

1. Among the leading contemporary revisionist histories are: Michael Katz, *The Irony of Early School Reform: Educational Innovation in Mid-Nineteenth Century*

Massachusetts (Cambridge, Mass.: Harvard University Press, 1968); *id., Class, Bureaucracy, and Schools: The Illusion of Educational Change in America* (New York: Praeger, 1971); Stanley K. Schultz, *The Culture Factory: Boston Public Schools, 1789-1860* (New York: Oxford University Press, 1973); Joel H. Spring, *Education and the Rise of the Corporate State* (Boston, Mass.: Beacon Press, 1972); Clarence J. Karier, Joel H. Spring, and Paul C. Violas, *Roots of Crisis* (Chicago: Rand McNally and Co., 1973); and Colin Greer, *The Great School Legend: A Revisionist Interpretation of American Public Education* (New York: Basic Books, 1972).

2. Harold Isaacs, *Idols of the Tribe* (New York: Harper and Row, 1975), 3.

3. Diane Ravitch, *The Great School Wars: New York City, 1805-1973* (New York: Basic Books, 1974), 7, 21.

4. James G. Carter, *Essays upon Popular Education* (Boston, Mass.: Bowles and Dearborn, 1826), 19.

5. Lloyd P. Jorgenson, *The Founding of Public Education in Wisconsin* (Madison: State Historical Society of Wisconsin, 1956), 7; Cornelius J. Heatwole, *A History of Education in Virginia* (New York: Macmillan, 1916), 102; and Albert Fishlow, "The American Common School Revival: Fact or Fancy?" in Henry Rosovsky, *Industrialization in Two Systems: Essays in Honor of Alexander Gerschenkron* (New York: John Wiley, 1966), 40-67.

6. David Tyack, "The Perils of Pluralism: The Background of the Pierce Case," *American Historical Review* 74 (October 1968): 74-98.

7. *Pierce* v. *Society of the Sisters of the Holy Names,* 268 U.S. 510 (1925).

8. Jane Addams, *Newer Ideals of Peace* (Chautauqua, N.Y.: Chautauqua Press, 1907), 77.

9. Timothy L. Smith, "Immigrant Social Aspirations and American Education, 1880-1930," *American Quarterly* 21 (Fall 1969): 523-543.

10. Mordecai Soltes, *The Yiddish Press: An Americanizing Agency* (New York: Bureau of Publications, Teachers College, Columbia University, 1925), 151-152.

11. *Meyer* v. *Nebraska,* 262 U.S. 390 (1923); Arnold H. Leibowitz, "Educational Policy and Political Acceptance: The Imposition of English as the Language of Instruction in American Schools" (Washington, D.C.: Center for Applied Linguistics, ERIC Clearinghouse for Linguistics, March 1971), 34.

12. Leibowitz, "Educational Policy and Political Acceptance"; John B. Shotwell, *A History of the Schools of Cincinnati* (Cincinnati, Ohio: School Life Co., 1902), 289-301; Joshua A. Fishman, *Language Loyalty in the United States* (The Hague: Mouton & Co., 1966), 233; and Heinz Kloss, *Excerpts from the National Minority Laws of the United States of America* (Honolulu, Hawaii: East-West Center, 1966), 48-55.

13. Kloss, *Excerpts from the National Minority Laws,* 62.

14. Fishman, *Language Loyalty in the United States,* 29-30.

15. Theodore Andersson and Mildred Boyer, *Bilingual Schooling in the United States* (Washington, D.C.: U.S. Government Printing Office, 1970), 211.

16. Robert F. Berkhofer, Jr., *Salvation and the Savage: An Analysis of Protestant Missions and American Indian Response, 1787-1862* (New York: Atheneum, 1972), 16-43.

17. Leibowitz, "Educational Policy and Political Acceptance," 67-78.

18. U.S. Senate Committee on Labor and Public Welfare, Special Subcommittee on Indian Education, *Indian Education: A National Tragedy—A National Challenge* (Washington, D.C.: U.S. Government Printing Office, 1969), 147-148.

19. G. E. E. Lindquist, *The Red Man in the United States* (New York: George H. Doran, 1923), 40-41.

20. Institute for Government Research, *The Problems of Indian Administration* (Baltimore, Md.: Johns Hopkins Press, 1928), 22, 403, 408, and 412.

21. U.S. Senate Committee on Labor and Public Welfare, Special Subcommittee on Indian Education, *Indian Education,* 186-189.

22. Carter G. Woodson, *The Education of the Negro Prior to 1861* (Washington, D.C.: Associated Publishers, 1919), 1.

23. *Ibid.,* 205-208; Henry Allen Bullock, *A History of Negro Education in the South: From 1619 to the Present* (Cambridge, Mass.: Harvard University Press, 1967), 5-15.

24. Bullock, *History of Negro Education in the South,* 10-13, 21-26: Woodson, *Education of the Negro Prior to 1861,* 128-144, 205-208.

25. Woodson, *Education of the Negro Prior to 1861,* 317; Schultz, *Culture Factory,* 160-162.

26. Horace Mann Bond, *Black American Scholars: A Study of Their Beginnings* (Detroit, Mich.: Balamp Publishing, 1972), 23, 53.

27. Bullock, *History of Negro Education in the South,* 23-25, 57-58.

28. *Ibid.,* 77-78. On the role of northern philanthropists, see Louis R. Harlan, *Separate and Unequal: Public School Campaigns and Racism in the Southern Seaboard States, 1901-1915* (Chapel Hill, N.C.: University of North Carolina Press, 1958).

29. Fishman, *Language Loyalty in the United States,* 92.

Olneck and *Lazerson:* **The School Achievement of Immigrant Children**

1. Contrast Timothy Smith, "Immigrant Social Aspirations and American Education, 1880-1930," *American Quarterly* 21 (Fall 1969): 523-543, with Colin Greer, *The Great School Legend: A Revisionist Interpretation of American Public Education* (New York: Basic Books, 1972).

2. For a critique of the melting pot belief, see Nathan Glazer and Daniel P. Moynihan, *Beyond the Melting Pot* (Cambridge, Mass.: M.I.T. Press, 1963) and Milton M. Gordon, *Assimilation in American Life* (New York: Oxford University Press, 1964). Oscar Handlin *(The Uprooted* [Boston: Little, Brown and Co., 1951]) sets out the themes of alienation and disorientation in the immigrant experience.

3. Recent studies emphasize diversity among immigrant groups. See Rudolph J. Vecoli, "Ethnicity: A Neglected Dimension of American History," in *The State of American History,* ed. Herbert J. Bass (Chicago: Quadrangle Books, 1970); Rudolph J. Vecoli, "Contadini in Chicago: A Critique of *The Uprooted,"Journal of American History* 51 (December 1964): 404-417; *id.,* "Prelates and Peasants: Italian Immigrants and the Catholic Church," *Journal of Social History* 2 (Spring 1969): 217-268; Victor R. Greene, "For God and Country: The Origins of Slavic Catholic Self-Consciousness in America," *Church History* 35 (December 1966): 446-460.

4. For a similar, though more limited example, see David K. Cohen, "Immigrants and the Schools," *Review of Educational Research* 40 (February 1970): 13-27.

5. For example, see Leonard P. Ayres, *Laggards in Our Schools* (New York: Russell Sage Foundation, 1908).

6. Calculated from U.S. Immigration Commission, "The Children of Immigrants in the Schools," *Reports,* Vol. 29 (Washington, D.C.: Government Printing Office, 1911), 63-64.

7. Ratios of the number of eighth-grade students to the number of seventh-grade students were calculated for nativity groups for Boston, Chicago, and New York. The differences were trivial. *Ibid.,* Vol. 31, 190-193, 564-568; Vol. 34, 624-628.

8. J. B. Maller, "Economic and Social Correlatives of School Progress in New York City," *Teachers College Record* 34 (May 1933): 664.

9. In Detroit, for example, by 1935, 70 percent of the Jewish youth had graduated from high school compared to 40 percent of the non-Jewish youth. Nathan Glazer, "Social Characteristics of American Jews," in Louis Finkelstein, *The Jews* (New York: Jewish Publication Society of America, 1949), Vol. II, 1712.

10. George S. Counts, *The Selective Character of American Secondary Education* (Chicago: University of Chicago Press, 1924), 111-112.

11. See Mark Zborowski and Elizabeth Herzog, *Life Is with People: The Culture of the Shtetl* (New York: International University Press, 1952), Pt. II, Chap. 2.

12. Counts, *Selective Character of American Secondary Education,* 112.

13. See especially Leonard Covello, *The Social Background of the Italo-American School Child* (Leiden: E. J. Brill, 1967; first published in U.S. in 1972 by Rowman and Littlefield, Totowa, N.J.), 292. We believe similar attitudes held true among Poles.

14. U.S. Immigration Commission, *Reports,* Vol. 29. The data in the *Summary* volume are suspect. They are drawn from an unrepresentative sample of the cities and schools in the Commission's data, and they exaggerate the differences in performance between nationality groups. Nevertheless, they are the only data that permit attempts to control the effects of independent variables on nationality differences in retardation, and so we have used them.

15. *Ibid.,* 92.

16. *Ibid.,* 61.

17. *Ibid.,* 98, 92. Italian English-language acquisition continued to lag in subsequent decades; in 1930, at every age level the proportion of Italians who could not speak English exceeded the proportion of Russians who could not.

| | Percent unable to speak English — 1930, by age group | | | |
Nationality, by birth	10-24	25-44	45-65	65 and over
Russian	2	3	9	28
Italian	7	12	20	41

Source: U.S. Bureau of the Census, *Abstract of the Fifteenth Census* (Washington, D.C.: Government Printing Office, 1933).

18. A number of "IQ" issues are not raised here. One is the possible genetic base of group IQ differences. Our presumption is genetic equality between groups with

respect to the determinants of IQ scores. That presumption is consistent with the available evidence, provided we also assume that genes play a larger role in determining IQ than they do in determining educational attainment. Put another way, we assume that the impact of cultural differences is relatively greater on educational attainment than it is on IQ differences. If this is true — and it is difficult to conceive an important effect of genes on educational attainment that is not mediated by IQ (Athletic prowess, musical talent, and physical attractiveness are important to only the lucky few, and add little to explaining variation in educational attainment among the general population.) — and if groups were equal in genetic endowment affecting IQ, we would expect smaller differences on IQ than on educational attainment. Our best estimate for the period in question is the Jews exceeded Southern Italians by one-half standard deviation in tested IQ, but exceeded them by two-thirds of a standard deviation in educational attainment.

A second set of issues concerns the impact of individual IQ scores on individual attainment within ethnic groups. All of our estimates about the role of IQ differences between groups assume that the relationship between IQ and educational attainment is the same within each group. There is reason to believe that this may not be true. We think it is fair to speculate that among Jews IQ differences mattered less for educational attainment than they did among Italians. We suspect that lower-ability Jews were more likely to pursue schooling relative to high-ability students than were lower-ability Italians. Put another way, a high-IQ Italian would stand at a greater advantage over his lower-IQ peers than would a high-IQ Jew, with respect to educational attainment. If this reasoning is correct, our present estimate of the part group IQ differences played in accounting for Jewish-Italian schooling differences is high, and our confidence in the importance of cultural values for explaining differences in educational attainment is strengthened.

19. Katharine Murdock, "A Study of Race Differences in New York City," *School and Society* 11 (January 31, 1920): 147-150. The first discussion of the test in the literature reports results for over 1,000 subjects in Bloomington, Indiana. Standard deviations appear to be 24 for ten-year-olds, 28 for eleven-year-olds, and 25 for twelve-year-olds. Calculated from S. L. Pressey and L. W. Pressey, "A Group Point Scale for Measuring General Intelligence, with First Results from 1,100 School Children," *Journal of Applied Psychology* 2 (September 1918): 266. This means that Italians in Murdock's sample scored well over a half standard deviation below Jewish subjects. These results are at variance with our other evidence, and are discounted on the assumption that the Pressey test was overly reliant on language acquisition. See also Dorothy W. Seago and Theresa S. Koldin, "A Comparative Study of the Mental Capacity of Sixth Grade Jewish and Italian Children," *School and Society* 22 (October 31, 1925): 566, and Gustave Feingold, "Intelligence of the First Generation of Immigrant Groups," *Journal of Educational Psychology* 15 (February 1924): 70, cited in Cohen, "Immigrants and the Schools," 27.

20. See Arthur I. Gates, "The Correlation of Achievement in School Subjects with Intelligence Tests and Other Variables," *Journal of Educational Psychology* 13 (April 1922): 281; Maller, "Economic and Social Correlatives," 659; Carl W. Ziegler, *School Attendance as a Factor in School Progress* (New York: Teachers College, Columbia University, 1928), 26.

21. Feingold, "Intelligence of the First Generation of Immigrant Groups," 77-82.

22. Christopher S. Jencks et al., *Inequality: A Reassessment of the Effect of Family and Schooling in America* (New York: Basic Books, 1972), 337.

23. *Ibid.*, 323-325.

24. Beverly Duncan and Otis Dudley Duncan, "Minorities and the Process of Stratification," *American Sociological Review* 33 (June 1968): 356-364.

25. See, for example, James W. Bridges and Lillian E. Coler, "The Relation of Intelligence to Social Status," *Psychological Review* 24 (January 1917): 1-31; Emily Dexter, "The Relation between Occupation of Parent and Intelligence of Children," *School and Society* 17 (June 2, 1923); S. L. Pressey and Ruth Ralston, "The Relation of the General Intelligence of School Children to the Occupation of Their Fathers," *Journal of Applied Psychology* 3 (December 1919): 366-373.

26. In addition to Bridges and Coler, Dexter, and Pressey and Ralston cited in note 25, above, see Counts, *Selective Character of American Secondary Education*, and Joseph K. Van Denburg, *Causes of the Elimination of Students in Public Secondary Schools of New York City* (New York: Teachers College, Columbia University, 1911).

27. Samuel Joseph, *Jewish Immigration to the United States from 1881-1910* (New York: Columbia University, 1914).

28. Isaac Rubinow, "Economic and Industrial Conditions—New York," in *The Russian Jew in the United States,* ed. Charles S. Bernheimer (Philadelphia, Pa.: J. C. Winston Co., 1905).

29. United States Industrial Commission, *Reports,* Vol. 15 (Washington, D.C.: Government Printing Office, 1901), 478, 343-369.

30. Not all income was earned by male members of the family, so not all of the Jewish income advantage can be attributed to male occupational superiority. Of the Russian-Jewish households in the seven cities surveyed by the Immigration Commission, 43 percent received income from boarders, compared to 27 percent for Southern Italian households; 36 percent of the Russian-Jewish households received income from offspring, compared to 22 percent for the Southern Italians. These differentials were somewhat offset by the fact that 17 percent of the foreign-born Italian wives worked, compared to 8 percent of the Russian-Jewish wives. (U.S. Immigration Commission, *Reports,* Vol. 1, 766.)

31. On the impact of cultural values on economic decisions, see Virginia Yans McLaughlin, "Patterns of Work and Family Organization: Buffalo's Italians," in *The Family in History,* ed. Theodore K. Rabb and Robert I. Rotberg (New York: Harper and Row, 1973), 111-126.

32. Duncan and Duncan, "Minorities and the Process of Stratification."

33. Knowledge of the intercorrelations between educational attainment, test scores, and father's occupation permits the estimation of the regression coefficients in a path model in which attainment is assumed to be determined by scores and father's occupation. These results are maximum effects, unless either test scores or father's occupation is negatively related to an omitted variable that affects attainment positively. We then substituted the average differences in standard deviations between Russian Jews and Southern Italians on father's occupation and test scores into the resultant equation predicting education. Our prediction of the difference between the two groups on educational attainment fell short by one-third, as the text notes. Inclusion

of family size did not alter the results importantly. At least 30 percent of the attain-ment gap remained unexplained when family size, test scores, and father's occupation were taken into account. For an explanation of the method of path analysis, see Otis D. Duncan, "Path Analysis: Sociological Examples," *American Journal of Sociology* 72 (July 1966): 1-16.

34. Zborowski and Herzog, *Life Is with People,* 118-123; Mark Zborowski, "The Place of Book-learning in Traditional Jewish Culture," *Harvard Educational Review* 19 (Spring 1949): 87-109; Mary Antin, *The Promised Land* (Boston, Mass.: Houghton Mifflin Co., 1912), 204-217.

35. Charles Angoff, *Journey to the Dawn* (New York: Beechhurst Press, 1951), 196; Elias Tobenkin, *Witte Arrives* (New York: Frederick A. Stokes Co., 1916), 16.

36. The Exodus is the central myth exemplifying this theme.

37. From the *Daily Forward,* May 6, 1906, cited in Robert E. Park and Herbert A. Miller, *Old World Traits Transplanted* (New York: Harper and Brothers, 1921), 7.

38. Tobenkin, *Witte Arrives,* 23; Angoff, *Journey to the Dawn,* 238.

39. Melvin Kohn, *Class and Conformity: A Study in Values* (Homewood, Ill.: Dorsey Press, 1969), 63; Fred L. Strodtbeck, "Family Interaction, Values, and Achievement," in David C. McClelland *et al., Talent and Society* (Princeton, N.J.: Van Nostrand, 1958); Bernard Rosen, "The Achievement Syndrome: A Psychocultural Dimension of Social Stratification," *American Sociological Review* 21 (April 1956): 203-211. See also George Psathas. "Ethnicity, Social Class, and Adoles-cent Independence from Parental Control," *American Sociological Review* 22 (August 1957): 415-423, where Jews scored higher than Italians on measures of "parental regard for child's judgment."

40.   Like most generalizations, these should be treated with care. For example, it appears that Southern Italian districts that had undergone some land tenure changes and whose economic base was more oriented toward "economic individualism" sent a larger proportion of migrants to the U.S. than the more feudal districts. J. S. McDonald, "Italy's Rural Social Structure and Emigration," *Occidente* 12 (September-October 1956): 437-456. On Southern Italian life, see Covello, *Social Background of the Italo-American School Child;* Phyllis Williams, *South Italian Folkways in Europe and America* (New Haven, Conn.: Yale University Press, 1938); Edward Banfield, *The Moral Basis of a Backward Society* (Glencoe, Ill.: Free Press, 1958); Vecoli, "Contadini in Chicago" and "Prelates and Peasants."

41. Carlo Levi, *Christ Stopped at Eboli* (New York: Farrar, Strauss, 1963, 1947), 76 *et passim;* Covello, *Social Background of the Italo-American School Child,* Chaps. 6-8; Vecoli, "Prelates and Peasants"; Banfield, *Moral Basis of a Backward Society.*

42. Herbert Gans, *The Urban Villagers* (New York: Free Press of Glencoe, 1962); and William F. Whyte, *Street-Corner Society: The Social Structure of an Italian Slum* (Chicago: University of Chicago Press, 1943). Jews traditionally characterized the world as a dichotomy, contrasting Jewish with Gentile. In America, however, except for the very Orthodox, that dichotomy did not inhibit participation in secular and civic society.

43. Whyte, *Street-Corner Society,* 105, 107.

44. Covello, *Social Background of the Italo-American School Child,* 254-273. Gans reported that the actual mode of child rearing among Southern Italians in

Boston's West End mitigated against school success. The West Enders were episodic and impulsive in their responses to children, stressed immediate person-to-person contact, and showed limited interest in the use of words and concepts.

45. Covello, *Social Background of the Italo-American School Child,* 241-247; Vecoli, "Prelates and Peasants,"

46. Covello, *Social Background of the Italo-American School Child,* 286-329; McLaughlin, "Patterns of Work and Family Organization"; Gans, *Urban Villagers,* 150, 297. Hostility to schooling, especially to compulsory attendance, as being inimical to the immigrants' economic needs was accentuated by the high proportion of Southern Italians who came to the U.S. with the intention of returning home. Youth who could contribute to that goal by working were an economic asset not lightly given up.

47. For an alternative to this assessment of the relationship between school success and Southern Italian-American culture, see Luciano Iorizzo and Salvatore Mondello, *The Italian-Americans* (New York: Twayne Publishers, 1971), 92-93, and, more generally, Smith, "Immigrant Social Aspirations." Covello notes that a change in attitudes toward schooling became noticeable during the 1920s as more and more Italians began to abandon the idea that they would soon return to Italy. *Social Background of the Italo-American School Child,* 298.

Seller: Success and Failure in Adult Education

1. See, for example, David Tyack, *The One Best System: A History of American Urban Education* (Cambridge, Mass.: Harvard University Press, 1974); Diane Ravitch, *The Great School Wars: New York City 1805-1973* (New York: Basic Books, 1974); Colin Greer, *The Great School Legend: A Revisionist Interpretation of American Public Education* (New York: Basic Books, 1972).

2. Frank Thompson, *The Schooling of the Immigrant* (New York: Harper and Brothers, 1920), 30-31.

3. Robert E. Park, *The Immigrant Press and Its Control* (New York: Harper and Brothers, 1922), 25-33.

4. *Ibid.,* 105. Park quotes Abraham Cahan, editor of the *Jewish Daily Forward,* in an interview: "Now if you take a German or Irish teamster . . . and you speak of the equator, or the North Pole, . . . he understands you. . . . But a Jewish intellectual does not know what the equator is. These intellectuals can discuss the most abstruse problems in philosophy, but they know nothing about geography; that is Gentile learning."

5. Timothy Smith, "Immigrant Social Aspirations and American Education, 1880-1930," *American Quarterly* 21 (Fall 1969): 523-543. See also John Bodnar, "Materialism and Morality: Slavic-American Immigrants and Education, 1890-1940," *Journal of Ethnic Studies* 3 (Winter 1976): 1-17.

6. John Higham, *Stangers in the Land: Patterns of American Nativism, 1860-1925* (New Brunswick, N.J.: Rutgers University Press, 1955), 213-214.

7. The state of Utah required every alien between the ages of 16 and 45 who could not read, write, or speak English at a fifth-grade level to attend night school. This and other state laws concerning Americanization education for adults are summarized in

Edward George Hartmann, *The Movement to Americanize the Immigrant* (New York: Columbia University Press, 1948), 237-252.

8. "Working Plan of the Detroit Campaign," in *Report of the Commission of Immigration and Housing of California* (Sacramento, Calif.: California State Printing Office, 1916), 128.

9. Edwin A. Rumball, *Participating Americans: The Story of One Year's Work for the Americanization of Buffalo* (Buffalo, N.Y.: Civic Education Association, 1918), 8.

10. For descriptions of adult immigrant education written by people involved in these projects, see Thompson, *Schooling of the Immigrant;* William Sharlip and Albert Owens, *Adult Immigrant Education: Its Scope, Content, and Methods* (New York: Macmillan Co., 1928); Peter Roberts, *The Problem of Americanization* (New York: Macmillan Co., 1920); Robert A. Woods, *Americans in Progress: A Settlement Study of Residents and Associations of the South End House* (New York: Riverside Press, 1903); and, for a representative compilation of articles from the periodical press and a bibliography, see *Americanization,* ed. Winthrop Talbot, Handbook Series (New York: H. W. Wilson Co., 1917).

For accounts by historians, see Hartmann, *Movement to Americanize the Immigrant;* Robert A. Carlson, *The Quest for Conformity: Americanization through Education* (New York: John Wiley and Sons, 1975); Gerd Korman, *Industrialization, Immigrants, and Americanizers: The View from Milwaukee* (Madison: State Historical Society of Wisconsin, 1967); and Allen Davis, *Spearheads for Reform: The Social Settlements and the Progressive Movement, 1890-1914* (New York: Oxford University Press, 1967).

These works are mainly descriptive. In a work of 273 pages, Hartmann devotes only one paragraph to an assessment of the effectiveness of the programs. He admits that, "the number of immigrants who became Americanized along the formal lines advocated by the Americanization groups must have been small, indeed, when compared with the great bulk of their fellows who never saw the inside of an American schoolroom or settlement house." Hartmann (p. 271) attributes eventual Americanization to immigrants' contacts with native-born Americans, ignoring the educational efforts of immigrant communities.

11. Margaret D. Moore, *Citizenship Training of Adult Immigrants in the United States: Its Status in Relation to the Census of 1920* (Washington, D.C.: Government Printing Office, 1923), 3.

12. *Ibid.,* 4.

13. *Ibid.,* 11.

14. Rumball, *Participating Americans,* 6-9.

15. Grace Abbott, "The Education of the Immigrant," in *The Immigrant and the Community* (New York: Century Publishing Co., 1917), reprinted in part in Talbot, *Americanization,* 225-232; Frank D. Loomis, *Americanization in Chicago* (Chicago: Chicago Community Trust, 1920), 22-24.

16. Vernon M. Riegel, *Adult Education in Ohio: Facts and Figures Issued by the State Department of Education* (Columbus, Ohio: State Department of Education, 1925). See also Grace Abbott, *The Educational Needs of Immigrants in Illinois,* Bulletin no. 1 of the Immigration Commission (Springfield, Ill.: Office of the Super-

intendent of Education, 1920), and *The Problem of Adult Education in Passaic, New Jersey,* Bureau of Education Bulletin no. 4, Department of the Interior (Washington, D.C.: Government Printing Office, 1920).

17. Abbott, "The Education of the Immigrant," 225.

18. Albert Shiels, *Americanization* (Los Angeles, Calif.: Los Angeles *Examiner,* 1919), 30.

19. John Daniels, *America via the Neighborhood* (New York: Harper and Brothers, 1920), 357-358.

20. *Ibid.,* 194-195.

21. Abbott, "The Education of the Immigrant," 226.

22. Herbert A. Miller, *The School and the Immigrant* (Cleveland, Ohio: Cleveland Foundation, 1916), 91-94.

23. Abbott, "The Education of the Immigrant," 226. See also Sarah Moore, "The Teaching of Foreigners," *Survey* 24 (June 4, 1910): 386.

24. *The Problem of Adult Education in Passaic, New Jersey,* 17.

25. Attempts to Americanize and educate South Italian women were often unsuccessful because they went against strong South Italian mores and traditions. For example, educators insisted on teaching personal hygiene, a subject these women did not discuss with strangers; and a YWCA pamphlet urged South Italian women to be "chums" with their children, when their culture dictated a much more formal relationship. See Virginia McLaughlin, "Like the Fingers of the Hand: The Family and Community Life of First Generation Italian-Americans in Buffalo, New York, 1880-1930," unpub. diss., University of Buffalo, 1970, 234-235; and Cecile L. Griel, *I Problemi Della Madre in un Paese Nuovo* (New York: National Board of YWCA, 1919), reprinted in *Italians in the United States: A Repository of Rare Tracts and Miscellanea* (New York: Arno Press, 1975), 37-40.

26. Tyack, *The One Best System,* 22, 131-132. For a view from a national official involved in wartime Americanization work, see George Creel, "Hopes of the Hyphenate," *Century,* No. 91 (January 1916): 350, reprinted in Talbot, *Americanization,* 168.

27. Daniels, *America via the Neighborhood,* 260.

28. Korman, *Industrialization, Immigrants, and Americanizers,* 142; Hartmann, *Movement to Americanize the Immigrant,* 140-146; *Problem of Adult Education in Passaic, New Jersey,* 19-20.

29. Carol Aronovici, "Americanization," *Annals of the American Academy of Political and Social Science* 93 (January 1921): 134. See also Rumball, *Participating Americans,* 12.

30. Higham, *Strangers in the Land,* 259-260: Hartmann, *Movement to Americanize the Immigrant,* 175, 231-232.

31. "Proceedings of the National Conference on Americanization in Industry," Nantucket Beach, Mass., June 22-24, 1919.

32. *The Immigrant Jew in America,* ed. Edmund James (New York: National Liberal Immigration League, 1907), 209.

33. John I. Kolehmainen, *The Finns in America: A Bibliographical Guide to Their History* (Hancock, Mich.: Finnish American Historical Library, Soumi College, 1947), 110-111.

34. Daniels, *America via the Neighborhood,* 136-137.

35. *Ibid.,* 137-139.

36. *Ibid.,* 142-145.

37. *Ibid.,* 140-141.

38. *Ibid.,* 150-151.

39. By 1925, the Croats had four national federations with 84,000 members; the Serbs had four with 20,000 members. See Gerald Gilbert Govorchin, *Americans from Yugoslavia* (Gainesville: University of Florida Press, 1961), 109-122; Joshua Fishman, *Language Loyalty in the United States* (The Hague: Mouton & Co., 1966), 337-338; and Joseph Wytrwal, *America's Polish Heritage: A Social History of the Poles in America* (Detroit, Mich.: Endurance Press, 1961), 195-197.

40. Frederick G. Bohme, *A History of the Italians in New Mexico* (New York: Arno Press, 1975), 194.

41. Sophonisba Breckenridge, *New Homes for Old* (New York: Harper and Brothers, 1921), 211-212.

42. *Ibid.,* 216.

43. Daniels, *America via the Neighborhood,* 129-131; Govorchin, *Americans from Yugoslavia,* 122-124.

44. Park, *The Immigrant Press and Its Control,* 129-130; Kolehmainen, *The Finns in America,* 111; Dominic J. Cunetto, "Italian Language Theater Clubs in St. Louis, Missouri, 1910-1950," unpub. diss., University of Florida, Gainesville, 1960, and Giovanni E. Schiavo, *The Italians in Chicago: A Study in Americanization* (Chicago: Italian-American Publishing Co., 1928), 69-70.

45. David Lifson, *The Yiddish Theater in America* (New York: T. Yoseloff, 1965); Walter Mattila, *The Theater Finns* (Portland, Ore.: Finnish American Historical Society of the West, 1972); Lawrence Estavan, *The Italian Theater of San Francisco* (San Francisco: U.S. Works Progress Administration, North California District, 1939).

46. Daniels, *America via the Neighborhood,* 325-327.

47. Florence Hemley Schneider, *Patterns of Workers Education: The Story of the Bryn Mawr Summer School* (Washington, D.C.: American Council on Public Affairs, 1941); Juliet Poyntz, "The Unity Movement: The Soul of a Union," *Life and Labor* 7 (June 1917): 96-98.

48. Kristen Svanum, "What Life Means to a Worker: The Story of the Winter Semester at the Work People's College," *Industrial Pioneer* 4 (May 1926): 14-18.

49. Daniels, *America via the Neighborhood,* 116.

50. Richard M. Linkh, *American Catholicism and European Immigrants, 1900-1924* (Staten Island, N.Y.: Center for Migration Studies, 1975), 148-156.

51. *American Newspaper Annual and Directory* (Philadelphia: N. W. Ayer and Son, 1920), 7.

52. Govorchin, *Americans from Yugoslavia,* 139.

53. Park, *The Immigrant Press and Its Control,* 99.

54. *Ibid.,* 108-109.

55. *Ibid.,* 7-8.

56. Irving Howe, *World of Our Fathers* (New York: Harcourt Brace Jovanovich, 1976), 238-244.

57. *Ibid.*, 229-235.

58. Newspaper circulation not only rose during the war years; it continued to rise, reaching a peak in 1930.

59. Daniels, *America via the Neighborhood*, 108-110.

60. Irving Howe records a similar anecdote of an elderly socialist who says: "In my home the *Forward* was treated like the Bible. You didn't tear, cut, or muddy the pages of the *Forward* any more than you did the Torah" (Howe, *World of Our Fathers*, 528).

SIX

The Control Problem

History of an Urban System of School Governance, by
Robert L. McCaul

Pedagogy as Intrusion: Teaching Values in Popular Primary Schools
in Nineteenth-Century America, by   *Barbara Finkelstein*

Historical analysis of educational control in the United States
focuses on a variety of agencies and individuals in both the private and
public sectors. Studies of family structure, ecclesiastical authority,
corporate organization, and divisions of power among the branches of
government at local, state, and federal levels illustrate the array of
possible research topics. Interactions between private and public
agencies must also be taken into account. There are, of course, grada-
tions of control, ranging from indirect influence to mandated authority. Which means of control are most potent may not, however, be immediately evident, given the several settings and forms in which education occurs and the possibility that effective control may not be
highly visible. In regard to American public schools, control is exercised through various means at different levels of government, and
these arrangements have changed over time. An added complication
for historical research follows from the necessity of charting alterations in the scope of public policy relative to public and private schools
and other educational institutions. For historians, educational control
represents an intriguing research problem because of its complexity
and convoluted development. On another level, it represents a policy

problem. Inevitably, historical research on educational goals, structures, and outcomes touch upon political considerations: Who is in
charge? Who benefits from current arrangements? Where is the effective power to institute changes located?

The two articles that follow offer examples from the growing body
of historical research on educational control in the United States.
With increasing interest in the history of urban education, historians
in recent years have devoted considerable attention to school bureaucratization and the role of educational professionals in school control.
Robert McCaul adds to this literature a study of the history of school
governance in Chicago that identifies both the central participants in
the story and the influences exerted by local politicians and the state
legislature. Barbara Finkelstein's analysis of some of the goals and outcomes of schoolkeeping illustrates that control can be exercised subtly
and without the sanction of formal policy.

History of an Urban System
of School Governance

Robert L. McCaul

There are, of course, many ways of "explaining" the events of which
the history of public school governance in Chicago is composed. These
events may be seen as the results of actions by strong-willed men and
women — by superintendents like E. Benjamin Andrews, Ella Flagg
Young, or Benjamin C. Willis, or by presidents of the board of education like Graham H. Harris, Jacob M. Loeb, or James B. McCahey, or
by mayors like Carter Harrison, William Hale Thompson, or Richard
J. Daley. Or the structure of school governance may be seen as evolv-
ing in stages corresponding to the evolution of the structure of municipal government; or as moving from decentralization to centralization to decentralization to centralization, sequentially through time,
in response to intrainstitutional and extrainstitutional rhythms largely
unknown. Or as a system subject to a kind of entropy that afflicts all

Reprinted, with permission, from *Rethinking Urban Education,* ed. Herbert J.
Walberg and Andrew T. Kopan (San Francisco: Jossey-Bass, Inc., Publishers, 1972):
247-260.

human institutions and that as they enlarge and elaborate renders them more and more inefficient. Or as a system developing certain characteristics because the principles by which it is administered, organized, and financed have been borrowed from noneducational human enterprises. Or, to come at last to the approach of this [essay], the events of which the history of Chicago public school governance is composed may be viewed as the consequences of a series of struggles on the part of various groups of persons and their allies for a share in the possession of the powers of governance or for participation in the exercise of these powers. (Although this . . . is a case study of developments in Chicago school governance during the last century and a third, it will be obvious to anyone acquainted with urban school history that the Chicago experience is not altogether unique and that the data and discussion presented . . . have relevance for other urban school systems.)

From 1835 to the present day various groups of persons, one after another, have attempted to make changes in public school governance, and other groups of persons have resisted change. The changes sought have been in the personnel possessing and exercising the powers of governance or in the mechanisms by which the powers have been possessed, allocated, and used. Certain groups have been actuated by some of the highest of motives—by love of their children or concern for the commonweal; other groups, by some of the lowest of motives—by prejudice or selfishness or by hope of graft and loot. Certain ' groups have sought to gain or retain powers for themselves because they hungered for the pleasures of dominance and authority or because they wished to protect pupils of their own ethnic, religious, or socioeconomic background or because they wanted security in their occupation or profession or because they genuinely believed that their individual knowledge and experience would enable them to improve the quality of policymaking or policy execution within the system. Certain groups have sought to gain or retain powers not for themselves but for others, expecting that participation in governance by those others would bring the school system into closer accord with their ideals of democracy, civic virtue, effectiveness, or fiscal prudence. Certain of the groups engaging in struggles over the powers of school governance have consisted of persons within the school system itself—of members of the board of education, superintendents of schools and other administrators, teachers, nonteaching employees, and pupils. Certain groups have consisted of persons outside the system—of members of parent organizations or of the political, church, ethnic, business, or communications institutions of the city or of the agencies of state and federal governments.

BOARDS OF EDUCATION

The first law dealing specifically with public education in Chicago was passed by the Illinois General Assembly in 1835 and approved by the governor on February 6. "An Act relating to Schools in Township thirty-nine North, Range fourteen East" provided for a decentralized structure of school government, with powers distributed among four sets of officials (the Cook County Commissioners, the County Commissioner of School Lands, a township board of common school inspectors, and district boards of common school trustees) and among the legal voters of the township and school districts. The most important of the powers held by the legal voters was that of electing the inspectors and trustees.

This structure lasted only two years and was then replaced by a centralized structure, with power of appointment of school inspectors and trustees vested in the city council. Sections 83 to 92 of the first city charter, March 4, 1837, and "An Act relating to Common Schools in the City of Chicago and for other purposes," approved March 1, 1839, transferred the powers of school governance to the Common Council of the City of Chicago. The members of the council were made "commissioners of common schools" and were to do "all acts and things in relation to said school funds which they may think proper to their safe preservation and efficient management." As commissioners, the councillors were given the power of raising by taxes sufficient money for building schoolhouses, supporting and maintaining public education, and paying teachers. They also received the powers needed to fix the salaries of teachers, prescribe the schoolbooks to be used and the studies to be taught, and "pass all such ordinances and by-laws as they from time to time deem necessary in relation to said schools and their government and management." Finally, the council was to appoint annually seven persons as inspectors of common schools and three persons in each district as common school trustees, the inspectors and trustees to have such powers and duties as might be prescribed by the council.

The provisions of the charter of 1837 and act of 1839 yielded marked advantages. The school and political territories of the city were made coextensive, and the city was freed from dependence on the county in school finances. Because the council had become the sole repository of the powers of school governance, coordinated action on school matters was facilitated and a "system" of public schools could be more readily organized. The new structure soon exhibited serious disadvantages, however. Very quickly the council found that it could not spare the time and attention needed for running the schools. It was saddled with responsibility not only for education but also for sanitation, police, fire, and other municipal services, all of which were proliferating as the city's population doubled, tripled, and quadrupled in the middle decades of the century. To lighten its burdens, the council gradually delegated the exercise of its school powers to the board of school inspectors. Besides, the revised city charter of February 16, 1857, abolished the position of district school trustee, imposing on the board of education (the new title of the old board of school inspectors) the business duties formerly transacted by the district trustees. Yet the board was still left in the awkward position of running the schools under a delegated authority.

The board chafed under its subservience to the council and under the uncertainty and inefficiency introduced into financing and managing the schools by the council's possession of statutory powers. In 1868 and in 1871 the presidents of the board requested the legislature to confer upon the board in law the powers delegated to it by the council. These pleas did not go unheeded by the Illinois General Assembly. Section 80 of "An Act to establish and maintain a System of Free Schools," approved April 1, 1872, contained paragraphs applying only to cities exceeding 100,000 in population; that is, only to Chicago. Of twenty-two powers of school governance listed in those paragraphs, sixteen were vested wholly in the board of education, three were vested in the board but could be exercised only with the concurrence of the council, one (the selling of school lands) was vested in the council but could be exercised only on written petition of the board, and one (the levying and collecting of school taxes) was vested wholly in the council and officers of city government. The act was explicit about the board's possession of the sixteen powers, stating that "no power given to the board shall be exercised by the city council."

Under the act the council was deprived of its power of appointing

members of the board of education, this power now being committed
to the major. No restrictions were put upon the mayor's right of appointment save that his nominations had to be by and with the advice
and consent of the council and his nominees had to have been residents of the city for the preceding five years. The appointment of
school board members has been a mayoral prerogative since 1872.
Since councils have generally rubber-stamped the mayor's nominations and since residence, age, citizenship, and other formal requirements for eligibility have been merely circumstantial, the prerogative
has been naked of legal safeguards that would prevent an unscrupu-
lous or irresponsible mayor from appointing inferior people or worse
to the board.

Section 80 of the act of April 1, 1872, brought to an end a period of
council supremacy that had lasted a third of a century. It had taken
the board thirty-three years to wrest from the city council the powers
of governance centralized in the council by the charter of 1837 and the
law of 1839. The board did not make a clean sweep, however; the
council still held rights in the field of finance, and these rights were to
be a source of friction between the council and the board for many
years. Otherwise, the powers of school governance passed over to the
board. Now these powers were as centralized in the board as they had
been in the council, and the board proved as tenacious in its grip on
them as the council had been. From 1872 on into our own day, and
sure to continue beyond, battles have been waged to secure for the
superintendents, the teachers, the nonteaching employees of the
board, the pupils, and the people a share in the powers of school
governance.

SUPERINTENDENTS OF SCHOOLS

The ordinance of November 28, 1853, creating the office of
Chicago Superintendent of Schools made the occupant completely
menial to the board. He was to "act under the advice and direction" of
the board in performing his duties, which the board would "from time
to time direct." He had no authority over business and legal affairs;
over the appointment, transfer, and promotion of teachers; or over
the choice of textbooks or content of the curriculum. According to the
ordinance, his only plenary power was to be that of granting pupils
permission to enroll in the middle of semesters and attend schools outside of their home districts.[1] Section 80 of the law of 1872 did not even

mention the office of Superintendent of Schools, merely affirming that the board would have the entire superintendence and control of the schools.

Nor were the boards in the 1860s, 1870s, and 1880s disposed to delegate any fraction of their authority to the superintendent, although some boards were more relaxed on this score than others and some superintendents were more trusted and allowed more independence. Mostly the board acted as its own executive and ran the schools through standing committees of its own members. Yet all this while, from 1853 into the next century, the number of educational alternatives had [been] augmented and the range of educational alternatives had expanded. A wise and appropriate selection among priorities and alternatives required familiarity with a specialized literature in psychology, sociology, and pedagogy that was becoming more extensive, technical, and recondite. Boards of education, composed of unpaid laymen with other responsibilities and other drains on their time, were being confronted with a multiplying volume of school business and a bewildering array of educational options. And civic, professional, and business groups were demanding higher standards of efficiency and honesty in the conduct of school affairs.

However resistant the board was to sharing its powers with the superintendent, it was not able to withstand forever the stimuli impinging upon it. In the 1890s some members began to realize that the board could not obtain the assistance it needed from the superintendent if it continued its "tyranny" over him.[2] Moreover, from 1898 to 1900 and from 1909 to 1915, Chicago had two superintendents, E. Benjamin Andrews and Ella Flagg Young, who were unwilling to wait docilely for the board to get around to conferring executive powers upon the office of superintendent. Andrews reached out for control of the hiring, promotion, and discharging of teachers, and Mrs. Young for control over the selection of textbooks and the program of courses. She also sided with the teachers in their efforts to extract from the board increases in salary and improvements in job security and teaching conditions. Although the board since 1895 had been talking about transferring executive powers to the superintendent in order to eliminate "pull" in hiring and promoting teachers and in order to achieve greater expertness in educational decisions, it took fright at Andrews's and Mrs. Young's aggressiveness and fought to keep them as powerless as preceding superintendents had been.

By 1916 wrangling and strife between the boards and superintendents and boards and teachers had pushed the school system to the brink of destruction, or so it seemed to the city council. The council ordered its committee on schools, fire, police, and civil service to investigate the disorganization of the schools, and the committee concluded that it was imperative to enact a new state law reserving to the board the right of making policy and giving to the superintendent power to organize and administer the system without interference from the board.[3]

Such a law was enacted by the Illinois General Assembly at its next session. The Otis law (named after Ralph Chester Otis, the member of the Chicago board of education who had drawn it up) was approved by the governor on April 20, 1917. Like the act of 1872, it provided for the mayoral appointment of school board members, with concurrence by the city council; and it stated explicitly that the powers vested in the board were not to be exercised by the council. Where the Otis law differed from the act of 1872 was in its assignment of specific powers to the superintendent of schools, business manager, and school attorney. The superintendent was to prescribe and control, subject to the approval of the board, the courses of study, textbooks, educational apparatus and equipment, and discipline in and conduct of the schools; and he was to perform such other duties as the board by rule might decide. *Only* upon recommendation of the superintendent (or by a two-thirds vote of all board members), was the board to make appointments, promotions, and transfers of teachers, principals, assistant and district superintendents, and all other teaching employees; select school sites; locate schoolhouses; and adopt and purchase textbooks and educational apparatus. Equivalent powers in the business and legal departments were allocated to the business manager and school attorney. All three officers were granted the right of attending board meetings and entering into its deliberations, but not the right to vote.

Just as the charter of 1837 and the act of March 1, 1839, had set the pattern of governance for the period from 1840 to 1871, and just as the act of April 1, 1872, set the pattern from 1872 to 1916, so has the Otis law set the pattern from 1917 to the present day.

This is not to imply that the Otis law and the procedures outlined in it have gone unaltered. The law kept the method of mayoral appointment without safeguards as it had been. A mayor could, if he wished, reach the superintendent through his appointees to the board, as

Mayor Thompson had in maneuvering the ousting of Charles E. Chadsey and his impeachment of William E. McAndrew. A second flaw in the Otis law was that it made the superintendent, the business manager, and the school attorney coequals, each enjoying direct and independent access to the board. The superintendent did not have supervision over the planning of expenditures, nor did he have control over appropriations. In the depression, when finances became the most critical of all the elements involved in running the schools, Superintendents Bogan and Johnson were reduced to much the same state of powerlessness as superintendents had been prior to the Otis law. The president of the board, James B. McCahey, was able, on account of the *troika* administrative structure, to usurp the powers of the superintendent and business manager and act as the school system's top executive.

Groups of concerned citizens and teachers charged that the McCahey administration was destructive to teacher morale and the proper functioning of the schools. They also accused Mayor Kelly of using the system as a source of patronage for his political machine, and Superintendent Johnson of intimidating teachers and reaping personal profit from his position. Unable to prevail upon Kelly to appoint persons sympathetic to their views to the board, these groups succeeded in getting the North Central Association of College and Secondary Schools to issue an ultimatum warning Kelly that accreditation would be withdrawn from Chicago public high schools unless administrative responsibility were centered in the office of Superintendent of Schools and a new superintendent and a new independent board of education [were] installed. Kelly, alarmed at the prospect of blacklisting by the North Central Association, appointed a committee of five university presidents (of DePaul, Illinois Institute of Technology, Loyola, Northwestern, and University of Illinois) and the president of the North Central Association to consider the association's decree and any other features of the school system the committee wished. Henry T. Heald, president of Illinois Institute of Technology, was elected chairman, and his committee published a report suggesting the formation of a Mayor's Advisory Commission on School Board Nominations and a revision of the Otis law to make the superintendent the chief administrative officer of the system.[4] Kelly accepted these proposals and immediately established an advisory commission. The reform groups of the city, having failed to place persons of their choice on the board through the structure provided by the Otis law, had won their battle to add to that structure a mechanism that would, they anticipated, ensure the appointment of persons with ideals compatible with their own.

Since 1946 the Mayor's Advisory Commission on School Board Nominations, revamped by Mayor Daley in 1969, has submitted to the mayor slates of qualified candidates for the board. On the commission sit representatives from civic organizations and the universities, and their selection of candidates has reflected the upper-middle-class, professional orientation of the commission's membership. The commission is not a statutory body, and the mayors are not bound to confine themselves to its slates. Nevertheless, there is a movement underway in the legislature to enact a law that would legalize the commission and compel the mayor to appoint one of three candidates recommended to him by the commission for every vacancy on the board.

A second proposal of the Heald committee—that the Otis law be amended to eliminate the *troika* set of administrative officers at the head of the system—was carried out after Mayor Kennelly's election. On June 4, 1947, a law was enacted creating the office of General Superintendent of Schools, the incumbent to be "chief administrative officer of the board" and to "have charge and control, subject to the approval of the board, of all departments and of the employees therein of the public schools, except the law department." For reasons not altogether clear, the amendment left the school attorney still on the same plane as the superintendent, but it did straighten out the line of authority in the executive branch by subordinating the business manager to the superintendent.

Manifestly, since the 1890s there has been a trend toward involving the superintendent, as an "expert," more and more in policymaking and policy execution by bestowing on him powers of initiative in certain phases of school governance and by making him the officer in the formal structure of governance to whom the responsibility of furnishing the board with information and counsel is entrusted. But the need for expertness has passed beyond the point where a board can safely rely on one expert or where a superintendent can act as a universal expert on all school matters. It is platitudinous to remark that school problems have become so complex that the task of framing appropriate solutions crosses many academic disciplines and fields of knowledge. Perhaps there would be some merit in attaching to the board a permanent consultative panel of professors from the departments of

education, sociology, political science, and business of the local universities and an executive secretary and a small clerical and statistical
staff. To this panel both the board and the superintendent could turn
for counsel and for documentary and quantitative data focused on the
particular problems confronting them.

THE PEOPLE

Various groupings of citizens — ethnic, economic, social, religious,
and professional — have endeavored to obtain for themselves or for
persons sympathetic to their needs, views, aspirations, or ideals some
participation in school governance. These groups have begun by seeking to set their own representatives, or representatives to their liking,
on the board of education. If defeated, they have then tried to accomplish changes in the structure set forth in the charter of 1837 and the
law of 1839 or in the law of 1872 or in the Otis law.

A frequent target of the "outs" has been the method of mayoral appointment. For example, as noted previously, the civic reform groups
who were outraged at what they thought was unethical, inefficient
management of the schools by Kelly, McCahey, and Johnson were able
to get the Mayor's Advisory Commission on School Board Nominations added to the procedural machinery. Other groups have attempted to divest the mayor wholly of his power of appointment. The substitute most commonly proposed has been election by the people at
large or by areas or districts. Efforts to amend the school law so as to
have an elected board were made in 1893, 1904, 1916, 1919, 1922,
1943, 1967, and 1971. All of these efforts have failed. The usual alle-
gation brought against popular election is that it would introduce partisan politics into school affairs. How and why election should be more
perniciously partisan and political than mayoral appointment is
somewhat difficult to understand.

There is no denying that the method of mayoral appointment has
left many groups in the city unrepresented on the board. Eventually
Chicago may have a board, categorical in composition and blending
appointees and electees, with some members appointed by the mayor
from the city-at-large; with the superintendent of schools a member ex
officio; and with a city councillor, a Chicago public school teacher, a
nonteaching employee of the board, a Chicago public school pupil,
and a citizen from each of the three areas of the city as members elec-

ted by their respective constituencies. All members of the board, including the superintendent, would have voting rights.

Another tactic pursued by groups excluded from the board has been that of agitating for the creation of additional agencies of school government at the area, district, and neighborhood levels to which they can have access. Typically, these groups have been the poor, the depressed, and the repressed of the city; but they have often found allies among more affluent, higher-status groups, who have argued on grounds of equity or efficiency that an all-city board should be balanced out by localized agencies of governance. The question of what kind of local agency would prove most effective was first debated in Chicago in the 1890s. Some persons believed that Chicago should follow New York's example and organize district school boards under the central board.[5] A less extreme remedy was proposed by Mayor Harrison's Educational Commission in 1899. It recommended that the mayor appoint for each school district a committee of six residents, who would visit the schools of their district and report their observations and recommendations to the board. The district resident commissioners were to serve three-year terms. Such a plan, the commission promised, would ward off two dangers: first, the danger of excessive conservatism produced by the administration of the schools by a superintendent and other "experts"; and, second, the danger of rigidity and standardization produced by a structure in which only one agency, an all-city school board, makes policy for an entire, heterogeneous school system.[6]

The commission's bill was defeated in the state legislature, and the issue of centralism versus localism lay dormant until it was awakened in the 1960s by black and white militancy. The board then reacted by forming local school councils, principal selection committees, school area committees, and a subordinate school board in the Woodlawn area. The trouble with these area and neighborhood committees is that they are afflicted with weaknessses that may destroy their usefulness. Often they mix teachers and principals with parents and so are vulnerable to domination by the school administration; their lines of communication with the board and superintendent are uncertain; their opinions and suggestions need not be considered by the board and superintendent; their existence is at the pleasure of the board and superintendent and is not secured by statute or ordinance. Unless these defects are eliminated, more drastic forms of decentralization and local participation may become the objective of a crusade on the part of dissatisfied groups in the city. If they succeed, the consequences may be disruptive.[7]

CONCLUSION

Other groups than those already mentioned have come to share in school governance. For many years the teachers and their allies struggled to win for the teachers a say in school governance. In May 1967 they finally won their battle: the Chicago Teachers Union and the board signed a collective bargaining agreement providing for "the first formalized participation of teachers at the city-wide level in the determination of board of education policy and in the administration of the schools."[8] The pupils — through student councils, liaison committees, interschool councils, and places on faculty committees — may now express their grievances and their views on school policy. The custodians, clerks, and craftsmen employed by the board are civil service employees and unionized; therefore, the Civil Service Commission and the unions, as well as the board, join in making decisions on working conditions, hiring, firing, and salaries. Some departments of the federal and state governments have forced certain patterns of teacher assignments and pupil enrollment and attendance upon the Chicago board.

As we have seen, the law of 1872 vested most of the powers of school governance in the board of education. During the century that followed, various groups sought to gain for themselves, or for others sympathetic to their ideals and views, a share in the possession and exercise of these powers. Their efforts resulted in an addition to the number of agencies and mechanisms of governance and a wider distribution of the powers of governance. The implications for educational change of these movements have been discussed toward the end of each section of this paper. In brief, the more significant of these are the following: (1) The movement to involve professionals like the superintendent and teachers in policy formulation and execution and the increase in the complexity of educational problems suggest the desirability of expanding the range of expert advice and information available to the board, perhaps by some such device as a permanent consultative panel. (2) The movement for broader, representation on the board of education and the dissatisfaction with the method of mayoral appointment suggest that there will be a change in appointment procedures and the composition of the board, perhaps by the creation of a board blending appointees and electees and categorical in composition. (3) The movement to give parents and citizens a voice in school affairs at the local level will not cease until the present neighborhood and area councils and committees are secured in their organization and regularized in their operation.

By improving the quality of the board's leadership and broadening its composition, these measures may partially offset the historic weakening of the board's power that has occurred through the process of fragmentation. But the decline of the local board as an effective unit of control in school governance seems bound to continue apace.

The reasoning behind this prediction may be roughly summarized in this manner. Since the middle of the twentieth century, it has been generally agreed that individual differences are in the main produced by variations in home and school environments. And variations in home and school environments—causing as they do differences in scholastic aptitude, aspirations, and training—instigate differences— that is, inequalities—in educational opportunity. To equalize educational opportunity, and equal educational opportunity is one of the traditional American ideals, it will be necessary to equalize school environments.

Cases involving these considerations have come into the courts, and verdicts have pronounced equal educational opportunity as one of the rights guaranteed citizens by the "equal-protection" clause of the Fourteenth Amendment. We may expect, therefore, that the ruling ideal of equal educational opportunity, backed by the might of the courts, will initiate a trend toward standardizing the means of education.

What effect will the trend toward uniformity have on the distribution of the powers of governance? Clearly, uniformity can be achieved only by an agency superior to the districts and possessing the powers needed for imposing uniform policies, practices, and conditions upon them. Such an agency must be at the state or federal levels in the hierarchy of government, though the possibility of its being a federal agency is remote. Thus, a struggle between state and local agencies of school governance is in immediate prospect. Very probably this struggle can have no other outcome than that state boards of education (or their equivalents) will emerge victorious and in possession of the controlling powers of governance, with a corresponding loss of powers by district boards of education, district superintendents, district teachers, and district citizens. Then another phase in the sequence of struggles over school governance will commence, as the state superintendent of schools, the state organizations of teachers, and the state groups of citizens strive to gain for themselves or sympathetic others a share in the possession and exercise of the powers centralized in the state board.

Pedagogy as Intrusion: Teaching Values in Popular Primary Schools in Nineteenth-Century America

Barbara Finkelstein

One function of teachers in popular primary schools in nineteenth-century America was then, as it is now, to instruct students in the fundamentals of literacy.[1] But there is considerable evidence suggesting that teachers engaged in activities which can be understood as attempts to direct the social and moral as well as the intellectual behavior of their students — to shape their attitudes, to form their patterns of behavior, and to endow them with manners and morals. Indeed, the literature of school description suggests that teachers in popular primary schools throughout the nineteenth century conveyed values to students in a rigid and highly controlling manner.[2] Their behavior toward students within classroom settings both complimented and extended the intrusive mode of child-rearing as defined recently in the pioneering work of Lloyd deMause.[3] Teachers, it would seem, had responsibility for maintaining and transmitting traditional values in a society undergoing drastic economic and social dislocations.

Both deMause and Phillipe Aries (in a rare instance of agreement) have emphasized the simultaneity of the discovery or recognition of modern childhood and the emergence of parental attitudes of vigilance over the lives of their children. Both have agreed that these two concurrent, if not causally related events, conferred a new quality and possibility to child rearing — that of an "over-controlling," carefully planned regimen of protection and supervision.[4] For parents, it meant

Reprinted, with permission, from *History of Childhood Quarterly* 2 (Winter 1975), 349-378.

minute attention to, and constant preoccupation with, their children. "The child raised by intrusive parents was nursed by the mother, not swaddled, not given regular enemas, toilet trained early, prayed with but not played with, hit but not regularly whipped, punished for masturbation, and made to obey promptly with threats and guilt as often as with other methods of punishment."[5] While neither child-oriented nor, as deMause puts it, empathic, intrusion nonetheless represented an alternative to the shocking history of infanticide, abandonment, negligence, and indifference which appears to have characterized the treatment of children until well into the eighteenth century.

Phillipe Aries has linked the recognition of modern childhood and the emergence of what deMause calls the intrusive mode of child rearing to the growth of systematic, deliberate, and sustained age-graded schooling outside the household.[6] No such link appears to have existed in colonial America, but there is reason to believe that the commitment of American parents to intrusive modes of child rearing helps to explain why, by the mid-nineteenth century, schools had become important agencies of acculturation — as important in many respects as the family and the church.

Colonial Americans were heirs to the tradition of intrusive child rearing. The manuals of conduct, the prescriptions of preachers, the injunctions of selectmen, and the corpus of colonial law, all suggest the need for eternal parental vigilance over the lives of children. A well-ordered family was expected to induce children to be obedient, pious, diligent, civil, mannerly, and clean. The family also assumed principal responsibility for preparing children in learning and in labor and for seeing to their ability to read and understand the "principles of religion" and the "capital laws of the country."[7] Lawrence A. Cremin has made the interesting point that the colonial household was an even more important agency of education than was its English counterpart.[8]

The variety of nurturing practices thus far documented[9] — early weaning from mother or wet nurse, and generous, if not brutal, use of the rod in order to break the will, harden the emotions, and discipline the intellect — were carried out chiefly by the family, but with the help of churchmen and schoolmasters. Churchmen sermonized and catechized with the sanction of public authority to enforce their preachments.[10] Less commonly, schoolteachers, in an infinite variety of contractual relationships and environmental settings, supplemented the educational efforts of families.[11]

The ability and the desire of colonial parents to transmit culture in accordance with moral and legal precepts within the household was undermined by the time of the American revolution. Bernard Bailyn has brilliantly argued that the social as well as educational functions of apprenticeship and bonded servitude were being subverted as servants and apprentices escaped to freedom and independent wage labor. Without the help of skilled indentured servants, colonial parents had to share the extraordinary responsibilities of intrusive child rearing with educational agencies outside the home. The emergence of evening schools and of independent masters to transmit vocational and even literary skills represented, as Bailyn has suggested, the differentiation of household functions into new social structures.[12]

Both Bailyn and Cremin have advanced the idea that the ability of churchmen to secure conformity to their faith through public utterance and indirectly through the household was limited in the unstable, highly mobile, and heterogeneous society of the eighteenth century. As they gradually lost the full sanction of public authority, churchmen built schools and colleges which were designed to persuade and exhort, to secure uniformity of belief as well as to convey literacy. Church schools, like evening schools, provided parents with yet another differentiated institution of education.[13]

Schools were becoming more important adjuncts of the home, not only because families and masters could no longer assume all of the responsibilities of intrusive child rearing within the household, not only because churchmen built schools when they were no longer able to compel piety effectively through public utterance, but because parents themselves felt ambivalent toward their children. John Walzer, identifying, analyzing, and documenting ambivalence in the attitudes of some eighteenth-century colonial parents toward their children, intriguingly suggests that sending children to school at an early age represented, on the one hand, a parental desire to be rid of children, while at the same time, represented a holding-on — an important part of inculcating proper attitudes and ideals and at the same time providing a place of confinement, protection, and restraint outside the home.[14]

Schools continued to become increasingly available to parents after the revolution. The story of their growth and development has been told many times over, in different ways by different historians.[15]

The fact that parents supported schools by sending their children—and in increasingly large numbers over time in the nineteenth century—might well reflect the institutionalization of ambivalence as well as the recognition by parents of their inability to protect, to restrain, to transmit values, and to purvey literacy effectively without the support of educational institutions outside the household.

On isolated homesteads scattered throughout the country in the nineteenth century, nuclear families were widely dispersed. Thousands of yeomen farmers who needed the labor of their children, nonetheless sent their children to school during slack seasons—usually the winter and/or summer. Young children between the ages of three, four, and five frequently accompanied older brothers and sisters to school when their labor was not needed at home. Indeed, the literature of school description indicates that the thousands of one-room schools, scattered throughout the nation, almost always housed a compliment of the very young. Doubtless, overworked parents were relieved to be rid of their small charges for a time, in an arrangement that would secure literacy as well as keep the children from idleness.[16]

In the cities there were even more compelling reasons for sending children to school. Rapid alterations in family patterns in middle-class urban America—as suggested to date—placed the responsibility of child rearing almost exclusively in the hands of mothers. In cities—and their growth was impressive during the nineteenth century—opportunities for work drew fathers physically away from the domestic sphere. Isolated from informal ties to relatives and neighbors, without a rich network of kinship and friendship, urban middle-class women and men were hindered from meeting other city dwellers in an intimate or communal manner.[17] Forced to rear their children unassisted by wet nurses, with limited help from domestic servants, relatives, or husbands, advised by popular writers such as Catherine Beecher, Sarah Hale, and Lydia Sigourney to keep the domestic hearth free of pollution from the values of the marketplace, enjoined by the likes of Jacob Abbott and Horace Mann to do a mother's duty by rearing children vigilantly and by sending them to school,[18] it is hardly surprising that the common school reformers found a sizable public that was ready to support the public schools by sending their children. For parents who did not require the labor of their children, and who were committed to intrusive nurture, the schools must have appeared to be an alternative to the streets, and the teachers to be parent-surrogates with special skills.[19]

For the poor and unskilled—whose ethnicity and social origins varied—survival depended on the wages of all members of the household. Before 1850, children and mothers as well as fathers were likely to work.[20] While there is evidence to suggest there were immigrant and poor parents who willingly sent their children to school,[21] there is also reason to believe that any children of poverty were in school because they were persuaded by the church, or often by civil authority. What had been a useful extension of home rearing for the English-speaking middle classes was, for many poor, to become a lesson in the virtues of intrusive nurture.[22]

While the literature concerning the noncognitive aspects of teacher behavior is at best sparse, it is clear that there were teachers, students, and observers who understood that pedagogues undertook moral and political as well as intellectual responsibilities within the classroom setting. Some obviously believed that children were by nature not only imperfectly literate, but morally deficient, and proceeded as though the teacher should act not only as mental disciplinarian to students, but as moral overseer. This attitude was beautifully rationalized in the poetry of a rural schoolmaster: "an endless throng of heedless children in mad pursuit of illusive childish joys dance by his station. If left unwarned they would surely choose the downward way . . . ."[23] A Pennsylvania teacher of the 1850s expressed similar fears about his first class when he intoned that the whole future life of these boys and girls "might be rightly shaped or malformed" in his classroom. His intention was to instill "a right appreciation of the world, its people and its destiny."[24] A woman teacher suggested that she never neglected to "instill into the minds of pupils a sense of the nobleness of doing right because it was right. . . ." Less grand, but no less to the point, was this assertion of the Boston grammar schoolmasters who had controlled popular schooling in Boston in the 1830s and 1840s:

The object of the elementary instruction of our schools . . . is, not alone to impart a certain amount of knowledge to the pupils, but to give . . . training . . . to discipline and strengthen their minds, and prepare them, as far as possible, for that independent action, which will be required of them in the discharge of the duties of life.[25]

Twenty years later, the Boston School Committee defined the teacher's obligation as moral and spiritual as well as intellectual:

Taking children at random from a great city, undisciplined, uninstructed, often with inveterate forwardness and obstinacy, and with the inherited stupidity of centuries of ignorant ancestors; forming them from animals into intellectual beings, and . . . from intellectual beings into spiritual beings; giving to many their first appreciation of what is wise, what is true, what is lovely and what is pure.[26]

The Baltimore school commissioners also emphasized moral intrusion when they asserted that the successful teacher had to raise the moral and intellectual powers of the youngest citizens and suppress the lower passions and propensities.[27]

Other teachers, characterizations of whom appear with greater frequency in the second half of the century in populous village and large urban schools, expressed their supraintellectual aspirations using political rather than moral metaphors. One woman, for example, likened her role in the classroom to that of a governor, whose primary function was to secure a voluntary compliance to law and order without recourse to police powers. "Always a governor, never a tyrant," hung on her walls.[28] A teacher in a New Jersey village school confiscated a knife from a violent student, not with an exclamation of moral censure, but with a concern for social order. "I confiscate this weapon . . ." he cried, "in the name of the commonwealth."[29] Similarly, a mother-teacher, writing in a popular magazine, likened the school to a "miniature kingdom, with its rulers and executive officers, its honors, penalties and forfeitures . . . rewards and punishments."[30]

The social and political concerns of the teachers can be inferred, not only from their stated aspirations, but from characterizations of the classroom situation. William A. Mowry, a professional teacher in rural schools for over half a century, suggested that country schools and teachers performed a unique socializing function. The farm, he explained, "furnishes the members of only one family as companions." But the district school, to a large extent, remedies this defect and gives the very best social stimulus to children:

Here the boys receive their first lessons in true democracy. All children of the neighborhood meet on a common level. To all are accorded the same rights, to all are assigned the same tasks, in all the same powers are developed, and all are subject to the same discipline. Each boy measures himself with his peers. . . .[31]

"A school . . . ," recalled a southern gentleman who had attended old field schools in the South in the 1840s and 1850s, "is a world within itself. In it the inhabitants learn to give and take as they must do in the larger world after school days are over."[32] And a New England master who had taught in the 1820s, 1830s, and 1840s remembered years later that he "had charge of forty children . . . from every kind of family, representing every phase of human nature. The bright and the stupid, the roguish and the ugly, the restless and the turbulent were all huddled in together, a little world in embryo."[33] "Quite apart from any special subject matter," remarked Henry Johnson, "we received our most amazing practice in fundamental social virtues."[34] While some of this may well have reflected the romanticism or ideology of the viewer, much of it was doubtless accurate observation.

Foreign travelers were equally sensitive to the social and political possibilities of moral training. Education, explained Patrick Shirreff, "is most effectual when combining industrious and moral habits with the highest degree of mental cultivation. . . ."[35] David Macrae, another traveler who had observed schools in the 1870s, remarked that teachers "sent students forth not only instructed, but disciplined — taught how to behave themselves as little citizens of the republic in which every boy is to be a gentleman, and every girl a lady."[36] Alexander Macmillan was struck by the extreme sensitivity of Americans, and especially of American parents and teachers "as to character."[37]

While the literature, as we have seen, is not without descriptions of teachers who were conscious of and committed to their roles as moral overseers or political stewards, the typical teacher was not overly conscious of these roles. Nonetheless, he or she engaged in activities that even went considerably beyond moral training.

Even in their most narrow capacity as mental disciplinarians, teachers were indirectly, and probably unconsciously, involved in the formation of social loyalties. Their tendency to rely almost completely on the texts meant that students, as they learned to read, write, cipher, and draw maps, imbibed the moral maxims, the political pieties, and the economic and social preachments of the writers whose books the students were commonly asked to memorize.[38] And, in the process, the teachers served as agents of the adult community, not only by insisting that students accept the pieties of the texts, but by creating relationships which rested on the assumption that the students, if not morally evil, were at least morally and rationally undefined, incapable of proper behavior without external compulsion. Indeed, teachers behaved as though they believed that one of their principal duties was to create an environment that would suppress spontaneity, would discourage communication between students, and they would force pupils to suspend their impulses and derive standards of conduct solely from the teacher.

East, west, north, and south, in every kind of teaching situation, we find that teachers consistently pressured students to learn the value of conformity to law. One expression of the commitment was, of course, their near universal demand for obedience. Even the most humanitarian pedagogues insisted that schooling could not proceed properly without the recognition of the absolute authority of the teacher. "The first step which a teacher must take," enjoined Jacob Abbott in a lecture to the American Institute of Instruction in 1831, "is to obtain the entire unqualified submission of the school to his authority."[39] Francis Wayland echoed these sentiments in a widely publicized book on moral science: "it is the duty of the instructor to enforce obedience, and of the pupil to render it." He goes on to explain that the pupil is inferior and is under the obligation of obedience.[40] Millard Fillmore Kennedy, a New England schoolmaster for some thirty years, recalled these requirements for a successful teacher: "the teacher has to have absolute power. . . . He was expected to rule by 'suasion, if he chose, by rough-and-tumble force if necessary."[41]

Not surprisingly, the need for classroom obedience was often portrayed as indispensable to the preservation of social order in the larger society. The grammar schoolmasters of Boston, distressed with what they believed to be Horace Mann's misunderstanding of authority lines in the school, posited this maxim:

Implicit obedience to rightful authority must be inculcated and enforced upon children as the very germ of all good order in future society; no one, who thinks soundly and follows out principles to their necessary results, will presume to deny.[42]

Little different were the sentiments expressed some forty years later in the report of a national commission of school administrators in 1874: "The teacher has an obligation to train the pupils into habits of prompt obedience to his teacher . . . in order that he may be prepared for a life wherein there is little police-restraint on the part of constituted authorities."[43] C. D. Arfwedson, who observed scores of schools in New York City in the early 1840s commented that social order was well served by teachers who kept students in strictest subordination.[44] Another observer quipped that "turbulent boys soon learned they had no power and submitted."[45] David Macrae, who visited schools in New York in the 1870s, admired the ability of the teachers to inspire respect for and conformity to law.[46]

Needless to say, the insistence of teachers on obedience was not lost on their students. "Pedagogues . . . ," quipped one, "were installed to rule in dominant dignity and undisputed sway in their learned domain, with something like the divine right of kings."[47] An anonymous pupil who described his teacher in Kingston, New York, in the 1820s claimed that he embodied all the characteristics of a "dread monarch."

> The district school is often taught by
>   some stern and robust man
> Who thinks all virtue must be sought
>   in his coercive plan;
> Who like a power none can evade,
>   would but command and be obeyed.[48]

Even more astute was this judgment rendered by an urban teacher who recalled his most severe teacher in New York City in the 1830s:

It must not be inferred that he was a brutal tyrant. It was only that the fundamental law of the school was obedience to rules, and seldom did any fellow incur chastisement, that he did not also have to listen to the quotation of Solomon's proverb, "The way of the transgressor is hard!" With all his severe discipline, there was no teacher in the school who was so generally loved.[49]

Alfred Holbrook described what was probably a near universal sentiment in the schools of the 1820s and 1830s, that "disobedient boys required a brand of 'muscular Christianity.' "[50] Apparently Solomon's injunctions against spoiling children were frequently invoked by teachers in disciplining their errant students—yet another example of their commitment to stamping-in conformity to law.[51]

In the one-room schools of the countryside, where teachers typically combined a career in teaching with a career in farming, and boarded at the houses of their students, and where they knew and played with students outside the schools, we find that teachers used a whole arsenal of measures to distinguish their office as teacher from their relationship as parent, confidante, or friend.[52] That they made this distinction was reflected in the differing relationships between students and teachers on the playground and in the classroom. Hiram Orcutt, a rural schoolmaster in New England, described the difference in this way:

Out of school hours I mingled familiarly with them, joined them in their sports, and sympathized with them in all their joys and sorrows. In their homes . . . and on the playground we stood on a common level. In the classroom, however, I was recognized as master, and so complete was their loyalty . . . that I could punish . . . without the least opposition on the part of the offender.[53]

A student who was raised in Andover, Massachusetts, recalled a lady who she was sure, "would have liked to kiss away the tears that followed the snaps [of a thimble] . . . but," she continued, "she was too much of a martinet for that so she contented herself with sniffs so loud and peculiar that we came to consider them a natural and necessary part of the proceeding."[54]

The most frequently described distancing device was, of course, the unilateral use of the rod which teachers displayed prominently and used consistently.[55] Conspicuous placement of quince, birch, maple, or hazel tree whips, and of whipping posts "spoke volumes as to order and lessons well-learned." In the words of an Oregon teacher, "they were silent but forceful admonitions" to potentially disruptive or inattentive scholars.[56] Some particularly well-organized pedagogues had several rods hung behind their desks and developed thrashing into a fine art. A Texas student explained his teacher's system in this way: "The larger switches were graded, partly by the size of the boys and partly by the gravity of the offense." Some of the rods were little hazel tree twigs while "the fourth size . . . was of oak and would have been better called clubs."[57]

Some teachers asserted their physical superiority in the opening days of school — a necessary distancing mechanism perhaps — in a classroom where students equated authority with muscle. A teacher who recalled his boyhood on the Tennessee frontier praised his favorite mentor as the one who could "beat them all at ball, jump a great distance and keep order. . . ."[58] Another, who was raised in the 1820s, admired his schoolmaster, Uncle Hugh, who could "fight for and with his flock even to the extent of engaging in duels."[59] A New England teacher prided himself on his ability to use "Muscular Christianity,"[60] and another physically overpowered the big boys during the first day of class because he knew that "muscle was considered to be almost as important as brains."[61] There is even a story of a teacher who kept an unloaded Colt revolver in his desk in order to impress unruly boys in the opening weeks of class.[62]

Descriptions are legion of teachers who combined the cruelest physical torture with the more subtle persuasion of humiliation to maintain their authority and to secure obedience.[63] A normal school principal described schooling in Oregon in the 1860s and 1870s recalling that recalcitrant students would be "sent [to the] front to stand and face the pupils until his memory returned."[64] The experience of a Hardin County, Iowa, man who attended schools in the 1860s suggests that his teacher had incorporated the collective wisdom of all other experts at humiliation. Not only did his teacher require disobedient students to stand with their arms extended or with a finger on a certain nailhead in the floor for a considerable time, but he often compelled them to sit on the girl's side, or forced them to squat in tortuous positions for hours on end.[65]

The fact that encounters between students and teachers in class-rooms were likely to be physical as well as intellectual may well explain the characterizations of teachers by amateur wits and poets who recognized a muscular basis of pedagogical authority. An anonymous student described a Kingston, New York, teacher of the 1820s in this way: "He was a pedagog of the old stamp, with a most hearty belief in the code of discipline inculcated in the proverbs of the wise Jewish monarch whose name he so aptly bore . . . his rod was his scepter. . . ."[66] Brief and to the point is this widely quoted poem, devised by a woman recalling her Hoosier girlhood in the 1820s and 1830s:

> Brisk wielder of the birch and rule
> The master of the district school.[67]

The school, recalled a Pennsylvania teacher, was governed all together by the physical force of the ferule or rod. "The masters were neither educators, instructors, teachers nor trainers," "They specialized, " he went on "in the use of the rod and cowskin, the rule and leather spectacles. . . ."[68]

In the second half of the nineteenth century, where teachers in country schools not infrequently graded students into classes of equivalent achievement, teachers sought to combine moral persuasion with physical coercion in order to establish voluntary compliance to rules and regulations.[69] The literature is replete with descriptions, both abortive and successful, to make students aware of and responsible for their wrongdoings.[70] One popular way was to require students to keep a record of infractions. Henry Johnson described one teacher's utter failure:

To develop a scrupulous honesty and a high sense of honor we kept a record of our deportment and reported the exact percentage in response to roll call at the end of each day. For our guidance, Miss Pember made a list of possible offenses with a scale of penalties . . . whispering: -2 points; hair pulling: -4; spit balls: -6; putting rubber in the stove: -15. If we fell below fifty, we had to stay after school and receive one tap of a ruler on the hand for each point below 50. This prompted competition for the lowest score. The taps became more numerous and the class, numbering 40, had to be divided into squads only one of which could be punished on the same day and the ruler taps lagged further and further behind. . . . She . . . lasted until Christmas vacation.[71]

No more successful were the efforts of another teacher who sought to encourage diligence by calling the roll at the end of each day and eliciting the words "perfect" or "imperfect" from his students. The rattan awaited students foolish enough to admit of imperfection.[72]

The tendency of the typical teacher to demand respect for and submission to his authority as master of the school, was in no way
qualified when he himself behaved in less than saintly fashion. Indeed,
the rural literature abounds with descriptions of teachers who com-
manded obedience to their office, at the same time as they vigorously
drank, courted the girls, swore, and smoked in the schoolrooms.[73]

Informality within the classroom occurred, it would seem, only as a
kind of ceremony or ritual, which eventually became part of the tradition of country schooling. Barrings-out—annual events during which
students sought to fortify the schoolhouse in order to prevent the entrance of the master, and where the masters used every artifice to enter
the classroom and reassert their authority as pedagogues—also symbolize the authority that the office of teacher was supposed to carry.[74]
The following description of a barring-out in Pennsylvania schools in
the 1840s and 1850s conveys a sense of ritualized informality that suffuses . . . the rural literature:

On arriving at the door and finding it fastened, the teacher, affecting to be greatly
enraged at the audacity of his school demanded . . . that it be immediately opened;
but the answer from within was cool and defiant . . . when the conditions of surrender
were presented to him . . . [he] indignantly pronounced them outrageous, and tore
the paper into ribbons. He then declared that he was coming in if he had to pull the
house down . . . and soon returned with the ax on his shoulder. . . . At this juncture
the teacher vigorously assaulted the door, pounding it with an ax until he split it in
several places. This availing him nothing, he climbed to the roof and commenced
tearing away the clapboards. . . . His next point of attack was the south window. With
the ax he tore off the cleats which held the sash in its place. . . . A little parley now en-
sued, when it was agreed that neither party was to strike or injure the other, but by all
fair means at his command the master was to get in if he could, and the school [*sic*]
were to keep him out if they could.[75]

That some teachers in rural schools in the last half of the nineteenth
century seemed to be breaking with a tradition of corporal punishment seems evident. The new emphasis, at least as depicted in the
literature, on fear of parental punshiment and on the confinement of
caning and whipping to blatantly disruptive students, suggests a profound and basic change in attitude toward education, a change . . .
manifested as much as twenty years earlier in the cities.

Throughout the nineteenth century teachers in cities relied less
completely than their rural counterparts on physical coercion to
assure their authority. The commitment to inducing obedience took
on other forms and flourishes. Teachers sought to secure conformity,

not only by emphasizing the distinction between the office and the person of the teacher, not only by expelling students for violations of rules and regulations, not only by delivering sermons on the necessity of respecting constituted authorities, but by applying principles of military discipline to the classroom situation.[76] Joseph Lancaster provided the model for countless teachers in the early generation, and exemplified the spirit of the typical urban teacher throughout the period under discussion. In his manuals Lancaster left no minute of the day unexplained, left no student unattended. The plans were symbolized by his declaration, "A place for everything and everything in its place."[77]

Lancaster arranged the instructional system so that students would at all times be responsible to a designated authority. There were monitors to take attendance, monitors to keep order, monitors for recess, and monitors in charge of monitors. The assignment of monitorial status to students had the advantage not only of enticing each student to seek superior rank, but of providing supervision and instruction for each student all of the time.[78] The beauty of the system, remarked an English traveler, "is that nothing is trusted to the boy himself; he does not only *repeat* the lesson before a superior, but *learns* it before a superior . . . under the eye and command of a master."[79]

Not only did the monitorial system provide for a hierarchy of offices to which every student was bound by threat of physical or mental punishment, but the Lancasterian masters enforced rules and regulations which proscribed every conceivable physical movement of the students as well. In effect, teachers forced students to suspend their impulses; to derive their standards of conduct from the will of the master. The elaborate and carefully enforced rituals and ceremonials were designed, in the words of one Lancasterian master, "to beget a love of order and propriety and dispose students to the habit generally of doing things in a mechanical and systematic manner."[80] Not only did students have to hang their coats on signal, move to their seats on signal, rise and sit on signal, they had to perform their intellectual tasks in proper physical form.[81] Opening exercises, for example, were conducted in this manner: "He [monitor] opens the door, rings the bell, and the scholars without, leave off their sports and pour into school. They array themselves against the wall around the room as military companies, each class under its own monitor as captain. . . ."[82]

Physical regulations were no less stringent during recitations:

While reading, as the eye rises to the top of the right hand page, the right hand is brought to the position seen in figure 4, with the forefinger under the leaf, the hand is slid down to the lower corner, and retained there during the reading of the page . . . This also is the position in which the book is to be held when about to be closed; in doing which the left hand, being carried up to the side, supports the book firmly and unmoved, while the right hand turns the part it supports over the left thumb . . . The thumb will then be drawn out between the leaves and placed on the cover; when the right hand will fall by the side.[83]

A student who attended a Lancasterian school in New York recalled that every boy had to have his "left palm enclosed in his right behind his back, in a sort of self-handcuffed state, and woe be to him who is not paying attention when the order is given, or if tardy in obeying it . . . . '[H]adn't hands behind' . . ." was a significant offense in this school.[84]

The intrusive pedagogical mode that characterized monitorial schools in the first half of the nineteenth century was also characteristic of teacher behavior in non-Lancasterian urban schools—legion after 1850. Like their predecessors, teachers who were now teaching in classes grouped by age, tended to identify the enforcement of physical ritual with the development of obedience, virtue, and conformity to rules of whatever nature. Some observers from Baltimore admired this procedure in a New York Primary School:

The regularity of their movements, their simultaneous enunciation, their young voices mingling in the melody of their childhood's songs. . . . When they sing "Now we all stand up," they spring to their feet, the entire mass with apparently a single motion. When they sing "Now we all set down," they drop into their seats. "Now we fold our arms," all arms are folded. "Now we are nodding, nid, nid, nodding," the sea of little heads move to right and left. . . .[85]

An anonymous critic of other New York City public schools interpreted what he saw in this way:

They sat, the girls on the one side and the boys on the other, each eyes fixed upon the wall directly in front. There was no motion. . . . The rows of children, right and diagonal, were as regular as rows of machine-planted corn. A signal was given at which every face turned instantly, as though on a pivot toward the face of the directress. She bade them good-morning, and in one breath, the whole school responded. At another signal every face swung back on its pivot to the original position. . . .[86]

The observations, criticisms, and recollections of various writers all suggest that the physical uniformity symbolized in the opening exercises carried over to the classroom recitations.[87] When a mathematics problem was proposed by the teacher, recalled one writer who described New York schools in the 1860s, "down would go all the slates and the work of ciphering would proceed . . . as the work was completed . . . the slates would pop up against the breast, one after another; and when a boy was called upon to explain, up he would jump, rattle off his explanation, and then thump down again amongst the perfect stillness of the rest. . . ."[88]

The attempt to instill habits of obedience and conformity is most dramatically illustrated, perhaps, in a description written by Joseph Mayer Rice. In the New York City classroom which he described, the teacher had carried the passion for obedience and mechanical submission to regulations so far that she had confused them with the instructional task at hand:

During several daily recitation periods, each of which is from twenty to twenty five minutes in duration, the children were obliged to stand on the line, perfectly motionless, their bodies erect, their knees and feet together, the tips of their shoes touching the edge of the board in the floor. The slightest movement on the part of the child attracts the attention of the teacher. The recitation is repeatedly interrupted with cries of "Stand straight," "Don't bend the knees," "Don't lean against the wall," and so on. I heard one teacher ask a little boy: "How can you learn anything with your knees and toes out of order."[89]

The descriptive literature also suggests that the typical urban teacher of the late nineteenth century substituted social and psychological pressures for physical coercion to induce obedience. Thus, we find not only a dearth of descriptions and recollections of physical coercion by students, teachers, or observers in these city schools, but explicit statements applauding its demise. The school commissioners of Baltimore, for example, whose report of 1873 followed a school-by-school inspection of the city's primary schools, declared that "our teachers are now generally abandoning corporal punishment except in extreme cases, and resort to milder and more successful methods of controlling their students."[90] By 1874 they declared, probably with undue optimism, that corporal punishment had been abandoned entirely in a few schools.[91]

Complaints about soft pedagogy, all but nonexistent in the earlier literature, confirm its abandonment by many city teachers. Detroit schools in the 1870s, for example, inspired this poetic caveat:

About this time the schools began
To slack the use of the *rattan;*
They said "O, no, it will not do
To use the rod on children so."

> Parents have ceased to remonstrate,
> So children begin to demonstrate;
> And teachers try with various plans,
> Coax, plead, entreat, and keep off hands.
>
> Some teachers fall into the way
> of letting the children sleep and play. [92]

One finds in the urban literature of the second generation, the emergence of measures designed by teachers to tweak the consciences of their students.[93] Moral "suasion" seemed to be a tactic used often by women in order to control disruptive behavior.[94] A mother recalled the response of a teacher to a student who had shouted "By Moses. A'int it cold!" as he entered a Boston school room. Moral "suasion" took the form of a gentle lecture:

> . . . she sketched, in language suited for childish comprehension, the early history of the exposure of the "pretty infant" in a "little rush cradle" on the shore of the Nile . . . how the good God called him to set free so many slaves; what a humility and reverence he always showed . . . how many trials he went through . . . how, at last, after all his labors, he was not allowed to enjoy the beautiful prospect along the Jordan. . . . Don't you think Moses deserves more respect and honor than Oscar showed to his name when he used it in the form of swearing, yesterday?

After she had finished the lecture, she sent the students home in order to think about the processes through which they had gone to expunge improper words from their vocabularies.[95] A less gentle, though nonetheless real, appeal to conscience is described by a student whose teacher announced publicly that she was not a fit person to be in school with such a good name.[96] A New York City teacher explained to a visitor that they maintained order by appealing "to the self-respect of the girls themselves, and the older show an example to the younger."[97] It is noteworthy that the element of rivalry was not absent in these attempts to control the social behavior of students.

What we find in urban schools is that the regulations required students to consult an authority for the most minute standards of conduct. They could satisfactorily submit to the rules and regulations of the teachers only by purging themselves of their individuality, by submerging their identities, and by incorporating the goals of the teachers as their own. In fact, the teachers demanded nothing less than perfect adherence to the values of self-control, self-restraint, and self-government.

The classroom deportment of the teachers reflected not only a commitment to developing in students a respect for and submission to constituted authority, but a devotion as well to cultivating their capacity for self-reliance. Somewhat paradoxically, we find that with all the stress on conformity, teachers engaged also in a series of activities designed ultimately to isolate students from each other, to make them intellectually as well as socially independent within the classroom setting.

In all the descriptive literature I was able to discover only three descriptions of teachers who proceeded as though students should or could, through informal discussion, assist each other in learning their lessons.[98] Indeed, almost every related description suggests that recitations were organized so that students would learn independently. In the so-called loud schools of the 1830s and 1840s, teachers literally forced students to learn their lessons in isolation, by demanding that each one "con" his lesson aloud.[99] Other teachers who abandoned the loud school format transmitted the value of self-reliance by demanding silence and by punishing whispering with abandon. Indeed, the descriptive literature is burdened with both praise and censure of teachers whose demands for silence were vigorously enforced, who consistently discouraged communication, and who punished with enthusiasm any abridgements of the rule of silence.[100]

The widespread popularity of competition in all its forms can also be interpreted not only as an incentive to instruction, but as a vehicle for heightening the desire of students to work independently, to seek out the variety of prizes provided in every classroom situation by surpassing rather than helping fellow students.

Still another expression of the commitment of the teachers to self-reliance through intellectual independence was their harsh treatment of cheating, which they apparently viewed as the ultimate violation of their assumption that children could best learn through their own efforts and without the collaboration of their classmates. The literature is filled with descriptions of punishments administered for aiding and abetting, or for receiving help in answering questions.[101] A southern man recalled the following punishment after he had helped a girl with her lessons:

[The teacher] . . . carried me down to the spring . . . in the shadow of an old cotton-wood log; he repeated a verse from the Bible, about sparing the rod and spoiling the child; he then knelt, and prayed a short prayer, in which he asked his Heavenly Father to forgive the awful crime of which I had been guilty, and then rose, and catching me by my long hair, almost lifting me from the ground, he administered an awful whipping.[102]

In city schools and in large village schools of the 1880s and 1890s, we find that teachers, commensurate with their new view of corporal punishment, were more likely to punish cheating by humiliating or suspending students, or by reporting them to their parents.

Teachers also sought to isolate students from one another by preventing eye contact among them. "My first teacher . . . ," recalled a Pennsylvanian, who had attended school in the 1850s, "was Robert Venable. I do not know where he came from, but one thing I do remember, the scholar had to keep his eye on his book whether he was studying his lesson or not."[103] Another description of a rural schoolmaster in Tennessee explains that he single-handedly fashioned desks for his students and placed them in neat rows before him. "This placement of desks and benches had . . . ," he explained, "the advantage of making it difficult for students to look at one another."[104] "No playing or visiting was tolerated," recalled an Iowa man who had attended a one-room school in the forties. A breach of that rule resulted in a "heavy . . . stroke from the [master's] open palm."[105] A student who attended schools in Fort Henry, New York, in the 1870s, lamented this regulation in a bleak bit of poetry:

> There's another about as difficult,
> But it's one he often repeats,
> For we like to see what our neighbor is doing,
> And we turn about in our seats.[106]

In the monitorial schools of the cities, masters literally forced students to look at the monitor and the textbook when they assumed their positions for recitation — a regulation designed to cultivate self-reliance along with self-discipline. Little different were the demands for correct posture in large urban schools of the 1850s, 1860s, 1870s, 1880s, and 1890s. Edward Austin Sheldon described a Boston school in the 1870s where the students who stood on the floor "had the attitude of soldiers. They stood in a perfectly straight line, held books equidistant from their noses."[107] And Joseph Mayer Rice made the following observations of a New York City teacher, whose principal had presided over the school for twenty-five years:

All children in the room stare fixedly at a point on the blackboard. When material of whatever nature, is handed to the children . . . [it] is then passed along sideways until each child in the row has been supplied. During this procedure the children are compelled to look straight in front of them, and to place their hands sidewise in order to receive the material, without looking whence it comes.[108]

Given the emphasis on the maintenance of order, it is hardly surprising that teachers embodied in their activities a respect for property, for the rights of propertyholders, for the legal order of things—sometimes, indeed, with an excess of zeal. Rules prohibiting students from touching the teacher's desk and its contents, harsh punishment for students who were caught stealing (an act which led one teacher to conclude that moral evil had contaminated his kingdom),[109] penalties for students who defaced the property of other students or who destroyed books or wrote graffiti on the walls of classrooms or cloakrooms, all were vigorously and consistently enforced in every teaching situation.[110] Indeed, there is even a description of a Hartford teacher who would not permit children to touch their books except when they were reading.[111]

Throughout the nineteenth century we also find ubiquitous descriptions of teachers who had conscientiously censored standards of social and emotional behavior, unrelated, it would seem to intellectual progress.[112] Even in the most primitive school settings, teachers praised and censored various kinds of social and emotional behavior. A Hoosier, for example, remembered an informal understanding with the parents of students whom he was teaching. "[We] agreed . . ." he explained, "in requiring children, at home and at school, to cultivate good habits and polite manners, to avoid profanity and all immoral and vulgar language or conduct." Indeed, he went on, "the teacher was censured if he did not punish offenses deservedly. . . ."[113] A New England teacher suspended a student from school for showing indecent pictures on the playground.[114] One southern lady complained that her pedagogue had usurped parental rights when he threatened to suspend any students who went dancing at night.[115] And the literature of the one-room rural school is laden with descriptions of teachers who imposed various sanctions on students who fought with one another outside the classroom. Some were whipped, others placed at the foot of the class as punishments for socially unacceptable behavior outside the school.[116]

Descriptions of rural pedagogues suggest that they were much concerned with the possibility of illicit contact between boys and girls. Observers describe a variety of means employed by teachers to separate the boys from the girls. Some teachers simply placed boys and girls on opposite sides of the room.[117] Others went at the problem of the sexes more enthusiastically. An Oregon normal school director recalled that "boys and girls never sat together." "Such," he said, "would have been 'awful.' "[118] Other observers remembered teachers who literally built barriers inside the classrooms to separate the boys and girls. Descriptions of this academic though perhaps not so cozy equivalent of a bundling board are not unusual.[119]

Descriptions of pedagogues in the urban schools throughout the nineteenth century, and in the village schools of the second half of the century, suggest that these teachers were considerably more preoccupied with parental prerogatives than their rural counterparts—a fact which might reflect the absence of homogeneous standards among the larger groups. Not only did they censor nonacademic deportment, but they consistently evinced interest in the personal habits of the students.[120] William Andrus Alcott related this incident in a Hartford, Connecticut, school in the 1830s: "The younger teacher had assisted them in taking off their clothes and placing them properly, and if personal cleanliness had been in any instance neglected," Alcott observed, "she possessed the requisite and appropriate means of remedying the evil." One day, he went on, "I found the teacher out of doors washing one of her pupils . . . it produced the desired effect: — that for some time past not one scholar had been sent to school dirty, to where there formerly were ten."[121] Another observer, David Macrae, explained that Americans have a punctilious attitude to the clothing and deportment of children. They are, he went on, "all clean—a point to which great attention is paid in American schools."[122] Indeed, observers were typically struck by the passion which urban teachers displayed for personal hygiene.[123] There is even a description of a teacher who administered medicine to ill-looking children.[124]

Good manners were encouraged. William Henry Venable described an exercise in a Buckeye village school, which, he adds, "was designed to fit students for the actual duties of life:

. . . [he] went so far as to require his pupils to imitate what he supposed to be the polite usages of people of "quality" . . . . Before beginning and after closing each recitation, every class, its members ranged in orderly rank, saluted the master with a becoming reverence. . . . All the boys formed a sort of military line, facing the girls arranged opposite in a seemly row, and when the word "Obeisance" was pronounced, the young cavaliers responded with an elaborate bow, receiving in return a profound curtsey. . . . Nor was the practice of conventional etiquette restricted to polite rehearsals on the puncheon floor of the humble log schoolhouse. The boys were admonished to practice gentlemanly deportment . . . and, above all, never to neglect the gallant habit of lifting the hat, on meeting a woman.[125]

Bronson Alcott remembered a teacher who gave the order to "go straight home, and be civil . . ." to everyone.[126] A Pittsburgh man who attended schools in the 1840s remembered two outstanding rules: No cursing or swearing as well as no fighting—in or out of the classroom.[127] Frederick Marryat recalled these signs in a New Jersey schoolhouse in the 1870s. "No kissing girls in school time," and "No *licking* the *master* during holydays."[128]

Some rare teachers even went so far as to try to inculcate certain linguistic niceties, not as a matter of correct speech, or effective expression, but as a matter of social style. A Boston lady, for example, bitterly recalled this scene:

Our new teacher was trying to establish the custom of having the pupils address her by her name rather than by calling her teacher. . . .
"Are these right, teacher?"
She smiled and replied, "Say Miss Mills."
". . . Miss Mills – er – er–teacher is this right?"
Then she looked serious and said, "Do not say teacher, just say Miss Mills."
Once again I tried, "Miss Mills — er teacher is this—" Oh, that awful habit!
. . . Then she said, "Now after me. Miss Mills, is this right?"[129]

And one teacher even considered facial expression to be matter of considerable importance. William Andrus Alcott described the following scene in his Hartford school in the 1830s:

About this time, one or two very young pupils became rather ill-humored. The teacher proposed, in a very gentle manner, to draw the appearance of their "sour faces" on the slate; which immediately soothed their countenances. . . .[130]

The behavior of the teachers as moral overseers, political stewards, and as parent surrogates involved them ultimately in the preservation of social order. By demanding diligence, industry, consideration for others, and achievement, they reinforced the moral order of society. By demanding conformity to rules and regulations, they upheld the legal order of things. By promoting competition and by protecting private property, they reinforced economic order. By demanding respect, they reinforced the order of age and youth. And the generality did all this by generous use of the rod, and by pedagogical authority designed to harden the emotions, to break the will as well as to discipline the intellect. The teachers were indeed extending the intrusive mode. There were, of course, the inevitable exceptional teachers who transmitted values in a gentle, guiding, "socializing mode," but they were unusual throughout the century.

NOTES

McCaul: History of an Urban System of School Governance

1. Chicago Board of Education, *Twenty-fifth Annual Report of the Board of Education* (Chicago: Clark and Edwards, 1880).

2. *Id., Forty-first Annual Report of the Board of Education* (Chicago: J. M. W. Jones & Co., 1895); *id., Forty-second Annual Report of the Board of Education* (Chicago: J. M. W. Jones & Co., 1896); Chicago Educational Commission, *Report* (Chicago: Lakeside Press, 1899).

3. Committee on Schools, Fire, Police, and Civil Service of the City Council of the City of Chicago, *Recommendations for Reorganization of the Public School System of the City of Chicago* (Chicago: Barnard and Miller, 1916).

4. North Central Association of Colleges and Secondary Schools, "Action Taken in Regard to the Chicago Public Schools, March 30, 1946," in Havighurst-McCaul project archives, University of Chicago; Committee of University Presidents, "Report on the Administration of the Chicago Public Schools to Mayor Edward J. Kelly, June 17, 1946," in Havighurst-McCaul project archives, University of Chicago.

5. *Chicago Tribune,* April 24, 1893.

6. Chicago Educational Commission, *Report.*

7. Robert J. Havighurst, "The Reorganization of Education in Metropolitan Areas," *Phi Delta Kappan* 52 (February 1971): 354-358.

8. F. M. Whiston, "Statement to Board and Teachers," *Agreement between the Board of Education and Chicago Teachers Union, January 1, 1967, to December 31, 1967* (Chicago: Chicago Teachers Union, 1967).

Finkelstein: Pedagogy as Intrusion

1. This essay examines schools which might be considered typical of the sort that were accessible to most people. Free schools, and low-cost subscription schools, both denominational and undenominational in character, are all exemplary. The role of teachers in fashionable and expensive seminaries, on Indian reservations, in schools where English was not the predominant language, in schools for the deaf, dumb, blind, or delinquent will not be considered.

2. The descriptive literature comprises recollections, observations, analyses, and criticisms of classroom procedures written by a multitude of individuals using a variety of methods. The inherently subjective character of each source and the limited number of schools described in each source require cautious use. The collected data can convey some sense of variety in classroom procedures, but cannot document with any certainty the frequency of each type of behavior in American schools. Because those who describe schools are a select group, and because the sources themselves are selectively published and preserved, there are bound to be distortions.

I have not generalized from one or two sources at any time. Each generalization reflects convergences in the observations of a variety of people—teachers and students recalling their experience, foreign travelers observing American schools, and interested Americans describing and analyzing schooling. For a complete bibliography, see Barbara Finkelstein, "Governing the Young: Teacher Behavior in American Primary Schools, 1820-1880," unpub. diss., Teachers College, Columbia University, 1970.

3. Lloyd deMause, "The Evolution of Childhood," in *The History of Childhood,* ed. *id.* (New York: Psychohistory Press, 1974).

4. Phillipe Ariès, *Centuries of Childhood: A Social History of Family Life,* tr. Robert Baldick (New York: Alfred A. Knopf, 1962). Ariès regards this development as the beginning of a loss of emotional freedom for children—a Romantic notion if one contemplates deMause's documentation of physical and psychological abuse toward children prior to the eighteenth century.

5. deMause, "The Evolution of Childhood," 52.

6. Ariès, *Centuries of Childhood.*

7. For good studies of the role of the family in the education of colonial children, see Lawrence A. Cremin, *American Education: The Colonial Experience, 1607-1783* (New York: Harper and Row, 1970), 113-138; Bernard Bailyn, *Education in the Forming of American Society* (Chapel Hill: University of North Carolina Press, 1960); Edmund S. Morgan, *The Puritan Family: Religion and Domestic Relations in Seventeenth Century New England,* new ed. (New York: Harper and Row, 1966); John Demos, *A Little Commonwealth: Family Life in Plymouth Colony* (New York: Oxford University Press, 1970); David J. Rothman, "A Note on the Study of the Colonial Family," reprinted in *Education in American History: Readings in the Social Issues,* ed. Michael Katz (New York: Praeger Publishers, 1973).

8. Cremin, *American Education,* 126-127.

9. *Ibid.;* Joseph E. Illick, "Child-Rearing in Seventeenth Century England and America," in *History of Childhood,* Chap. 7.

10. The various educational roles of the churchmen are described in Cremin, *American Education,* Chap. 5.

11. Illick analyzes the collective impact of the entire web of educational institutions concluding, as does Cremin, that people with a capacity for self-discipline and a desire for self-government were the end product of the systems of nurture.

12. Bailyn, *Education in the Forming of American Society.*

13. *Ibid.* We should note that differentiation was not accomplished in the same way, nor at the same time in all colonial communities. The general movement should not obscure the infinite diversity of the colonies.

14. John F. Walzer, "A Period of Ambivalence: Eighteenth-Century American Childhood," in *History of Childhood,* Chap. 8.

15. In order to comprehend the range of interpretation, see Laurence R. Veysey, "Toward a New Direction in Educational History: Prospect and Retrospect," *History of Education Quarterly* 9 (Fall 1969): 343-360; Lawrence A. Cremin, "Notes toward a Theory of Education," *Notes on Education,* No. 2 (June 1973); *id.,* "Further Notes toward a Theory of Education," *Notes on Education,* No. 4 (March 1974); Barbara Finkelstein, "Choose Your Own Bias: Non-Documentary Textbooks in the History of American Education," *Educational Studies* 5 (Winter 1974): 210-215.

16. The descriptive literature suffuses with ambivalence expressed in various ways by parents. We should note, however, that we have, as yet, no knowledge of the percentage of parents who sent their children to school, nor even of the configuration of communities that would encourage school attendance.

17. This thesis has been elaborated brilliantly in Kirk Jeffrey, "The Family as Utopian Retreat from the City: The Nineteenth Century Contribution," *Soundings* 55 (Spring 1972): 21-41; and William R. Taylor and Christopher Lasch, "Two Kindred Spirits: Sorority and Family in New England, 1839-1846," *New England Quarterly* 36 (March 1963): 231-241. See also William E. Bridges, "Family Patterns and Social Values in America, 1825-1875," *American Quarterly* 17 (Spring 1965): 3-11; Harvey J. Graff, "Patterns of Dependency in the Mid-Nineteenth Century City: A Sample from Boston, 1860," *History of Education Quarterly* 13 (Summer 1973): 129-143; Arthur W. Calhoun, *A Social History of the American Family* (New York: Barnes and Noble, 1960).

18. For an elaboration of the cult and practice of domesticity, see Kathryn Kish Sklar, *Catherine Beecher: A Study in American Domesticity* (New Haven, Conn.: Yale University Press, 1937); Anne L. Kuhn, *The Mother's Role in Childhood Education: New England Concepts, 1830-1860* (New Haven, Conn.: Yale Studies in Religious Education, 1947); Bernard Wishy, *The Child and the Republic: The Dawn of Modern American Child Nurture* (Philadelphia: University of Pennsylvania Press, 1968). Wishy's volume is, as Stanley Schultz has stated, no particular advance over the work of Anne Kuhn.

19. This perception has been documented, if elliptically, in four excellent histories. See Michael Katz, *The Irony of Early School Reform: Educational Innovation in Mid-Nineteenth Century Massachusetts* (Cambridge, Mass.: Harvard University Press, 1968); Marvin Lazerson, *Origins of the Urban School: Public Education in Massachusetts, 1870-1915* (Cambridge, Mass.: Harvard University Press, 1971); Stanley K. Schultz, *The Culture Factory: Boston Public Schools, 1789-1860* (New York: Oxford University Press, 1973); Carl F. Kaestle, *The Evolution of an Urban School System: New York City, 1750-1850* (Cambridge, Mass.: Harvard University Press, 1974); Selwyn K. Troen, "Popular Education in Nineteenth Century St. Louis," *History of Education Quarterly* 13 (Spring 1973): 23-41. Each of these historians includes data and bibliographies.

20. The work of Oscar Handlin is still definitive.

21. *The Family in History: Interdisciplinary Essays,* ed. Theodore K. Rabb and Robert J. Rotberg (New York: Harper and Row, 1973), 85-140, 171-180, 227-235.

22. This is Katz's central argument in *Irony of Early School Reform.* The descriptive literature indicates, however, that teachers in parochial schools were as committed to intrusion as were the masters and mistresses of the public schools.

23. Lawrence Daniel Washington, *Confessions of a Schoolmaster* (San Antonio, Tex.: Naylor Co., 1939), ix.

24. Mary B. King, *Looking Backward: Or Memories of the Past* (New York: Anson D. F. Randolph and Co., 1870), 14.

25. Boston Association of Masters of the Public Schools, *Remarks on the Seventh Annual Report of the Honorable Horace Mann, Secretary of the Massachusetts Board of Education* (Boston: n.p., 1844), 45.

26. Quoted in Katz, *Irony of Early School Reform,* 120.

27. Baltimore Commissioners of Public Schools, *Eighth Annual Report of the Commissioners of Public Schools to the Mayor and City Council of Baltimore, 1836* (Baltimore, Md.: Commissioners of Public Schools, 1836), 9.

28. William Milford Giffin, *School Days in the Fifties: A True Story with Some Untrue Names of Persons and Places* (Chicago: A. Flanagan, 1906), 31.

29. James P. Logan, "An Old-Time Pedagogue: Memories of a Country District School in Civil War Days," *Proceedings of the New Jersey Historical Society* 55 (October 1937): 268.

30. Mrs. E. W. Bellamy, "Rewards and Punishments," *Home and School* 2 (September 1873): 410; see also Horace Mann, "Sixth Annual Report of the Board of Education," *Common School Journal* 5 (1843): 220.

31. William Augustus Mowry, *Recollections of a New England Educator, 1838-1908* (New York: Silver, Burdett and Co., 1908), 15. For similar sentiments, see Meredith Janvier, *Baltimore in the Eighties and Nineties* (Baltimore, Md.: H. G. Roebuck and Son, 1933), 137.

32. John George Clinkscales, *On the Old Plantation: Reminiscences of His Childhood* (Spartanburg, S.C.: Band and White, 1916), 89.

33. Hiram Orcutt, *Reminiscences of School Life* (Cambridge, Mass.: printed by the University Press, 1889), 50; Mrs. Francis Edward Clark, *The Little Girl that Once Was I* (Boston: International Society of Christian Endeavor, 1936), 48.

34. Henry Johnson, *The Other Side of Main Street: A History Teacher from Sauk Centre* (New York: Columbia University Press, 1935), 34; Logan, "Old-Time Pedagogue," 265.

35. Patrick Shirreff, *A Tour through North America* (Edinburgh: Printed by Ballantine and Co., 1835), 56.

36. David Macrae, *The Americans at Home: Pen-and-Ink Sketches of American Men, Manners, and Institutions,* popular ed., rev. (Glasgow: John S. Marr and Sons, 1875), 476.

37. For descriptions of teachers and of their political function within the classroom setting, see Alexander Macmillan, *A Night with the Yankees* (Ayr: privately printed by R. MacLehose, 1868), 46. See also W. E. Baxter, *America and the Americans* (London: George Routledge and Co., 1855), 163; James Dawson Burn, *Three Years among the Working Classes in the United States during the War* (London: Smith, Elder and Co., 1865), 162.

38. There are several good studies of the social, political, economic, racial, moral, and cultural ideas contained in American textbooks: Ruth Miller Elson, *Guardians of Tradition: American Schoolbooks of the Nineteenth Century* (Lincoln: University of Nebraska Press, 1964); John A. Nietz, *Our Textbooks* (Pittsburgh: University of Pittsburgh Press, 1961); Richard Mosier, *Making the American Mind* (New York: Kings Crown Press, 1947); Charles H. Carpenter, *History of American Schoolbooks* (Philadelphia: University of Pennsylvania Press, 1963).

39. Jacob Abbott, *Lecture on Moral Education Delivered in Boston before the American Institute of Instruction, August 26, 1831* (Boston: Hilliare, Gray, Little and Williams, 1832), 48; *id., Right and Wrong: Or Familiar Illustrations of the Moral Duties of Children* (Boston: William Pierce, 1834).

40. Francis Wayland, *The Elements of Moral Science* (New York: printed for Cooke and Co., 1835), 367.

41. Millard Fillmore Kennedy, in collaboration with Alvin F. Harlow, *Schoolmaster of Yesterday: A Three-Generation Story, 1820-1919* (New York:

McGraw-Hill Book Co., 1940), 20. See also James Philbrick, "Second Annual Report to the Boston School Committee," *Boston School Committee Report, 1857,* 82; Clark Lewis Barzee, *Oregon in the Making: '60s to Gay '90s* (Salem, Ore.: Statesman Publishing Co., 1936), 59.

42. Boston Association of Masters of the Public Schools, *Remarks on the Seventh Annual Report,* 84-87.

43. Duane Doty and William Torrey Harris, *A Statement of the Theory of Education in the United States of America as Approved by Many Leading Educators* (Washington, D.C.: Government Printing Office, 1874), 13. For similar sentiments, see James Pyle Wickersham, *Discipline as a Factor in the Work of the School* (Syracuse, N.Y.: C. W. Bardeen, 1898), 19.

44. Carl David Arfwedson, *The United States and Canada in 1832, 1833, and 1834* (London: Richard Bentley, 1834), 240.

45. John Griscom, *Memoir of John Griscom* (New York: R. Carter and Bros., 1859).

46. Macrae, *Americans at Home,* 475-476.

47. John Proffatt, "The Pedagogue in Literature," *American Educational Monthly* 9 (January 1872): 12-13.

48. William Reed, *Life on the Border Sixty Years Ago* (Fall River, Mass.: R. Adams, 1882), 34, quoted in Isaac Freeman Hall, *In School from Three to Eighty: Pictures of American Life, 1825-1925* (Pittsfield, Mass.: Press of the Eagle Printing and Bindery Co., 1927), 89. See also "An Old-Time Pedagogue," *Olde Ulster, An Historical and Genealogical Magazine* 7 (June 1911): 172.

49. John Howard Redfield, *Recollections of John Howard Redfield* (New York: printed for the author, 1900), 23. See also Clinkscales *(On the Old Plantation,* 93), who expressed the same sentiments about a pedagogue in an old-field school in the 1840s; William Andrus Alcott, *Confessions of a School Master* (Andover, Mass.: Gould, Newman, and Saxton, 1839), 394.

50. Alfred Holbrook, *Reminiscences of the Happy Life of a Teacher* (Cincinnati, Ohio: Elm Street Printing Co., 1885), 19.

51. For examples, see Barnabas C. Hobbs, "Early School Days," in *The Indiana Schools and the Men Who Have Worked in Them,* ed. James H. Smart (Cincinnati, Ohio: Wilson and Hinkle, 1876), 19; Logan, "Old-Time Pedagogue," 173 (New Jersey); T. W. Price, *The Life of T. W. Price* (Selma, Ala.: Daily Times Job Printing Office, 1879), 15; Richard H. Clark, *Memoirs of Richard H. Clark,* ed. Lollie Belle Wylie (Atlanta: Franklin Printing and Publishing Co., 1898), 86-87. For the cities, see "My School-Boy Days in New York City Forty Years Ago," *New York Teacher and American Educational Monthly* 6 (March 1869): 98; Daniel Carter Beard, *Hardly a Man Is Now Alive* (New York: Doubleday-Doran, 1939), 98; J. F. F. Gray, *The Story of My Life* (Baltimore: M. E. Church, 1924), 5; A. H. Nelson, "The Little Red Schoolhouse," *Educational Review* 23 (January-May 1902): 307; Henry H. Fetterolf, "Going to School Eighty Years Ago," *Historical Society of Montgomery County Bulletin* 1 (April 1937): 86-89.

52. The descriptive literature is literally dominated by descriptions of the life of teachers outside the classroom situation. For particularly effective characterizations of the social relationships of students and teachers, see James William Turner, *Half a*

Century in the School Room, or Personal Memoirs of Jas. William Turner (Carrier Mills, Ill.: Turner Publishing Co., 1920), 19; Washington, *Confessions of a School Master,* 17; Holbrook, *Reminiscences,* 95.

53. Orcutt, *Reminiscences of School Life,* 59.

54. Sarah Stuart Robbins, *Old Andover Days: Memories of a Puritan Childhood* (Boston: Pilgrim Press, 1908), 61.

55. So universal are descriptions of this kind of apparatus that exceptions stand out. For examples of exceptions, see Harvey Washington Wiley, *An Autobiography* (Indianapolis: Bobbs-Merrill Co., 1930), 36; William Smith Knowlton, *The Old Schoolmaster, or Forty-five Years with the Girls and Boys* (Augusta, Me.: Burleigh and Flynt, 1905), 29.

56. Barzee, *Oregon in the Making,* 60.

57. E. E. Kenney, "Recollections of Early Schools," University of Texas *Bulletin,* No. 1824 (April 25, 1918), 137.

58. Turner, *Half a Century in the School Room,* 19-20.

59. Washington, *Confessions of a School Master,* 17.

60. Holbrook, *Reminiscences,* 95.

61. Rufus Matthew Jones, *A Small-Town Boy* (New York: Macmillan Co., 1941), 77; Fassett Allen Cotton, *Education in Indiana, 1793-1923* (Bluffton, Ind.: Progress Publishing Co., 1923), 57; L. B. Balliet, "A Lehigh County English School Seventy Years Ago," *Pennsylvania German* 9 (January 1908): 526; Mowry, *Recollections of a New England Educator,* 35; James Albert Woodburn, "Hoosier School Master," *Indiana Magazine of History* 32 (September 1836): 231-247; Logan, "An Old-Time Pedagogue," 263-269.

62. Nelson, "The Little Red Schoolhouse," 308.

63. Descriptions of these procedures also appear to have been universal. For particularly graphic descriptions of the combining of physical torture and humiliation, see Warren Burton, *The District School as It Was, by One Who Went to It* (Boston: Carter, Hendee and Co., 1833), 39; Walter Brooks, *A Child and a Boy* (New York: Brentano's, 1915), 110.

64. Barzee, *Oregon in the Making,* 61.

65. Frank T. Clampitt, *Some Incidents in My Life: A Saga of the "Unknown" Citizen* (Ann Arbor, Mich.: Edwards Brothers, 1935), 15-16.

66. "An Old-Time Pedagogue," *Olde Ulster,* 173.

67. Rachel Quick Buttz, *A Hoosier Girlhood* (Boston: Richard G. Badger, Gorham Press, 1924), 51.

68. Balliet, "A Lehigh County English School," 526.

69. The following sources contain particularly graphic descriptions of this universally described phenomenon: George Henry Gerberding, *Reminiscent Reflections of an Octogenarian* (Minneapolis, Minn.: Augsburgh Publishing Co., 1928), 12; Joseph Garner Estill, *Episodes in the Life of a Commonplace Man* (Lakeville, Conn.: privately printed, 1939), 25: Paul Henry Hanus, *Adventuring in Education* (Cambridge, Mass.: Harvard University Press, 1937), 28; Jeremiah Hubbard, *A Teacher's Ups and Downs from 1858 to 1879* (Richmond, Ind.: Palladium Steam Printing Co., 1879), 48.

70. There are, of course, descriptions of teachers who abandoned physical coercion for moral persuasion.

71. Johnson, *Other Side of Main Street.*

72. Estill, *Episodes in the Life of a Commonplace Man,* 25.

73. For examples, see Alice Mendenhall George, *The Story of My Childhood* (Whittier, Calif.: William A. Smith, 1923), 65; James Marion Sims, *The Story of My Life* (New York: D. Appleton and Co., 1884), 60, 64. Matters were very little different in urban centers. See William Graham Johnston, *Life and Reminiscences from Birth to Manhood of William Graham Johnston* (New York: Knickerbocker Press, 1901), 203; *Report of the Committee Appointed to Visit Public Schools of Philadelphia, New York, Brooklyn, and Boston to the Board of Commissioners of Baltimore* (Baltimore, Md.: H. A. Robinson, 1867), 35-36.

74. Descriptions are legion of barrings-out in rural schools. For particularly graphic illustrations, see I. L. Kephart, "Barring-Out the Teacher," in Asa Earl Martin and Herr Hiram Shenk, *Pennsylvania History as Told by Contemporaries* (New York: Macmillan Co., 1925), 392-396; Joseph S. Williams, *Old Times in West Tennessee* (Memphis, Tenn.: W. G. Cheeney, 1873), 285-286; John Massey, *Reminiscences* (Nashville, Tenn.: Church, South, Smith, and Lamar, 1916), 51; John S. Van Voorhis, *The Old and New Monongahela* (Pittsburgh: Nicholson Printer and Binder, 1893), 53; Judge Decatur Franklin Morrow, *Then and Now: Reminiscences and Historical Romance* (Macon, Ga.: J. W. Burke Co., 1926), 228.

75. John Lewis Franklin, "Life of Ezekiel Boring Kephart: Statesman, Educator, Preacher," quoted in Martin and Shenk, *Pennsylvania History as Told by Contemporaries,* 392-396.

76. There is evidence to suggest that teachers in the city also distinguished their person and their office by whipping students and delivering sermons. For examples, see Sarah Smith Bixby, *Adobe Days* (Los Angeles, Calif.: Zake-Zeitlin, 1931), 122-123; Arthur Howard Hall, *Old Bradford School-Days* (Norwood, Mass.: Plimpton Press, 1910), 156.

77. Joseph Lancaster, *The British System of Education: being a complete epitome of the improvements and inventions practised by Joseph Lancaster, to which is added a Report of the Trustees of the Lancaster School at Georgetown, Columbia* (Washington, D.C.: Joseph Milligan, 1812); *id., The Lancasterian System of Education with Improvements by Its Founder* (Baltimore, Md.: published for the author, 1821), 4. The sources around which this discussion of Lancasterian schools turns portray schools in eastern cities—New York, Philadelphia, Washington, Baltimore, Pittsburgh. But there is evidence to suggest that monitorial schools in cities further west resembled those of the eastern metropolises. Civic leaders from places such as Cincinnati and Lexington dispatched men to study schools in Baltimore, Philadelphia, New York, and Boston. Richard C. Wade, *The Urban Frontier: The Rise of Western Cities, 1790-1830* (Cambridge, Mass.: Harvard University Press, 1959), 105-125. Articles appear frequently in the *American Annals of Education and Instruction* and describe the progress made by western cities in establishing monitorial schools.

Allusions to Lancasterian schools can also be found in other periodicals. For examples, see *American Journal of Education,* 1826-1830, and *Western Academician and Journal of Education and Science.* The Joseph Lancaster Papers located in the American Antiquarian Society in Worcester, Massachusetts, also contain references to Lancasterian schools in many cities. Manuals, prepared by masters of Lancasterian schools in particular locations, also indicate their omnipresence. See, for example, William Dale, *A Manual of the Albany Lancasterian School* (Albany, N.Y.: n.p., 1820).

There are also monographs that describe the development of Lancasterian schools. See Charles Calvert Ellis, *Lancasterian Schools in Philadelphia* (Philadelphia: n.p., 1907); John Franklin Reigart, *The Lancasterian System of Instruction in the Schools of New York City* (New York: Teachers College, Columbia University Press, 1916). Several other historians allude to the presence of Lancasterian schools in particular states. See, for example, Moses Edward Ligon, *A History of Public Education in Kentucky* (Lexington: University of Kentucky Press, 1942), 33; Charles Lee Coon, *North Carolina Schools and Academies: 1790-1840: A Documentary History* (Raleigh, N.C.: Edwards and Broughton Printing Co., 1915), 722-745; William Arthur Maddox, *The Free School Idea in Virginia before the Civil War* (New York: Teachers College, Columbia University, 1915).

78. Lancaster, *Lancasterian System of Education.*

79. Quoted in Paul Monroe, *Founding of the American Public School System: A History of Education in the United States* (New York: Macmillan Co., 1940), 369.

80. Joseph Lancaster, "On the Science of the Human Mind," American Antiquarian Society, Manuscript Collections, Joseph Lancaster Papers.

81. Almost all authors describe this kind of physical uniformity. For examples, see "My School-Boy Days in New York City Forty Years Ago"; Edward Strutt Abdy, *Journal of a Residence and Tour in the United States and North America* (London: John Murray, 1834), 152-153; Anne Royall, *Sketches of History, Life, Manners in the United States* (New Haven, Conn.: printed for the author, 1826), 256; William Bentley Fowle, "Boston Monitorial Schools," *American Journal of Education* 1 (January 1826): 39-40; Griscom, *Memoir*, 209; Thomas Hamilton, *Men and Manners in America*, 2d American ed. (Philadelphia: Carey, Lea, and Blanchard, 1833), 52-57; Basil Hall, *Travels in North America in the Years 1827 and 1828* (London: Simpkin and Marshall, 1829), 24-30; Arfwedson, *The United States and Canada*, 240.

82. "My School-Boy Days in New York City Forty Years Ago," 95.

83. Quoted in Monroe, *Founding of the American Public School System*, 367-368.

84. "My School-Boy Days in New York City Forty Years Ago," 95.

85. *Report of the Committee Appointed to Visit Public Schools*, 35-36.

86. "Two Representative Schools," *New York Teachers, and American Educational Monthly* 5 (July 1868): 275-278.

87. Joseph Mayer Rice, *The Public School System of the United States* (New York: Century Co., 1893); Hanus, *Adventuring in Education*, 28-29; Ellwood P. Cubberley, *The Portland Survey: A Textbook on City School Administration Based on a Concrete Study* (Yonkers-on-Hudson, N.Y.: World Book Co., 1916); Andrew J. Rickoff, *Past and Present of Our Common School* (Cleveland, Ohio: Leader Printing Co., 1877), 79.

88. "Two Representative Schools," 256.

89. Rice, *Public School System of the United States*, 98.

90. Baltimore School Commissioners, *Forty-first Annual Report, 1872* (Baltimore: Baltimore School Commissioners, 1873), 55.

91. *Id., Forty-second Annual Report, 1873* (Baltimore: Baltimore School Commissioners, 1874), 54.

92. Hubbard, *A Teacher's Ups and Downs*, 14.

93. See James Howard Patterson, *Of Me I Sing, or Me and Education* (Nappanee, Ind.: E. V. Publishing House, 1940), 34. Similar complaints can be found in the following descriptions: Gail Hamilton [Mary Abigail Dodge], *Our Common School System* (Boston: Estes and Lauriat, 1880), 255; Frederick C. B. Marryat, *A Diary in America, with Remarks on Its Institutions* (London: Longman, Orme, Brown, Green, and Longmans, 1839), Vol. III, 280-287.

94. I do not mean to imply that teachers in other settings in the early generation did not use moral persuasion. Indeed, they did, but they typically coupled it with physical coercion of one kind or another. In the descriptive literature of the 1850s, 1860s, and 1870s, teachers consistently and consciously preferred this method. There are, of course, the inevitable exceptions. Roger W. Babson, *Actions and Reactions* (New York: Harper and Brothers, 1949), 19; Hanus, *Adventuring in Education*, 136-137; Janvier, *Baltimore in the Eighties and Nineties*, 136-137. Nor do I mean to imply that all women depended exclusively on moral persuasion. For an example of one who preferred physical coercion, see Isabella Bacon Bond, *Memoirs of Isabella Bacon Bond* (Boston: privately printed, 1934), 55; "A Mother's Visit to a Primary School," *Massachusetts Teacher* 22 (April 1869): 159-160.

95. "A Mother's Visit to a Primary School," 159-160.

96. *Old School Days: Being Reminiscences of a Passing Generation*, ed. Thomas Garth (Ann Arbor, Mich.: Edwards Brothers, n.d.), 40. Tardiness was probably a problem since teachers typically constructed rituals to prevent it. Macrae, *Americans at Home*, 473-474; Frederick William Ballinger, *Recollections of an Old Fashioned New Englander* (New York: Round Table Press, 1941), 15.

97. Macrae, *Americans at Home*, 473.

98. When teachers used students as monitors, they endowed the monitors with special status, differentiating them from fellow students and formalizing relationships between students. For exceptions to this rule, see Leila Partridge, *The "Quincy Methods" Illustrated: Pen Photographs from the Quincy Schools* (New York: E. L. Kellogg and Co., 1885); Edward Austin Sheldon, *Autobiography of Edward Austin Sheldon*, ed. Mary Sheldon Barnes (New York: Ives-Butler Co., 1911), 168; Elizabeth Palmer Peabody, *Record of Mr. Alcott's School*, 3d ed. (Boston: Roberts Brothers, 1874).

99. For good descriptions of loud schools, see Rebecca Latimer Felton, *Country Life in Georgia in the Days of My Youth* (Atlanta, Ga.: Index Printing Co., 1919), 58-60; Hobbs, "Early School Days," 20; Morrow, *Then and Now*, 227.

100. The demand for silence appears to have been near universal. For an exception, see Sheldon, *Autobiography*, 168.

101. For examples, see Hall, *Old Bradford School-Days*, 12; Barzee, *Oregon in the Making*, 61; Macrae, *Americans at Home*, 475-476.

102. Lamar Fontaine, *My Life and My Lectures* (New York: Neale Publishing Co., 1908), 14-15.

103. J. F. Schaeffer, "Letter," in Myron Carleton Lough, "Early Education in West Virginia," *Transallegheny Historical Magazine* (January 1902): 152.

104. Orcutt, *Reminiscences of School Life*, 67.

105. George Duffield, *Memories of Frontier Iowa* (Des Moines, Iowa: Bishard Brothers, 1906), 53.

106. L. Adda Nichols Bigelow, *Reminiscences* (Chula Vista, Calif.: Denrich Press, 1917), 3.

107. Sheldon, *Autobiography*, 168.

108. Rice, *Public School System of the United States*, 33. See also *Report of the Committee Appointed to Visit Public Schools*, 83.

109. Orcutt, *Reminiscences of School Life*, 67.

110. For examples, see Holbrook, *Reminiscences of the Happy Life of a Teacher*, 32; Hubbard, *A Teacher's Ups and Downs*, 59; Knowlton, *Old Schoolmaster*.

111. William Andrus Alcott, *A Word to Teachers: or, Two Days in a Primary School* (Boston: Allen and Ticknor, 1833), 37.

112. Though one finds descriptions of teachers engaging in activities usually associated with motherhood, the ties between teachers and pupils do not appear to have been affectional. Instances of kissing or hugging or of consoling students are rarely encountered. For a lonely example, see Holbrook, *Reminiscences of the Happy Life of a Teacher*, 30.

113. Hobbs, "Early School Days," 17-18.

114. Mowry, *Recollections of a New England Educator*, 50.

115. Felton, *Country Life in Georgia*, 61-62.

116. For examples, see Buttz, *Hoosier Girlhood*, 62; Reed, *Life on the Border Sixty Years Ago*, 32; Gerberding, *Reminiscent Reflections of an Octogenarian*, 12.

117. Flo V. Knisely Menninger, *Days of My Life: Memories of a Kansas Mother and Teacher* (New York: Richard R. Smith, 1939), 40; Knowlton, *Old Schoolmaster*, 45; Bernard G. Burtnett, "The Old Marble School at Union Corners," *Quarterly Bulletin of the Westchester County Historical Society* 10 (January 1933): 13; Barzee, *Oregon in the Making*, 65.

118. Barzee, *Oregon in the Making*, 62.

119. Hall, *In School from Three to Eighty*, 142; John Morris Dodd, *Autobiography of a Surgeon* (New York: Walter W. Neal, 1928), 147.

120. The censoring of nonacademic deportment is present in almost every school according to descriptive literature. But in cities, teachers consistently attended to matters relating to hygiene, cleanliness, speech, and dress. These activities suggest that they sought to correct as well as to supplement the training that pupils received at home.

121. Alcott, *Confessions of a Schoolmaster*, 3.

122. Macrae, *Americans at Home*, 472-473.

123. Even in the early period we find these observations. See, for example, Joseph Lancaster, "Memoranda of Visits to Public Schools in New York and in Philadelphia, 1838," American Antiquarian Society, Manuscript Collections, Joseph Lancaster Papers; Baltimore School Commissioners, *Annual Reports for the Years 1826-1834* (Baltimore, Md.: Public School Commissioners, 1936); Francis Milton Trollope, *Domestic Manners of the Americans* (London: Printed for Whitaker, Treacher and Co., 1832).

124. Massey, *Reminiscences*, 48.

125. William Henry Venable, *A Buckeye Boyhood* (Cincinnati: Robert Clarke Co., 1911), 47-48.

126. Amos Bronson Alcott, *New Connecticut: An Autobiographical Poem* (Boston: Roberts Brothers, 1889), 135.

127. Gerberding, *Reminiscent Reflections of an Octogenarian*, 12.

128. Marryat, *Diary in America*, 287.

129. Bond, *Memoirs of Isabella Bacon Bond*, 55.

130. Alcott, *Word to Teachers*, 25.

SEVEN

A Past for the Future: Historiographical Perspectives

Perspectives on the History of Women's Education in the United States, by *Jill K. Conway*

Essay Review of Charles Silberman, *Crisis in the Classroom,* by *Michael B. Katz*

Identities and Contours: An Approach to Educational History, by *Maxine Greene*

Conflict and Consensus Revisited: Notes toward a Reinterpretation of American Educational History, by *Carl F. Kaestle*

While it is true that impressive work in the history of American education has been completed over the past two decades, noticeable gaps remain. The enlarged definition of the field notwithstanding, the forms of education other than schools are only beginning to receive their due. As the preceding chapters illustrate, the history of American education is still focused on schools and related matters. This emphasis is understandable, given the importance of schooling in American life and the amount of it that has been available relative to other educational forms. Recent school histories, however, exhibit a new sophistication in both the analytical techniques employed and the examination of school-society relations. They are not, strictly speaking, institutional biographies, and they are not designed to be

271

laudatory or inspirational. Exceptions can be found, but the model school histories tend to be rigorously analytical and policy oriented.

The knowledge gaps in the history of American education reflect in part historiographical problems, including intramural quarrels over techniques, sources, and perspectives. In addressing these problems, historians risk narrowing their audience to themselves. The history of American education, like history generally, has a larger public. The interpretations may be varied and even conflict, but they make possible an enlarged memory and help to develop an appreciation of the connections and discontinuities between past and present. History can contribute significantly to the education of the public. Such assignments require historians to produce, at some point, coherent stories. All of which serves as reminder that they do not write only for each other, but for their contemporaries and the future as well.

The essays in this chapter offer guidelines for histories of American education intended for this larger audience. Some of the four authors are in direct disagreement, but in combination their advice amounts to a listing of elements necessary for honest, critical accounts. Jill Conway speaks to the importance of interpreting the history of education for women from the perspectives of women, with the caveat that those perspectives require close inspection. Educational "progress" for women, she warns, has not always delivered what it seemed to promise. The argument has general applicability to educational history, which in part and to the extent permitted by sources is a story to be told from the inside out.

Michael Katz's review essay touches on themes developed more fully in published monographs. American public schools have functioned within a political climate that is reflected in their goals, organization, and outcomes. To be intelligible or useful, interpretations of their past development necessarily include analyses of the schools as political institutions and accounts of their connections with the distributions of power in American society. Katz, to be sure, is far more specific than these summary guidelines suggest in directing attention to the schools' political and ideological character. Without straying from the evidence or relying on untested assumptions, historians may disagree with Katz's profoundly negative assessment. But they cannot avoid subjecting the schools to political analysis.

Maxine Greene's article illustrates her long-standing concern for utilizing imaginative literature in historical analyses of education.

Such sources reflect the dimensions and complexities of human experience and shed light on those times and episodes in which it
becomes necessary for individuals to "say *no* in thunder." In short,
they can keep historians honest and help protect them from reductionism. Being fundamentally a human story, the history of American
education requires rich appreciation of the meaning of education as a
dynamic within civilization. That level of understanding cannot be
achieved, Greene argues, solely through quantitative assessments of
schooling outcomes or critical social-class analyses. Important as those
matters are, there is a larger, more valuable and instructive history to
be recovered.

Carl Kaestle is perhaps best known for his thorough and innovative
research on the origins of urban education. He has proved to be especially persuasive in establishing connections between history and educational policy studies. His deceptively brief article, which concludes
this volume, argues the need for nothing less than new, refined research models to enable more accurate interpretations of American
educational history. The traditional conflict and consensus models, he
finds, cannot explain the available evidence; thus, they promote simplistic and misleading versions of the educational past.

Perspectives on the History of
Women's Education
in the United States

Jill K. Conway

The lively current debate about developing programs of study
which will raise women's consciousness and bring them into American
intellectual life on a level of equality with men tends to be ahistorical
and to subscribe to many of the unexamined assumptions of American
educational history. Among the most revered of these is the interpretation unhesitatingly advanced by historians of education[1] that coeduca-

Reprinted, with permission, from *History of Education Quarterly* 14 (Spring 1974),
1-12.

tion automatically was a "liberating experience" for American women and that access to professional education naturally placed women on a level with male professional peers. Advocates of increased participation for women in the creation and transmission of American culture had better examine these assumptions with the skepticism which feminists normally extend to male interpretations of women's experience if they are not to devise a faulty strategy for reform through inability to perceive some of the concealed hazards of the landscape.

Although cultural historians have universally concluded that the development of educational institutions in colonial America and in the young republic of the early national period played a decisive role in the creation of an American democratic culture, little effort has been expended in analyzing the impact of these institutions on women's social role or on their consciousness of themselves as independent intellects. To understand the dimensions of this impact, we must begin, as in all questions of American cultural history, with the colonial period and the Puritan heritage. Governor Winthrop of Massachusetts Bay gave as succinct an expression of Puritan attitudes to women with aspirations to learning as it would be possible to find in his diary entry after meeting the emotionally disturbed wife of a friend.

Her husband, being very loving and tender of her was loath to grieve her; but he saw his error, when it was too late. For if she had attended her household affairs, and such things as belong to women, and not gone out of her way and calling to meddle in such things as are proper for men, whose minds are stronger, etc., she had kept her wits, and might have improved them usefully and honorably in the place God had set her.[2]

Although the Puritans placed a high value on literacy for women, its purpose was to enable them to study the scriptures under the appropriate male guidance, not to think for themselves as the trial and judgment of Anne Hutchinson vividly illustrates. There was in fact a Puritan prohibition against women publishing books and even so strong-willed a woman as Anne Bradstreet felt called upon to excuse her devotion to writing poetry as an occupation carried out at the expense of sleep after all her household duties and her devotions were finished. Thus, the Puritan concern for literacy in women was designed to serve a special purpose, to ensure their salvation, but only in the deviant few did the ability to read encourage an independent and self-directing intellectual life.

The transmission of Enlightenment ideas to the American colonies brought to colonial intellectual life characteristic debates of Western

European thought, designated by the shorthand phrase, the "querrelle des femmes." This was a debate, between feminists and antifeminists concerning the extent of women's rationality and the purpose and degree to which the female mind might be educated, which had continued from the early Renaissance period through to the Enlightenment. The discussion of this question in eighteenth-century colonial thought was for the most part not original and drew mainly on English and French sources.[3] However, as with so much of his writing, Benjamin Franklin was able to take the European terms of this discussion about female rationality and recast them in uniquely American theories and conclusions. Franklin was willing to abandon the Christian view of the female — as a lesser creation marked by greater impulsiveness and less able to use reason in control of the emotions than men — and to put in its place a view of the female as a rational being engaged in the pursuit of happiness. However, the revolutionary potential of such a view was not worked out in his thought because of the biological determinism which was inherent in his view of natural law. Thus, it never occurred to Franklin, the archetypal self-made and self-educated man, that the freedom to create the self might be extended to women. His *Reflections on Courtship and Marriage* of 1746 instead developed an approach to female education with which Americans were to become familiar.[4] A woman's education, he thought, should develop in her those qualities which would ensure her happiness in marriage since marriage and reproduction were her natural destiny. It was axiomatic for him that women's happiness was to be found in marriage, and reason therefore decreed that women should be educated to use their rational powers in the role of wife and mother. In bringing together the consideration of marriage, the pursuit of happiness, and the education of women, Franklin was squaring up to one of the most troublesome problems which were to perplex the leaders of the revolutionary generation. How could the rational scrutiny of the basis of power and authority in the political realm be undertaken without setting off the kind of radical debate about other patterns of domination and subordination in society which the revolutionary leaders profoundly wished to leave unquestioned? In particular, if the nature of tyranny inherent in monarchical institutions [were] to be laid bare for all to see, how could such matters be discussed without a consideration of the nature of tyranny within the patriarchal family? If the goal of the individual was to be the pursuit of happiness how could such a pursuit be so defined that women would accept the subordination necessary for harmony in family life and order in society? Franklin's answer was to make some concessions toward acceptance of female rationality and to argue for the creation of a system of female education which would make women rationally convinced that their true happiness lay in marriage and would develop in the female mind only those traits and tendencies likely to find satisfaction in domestic life.

Since formal educational institutions for women did not form any part of Franklin's scheme of things, the agency by which women were to be educated was to be through their contact during the process of courtship with the more finely disciplined male intellect. Franklin's aspiring suitor came armed with improving books, ready to convey good commonsense philosophy, sound moral principles, and a grasp of arithmetic. He also came prepared to set limits on the intellectual aspirations of his bride-to-be, to steer her away from the realm of abstract thought because a critical intellect would not be conducive to marital happiness, whereas a grasp of accounting would be of practical use in future domestic life.

It only remained for educational theorists to elaborate this view after the Declaration of Independence in accord with the national purpose. The task was ably taken up by Benjamin Rush whose writings on the education appropriate for women in a republic steered clear of the question of female rationality and placed great emphasis on the patriotic duties of republican women.[5] Rush took up another educational theme, echoes of which were still to be heard in twentieth-century discussions of women's education. In a republican society, since all men were equal, there could be no servant class. It followed, therefore, that women would have to be educated to understand domestic economy because the sound ordering of the household would now become their responsibility. The implicit assignment of women to a service role did not trouble Rush in the slightest since, like all his contemporaries, he assumed the correctness of the traditional subordination of women, though the upheaval of the Revolution required that this status be squared with republican ideology.

Thus when one looks at the roles taken up by women intellectuals in the early national period, one sees an immediate contrast between the life patterns of women who were to live and work with ideas within the context of American culture and those who took on the role of intellectual in Europe. In Europe the woman intellectual developed her creativity in the hurly-burly of literary life almost to the degree that she was deviant from her society. European women intellectuals were either déclassé (cast out from respectable society, detached from family and family responsibilities, living by their wits as self-supporting individuals), or else they lived a contemplative life in a religious community which was a recognized counter-institution for escape from the family.

It was otherwise in the United States in the period from 1790 to 1830 when new roles were emerging for the few women who had somehow acquired education. The early national period was one of intense and anxious questioning about what an appropriate republican culture would be like and about what social forces could be expected to keep republican society stable. The cause for worry and uncertainty about the future came from what was known from classical history of republican societies. Classical parallels suggested that the stability and prosperity of republics rested upon their capacity to maintain virtue and discipline among the citizenry. The United States of the 1790s had no standing army to impart discipline and had recently decided that there should be no national religious establishment which could undertake moral instruction. This meant that the family unit assumed an unprecedented political significance because the family was the only social unit which could be relied on to provide both moral training and discipline for the young of the Republic.

The result of these unique political pressures was the development of a new division of labor between the sexes. Males were thought of as having political and economic responsibilities: they were to be citizens and to provide the economic support for the family. Women had new responsibilities of a very important kind. They were to have the responsibility for the administration of the domestic establishment (something European men and eighteenth-century Americans expected to share with their wives), they were to play the primary role in educating the young, and, because of this primary responsibility, they were to serve as the moral guardians of the young. This new role for women as guardians of moral standards was unique to American culture. It immediately paved the way for the emergence in the 1830s of the woman teacher who could safely be charged with the education of the young of both sexes.

The first generation of women educators was born in the 1790s when these new cultural forces first began to operate. Their intellectual aspirations thus took them not into deviance but into intense patriotism and affirmation of American values. In explaining their careers they produced the first writing by women on women's education to be published in America. The textbooks, speeches, and lectures of Emma Willard and Catharine Beecher[6] were hardly clarion calls to independence for women scholars though both women lived for ideas and supported themselves entirely by their teaching and writing. Both were celebrators of the Republic and of American virtues, both rejoiced in the new calling which republican culture had created for the patriotic woman teacher, and both were impeccably correct in restricting women's teaching role to the moral guidance of the young in insisting that politics, theology, and philosophy were the unquestioned concerns of men. This kind of respectability was not unique to women educators. Women moralists and religious writers of the early national period likewise celebrated the family and the moral strength to be derived from maternity though poets like the popular Lydia Sigourney and famous preachers like Mrs. Phoebe Palmer clearly honored their domestic calling more in prose and sentiment than in hard days in the kitchen or the nursery. Sarah J. Hale, the moralizing editor of *Godey's Lady Book,* likewise earned middle-class status though she broke the genteel code about respectable women working because she was such a determined celebrator of the virtues of family life and the responsibilities of women for preserving moral standards.[7] By conforming their concerns as teachers, writers, preachers, or publicists to the conventional areas of female expertise and assuming responsibility for the preservation of "respectable" morality, women intellectuals in the early national period took on a role for themselves which was compensatory to that of men, rather than in competition with the work of male scholars, theologians, and writers. By doing so, they gave actual currency to the theories of writers on women's education, like Franklin and Rush, and so fostered the belief carried on by their students and readers that women's intellectual life found its purpose in achieving for American culture some of the tasks which men, because of their economic and political responsibilities, could not fulfill.

We might expect that this view of the compensatory value of the female intellect would be modified by the development of coeducational experiments in college education in the 1830s. However, coed-

ucational colleges, when they came, developed with the same notion of
the compensatory role of the educated woman. Since the early coeducational colleges had as their goal the training of effective ministers
for the West, they aimed to train women for useful work so that they
could function efficiently as the helpmates of the men who were to
evangelize the frontier and keep America from falling away from
Christian culture. The most striking example of an early coeducational experiment dictated by this practical goal was the founding of
Oberlin College. Oberlin was founded as a manual labor school which
had a farm attached to it where it was expected that men students
could work to produce the crops which were to pay for their education. Shortly after Oberlin was opened, however, it became apparent
that the school would also require a domestic work force to take care
of the chores of cleaning the residences, producing the meals and
clearing up afterwards, and laundering and mending the men's
clothes. Women students were thus essential if real economies were to
be achieved in the cost of providing education. The routine of Oberlin's first women students (so incorrectly cited as examples of the liberated woman scholar) was as follows. On Mondays there were no classes
held while women students did duty in the laundry, laundering the
men's clothes and carrying out any chores of mending or repairs that
were necessary. No time, however, was set aside for the laundering
and repair of women students' clothes. This was managed in spare
time at night after classes. Every day of the week women students
cooked, served meals, and waited on tables, thus duplicating in the
college environment the conventional role of the female.

Their presence at Oberlin was compensatory in another important
respect. By being there they were thought to contribute to the mental
and emotional balance of the men students, thus ensuring that the
male scholar's time was expended to maximum effect. This is an argument for coeducation which has a contemporary ring about it as we
observe the adoption of coeducation by the male elite colleges on the
ground that the presence of women (no matter how marginal they may
be) is beneficial to the mental health of men students. Women's presence at Oberlin was justified with disarming frankness for its contribution to the mental health of the males. After a generation of coeducational experience the essentially remedial role of the woman student
was thus defined. The presence of women "enkindles emulation; puts
each sex upon its best behaviour; almost entirely expels from the Col-

lege those mean trickish exploits which so frequently deprave monastic society, and develops in the College all those humanizing, elevating influences which God provided for in the well ordered association of the sexes together . . . ."[8] There was not in the entire discussion of the Oberlin experiment a sustained and serious debate about what coeducation might provide for the training of the female mind, except an adequate preparation for marriage and the capacity to serve as a companion for a frontier minister who might otherwise suffer from cultural deprivation. Women's minds during and after college education were thus considered only from the point of view of the services they might provide for men. We should not therefore be surprised to discover that the coeducational life of Oberlin was not one which encouraged women to think of themselves as the intellectual peers of men. Indeed, those few women's rights advocates who were educated at Oberlin were radicals before they came there and they sustained their interest in feminism in the face of very strong pressures against it during their undergraduate experience. The same conspicuous lack of discussion of the educational purpose of coeducation may be found in the decisions taken during the middle decades of the century to make tax-supported high schools coeducational. The arguments in favor of the movement toward coeducation were strictly economic as were the arguments which finally won admission for women into the midwestern state universities.[9]

We must, therefore, look elsewhere if we are to locate the causes for the drive toward independent careers for women which was to develop in the post-Civil War period. It was not the product of serious discussion of male and female intellectual equality in coeducational institutions. Instead, the experience, which proved to be consciousness raising, came out of the experience of role conflict which was almost universal for women participants in the antislavery movement. Coeducational institutions neatly adapted existing sex roles into their educational goals whereas women activists in the reform movements of the Jacksonian period would not accommodate their moral purpose to the traditionally subordinate position accorded their sex. The women reformers' role conflicts arose from their attempts to act out the now accepted women's role of guardian of society's moral standards through a concern for the situation of slaves rather than through child rearing and teaching. Because of the political implications of the antislavery movement, they encountered strong opposition as soon as their moral concerns took them beyond the family and the nurturing of the young. Women reformers like the Grimké sisters were forced to recognize that women's supposed moral tasks in society were strictly confined to the domestic sphere and that any effort to confront serious social issues would be constrained by women's subordination in all other areas of intellectual and political life. In attempting to act out women's assigned role of moral guardian within the contentious political sphere of the abolition movement, the Grimké's were brought to a radical perception of women's actual subordination within American society and hence toward serious thought about a wide range of feminist issues. This kind of radicalizing role conflict for women reformers was virtually ended with the conclusion of the Civil War when women's philanthropic concerns were once more directed along paths of conventional charity. The experience of this early feminist generation, however, provides us with an insight into the real sources of changing consciousness for women in the mid-nineteenth century.

In the post-Civil War era the source of important kinds of role conflict for women came from the establishment of women's colleges on the model of male elite schools on the East Coast. These women's colleges provided women with a collective female life and gave them a training for the mind which was not derivative and did not assume a role for women scholars compensatory to that of male students. Access to this kind of higher education modeled on the classical and literary curriculum of the male elite schools produced a batch of women reformers in the 1890s who were different from any preceding generation. They could not accept conventional marriage because their minds had been trained along lines which required discipline and independent effort, and they expected to put this training to a practical use which was not to be found within the narrow confines of domestic life. Estimates differ about the number who remained single, but approximately 60 to 70 percent of the first generation of graduates from women's colleges did not marry and many pursued specifically identifiable careers. The search for a career, however, was only briefly and partially radicalizing. Intense conflict was experienced by women of this generation in reaching the decision not to marry and to pursue some nondomestic career. However, once the decision had been made, the search for a career did not take women into the life of déclassé, alienated intellectual because intellectual life was becoming professionalized in post-Civil War America. Educated women could thus cling to their respectable status and develop new social roles for themselves in founding the service professions for women. The careers of Jane Addams, Lillian Wald, and Ida Cannon all illustrate the contribution of the new elite colleges for women to the founding of the service professions. Indeed, of all the founders of women's professions, only Mary Richmond lacked this kind of educational background.[10]

Although the founders of the women's professions had developed a strongly feminist consciousness because of the conflict between the accepted social role for women and the expectations of careers created by their education, this feminism was not sufficiently radical to produce questioning of the scientific culture of the high Victorian era. In developing service professions for women, the pioneering generation continued the acceptance of sex-typed roles for women because evolutionary biology told them that there was a separate nurturing female temperament which was complementary to that of the male. It is worth remembering that access to higher education need not liberate the student from the fundamental biases of Western culture, since women of this generation learned from Darwin and Spencer that there were biologically determined sexual temperaments, the male being warlike and aggressive and the female being nurturing and passive. The founders of the women's professions built their idea of a proper professional role for women around the systematic development of what they regarded as a biologically determined nurturing female temperament. There was, thus, no possibility that access to education might liberate them to view themselves as disciplined intellects who could operate without inhibition in traditionally male spheres of competence.

Even when women gained access to scientific and technological education, sex stereotypes dictated the roles which they defined for the scientifically educated female. The best example of a pioneer woman professional with early access to scientific education may be found in the career of Ellen H. Richards. In 1870 she went to the Massachusetts Institute of Technology as a student of chemistry. Her understanding of her place there is neatly defined in her own words. "Perhaps the fact that I am not a radical or a believer in the all-powerful ballot for women to right all her wrongs and that I do not scorn womanly duties, but claim it as a privilege to clean up and sort and supervise the room and sew things, etc., is winning me stronger allies than anything else."[11] Life in the laboratory did not raise her consciousness. Instead it prompted her to become one of the founders of the home economics movement. In promoting the new field of study for women, she claimed that the home was becoming so important a center of consumption for American society that a housewife with scientific expertise was required to manage it efficiently. Scientific education was thus to be used to bolster and inflate the traditional female domestic role, and in the development of the new field there was no effort to channel women's scientific creativity into more challenging intellectual spheres. Here we see a reductio ad absurdum of the unexamined assumption that access to education automatically changes consciousness, because contact with scientific education for Ellen Richards merely meant trying to make a profession out of domestic work.

The development of the women's professions should thus be interpreted as a conservative trend by which the potential for change inherent in changed educational experience was stillborn and women's intellectual energies were channeled into perpetuating women's service role in society rather than into independent and self-justifying intellectual endeavor. It was also a trend by which the direction and support of most kinds of intellectual inquiry remained unquestionably male controlled. Thus, the development of women's professions has not significantly altered their status in intellectual life; nor has it fostered women's intellectual creativity.

It is essential, then, to grasp that, contrary to what educational historians have had to say up to now, it is not access to educational facilities which is the significant variable in tracing the "liberation" of women's minds. What really matters is whether women's consciousness of themselves as intellects is altered. This did not take place as a result of the development of coeducation in the United States. It did not occur when women entered the service professions. In fact, during the great educational changes of the nineteenth and early twentieth century women's awareness of their own value as intellects was inhibited by their search for a respectable bourgeois professional role. They were ready to expand women's domestic role into some kind of pseudoscientific profession and willing to see the only legitimate fields for female intellectual effort in extensions of the domestic sphere.

This trend accounts for the relative lack of creativity among the newly educated women professionals so far as thought about women's place in society is concerned. New ideas about women's place in society did not come from the "women's" professions and the research program of their professional schools. Instead, the revolutionary ideas about women's status came from the developing discipline of anthropology through the endeavors of conventional scholars to develop some general comparative perspective on sexual customs and cultural values. The relative lack of creativity which comes out of women's access to higher education must be stressed because there is a distinct possibility that many of the "women's studies" programs being developed today will be similarly uncreative. The danger lies in the fact that these programs will not be productive of change in women's sense of themselves as intellectuals if they assume an inherent female temperament which is intellectually or morally different from that of males. Women's studies programs will merely produce more sex-typed intellectual activity and no change in women's sense of their involvement in intellectual problems outside a sexually defined sphere of competence. There can be no drive to intellectual power, creativity, and mastery of a discipline while women's intellectual life is still inhibited by the sense that female intellect is in some obscure way complementary to that of men.

In making this point it is necessary to stress that the educational experience of women ought to provide them with some sense of collective life because female sociability is an important precondition for creativity in women's scholarly endeavor, just as male sociability has been carefully institutionalized in all communities devoted to higher learning. There can be no question that the development of coeducation in the United States during the mid-nineteenth century deprived women students of the opportunity to experience a self-supporting and self-directing female community, such as existed and continues to exist in the religious and lay schools of many European countries. Experience of a female controlled and directed world is essential, if women are to discover a sense of their own potential for self-directing activity. However, this is an institutional problem having to do with the way in which intellectual activity is organized and pursued. It is not an intellectual problem having to do with different ways of knowing or validating truth.

There is another very practical problem posed by the mushrooming of special women's studies programs. It is a problem related to the correct strategy to be pursued in encouraging women's intellectual creativity, given the manner in which society's resources are channeled toward the support of intellectual life. Should women scholars bore from within established male professions, thereby tapping the resources committed to supporting them and attempting to transform the dominant style of intellectual life? Or should they attempt to attract scarce resources to women's programs which will be staffed by women scholars? Quite apart from the intellectual dangers inherent in such an approach, it is tactically weak. Separate and unequal women's programs will be poorly funded. They are and will continue to be denigrated intellectually and therefore they cannot possibly lead to the establishment of strong female professional identities. They will certainly be among the first expendable academic ventures to be cut when budgets require economies, and their graduates will be the first to be let go when there is any question of professional priorities in the maintenance of established faculties.

This is an unfashionable position to adopt in the current discussion of women's educational needs. However, the history of the women's professions illustrates the dangers inherent in institutionalizing certain kinds of feminine intellectual activity within an existing pattern of male controlled professions. The acceptance of any sexual division of labor is bound to channel creativity and to perpetuate existing patterns of socialization. Only the abandonment of a sexual division of labor in the life of the mind can effectively change women's consciousness of their worth as scholars and creative intellects.

Essay Review of
Crisis in the Classroom

Michael B. Katz

Charles Silberman has written a strangely comforting indictment of American education. The cause of the "crisis in the classroom," he would have us believe, is a simple failure to think clearly and honestly. Consequently, remedies for the schools' problems do not require the replacement of present social or educational structures; they demand,

Reprinted, with permission, from *Interchange* 3 (No. 1, 1972), 96-101. The volume reviewed is Charles Silberman, *Crisis in the Classroom: The Remaking of American Education* (New York: Random House, 1970).

rather, the introduction of sensible and humane reforms into institutions that now exist. Mr. Silberman, in fact, has little use for most educational radicals, and his book will stand as a classic example of the liberal reform approach to American education in the late twentieth century. Therein lie its strengths and weaknesses. As a catalog of educational horrors and a dissection of the weaknesses of several reform theories and practices, *Crisis in the Classroom,* though not original, is intelligent, clear, and compelling. As an analysis of the causes of educational failure, it is shallow and, even, evasive. Finally, as a program for change, *Crisis in the Classroom* is inadequate and, worse, misleading.

Crisis in the Classroom is the result of the Carnegie Corporation's Study of the Education of Educators, of which Mr. Silberman served as director. The corporation's funding, Mr. Silberman reports, enabled him to spend three and one-half years in research and writing, assisted by an administrative staff of four. It is apparent that he used the time and resources available to him vigorously and responsibly, reading an immense quantity and variety of literature about education and visiting schools and schoolmen throughout the United States and England. The outcome is a book of more than five hundred pages, written with the lively and graceful style that one would expect from an editor of *Fortune,* in which capacity Mr. Silberman also serves. The length of the book, its wealth of detail, its professional presentation, its sponsorship, its publicity—all of these factors lend to it an air of authenticity and, almost, a legitimacy. There is no doubt that it will be as widely read, considered, and influential as a book about education can be. For that reason it is all the more important to explore with some care its adequacy as a diagnosis and proposed treatment for American education.

First of all, consider Mr. Silberman's indictment of American education, which, in its way, is as severe as most of the critiques offered in more radical contexts. Most of his criticisms have been made before by other observers, but it is useful to have the case against the schools gathered together and put before the general public in such a persuasive fashion. Mr. Silberman's first major indictment is that the schools fail, and indeed have always failed, to act as equalizers of opportunity. The rhetoric of social mobility notwithstanding, schools have done remarkably little to counteract racial, social, and economic inequities within American society. Their failure, in fact, has touched off "burning anger" (p. 69), especially on the part of "Negro Americans . . . Puerto Ricans, Mexican Americans, and Indian Americans . . . furious because the schools are not moving their children into the middle class rapidly enough."

Mr. Silberman's second major indictment against the schools is their repressive and spirit-breaking quality. Preoccupied with order and control, schools, he observes, operate on an assumption of distrust, which creates an antagonistic and authoritarian atmosphere. Students, deprived even of the freedom to go the bathroom at will, become totally dependent upon authorities for direction, unable to assume any responsibility even if it is offered. They learn from the school that docility and conformity are the best strategies for survival. Mr. Silberman gives to these by now sadly familiar points special poignancy through interspersing his argument with spine-chilling vignettes drawn from his own observations within contemporary schools.

Throughout the twentieth century, school reformers, including those of the 1960s, have accomplished remarkably little, Mr. Silberman correctly observes. In fact, he is most acute as he analyzes the failures and weaknesses of a number of recent, widely proclaimed, but ultimately disappointing innovations: educational television, the new physics and related curricular reform movements, team teaching, the nongraded classroom, and computer-assisted instruction. In particular, his discussion of the latter—his effective debunking of the new myth that computers are the key to an educational revolution—is one of Mr. Silberman's most valuable achievements.

Of all educational institutions, Mr. Silberman argues that the high school is the worst:

Because adolescents are harder to "control" than younger children, secondary schools tend to be even more authoritarian and repressive than elementary schools; the values they transmit are the values of docility, passivity, conformity, and lack of trust. These unpleasant attributes might be tolerable if one could view them, so to speak, as the price of a "good education"—good, that is to say, in academic terms. Such is not the case. . . . And the junior high school, by almost unanimous agreement, is the wasteland, one is tempted to say cesspool—of American education [p. 324].

The schools at all levels fail: they do not teach skills or produce knowledge in the conventional sense; they reinforce the handicaps of poverty and race; and they try to root out whatever traces of independence and individuality they can find in the personalities of their students. The weaknesses of teacher education, Mr. Silberman bluntly but fairly claims, compound all of these problems. Intellectually vapid, inheriting a tradition that neglects questions of purpose, nearly useless in a practical sense: teacher education is a disgrace. Its quality is not helped by snobbish professors of liberal arts who offer their criticism, but rarely their help, from a safe and jealously guarded distance. In fact, as Mr. Silberman points out, the liberal arts professors are also in trouble. They, too, lack a clear sense of purpose and face growing public dissatisfaction with their work. Mr. Silberman is quite right to say that "the weakness of teacher education is the weakness of liberal education as a whole; if teachers are educated badly, that is to say, it is in large measure because almost everyone else is educated badly, too" (pp. 380-381).

If any people remain unconvinced that there is a crisis in education and that the schools are failing miserably (and unfortunately those people may still be a majority), Mr. Silberman's book should shatter their complacency and arouse their indignation. More important for those already indignant are questions that move beyond descriptivism. How are we to account for the awful situation that confronts us, and what are we to do about it? Here, as I have already observed, Mr. Silberman unfortunately has much less to offer the troubled and confused observer, consumer, or casualty of American education.

Mr. Silberman has a straightforward view of the cause of educational failure: "what is mostly wrong with the public schools is due not to venality or indifference or stupidity, but to mindlessness" (p. 10). Mindlessness, Mr. Silberman defines as "the failure or refusal to think seriously about educational purpose, the reluctance to question established practice" (p. 11). According to Mr. Silberman, mindlessness pervades all of American society, accounting not only for its bad schools but for other major social difficulties as well. We have simply been too preoccupied, too lazy, or too self-interested to think seriously and reflectively about the purposes of our activities and institutions. The lack of correspondence between the complexity of the problems Mr. Silberman describes and the reasons he gives for their continued existence is startling. To attribute the persistent failure of a major social institution to a 125-year fit of mindlessness appears almost tongue-in-cheek from an observer as acute, informed, and intelligent as Mr. Silberman.

However, his explanation has two functions, positive or negative depending on one's point of view. First of all, it removes the hint of personal threat implicit at least in most social criticism. No one in particular is at fault for what has happened. We can all—educationist, parent, citizen—be comfortable in the knowledge that our motives and our intentions have not been blameworthy. Mr. Silberman is not attacking us; despite his portrait of our failure, he is really doing little more than giving us a strong exhortation to pull up our socks.

Second, and more seriously, attributing educational failure to mindlessness removes the blame not only from individuals but from the larger social and economic system in which schools operate. Unlike the educational radicals whom he criticizes, Mr. Silberman does not even hint, to paraphrase Paul Goodman, that the problem of education is that young people do not have a worthy society in which to grow up. There is no question in Mr. Silberman's view that schools can be made well without a major overhaul of the structures that surround and sustain them. It is not the requirements of industrial capitalism, the obsession with law and order on the cheap, or the persistence of class bias and racism that have produced educational disaster. It is simply mindlessness. It would be comforting to believe that Mr. Silberman is right.

Unfortunately, it would be difficult for anyone reasonably versed in the history and sociology of education to accept Mr. Silberman's explanation. For example, take the first of his charges against the schools: they do not equalize opportunity. They were never seriously meant to. Throughout American history extensions of public education have given more benefit to middle-class or affluent people than to the poor. That was the case, for example, with the high school, which offered middle-class parents a chance to have the community as a whole pay for the education of their children. The alternative was relatively expensive private schooling. From the time of their founding in the middle of the nineteenth century until about 1930, high schools enrolled only a minority of eligible children; these were, insofar as one can tell, not very often the children of the poor. The poor, we sometimes forget, not infrequently saw through the rhetoric surrounding the high school and tried to delay or defeat its introduction; they were rarely successful. Today, perhaps, the greatest inequality exists in public higher education, which offers greater benefits to the affluent in the same way that the high schools did earlier in the century. Within schools, tracking systems—ways of separating students— developed with the explicit purpose of neatly channeling poor children into occupations similar in status to those of their fathers. My point is that these inequalities have not resulted from mindlessness. They have been quite deliberate. The inequality in the educational system, it is not unfair to say, is a reflex of the inequality in the social structure. Schools are now, and they have always been, reflections of class structure, which they have reinforced rather than altered. Thus, it was no accident, or example of simple mindlessness, when a white teacher told Malcolm X that he had better give up his hope of becoming a lawyer and be a carpenter instead. That, in fact, is the message that public schools have been designed to give the average lower-class boy, black or white.

The same sort of explanation must be offered for Mr. Silberman's second major indictment of the schools: their emphasis on docility. Here the case is crystal clear because it can be made from explicit statements in educational documents spanning a period from early in the nineteenth century until the present. People urged the introduction of systems of public education, including compulsory schooling, to socialize the poor. Educational history abounds with discussions of the dangers to law, order, and morality posed by unschooled lower classes. Educational promoters have argued quite explicitly throughout American history that the purposes of schooling should be more moral than intellectual; formation of attitudes, that is to say, has been of far greater importance than the development of intellectual or cognitive skills.

Mr. Silberman is quite wrong to imply that little thought has been given to educational purpose. School reformers have always considered the relation of the details of curriculum, pedagogy, and structure to larger social and educational objectives. The problem is that these objectives have usually stressed the inculcation of the virtues that, it has been thought, would ensure law and order at the lowest possible cost: restraint, reliability, punctuality, and docility. These are the qualities, as well, that employers have sought in their work force. When nineteenth-century schoolmen asked employers if educated laborers were any better than ignorant ones, the answers came back that they were indeed, not because they knew much more but because they were more acquiescent, more honest, and less likely to strike.

Mr. Silberman feels that the balance in American education has tipped too far toward the cognitive. On the basis of the evidence he presents—the preoccupation with order, control, and conformity at the core of the school experience—as well as on the basis of the historical record, it is not easy to accept that conclusion. It would be more appropriate to say that schools have been so deeply concerned with the affective, so committed to the primacy of attitude over intellect, that they have never paid sufficiently serious attention to cognitive skills, or to knowledge. Mr. Silberman's arguments, consequently, do not offer a new direction for American education. His stress on the need to emphasize the affective is a continuation of a very old tradition. The problem with that tradition, most starkly, is that poor people do not need another lesson in how to behave, even if that behavior is to be liberated rather than repressed. They need the knowledge and skills to move out of poverty. Affective schooling could become a particularly subtle form of "repressive desublimation," to use Marcuse's term. It could be a distraction rather than a benefit to people whose long-term interests would best be served by the redistribution of power and income. In this way affective education could, without too much difficulty, serve the purposes of social control for which traditional repressive schools have suddenly become inadequate.

Mr. Silberman's diagnosis of mindlessness as the cause of educational failure underlies his prescriptions for educational change. "If mindlessness is the central problem, the solution must lie in infusing the various educating institutions with purpose, more important, with thought about purpose, and about the ways in which techniques, content and organization fulfill or alter purpose" (p. 11). This argument misses the point, which I have made above, that the problem with American schools is not their lack of purpose but their continued dedication to purposes that have reflected the inequities of American society and the less appealing aspects of American culture. It is curious, moreover, that a man as concerned as Mr. Silberman with educational purpose gives us no more than the most general indications of his ideas on the subject. What is missing, in particular, is an elaboration of his views on the connection between educational purpose — the kinds of things he would like to see schools teach children — and the society of which the school is a part. The question is particularly important because Mr. Silberman champions a particular kind of educational innovation, and it is important to know his reasons. What difference will it make to the serious social problems of American society if schools change in the way that he hopes? Are changes in education part of a pattern of more widespread social change that he sees happening? I find myself unable to determine more than Mr. Silberman's most general answers to these questions. His school reform takes place, as it were, in a social vacuum.

Mr. Silberman is a champion of the English infant schools. He stands in a long tradition of American educational reformers who have found abroad a cure for America's educational problems. Among the first, in fact, were the champions of English infant schools, which started in the late eighteenth century as a way of relieving the pressure on poor families and seeing that poor children received a proper infusion of moral virtue. These schools enjoyed a brief vogue in the United States in the 1820s. Around the same time another English innovation, the Lancasterian or monitorial system, enjoyed enormous and rather more long-lived popularity in America. Later in the century Horace Mann returned from Europe holding up the example of Prussian and Scottish schools: university reformers, too, argued the excellencies of German models. So the list goes. It was, after all, less than two decades ago that Sputnik prompted an enormous wave of admiration for the achievements of Russian education. Reformers, and Mr. Silberman is no exception, have not looked to foreign examples primarily to gain new ideas. Rather, they have sought there proof that an innovation, to which they are already committed, works. Reports of educational travelers have always told at least as much about the preoccupations and ideas of the travelers themselves as about the systems that they describe. In the case of Mr. Silberman, the English infant schools show to his satisfaction that fundamental educational reform can occur within a system of public schools. He also finds within their type of informal education confirmation of a pedagogical style that combines a freeing of the learner with an important guiding and controlling role for the teacher. It offers, he believes, an alternative to the American educational radicalism, which, in his unfair caricature, seeks a total abdication of adult responsibility combined with a total capitulation to the whims of children.

I do not care to question the desirability of informal education; I am willing, for the sake of argument, to grant its superiority to what goes on in the average American classroom. But I do wish to ask, again, about its larger purposes. What can we expect from the widespread introduction of informal education into American schools? Mr. Silberman discusses British schools in a fashion similar to the way he discusses American ones: in a social vacuum. He nowhere probes the connections between the schools and the social order in an attempt to find out if informal education is making any difference to the quality of British life. Nor do we learn from him precisely what the connection is between educational and social improvement. In fact, as he admits early in his book, since the Second World War there has been a phenomenal increase in educational achievements within America. Americans are a more educated, more thoroughly schooled people than ever before. Yet few people would claim to discern much connection between that fact and any improvement in the quality or justice of American life.

At the conclusion of his book, Mr. Silberman claims that "we will not be able to create and maintain a humane society unless we create and maintain classrooms that are humane" (p. 524). This statement places him squarely in another tradition: those people who have seen in education a means to social reform. Presumably he believes that effort and money spent on the introduction of informal education into American schools will precipitate an improvement in American society. The danger in this belief is that educational reform may be used, as it has been so often before, as a smoke screen or diversion from the serious social and economic reforms required by American society. This utilization of the schools as a substitute for social reform has been a characteristic American response to social problems for a very long time. Early in the nineteenth century, school reformers argued that education could solve the problems of crime, poverty, immorality, and inequality within an emerging urban and industrial society. Since that time virtually every major social problem has found its way to the school, there to rest unsolved because education, quite simply, is powerless to solve it in the best of circumstances. Improving the schools has been a convenient way of avoiding the more difficult, contentious, and, to some, more ominous task of improving society.

Mr. Silberman's optimistic prediction that meaningful educational change can occur within existing school systems overlooks the connection between the structure of those systems and the educational outcomes that he deplores. However, two related features of those school systems have important consequences for the sort of learning that can go on within them and the objectives that they can reach; those features and their control—the powerlessness of the people whom they serve—and their form—bureaucracies. We often think of bureaucracy, or any other organizational form, as a disembodied, somewhat neutral shell. In fact, organizational form, as the history of bureaucracy reveals, reflects social values and social purposes. In education, as I have tried to show at length elsewhere [*Class, Bureaucracy, and Schools: The Illusion of Educational Change in America* (New York: Praeger, 1971)], bureaucracy became the dominant educational form by late in the nineteenth century because of a mixture of setting and priority. It was because men confronted particular organizational problems—mass schooling in an urban and industrial society—with particular priorities that they built bureaucracies. Those priorities—efficiency over responsiveness, order over participation, uniformity over cultural variety—reflected cultural values that became built into the very structure and functioning of school systems. Those systems still retain the shape given them in large cities by late in the nineteenth century, and they continue, consequently, to serve similar purposes.

The problem of control is related to the problem of bureaucracy. School reformers saw in centrally directed, professionally operated educational systems a way of reducing public control of education. They argued that earlier, more decentralized systems were hindered by partisan politics, nepotism, and the general ignorance of the people who made important decisions. The movement to centralize educational control coincided with attempts to centralize municipal government more generally and to transfer decisionmaking power to a small body of qualified, first citizens. Lurking behind this movement, of course, were a fear and distrust of ordinary people, in this case mainly immigrants. The centralization of city government, including schools, took place during a period of heavy immigration and of mounting nativist sentiment. Nativism, not infrequently, was sponsored by people leading the movement for municipal reform. Bureaucracy and centralized control have served as ways of keeping the common people from using government, including the schools, to express their own purposes.

The structure and control of education are issues that cannot be divorced from what happens within classrooms. That should be clear from their history. Introducing informal education into public educational systems without making other radical alterations will be, as was, for example, the project method, like moving around the furniture in a box. It is the walls of the box itself that must be torn down if education is to serve new purposes.

The argument that structural reform must precede a change in educational purpose and function raises the issue of community control. *Crisis in the Classroom* contains a long chapter on educational reform movements in the 1960s. That chapter does not mention the movement for community control or decentralization. Neither topic, strange to say, is mentioned elsewhere in Mr. Silberman's book. Yet, to many people, surely, these movements are where the action is in school reform. One can only conclude that Mr. Silberman is committed to the structure of public education as it exists. The voucher system, performance contracting, radical decentralization: these are not kinds of reforms he advocates or, even, cares to discuss. Insofar as one might gather from *Crisis in the Classroom,* the crisis at Ocean Hill-Brownsville never existed. Anyone unaware of the vitality of proposals for changing the control and funding of public education would leave Mr. Silberman's book without realizing that intelligent, informed, and sane people consider these radical measures to be live options. There are limits beyond which Mr. Silberman does not help or assist his reader to go.

In fact, Mr. Silberman's book rests comfortably within the long-standing style of elite reform that has marked American education since early in the nineteenth century. Consider, for example, his comments on the way in which informal education will come to American schools:

In the United States . . . the impetus is likely to come from the outside [of the school system] more often than from within. It is crucial, therefore, that the most careful preparations be made before the changes are introduced. As we have seen, American parents are perfectly capable of understanding and accepting informal education if it is explained to them, and American teachers can adapt informal teaching styles with grace and enthusiasm if—but only if—they receive sufficient training and support [p. 320].

As another instance, consider Mr. Silberman's admiration for the manner in which reform was brought about in Portland, Oregon. A group of people from Harvard developed a plan for an innovative high school and then looked around the country for a school in which they could put their idea into action. Portland allowed them to set up shop. The assumption underlying this sort of reform is that experts should decide what is best and then simply do it, though careful, perhaps, to mind their public relations. The people, one presumes, should be grateful.

This is how school reform has usually been carried out in America. Groups of influential people, considering themselves especially expert, have tried, often with success, to force educational change. Social policy and social change, it is assumed, issue from the top down. The problem is that this style of reform works badly. Innovations introduced in this way have not fared well; somehow they have not met the goals set by their sponsors, who remain unable to account for their failure. The example par excellence is the public school system, founded and developed in precisely this manner. Mr. Silberman himself documents its continued failure, but he fails to draw the correct moral, which is this: elite social and educational reform, like welfare bureaucracy, is bankrupt as social policy. At this point in history any reform worthy of the name must begin with a redistribution of power and resources. That is the only way in which to change the patterns of control and inaccessible organizational structures that dominate American life. It is the only way in which to make education, and other social institutions as well, serve new purposes.

There is no doubt in my mind that if we change the schools in the direction that Mr. Silberman suggests, they will become nicer places for children to be. This alone would be a great improvement. But, if that is all we do, we shall fail to make education more equal, to eradicate the class and race biases that adhere in educational structures, or to affect the society that surrounds the school. To move on those fronts requires not only considering solutions that Mr. Silberman does not discuss but raising questions that he seems reluctant to ask. Mr. Silberman has tamed educational discontent. By co-opting instead of resisting it, he has removed its threat and, unfortunately, its promise. He has shown the comfortable way to educational radicalism; others undoubtedly will follow, happy that they can enlist in the cause of justice without sacrifice.

Identities and Contours: An Approach to Educational History

Maxine Greene

Introducing *City of Words,* a study of recent American fiction, Tony Tanner writes:

Reprinted, with permission, from *Educational Researcher* 2 (April 1973): 5-10. Copyright 1973, American Educational Research Association, Washington, D.C.

I shall try to show that there is an abiding dream in American literature that an un-patterned, unconditioned life is possible, in which your movements and stillnesses, choices, and repudiations are all your own; and that there is also an abiding American dread that someone else is patterning your life, that there are all sorts of in-visible plots afoot to rob you of your autonomy of thought and action, that condition-ing is ubiquitous.[1]

This duality of dream and dread has haunted many of our writers since the days of James Fenimore Cooper's *Leatherstocking Tales*. Un-til the present day and the appearance of new or revisionist educa-tional history, it has not found expression in the literature of educa-tion. Educators and literary artists have traditionally looked upon the culture through different perspectives: educators, from the vantage point of concern with socialization and "improvement"; writers, from the vantage point of concern with the plight of the person in an am-biguous, often threatening world. Educational reformers, most par-ticularly, have given voice to what they chose to believe was a "public philosophy," a culture-wide consensus of opinion; whereas artists have concentrated on what Harry Levin calls "the dark other half of the situation, and their distinctive attitude has been introspection, dissent or irony." Levin, a literary historian and critic, goes on:

Where the voice of the majority is by definition affirmative, the spirit of independence is likeliest to manifest itself by employing the negative: by saying *no* in thunder — as Melville wrote to Hawthorne — though bidden by the devil himself to say yes.[2]

That "no" is not to be understood as either didactic or political. The independent artist is not interested in remaking institutions. Forming his own perceptions of reality, he is attempting (in gravity, ardor, and sometimes in despair) to provoke others to see for themselves, to order their own experiences of what it is to be alive and to exist in history.

Today's revisionist historians — Colin Greer, Clarence Karier, Michael Katz, Joel Spring, Paul Violas, and others like them — are say-ing "*no* in thunder." In the context of educational history they are employing the negative for the sake of exposing the myth of the com-mon school. They define the school, therefore, as "a vast social machine for the imposition of values and control,"[3] rather than as a means of promoting equality of opportunity, popularizing knowledge, teaching the young to learn how to learn. Within existing structures, the revisionists assert, legitimate educational reform is and always has been impossible. Any attempt to teach values or to do what is called "humanistic" teaching is, by definition, an effort to impose social con-trols. Katz wants the school to concentrate on teaching fundamental

skills and to exclude any "conscious attempt to formulate social attitudes."[4] The assumption seems to be that any concern with values,
moral issues, or even cognitive awareness, is inevitably transformed into "formulation," whether the teacher knows it or not. Given the
nature of our society, it is implied; given the pressure of our institutions, there is no hope of freeing students to choose themselves. Joel
Spring is even more explicit. Once the power of the family, church,
and community began waning at the beginning of this century, he
writes, the school became "*the* agency charged with the responsibility
of maintaining social order and cohesion and of instilling individuals
with codes of conduct and social values that would insure the stability
of existing social relationships."[5] If this is the case, the teacher within
the public school has no alternative but to be an accomplice of the
system.

There is, I think, a doubleness in revisionist educational history. On
the one hand, having broken with moralistic approaches, the new
historians are disclosing phenomena long hidden by official pieties.
Using techniques unknown in Ellwood Cubberley's "wonderful world,"
some of them have disclosed relationships between social structures
and social purposes, between demographic shifts and human plights
never examined before. They have demonstrated the long neglect of
pluralism, the maltreatment of immigrants and ethnic groups, the
curious conservatism of municipal and school reforms. Without the
new history, we might not have begun looking at the connections between schools and politics, education and social stratification, or
endemic racism. We might not have confronted the rationalizations
inherent in professionalism. We might still be treating the battle
against district control as an archetypical heroic battle, one absolutely
necessary if the Good were to be attained. It is clear enough that the
new history has effectively invalidated what Lawrence Cremin calls the
"narrowly institutional"[6] approach, in the light of which contemporary writing seems so liberating and so sound.

At the same time, however, the conceptual focus strikes me as
peculiarly narrow. The concern is almost exclusively with the patterning of presumably malleable, passive individuals—and the evils of
social control. The distinctions among types of control are overlooked.
Too little is said about the different ways in which individuals internalize control, experience the influences of community, order their
own life worlds. Nothing is said about variations in social reality, or

the possibility of individuals transforming it. The *problem* of social existence is overlooked, along with the inescapability of relationship for those who must learn to be human in a not always sustaining world. Yet these too are issues in human history, even when conditioning seems to be ubiquitous. The persons who compose the masses have chosen as often as they have blindly acquiesced, even if they have chosen to conform, to acquiesce. The so-called reformers—fearful, troubled, highly principled men—made decisions for their own good reasons, reasons ordinarily relevant to the world as it disclosed itself to them. We still know relatively little about their selective perceptions, the constructs actually available for interpreting the "real," the "others" most significant in their lives.

Because the school system has become the exemplar of all systems in revisionists' eyes, the very archetype of bureaucracy, differences among schools are glossed over, as are their roles as reflectors and producers of values and beliefs. Almost as if they were expiating the sin of being educationists, the new historians seem compelled to discover the primary threats to personality at the heart of education. This has led on occasion to a neglect of multiple causation, to an often groundless determinism. I find encouraging the dawning interest in exploring new connections within and around the schools, the studies of persons' behavior and consciousness in other places, the *different* responses to class status, even to social control.

Largely preoccupied with images of monoliths and patternings, nevertheless, the revisionists see all-pervasive victimization: they see us all submerged in a system we never chose. "It is not mere selection," writes W. H. Walsh, "but selection in accordance with criteria of importance, that the expositor brings into history. . . ."[7] "Our concerns shape the questions that we ask," says Michael Katz, "and, as a consequence, determine what we select from the virtually unlimited supply of 'facts.' "[8] The criteria being brought into history by the revisionists are partly derived from such constructs as those utilized by Paul Goodman and Theodore Roszak, both of whom Katz credits for affecting his concerns. Goodman, of course, believed that compulsory education was a "universal trap" and that the schools "less and less represent any human values, but simply adjustment to a mechanical system."[9] Roszak wrote at length about "centralized bigness," the "regime of expertise," and a technocratic system which generates its own legitimation.[10] Both were centrally concerned with the person and his survival, either by means of work, wandering, self-motivated inquiry, or (in Roszak's terms) through the proclamation of "a new heaven and a new earth so vast, so marvelous that the inordinate demands of technical expertise must of necessity withdraw in the presence of such splendor to a subordinate and marginal status in the lives of men."[11]

There is a sense, too in which the new history may have been af- fected by the same forces that have caused a general rebellion against formalism and moved novelists, as well as visual artists, to reject im- prisoning structures and seek out novel forms. The old forms, in the view of writers and painters, not only constrain and inhibit; they *de*form; they falsify what exists. In a mood somehow similar, the new educational historians describe the distortions caused by bureaucratic structuring and "an implausible ideology ever more divorced from reality."[12] This ideology, in its turn, distorts the perception of those who espouse it. They then go on to defile the identities of those they are assigned to teach. Consciously or not, the revisionists are portray- ing social reality as many modern novelists do. The overwhelming structures begin to resemble the "new machines, new forms of organization, new ways of increasing efficiency"[13] that have taken over the country in Kurt Vonnegut's *Player Piano*. They evoke the all-en- compassing bureaucracy, the syndicate in Joseph Heller's *Catch-22*. ("'They all belong to the syndicate,' Milo said. 'And they know that what's good for the syndicate is good for the country, because that's what makes Sammy run.'")[14] They are like the mental hospital, as perceived by Big Chief in *One Flew over the Cuckoo's Nest:*[15] a false, automated environment where processed pictures of the "real" are forever being projected on the walls. All these metaphors—machines, syndicates, hospitals—point toward rigidity and alienating controls. In a world so dominated, there is scarcely any hope for the individual. If he rebels, he will be reconditioned, lobotomized, or forced to run away to save his life.

This response to the technological society is in many ways war- ranted. There is no question of the threat to the person implicit both in technology and in what Hannah Arendt calls "rule by Nobody"—or "the rule of an intricate system of bureaus in which no men, neither one nor the best, neither the few nor the many, can be held responsi- ble. . . ."[16] The sociologists have for a long time talked of the inter- nalization of external "social facts" and their transformation into what

Emile Durkheim described as constraints upon the person—another way of describing social control.[17] The nineteenth-century pioneers of school reform obviously were convinced that control had to be imposed on human beings, most particularly the alien and the poor. Without such control, social stability could never be achieved, nor could "Americanization." The problem of the early twentieth-century progressives is far more complex and multidimensional, in spite of their unabashed gradualist orientations. John Dewey's commitment to what he called social control is clear enough; but it cannot be assumed, in consequence, that his overriding purpose was to perpetuate existing class structures and maintain the prevailing system of ownership. Nor can it be assumed that he developed his theories of education in the same mood and with the same fears as Horace Mann or Henry Barnard in time past.

Clarence Karier, in an almost paradigmatic revisionist treatment of liberalism, condemns John Dewey and his fellow progressives for the present crisis in our culture:

In a very real sense the crisis is a result of both the success and the failure of the enlightenment philosophy of progress. The collective side of that philosophy with its scientifically organized technology and computer-managed bureaucracy has become a reality; on the other side, however, individual freedom, dignity, and well-being have not fared so well. Caught up in collective institutional progress, the individual has become a means rather than an end to social order.[18]

Computer-managed bureaucracy must be granted; so must the scientifically organized technology. But what solid evidence exists for the claim that there is a causal connection between Dewey's "cultural participatory perspective" and the staving off of revolutionary change? What evidence exists for the claim that the masses were so indoctrinated with the uses of the scientific method as the key to progress that they readily acquiesced "in the face of political, economic, and military power"?[19] What evidence is there for the claim that Dewey was able to anticipate the corporate state and was, for that reason above all others, stressing the values of cooperative intelligence?

C. Vann Woodward once wrote with respect to our attitudes toward history:

In moods of disenchantment and cynicism and self-criticism, Americans have not contrived nihilistic or anarchist theories but have reinterpreted their past again, this time in an iconoclastic spirit, debunked their heroes, ridiculed the Puritan theocracy, and dwelt on the human motives of the Founding Fathers and the Constitutional Framers. Other moods, ranging from complacency to hysterical insecurity, have registered themselves in laboured reinterpretations of American history.[20]

The revisionists' approach to the history of the progressive era is anything but iconoclastic. In fact, this may be the first time that historians have contrived admittedly anarchist theories; and it is interesting that they should have been developed in the context of educational history. The explanation may have to do with the long persistence of a kind of educational hagiography. It may be that iconoclastic reinterpretations came too late, considering the inequities and injustices that multiplied as the years went by, considering the "legend" of the public school. In any case, whether due to preoccupations with the danger of manipulations or to a generalized disgust with school system qua systems, the new historians have pursued increasingly anarchist themes. This means that they have looked upon progressivism and, most particularly, Dewey's conception of experience and social control through a perspective founded in an opposition (to use Joel Spring's terminology) to "the existence of the state in any form because it destroys individual autonomy."[21] Beginning with the conviction that autonomy is threatened by most traditional rules, regulations, and forms of organization, then, the revisionists are bound to focus upon social control as the source of the damage done by schools.

There is some irony in the fact that Dewey and other progressives believed that they were rebelling against waste and exploitation, as well as against "formalism" in the early years of this century.[22] Concerned about "the constraints of previous morality and ideology," they honestly believed they were attending to real social problems and to those forces that hindered human growth. As Dewey saw it, the most damaging constraints were cognitive ones. The freedoms so long fought for in this country meant little if they were not backed up, he thought, by "intelligence and informed conviction"; and so he concentrated on creating classroom situations which would elicit both. He saw individualism as "a product of the relaxation of the grip of the authority of custom and tradition as standards of belief."[23] He saw cooperative intelligence as a way of reconstructing vitally shared experience, and shared experience as educative for those who participated and sought to affect connections within it. "To have the same ideas about things which others have," he wrote, "is to be like-minded with them, and thus to be really members of a social group, is therefore to attach the same meanings to things and to acts which others attach. Otherwise there is no common understanding, and no community life. But in a shared activity, each person refers what he is doing to what the other is doing, and *vice-versa*. That is, the activity of each is placed in the same inclusive situation."[24] It is difficult to see, in this descriptive treatment of how human beings live together, the evil of imposed controls.

When Dewey did explain what he actually meant by social control, he talked of the shared experience characteristic of competitive games and said it illustrated "the general principle of social control of individuals without the violation of freedom." And then:

Games are generally competitive. If we took instances of co-operative activities in which all members of a group take part, as for example in well-ordered family life in which there is mutual confidence, the point would be even clearer. In all such cases it is not the will or desire of any one person which establishes order but the moving spirit of the whole group. The control is social, but individuals are parts of a community, not outside it.[25]

It must be admitted that here, as well as in earlier writings, Dewey was concerned with the cultivation of dispositions he assumed to be "desirable," with meeting demands set up "by current social occupations," and with the assimilative or unifying power of the school. In his early writing, there were relatively few signs of concern with fundamental inequities in the culture; and, at the start, he appeared untouched by the exclusion of minority groups from the mainstream of economic life. He seemed convinced that little more was required than a confirmation of "the shared cooperative activities which are the normal source of order," so long as individuals were equipped to reflect upon those activities in their wholeness and in the light of their contribution to social life. Later on, of course, he became active in the NAACP and other organizations combating discrimination; but he did not always appear to comprehend the increasing feelings of powerlessness suffered by people who had no share in policymaking, whose participation was ultimately meaningless.

In 1916, he wrote that "A society which makes provison for participation in its good of all its members on equal terms and which secures flexible readjustment of its institutions through interaction of the different forms of associated life is in so far democratic. Such a society must have a type of education which gives individuals a personal interest in social relationships and control, and the habits of mind which secure social changes without introducing disorder."[26] There is no question that this sounds conservative, appallingly moderate, even classical in its cherishing of social harmony. It should be noted, however, that this is a normative statement: Dewey was describ-

ing the "good society," the one that might come into being if enough
constraints were broken, if planning were to be intelligent and humane. Looking back on it over half a century, aware of how far we are
from attaining "a society which makes provision for participation in its
good of all its members on equal terms," we are likely to discern a certain innocence in Dewey, if not a blindness to what was happening in
the world. The new historians, however, select out from normative
statements of this kind notions like the "habits of mind" intended to
bring change without "disorder." It is assumed that the object of
Dewey's efforts was to cultivate such habits: and this, in turn, appears
to be explicitly counterrevolutionary in intent. Moreover, it seems to
incorporate and crystallize the point of view (first defined almost a
century before) that public education could be relied upon to change
the world. By implication, more radical, more political options seem
to be closed. If this is how Dewey's normatives are read, his influence
cannot but be considered to be protective of the status quo. The
"direction" he spoke of cannot but be considered to be manipula-
tive—on behalf of social stability and the myth of the common school.
The revisionist, puncturing the liberal hope, concludes by categoriz-
ing Dewey as a proponent of a "controlled economy, state planning,
group thought and managed change."[27] The alternative? A concentration on the release of individuality; a deschooled society; an end to
social control; the "abiding American dream."

I understand the need to reevaluate both liberalism and progressivism at each stage of our development; but I believe it takes a very
selective reading to demonstrate that Dewey played an intentionally
counterrevolutionary role and deluded people with his talk of intelligence, like-mindedness, and the kind of social control that would not
violate freedom. More seriously, I do not see evidence provided that
those who were influenced by Dewey (and their names were not legion)
would have or could have invented the kinds of radical political
strategies that might have overthrown capitalism and effected revolutionary change.

As troubled by the heritage of pragmatism (in, say, the case of the
Pentagon Papers) as anyone else, I find questionable what I see as
historicism in the approach of the revisionists. I find questionable,
too, the oversimplification of social control and the strange, innocent
optimism that leads to a setting aside of the problem of socialization.
Even if it is the case that socialization in an inequitable society leads to